BECOMING

SOMETHING

MONA Z. SMITH

FABER AND FABER, INC.

AN AFFILIATE OF FARRAR, STRAUS AND GIROUX

NEW YORK

BECOMING

SOMETHING

THE STORY OF

CANADA LEE

For Roy,

who taught me to love a good story,

and Bud,

who tried to teach me how to write one.

Faber and Faber, Inc.
An affiliate of Farrar, Straus and Giroux
19 Union Square West, New York 10003

Grateful acknowledgment is made for permission to reprint the following previously published material:
"The Heart of Harlem," from *The Collected Poems of Langston Hughes*, by Langston Hughes,
copyright © 1994 by The Estate of Langston Hughes. Used by permission of Alfred A. Knopf,
a division of Random House, Inc., and Harold Ober Associates.

Library of Congress Cataloging-in-Publication Data
Smith, Mona Z., 1962–
    Becoming something : the story of Canada Lee / by Mona Z. Smith.— 1st ed.
        p.   cm.
    Includes index.
    ISBN-13: 978-0-571-21142-5
    ISBN-10: 0-571-21142-9 (alk. paper)
    1. Lee, Canada.   2. Motion picture actors and actresses—United States—Biography.
3. African American motion picture actors and actresses—United States—Biography.
I. Title.

    PN2287.L2898S65   2004
    792' .02'8'092—dc22

                                                                    2003027828

Designed by Jonathan D. Lippincott

www.fsgbooks.com

1   3   5   7   9   10   8   6   4   2

AUTHOR'S NOTE

A portion of the proceeds from this book benefit the Canada Lee Fellowship Fund at Columbia University, awarding scholarships to women and students of color pursuing theater as a career.

For more information, or if you would like to support the Canada Lee Fellowship Fund at the Columbia University School of the Arts, please contact the development office at (212) 854-7724, or email arts@columbia.edu.

CONTENTS

PREFACE

ow does a man die? Darkness comes, breath ends, the heart ceases
to beat.

How does a man's honor die? His glory, his fame, his good
name? Honor dies by a man's own hand, or by the hand of another—by
rumor and ruin, attack and abuse.

Sometimes, when a man's honor dies, his story dies with it, destroyed,
erased, deleted.

This is the story of a talented and ambitious black man, a musician
turned athlete turned artist turned activist, a patriot who fought tirelessly
for the rights of his people and for *all* people who did not enjoy the full
privileges of American democracy, a man viciously dishonored and virtually deleted from this nation's history. This is the story of Canada Lee, an
unsung hero, a voice of dissent silenced by the McCarthy-era blacklist.

In his classic book on the show business blacklist, *A Journal of the
Plague Years*, Stefan Kanfer writes, "Overlooked by almost every theatrical or film historian, unmentioned by such retentive and bitter victims as
Alvah Bessie and Dalton Trumbo, Lee is the Othello of the blacklist,
at once its most afflicted and ignored victim."

Ironically, Canada's story was also a relatively minor episode in Kanfer's book. When recounted at all, the tragic tale of this actor and activist
is usually treated as little more than a footnote in the history of the Cold

War and the anti-Communist crusade dubbed "McCarthyism" after its most notorious knight, Senator Joseph McCarthy. Most often, the only reason Lee is mentioned is to acknowledge him as one of a handful of people whose deaths are attributed to persecution by the blacklist—a complex machine of journalists, Hollywood executives, congressmen, businessmen, and government agencies that destroyed the careers of the famous and the not so famous.

Bibliographies list hundreds of articles, books, plays, and films written during the past five decades about the Red Scare and anti-Communism, about McCarthy and J. Edgar Hoover, the House Un-American Activities Committee (HUAC), as well as the blacklist and its most famous victims, a group of screenwriters and film directors known as the Hollywood Ten. Interest in the subject spiked in the early 1990s when the Cold War ended and information long buried in archives in Moscow, Washington, and elsewhere came to light. A new generation has become fascinated with those chilling decades of Soviet and American animosity, nuclear anxiety and espionage, Red Scare propaganda and the anti-Communist movement, including the blacklist.

Why, then, has Canada Lee's story not been told?

Certainly, he was not blacklisted in the usual manner. He was never called before HUAC and asked the infamous question: "Are you now, or have you ever been, a member of the Communist Party?" He wasn't sent to jail like the Hollywood Ten for refusing to answer that question. His name was never named by one of HUAC's glamorous movie-star witnesses. He was not cited in the notorious *Red Channels*, the "bible of the blacklist" that demolished the careers of so many entertainers. Instead, Lee was blacklisted as a result of one of the most peculiar episodes in the history of the Cold War, the now largely forgotten espionage trial of Judith Coplon.

Perhaps this is the reason.

Or perhaps it is because Canada Lee was black. Little has been written about the entertainers, teachers, labor leaders, artists, and activists of color who were blacklisted. Perhaps Lee's story hasn't been told because African Americans are generally under-represented in our history books; perhaps those who do chronicle black history view the blacklist as a relatively minor misdemeanor compared to nearly four hundred years of criminal human rights abuses in this country. In any event, of all the blacklisted African

Americans, we know the most about Paul Robeson, the internationally renowned singer and activist. A colleague and friend to Canada Lee, Robeson was also vilified as a Communist, his passport confiscated, his career sabotaged. Though he lived the last fifteen years of his life in virtual obscurity, Robeson's contributions to the arts and his struggle for civil rights have been reclaimed and celebrated, thanks in part to the indefatigable efforts of his only child, Paul Robeson, Jr. But Robeson's case is the exception.

Of the many stories that deserve to be told, I chose Canada Lee's because it was, in the beginning, a fascinating puzzle, a mystery to be solved.

While studying for a master's degree in theater, I wanted to write a play about the intersection of jazz and politics at the end of World War II. Leafing through a library book about McCarthyism, I came across a single-line footnote that attributed Canada Lee's death to the blacklist. Intrigued, I unearthed a few entries in reference books describing him as one of the greatest black actors of his time and mentioning some of his most noted roles. That was the extent of the information readily available. How could a man of such talent be erased from history with hardly a trace?

Surely, there was more to this.

Several years of research squeezed around day jobs, family, and other matters turned up more mentions in more books, including Kanfer's study of the blacklist and Victor S. Navasky's *Naming Names*. A slim but intriguing folder in the theater research collection of the New York Library of the Performing Arts tossed more crumbs my way. Celebrity profiles described in greater detail Canada's chameleon transformations from violinist to jockey to boxer to actor. Yellowed clippings showed he had worked in the Negro Unit of the Federal Theatre during the Depression before achieving Broadway stardom in Orson Welles's adaptation of *Native Son*. Movie reviews showed that Lee had landed significant roles in several films, including Alfred Hitchcock's *Lifeboat*. A newspaper photo of Canada helping to organize a rally against Jim Crow in the theater was the first tangible evidence of his political activism. Though tantalizing, Lee's story was still far from complete.

Then came a real breakthrough, followed by crushing disappointment. The Schomburg Center for Research in Black Culture in Harlem had acquired seven boxes of materials on Canada. After years of turning up bits and scraps, I thought I had hit the jackpot, only to discover that the materials were off-limits to researchers. Archivists said Lee's papers were fragile, and his files hadn't yet been sorted or microfilmed. However, an attorney who had overseen the transfer of these materials to the Schomburg said the donor was Lee's widow, who was still alive. Write a letter describing your project, the attorney suggested, and I'll forward it to her. Soon after, Frances Lee Pearson telephoned with an invitation to visit her in Atlanta. Meeting this woman was a revelation; now in her eighties and legally blind, Frances is an absolute dynamo. Determined to preserve Lee's story, she created a database about his life, copying his files into a computer with special equipment rigged for her by family and friends. When I told her how much I wanted to put Lee's story on the stage, Frances opened her late husband's files and shared her most treasured memories, bringing the richness of Canada's story to life at long last—his rise to stardom, his fight for civil rights, his persecution under the blacklist, his failing health, those final moments before he slipped away from her forever.

In one form or another, I have been writing his story ever since.

"All my life, I've been on the verge of being something," Canada Lee once said. He almost became a concert violinist, but ran away to the races instead. He tried to make a career as a jockey, but a growth spurt and race prejudice forced him to quit. He found success at last as a prizefighter, but an accident in the ring ended his quest for the world championship.

Then he tumbled into acting, and became a Broadway star. Canada Lee, who grew up in a blue-collar home in Harlem and left school at the age of fourteen, finally got what he wanted more than anything else in the world, the chance to be somebody: a name in the marquee lights, an artist hailed as one of the most important black actors of his day. Lee's achievement is all the more impressive because he earned these accolades when roles for black actors were even more limited and stereotyped than they are today. Most were forced to keep body and soul together by playing the Eternal Menial, characters Lee dismissed as "butlers and handkerchief-heads." He insisted on dignified roles. He created his own opportunities. He shattered barriers and won hearts.

Canada Lee got it all and then lost it all—his glory, his fame, his honor, his good name—because stardom was not enough for him. He had achieved the American dream of self-determination and success, but he knew he was luckier than most. He felt honor-bound to use his success as a platform to fight for equal rights for his people and for all people suffering social, political, and economic injustices.

The artist turned activist, and it would be his ruin.

Lee loved his country and believed in democracy. A man of little formal education, he spent much of his life critically studying and bravely acting upon those famous principles that so many of us learn by rote in civics class and then forget or take for granted: the self-evident truths that all men are created equal and endowed by their Creator with certain unalienable rights, including life, liberty, and the pursuit of happiness. Lee strived to make our union more perfect, to establish justice, promote the general welfare, and secure the blessings of liberty for all Americans.

The Constitution taught him that whenever a government becomes "destructive to these ends," when the powers-that-be seek to undermine our freedoms and infringe on our civil liberties, it is the right of the people to alter that government. As a patriot who put his faith and trust in this democracy, Lee fervently believed he had the right to oppose those laws and practices that violated our fundamental civil rights.

He demanded an end to segregation, Jim Crow, poll taxes, and lynching. During World War II, he condemned the military for its hypocrisy in sending black soldiers to fight a racist regime in a segregated army. He denounced discrimination in the workplace and the criminal justice system. He lobbied for fair and accurate representation of minorities in arts and media. He insisted on better child care, housing, education, and health care for the poor. He petitioned Congress to remove its white supremacists. He urged the government to take a stand against apartheid and colonialism, and to support the rights of Africans and others to self-determination. He lobbied for international cooperation, unity, brotherhood, and peace.

Canada Lee was an idealist, an eloquent, courageous, vigorous voice of dissent.

That is what made him so dangerous. To those in power, Lee was a troublemaker, a rabble-rouser, a militant, a subversive, a Communist sympathizer if not a card-carrying Red. Canada's political activities were tracked, investigated, and documented in government files, fueling the blacklist machine that finally crushed him.

At first, Lee had no idea the government was watching him. But in 1947, as the blacklist began to ravage the lives and careers of left-leaning artists, including his own friends and colleagues, the actor had to know that he was risking everything he had worked so hard for by continuing to speak out. Yet he spoke out anyway.

Sifting through crumbling newspaper clippings, marveling over those amazing career transformations and his valiant activism, it is devastating to see Canada's story come to an abrupt end. Once Lee was blacklisted, few reporters took interest in the only work he had left, his volunteer efforts for political and humanitarian causes. When the actor died, obituaries summed up his career in a few sentences and noted he had been labeled a Communist. After the obituaries were filed away and buried deep in the morgues of the newspapers, Canada Lee virtually disappeared from history.

Kelly Miller, the late journalist and dean at Howard University, once said that white America doesn't want to take the concerns of black artists and intellectuals seriously, "but tell them about the Negro jockey, banjo player, prizefighter, minstrel, mimic, buck dancer, cabaret critics, jazz orchestra, singer of jubilee glees or Memphis blues, and they will not only stop to hear, but linger to listen."

Negro jockey . . . prizefighter . . . musician . . . entertainer. The outsider who proves himself a talented player is cheered for performing a worthy service. But the outsider who proves himself an intelligent, impassioned critic is condemned and silenced.

As long as Canada Lee was the great Negro success story, the man who rose from humble beginnings to become a star, he was the darling of the media and beloved by his fans. But when he began to battle Jim Crow and racism, when he began to criticize America's stand on segregation and the state of its own democracy, when he assumed the role of the artist as activist, he was by turns attacked, boycotted, ignored, forgotten.

We listened to Canada Lee's story as long as it fit a stereotype we created. We stopped listening when his story challenged our political views, our prejudices, our patriotism, our democracy. We were upset because he achieved the American dream of becoming somebody, and then told America where it fell short of its own ideals.

Canada wasn't a perfect man. He was ambitious. He made mistakes. He was human. But he was nevertheless a good man, a brave man, a man who fought for justice and freedom for the poor, the disenfranchised, and the oppressed, an artist of color who demanded respect, a patriot who asked his country to live up to its own principles.

He accomplished so much. It should not be forgotten.

ACKNOWLEDGMENTS

will always be grateful to Frances Lee Pearson for supporting my efforts to write a play based on events in the life of Canada Lee, a work that is also titled *Becoming Something*.

I thank Greg, Emma Louise, and the rest of my family for their unflagging patience and good humor throughout this project and, indeed, my entire life. I'm only sorry that Roy, Lois, and Gay left us before they could read that. To my friends, I owe endless drinks for endless conversation about Canada Lee. I am grateful also to JoAnne Meyers, Peter Rubie, and Denise Oswald for making the book a reality.

Finally, I am indebted to the following people and institutions across the nation and abroad for their generous assistance with my research on this topic during the past ten years. If I inadvertently omitted anyone from this list, please accept my sincerest apologies: Sarah Almond, Giancarlo Ambrosino, New School for Social Research Library; Arnold Aronson, Columbia University; Peter Askin and Kim Merrill; Todd Bachmann, Production Manager, *This American Life*; Allida Black, Project Director and Editor, The Eleanor Roosevelt Papers, The George Washington University, Washington, D.C.; Howard Blue; William Branch; Beulah and Oscar Bullock; Brooklyn Information and Culture; Anitra Brooks; Bill and Evadney Canegata; Sharon Mornan-Cangieter, Virgin Islands; Becky Cape, Head of Reference and Public Services, The Lilly Library, Indiana

University; Allyn Chandler; Nicole Luongo Cloutier, Special Collection Librarian, Portsmouth Public Library; Amy Cooper, Special Collections Librarian, University of Iowa Libraries, Special Collections Department; Norman Corwin; Nancy Cott, Director, Arthur and Elizabeth Schlesinger Library on the History of Women in America, Radcliffe Institute for Advanced Study, Harvard University; Bernard Crystal, Butler Library, Rare Books and Manuscripts, Columbia University; Joan R. Duffy, Yale Divinity School Library; Federal Theatre Project Collection, Library of Congress; David E. Ferguson; Jack French, Editor, *Radio Recall*; Paschal Frisina III; Nataki Garrett, Tom Gilcoyne, historian, National Museum of Racing and Hall of Fame; Dr. Glenda E. Gill, Michigan Technological University; Donald L. Gillies; Erik Goebel, Senior Researcher, Danish National Archives, Copenhagen; Dorinda Hartmann, Archival Assistant, Film and Photo Archive, Wisconsin Center for Film and Theater Research, Madison; James V. Hatch, Hatch-Billops Collection; Carmen Hendershott, New School for Social Research Library; Evan B. Hocker, Archivist, The Center for American History, University of Texas at Austin; Franz Hoffmann, Berlin, Germany; Murell Horton; Marty Jacobs, Associate Theater Curator for Collections and Research Services, Museum of the City of New York; Jo Kadlacek and Chris Gilbert; Kentucky Derby Museum at Churchill Downs in Louisville, Kentucky; Johnny Kitt; Don Koss, Reference Librarian, Richard J. Daley College, Chicago, Ill.; Francis Lapka, The Lilly Library, Indiana University; Harold Lehman and Lisa Lehman Trager; Beth Lein; Kelly Leon; Sheila Lewandowski; Harriet Lyons, *New York Daily News*; Mike and Traci Mariano; Haydée and Al Meyers; Darlene Mott, Librarian/ Reading Room Supervisor, Sam Houston Regional Library and Research Center of Liberty, Texas; Katie and David Neuser; New York Public Library of the Performing Arts; Judge Konrad Nowakowski of Vienna, Austria; Bud and Anne Pagel; Michael Paller; Michael Patterson; Destiny Pierce; Elaine Plenda; Laura Reiner, Reference Librarian, Brandeis University Libraries; Patrick Riviere; J. Dennis Robinson; Fred Romanski, National Archives and Records Administration, Washington, D.C.; George Rugg, Curator, Department of Special Collections, Hesburgh Library, Notre Dame; Stuart Saks, Assistant Vice President, London Publishing Co. and *The Ring*; Terry Salomonson, Audio Classics Archive, Broadcast Audio Restoration, Preservation and Archives; Katharine

Salzman, Curator of Manuscripts, Southern Illinois University; Schomburg Center for Research in Black Culture; Ellen M. Shea, Head of Public Services, Arthur and Elizabeth Schlesinger Library on the History of Women in America, Radcliffe Institute for Advanced Study, Harvard University; Emily Silverman, Librarian, University of Massachusetts Amherst; Sally Sinclair; Howard Stein; Maya Thomas; University of North Carolina at Chapel Hill, Manuscripts Department; Ed Vermue, Special Collections and Preservation Librarian, Oberlin College Library; Linda May Wacker, Museum of Modern Art; Gloria Waller-Scott; Kris Wilhelm, National Archives and Records Administration, Washington, D.C.; Allen Walsh; Charles Walton; and Christopher Wisner.

BECOMING

SOMETHING

ONE

ALWAYS CHASING RAINBOWS

THE MUSIC

On May 8, 1952, in a cramped and gloomy apartment in Greenwich Village, a man opened his eyes after lying in a coma for more than a week.

The room was empty.

The man rose naked from his bed and walked a few steps across the room. He may not have understood where he was. The room was so quiet, it had never been this quiet before, always there had been music, jazz and blues, and people, talking and laughing. Where did the music go? Why was he alone?

Weak and tired, he stood without speaking, still as the shadows.

Footsteps tapped lightly across the floor behind him and suddenly stopped. The woman who loved the man saw him standing there in the room and she cried out in alarm. For a moment he was startled, confused. Then he felt her slender, strong arms close tightly around him, he heard her say his name, and he was instantly comforted.

The man returned to his bed and closed his eyes.

The next day, as evening fell in Greenwich Village, Canada Lee died. He was forty-five years old.

Canada Lee was born in New York City on March 3, 1907, and christened with the mellifluous if somewhat daunting name of Leonard Lionel Cornelius Canegata. Called "Lee" by his friends, the boy was in the first grade at Public School (P.S.) 5 in Harlem when he decided that he wanted to be somebody special. Somebody important.

Lee Canegata didn't know at first how to go about this. But he was absolutely certain that he *didn't* want to be "just a man who worked hard, came home, ate, slept, went out to work again the next morning, with no chance for advancing in the world."

How did a seven-year-old get that kind of ambition?

The Canegata family history might have had something to do with it.

As a boy, Lee was told that "Canegata" was a Danish name taken by his father's family back in St. Croix, a tropical island of rolling hills, rain forests, mangroves, and sandy shores that was originally christened *Santa Cruz* by Christopher Columbus in 1493. Ownership of St. Croix changed hands a few times before Denmark finally bought it from the French in 1733 for $150,000. Hoping to stimulate the island's rather desultory production and trade, the Danish West India and Guinea Company sold huge plantation lots to anyone who had the cash. Most buyers were English, though a smattering of French and Dutch purchased property as well. Sugarcane quickly boosted St. Croix into a prosperous agricultural center, and more workers were needed in the fields and processing plants. African slaves had been transported to the island since the early 1600s; landowners now stepped up the slave trade, importing thousands more.

Canada's paternal ancestors were among those who survived the dangerous three-month passage from Africa's Gold Coast to the West Indies. Between 1670 and 1807, Danish ships transported eighty-five thousand slaves on this route, and ships from other nations carried thousands more. Author Leif Svalsen has traced the journey of one Danish slave vessel, the *Fredensborg.* "The heat along the equator was stifling, the calculated space per slave was about the size of a coffin, and the provisions on board were frugal and foreign," Svalsen writes. "Slaves were often chained and separated from loved ones as they sailed into an unknown future." The death rate was high; eleven percent of the 265 slaves aboard the *Fredensborg* died before they could be sold on the block at St. Croix's market, where buyers included free black and mulatto farmers as well as white landowners.

Planters, shipping barons, smugglers, pirates, and merchants grew rich off sugar, slaves, rum, cotton, and molasses. They built windmills and factories and lavish mansions called great houses. Lush plantations bore whimsical names like "Estate Jealousy" and "Wheel of Fortune," as well as epithets more significant to slaves, such as "Hard Labor."

By 1803, St. Croix's population of thirty thousand included a few thousand well-to-do planters and their 26,500 slaves. There is an old saying on the island: "Some doin' well, some seein' hell." Every Cruzan slave knew misery, but working in the cane fields was the devil's own torture. Toiling ten to twelve hours in grueling heat, a slave received a dozen lashes or more if he slowed in his work. Some committed suicide; a few managed to escape to the mountains. Runaways who got caught were whipped, pinched with glowing tongs, maimed, broken on the wheel, or hanged. Bloody rebellions broke out.

Over fierce objections from planters, the Danish governor began to phase out slavery, first by banning importation of any more human cargo, and then, in 1847, by proclaiming that all children born to slaves were now free, while the rest of the slave population would be liberated in fourteen years. Unwilling to wait, eight thousand slaves marched on Frederiksted in July of 1848 and demanded immediate emancipation. Though he had no authorization from the Crown, Governor-General Peter von Scholten, long sympathetic to abolition, freed them. In so doing, he attempted to right centuries of injustice; he also helped to plunge an already precarious sugar economy into a full-on depression. Suddenly, 90 percent of the population had no money, property, or jobs. A labor act set wages at five cents a day for most freed slaves, who often were charged the same five cents a day for food from the company store, an arrangement tantamount to enslavement. In 1878, frustrated black laborers rioted for a week, burning fields, factories, and great houses. Wary of more revolts, government officials in 1880 offered higher wages, better land, and new opportunities to former slaves and their families.

James C. Canegata, a literate and ambitious man with an entrepreneurial spirit, saw his chance and seized it. Local accounts say he built a fleet of small merchant ships that sailed between St. Croix and American ports, becoming one of the wealthiest black merchants in the Virgin Islands. Reportedly, Canegata once owned the arcaded building on King Street where Alexander Hamilton had worked as a counting-house clerk before moving to the American colonies in 1772. He also operated a finely appointed dry goods store, which remained in the family for years. (David Hamilton Jackson, famed labor leader and civil rights activist, worked briefly for Canegata as a bookkeeper.)

As his business thrived and prospered, Canegata and his wife, Jane Gerard Canegata, started a family. James Cornelius was born in 1885, and a second son, David Cornelius, was born in 1887. Well-educated in private schools, these precocious and adventuresome boys were particularly keen on sports. James was an avid boxer, and both lads took up riding before they could reach the stirrups. Their father owned some of the finest horses on the island, and often employed jockeys to race his Thoroughbreds. James and David were fearless horsemen who "could sit a saddle or ride bareback the most ferocious animal," reported a St. Croix special correspondent in the *New York Age*.

As the eldest son, James might have expected to inherit his father's successful business. Despite this, the seventeen-year-old inexplicably shipped to New York City as a cabin boy in 1901. Perhaps James chafed under his father's rule and wanted to make his own way, or perhaps the allure of the great metropolis, with its glorious skyscrapers and teeming streets, its booming economy and ardent conviction that anything was possible, proved inexorable for an ambitious young man. As the teenager sailed into the New York harbor, excited and perhaps a bit fearful, he set eyes on the island that would be home for the rest of his life. St. Croix seemed a world away.

When James decided to stay in America, family lore holds that his father abruptly disinherited him and left the family fortune to David instead. After studying medicine at McGill University in Montreal, David Canegata returned to St. Croix, the first native to practice there. Appointed to the post of Municipal Physician, he strived to eradicate communicable diseases among the poor. During forty-five years of public service, Dr. Canegata held positions in all three branches of government, including eleven years as chairman of the legislature, ten years as a judge, and two years as the island's chief executive. His assiduous campaigns for self-rule, native suffrage, and a bill of rights for the territory earned him the admiration of his people. He died in 1972 and was buried on the island, where a popular park bears his name.

Canada Lee was very proud of his West Indian roots, his grandfather's successful business, and his uncle's careers in medicine and public service. When he became famous himself, Lee visited his relatives there and often spoke warmly of his Caribbean heritage to reporters, pointing out in one interview that the St. Croix Canegatas had been well educated for generations, "and I didn't finish grammar school."

While David set about his medical career in St. Croix, brother James struggled to find his place in New York. Arriving in the first major wave of West Indian immigrants to this country, James hoped for a bright future in his new home. He quickly learned that Afro-Caribbean émigrés often had advantages over native blacks. Better education and a long history of political and economic dealings with whites could work to their benefit, and many whites treated them more favorably than native blacks when it came to offering jobs or leasing apartments. This is one reason why interactions between native and West Indian–born blacks were notoriously prickly, especially in New York City where West Indians gained a reputation for arrogance and their vexation over the primitive segregation of American society. Many West Indians believed they had little in common with indigenous blacks; they saw themselves as a separate and distinct Caribbean community that could be further subdivided by island of origin. West Indians spoke with different accents, worshipped in different churches, wore different styles of clothing, and followed different codes of behavior within the family.

Canada's father, James, is usually described as a reserved, taciturn man, but he must have had an independent streak. Having defied his father by moving to New York, he then violated an unwritten code of Manhattan's West Indian community by marrying a black woman from the American South. Lydia Whaley Gadsen was a handsome, strong, and imposing daughter of deeply religious parents from South Carolina. She had a child from a previous marriage, a quiet little toddler named Robert Gadsen. After marrying Lydia, James treated the soft-spoken boy as his own son.

Together, James and Lydia Canegata had three children. First, in 1907, came a son, Leonard Lionel Cornelius, called "Lee." (There is some confusion over this name; Lee was also called "James" by certain family and friends, and his father would list him as "James C." in the 1920 U.S. Census.) A daughter, Claudia, was born two years later, followed in four years by another son, William, nicknamed "Lovey" by his mother for his sweet face and long, curly locks. When the children were small, their father worked as a porter in a factory; later, he took an office job at the National Fuel and Gas Corporation, where he would remain for decades. A loving but strict mother, Lydia raised her children to behave well and obey the Good Book. James, called Pop by his children, also ruled with a firm hand, warmly praising achievements but brooking no insubordination. The couple worked hard to make a comfortable home, but the household was modest by necessity. An American journalist describing Canada Lee's family history pointed out that in St. Croix, the Canegata clan "knew dignity and a measure of ease. Here, they knew humiliation and poverty."

Lee was born on West Sixty-second Street in a neighborhood known as San Juan Hill, a colorful but overcrowded section of Manhattan that sprawled from Amsterdam Avenue west to the Hudson River, between Fifty-third and Sixty-fourth streets. San Juan Hill may have earned its name when black veterans moved there after the Spanish-American War, although the military moniker also may stem from the turf wars that constantly broke out between poor blacks and immigrants.

Despite its mean streets and rough characters, San Juan Hill and the neighboring Tenderloin district were exciting places. Here was Black Bohemia, keeping time to the new rhythms of ragtime, the cakewalk, honky-tonk, and hot jazz that spilled out of the theaters, hotels, bars, and clubs. One can imagine Lee as a small boy playing on his stoop, listening to music by some of the great black musicians of the time, including Noble Sissle, Eubie Blake, James Reese Europe, W. C. Handy, and J. Rosamond Johnson. But before long, Lee's family was on the move, and so was Black Bohemia.

When Lee was four or five years old, the Canegatas pulled up stakes and joined the mighty river of black migration flowing north into Harlem. In the 1800s, Harlem had been home to a series of white immigrant communities, including Dutch, Irish, Germans, and European Jews. But the area was overbuilt with apartments, and when an economic depression hit, the real estate market slumped. An enterprising young African American realtor named Philip A. Payton, Jr., seized this opportunity and began filling apartments with reliable black tenants who, faced with a housing shortage in the city's segregated neighborhoods, were willing to pay steeper rents than whites.

The Canegatas and thousands of other black families streamed into a corridor east of Eighth Avenue between 130th and 145th Streets. Black Harlem, as historian David Levering Lewis has observed, "seemed to flash into being like a nova."

This was the Harlem that Lee would forever call his home. The Canegatas settled down at 141st Street between Seventh and Eighth avenues. They joined the local Salem Methodist Church, a congregation founded in a basement a decade earlier by the Reverend Frederick Asbury Cullen, poet Countee Cullen's adoptive father. James and Lydia "were church-going people," according to Lovey's son, Bill Canegata. "My grandmother was a healer. She would go off and pray and be religious and come back and lay hands on people and take away their sickness. She was called Sister Canegata . . . They were strong people for the church, my grandparents." Decades later, Canada Lee would say he joined only one organization in his life, and that was Salem Methodist.

As a boy, Lee was slight for his age but wiry and strong, a bundle of energy. Though not as conventionally handsome as his little brother, Lovey, Lee possessed a razor-sharp mind, indisputable charm, an impish smile, and a tendency toward mischief. One of the first friends he made in the new neighborhood was a boy some three years his senior named Billy Butler. One day Billy ran hell-for-leather out of a basement, chasing Lee, who "ducked behind something and put his foot out," Butler said. "I tripped over it, went up into the air, came down, and my tooth went through my lip." He ended up with two scars to remember Lee by, and often teased his lifelong friend about it.

Lee's parents enrolled him at P.S. 5 on 140th Street and Edgecombe Avenue. It was there, in the first grade, that he decided that he wanted to be somebody special. Somebody important.

He already *was* somebody important to other boys in the neighborhood. Lee Canegata was king of the block, the Robin Hood of 141st Street, who defended their turf against a gang of thugs called the "Syndicate." Armed with bottles and broomsticks, the Syndicate trolled the streets, stealing money and toys from smaller kids. Determinedly scrappy, Lee was the only boy brave enough to stand up to these bullies. Children bigger and older than Lee ran to him for protection when the Syndicate came calling. One day the plucky tyke challenged the leader of the gang. Friends and admirers gathered around to cheer their champion as Lee thrashed and pummeled the Syndicate leader in what one witness called "a fight almost to the death."

Lee battled his way to the top of the heap at school, too. Most days it seemed he was doing more skirmishing than learning. "I fought my way to and from school every day and learned that all I needed was as many fists as the next guy," Lee said. While he might have been a hero on his own block, he wasn't above a little bullying himself on the playground. When a monitor wrote his name down one morning for being tardy, he waited for the boy after school and punched him in the jaw. Lee also admitted that he rarely bothered to bring his own lunch to school. When it was time to eat, he simply waited until another boy opened *his* lunch box. Seizing his hapless victim, Lee would shout fiercely: "I gotcha!" His classmate either divvied up the grub or took a pounding. "It was a little game I invented," he recalled, laughing sheepishly. "Sometimes the boys didn't want to play. Then I just took what I wanted. I could whip them all, big or little."

He was king of the hill, but it wasn't enough. I want something more, he told himself, something better.

Maybe it was family history that put the notion in his head—the shipbuilding grandfather, the uncle on the Privy Council. Or maybe the heroes of his favorite stories inspired him. Lee may not have been a stellar student, but he was a born bookworm. "I was always reading stories and imagining myself a buccaneer," he said. "I was crazy about Grimm's fairy tales, and later the [Horatio] Alger books and Tom Swift stories."

An interesting reading list: Grimm's fairy tales of magical transformations, where frogs turn into princes. Tom Swift, boy genius, inventing his way out of countless perils. Alger's ragged boys rising to riches by dint of hard work, pristine morals, good manners, and physical cleanliness. In these books, success is not a question of luck, or wealth, or social class, or color. Success will be yours if your desire is fierce, your heart virtuous, your wits sharp, your back strong. These are stories that helped forge our great national myth that anyone can succeed in America if only he tries hard enough.

Lee Canegata was ready to try, but at what? What could a seven-year-old do?

His first stab was music. Maybe he saw those players around town, laughing and talking and dressing fine, and maybe he liked that hot music spilling out of the bars and clubs and rent parties. Maybe he chose music because his sister Claudia sang so well and his pal Billy Butler studied the violin.

Whatever the reason, Lee told his mother he wanted to take music lessons, and Lydia thought it was a good idea. Maybe music would keep the boy out of trouble.

She sent Lee to the new Music School Settlement for Colored People, where he studied with one of the academy's founders, J. Rosamond Johnson. A classically trained musician and composer, Johnson had made a name for himself writing hit songs for vaudeville and Broadway and later served as musical director of the Grand Opera House in London. He also composed the celebrated anthem *Lift Ev'ry Voice and Sing* with his brother, lyricist James Weldon. The Johnson brothers contributed much talent and energy to the Harlem Renaissance, and the Music School became a training ground and showcase for serious musicians. Lee Canegata showed an immediate aptitude for music. He studied violin and piano with Johnson, and also took lessons from Professor William Butler, who happened to be the father of Lee's pal, Billy.

Professor Butler was a neighborhood celebrity. At age twelve, he ran away from home to join the army as a drummer boy and left ten years later as bandmaster. He bought a townhouse on a tree-lined street in Manhattan's Chelsea neighborhood, where his white neighbors often mistook him for a janitor. One of his tenants was a six-foot-tall Irish beauty who made her living as a marketing gimmick. She was one of the "Seven Sullivan Sisters" who were unrelated but nevertheless blessed with identical heads of floor-length red hair, just the ticket for touting new toiletries. Butler married this Irish rose and eventually moved with her to Harlem. Lee Canegata never forgot the first time he saw Mrs. Butler send her crimson curtain of newly washed hair cascading down from a second-story window to dry.

Professor Butler reputedly made and lost several fortunes. In good times, the family enjoyed a houseful of servants, chauffer-driven limousines, and expensive tailored clothes. Butler began his day in a morning coat, striped pants, and a Homburg hat. In the afternoon, he changed into a "lounge suit," the equivalent of a Wall Street power suit. At dinner, he wore a tuxedo and expected his family to sit at the table in formal dress.

Lee's friend Billy Butler was also enrolled at the Music School Settlement. After months of violin lessons, Lee was deemed proficient enough to join Billy and his sister Celia in a community orchestra under Professor Butler's baton. Every inch the soldier-bandmaster, Butler ran his music program like a battalion. He could be patient with talented pupils, but his patience had limits and his expectations were high. Billy and Lee sometimes balked at the professor's strict discipline. Once, when they were supposed to be practicing, they sneaked into a local race-track instead. When the boys got home, Lee got a lecture and Billy got a whipping.

Possessing a natural talent for music, Lee advanced rapidly in his studies, despite the fact that he went days at a time without practicing. He could leave his violin in its case all week and then sight-read his way through his lesson, leaving many teachers none the wiser. When a piece of music fired his imagination, however, he worked on it hour after hour with discipline and concentration "while other kids played stickball," one reporter noted. At the age of eleven, he made his concert debut at a student recital in Aeolian Hall, an eleven hundred–seat venue at 29 West Forty-second Street that was almost as grand as its famous neighbor to the north, Carnegie Hall. Lee played Drdla's *Serenade*, admirably handling what must have been considerable pressure. A reporter noted that after the Aeolian Hall concert, "competent critics said he had a brilliant future."

But something went wrong. Though he continued to study seriously for three more years, Lee came to the decision that music would never bring him the fame and admiration he craved.

Decades later, Lee gave reporters different stories about why he decided to quit music. He told one that "a virtuoso's lot was not to his liking." He told another that "his inherited spirit of adventure interfered with his cultural improvement." Still another writer reported that Lee's parents had objected to the idea of a concert career—a rather unlikely explanation. A fourth account states that "to become his own man [he] had to leave his fiddle behind and run away from home."

Perhaps there's a bit of truth in all of this, or perhaps Lee realized that the odds were awfully long against a black man trying to make a career in classical music in the 1920s. Then—as now—orchestras were nearly if not completely lily white. Black classical musicians found few opportunities to work unless they were light-skinned and willing to pass for white.

As the son of an Irish mother, Billy Butler could have passed in order to work, but chose not to. He gave up the violin, switched to the saxophone and clarinet, and enjoyed a successful career playing jazz and conducting orchestras.

Lee admired Billy for refusing to pass. In Billy's place, he would have made the same choice, but because Lee was dark-skinned, this was never an option. After much thought, Lee decided not to follow Billy into jazz, nor would he try to follow Professor Butler into a teaching career, or Rosamond Johnson into black musicals and vaudeville revues. Instead, after seven years of intense study with some of Harlem's finest teachers and a successful student debut in one of New York City's premier concert halls, Lee carefully packed away his violin one day and, without telling his mother or father, bundled up some clothes, took a last look at home, walked out the front door, and disappeared.

What could drive a fourteen-year-old boy to run away from a loving, stable family?

If he couldn't be somebody as a concert musician, maybe he could be somebody racing horses.

TWO

RUNNIN' WILD

THE RACES

n 1921, a runaway boy from Harlem walked into the stable yard at the Saratoga Race Course with the wild idea of riding Thoroughbreds.

Lee could never really explain why he decided, of all things, to become a jockey. He'd read about famous races and winning riders in the newspapers, and listened to young sports in Harlem who came back from the track with thrilling stories. "Romance and excitement," Lee said. "I love it." He thought it beautiful to ride a horse, like those gallant knights in fairy tales. Astride his steed, dressed in bright racing silks, he would surely impress the girls he had lately become interested in impressing. And racing was in his blood. After all, the Canegata men back in St. Croix had been excellent horsemen.

Despite his family's equestrian history, Lee was utterly ignorant about horses. "I didn't know which end of the horse kicked and which end bit," he admitted.

When he arrived in Saratoga Springs, New York, he found plenty of other boys hanging around the stables and hoping to ride, most of them orphans or runaways. They slept in barns and begged for odd jobs, including scrubbing dishes in the track kitchen. Lee took a good look at the competition and put his considerable charm to work. After days of cajoling every trainer in sight, he got a job as a hotwalker, leading overheated horses around the stables or a dirt track to cool them down after a race or strenuous training run. Hotwalking was essential for the health of horses, but it was a monotonous, dusty grind for a young lad craving romance and excitement. Lee wanted to ride, and he pounced on any chance to get up on a horse, from the lowliest nag to the orneriest cuss. Persistent, cheerful, and seemingly fearless, he worked his way up to exercise rider, earning a few pennies galloping horses during morning workouts. Standing about five feet, five inches, Lee was slim, strong, and agile. A few trainers began to watch him in those early hours. "In a month I was wearing silks and booting horses home," Lee boasted.

In reality, getting in the saddle wasn't quite that easy. Racing was big business, and established owners would never risk money or horses on a greenhorn. Lee signed on with a "gyp," or gypsy trainer, who roamed from track to track. The gyp gave Lee a place to sleep, a bit of food, and a chance to ride in exchange for doing whatever he was told, including endless barn chores. Racing mostly at minor league courses and in backwater towns on inferior horses, Lee quickly learned that no rules applied when it came to winning. Jockeys would shove, punch, kick, and whip each other, cling to another horse's tail or saddlecloth, and crush other mounts against the inside rail. After months of brutal, bruising defeats, Lee finally posted his first win and earned the coveted status of apprentice jockey. Now maybe he would get a shot at riding better horses in bigger races.

His first ride as an apprentice was on a four-year-old named Jacobean at the Blue Bonnets in Montreal on September 7, 1922. They were entered in a Maiden Jockey's race at seven-eighths of a mile for a ten-thousand-dollar purse. As the horses went to post at 3:39 p.m., there was Lee, a hundred-pound boy perched atop a thousand pounds of genuine Thoroughbred, preparing to fly around the track at forty to fifty miles an hour. When the starting signal sounded, Jacobean broke well enough, but Lee shut his eyes and grimaced at the sudden shuddering in his stomach. Precariously balanced on his toes, body hovering in midair, the young jockey had never traveled this fast in his life. One small mistake, a momentary pitch forward or backward, could flip him off the horse and under the hooves pounding all around him. He heard the flick of whips and the clink of stirrups, smelled clouds of dust and his own sweat. He opened his eyes to find a blur of brilliant green infield streaking by on his left. A horse named Glenn had seized an early and comfortable lead, but

Jacobean was pouring on the heat now and closing the gap. Lee was convinced the horse was "about to chuck him on the chin." Rocketing through space, he tried to master his nerves by remembering how he felt the night he took the stage at Aeolian Hall, fiddle in hand, critics in the audience. I did well then, he told himself, I can do this now. He put his trust in Jacobean and gripped the reins for dear life. "I finished second," he said. "I mean the horse did. I couldn't do a thing but hang on."

Nevertheless, his confidence grew and the young jockey eagerly anticipated his next race on a horse named Ardito at Dorval, a relatively obscure Canadian track. During the morning training session, Lee gave the horse the rein but Ardito didn't move a muscle. "I spurred and he *still* didn't move," he recalled with a laugh. "The trainer picked up some dirt from the track and threw it at the horse." Ardito cast a baleful eye on the trainer and walked a few steps, just beyond the reach of the trainer's throwing arm.

"You're on a dog and he ain't never going to run," Lee muttered to himself.

This was pure humiliation for a young jockey eager to prove what he could do. Lee had placed second in his first big race, and now he was stuck on a horse that seemed destined to run dead last. He could barely hide his disgust that afternoon as he headed for the post at 5:49. The trainer knew Ardito's secret, however. He caught up to Lee and whispered, "Change your hold like he's running away with you. That'll encourage the nag!" Lee agreed to give it a try, but in the final moments before the race, he stared straight ahead a bit sulkily, prepared for the worst. "At the signal, my horse broke," he recalled. Ardito powered into the first stretch, leaving the rest of the pack in a cloud of dust. Lee was so shocked that he nearly slid off the horse. "When I get back on the seat again, I see I'm five lengths ahead," he recalled with a chuckle. Ardito never let up and won the race easily.

"I really thought I was pretty slick riding that one home," Lee said, "but the other jocks told me inside I looked like a washerwoman pumping down the stretch. All the time I thought I was riding so smooth like any big-time jockey, they said I was sitting bolt upright on the saddle like I had a rod down my back."

Moving on to Toronto, he placed second on a horse called Fair Game at Dufferin Park. After racing at a handful of other tracks on the Canadian circuit, he returned to New York. For months Lee continued to ride for gyps, forever hustling work and making very little money. Riding as a freelance apprentice, he was supposed to earn as much as fifteen dollars for a winner plus a cut of the purse, which could amount to forty dollars or more at the better tracks. But young riders rarely got paid what they were due, and Lee was no exception.

Luckily, he managed to attract the attention of a wealthy horsewoman named Mrs. F. Ambrose Clark, whose husband was heir to the ONT Thread and Singer sewing machine fortunes. The Clarks shared a passion for racing and built beautiful stables at their estate in Old Westbury on Long Island (now a campus of the State University of New York). Ambrose Clark also financed tracks and polo grounds including Aiken Steeplechase, part of the famous Triple Crown. Mrs. Clark hired Lee and before long he was racing her colors at Belmont, Aqueduct, Jamaica, and a dozen other tracks. He must have ridden fairly well to race for a horsewoman as respected as Mrs. Clark, but in later years he usually belittled his talent. "I never had a good hand on a horse," he said.

When Lee raced at tracks in New York City, his little brother would sneak off to watch him ride. Whenever Lovey disappeared, his father always knew how to find both of his boys: by reading the sports pages. According to Bill Canegata, "Pop would just look in the papers to see where Lee was riding and then he'd go down to the track and get them. There was no arguing with Pop. He was the boss."

Pop had conflicted feelings about Lee's jockey career. Though James himself had run away from home as a young man to seek his fortune, he had hoped his sons would stay in school and make better opportunities for themselves. Racetrack people had a reputation for being wild and immoral; no matter how successful they might be, polite folks still viewed them with disdain. "Lee made money," Bill Canegata said. "But Pop, I don't think he liked the track. The life."

Horseracing was glamorous, but it was also dangerous, and the track was a place where fun-lovers and hard laborers mixed with mobsters, petty crooks, rumrunners, and professional gamblers. As a teenager out on his own, Lee met up with some pretty tough characters at the track, as well as gambling joints and billiard parlors. These were "havens for ex-convicts, thieves, and cutthroats," he later said. The boy kept his nose clean, but Pop Canegata still had reason to worry. Before long, Lee was having his own second thoughts about earning a living in racing. As with his motives for taking up the sport, there's some question about exactly why Lee decided to quit. Later in life, he said he grew too tall and heavy to ride. He often blamed himself for not having the right stuff, and jockey records do indicate that he had a rather lackluster career—out of twenty-three documented races, he placed just twice and won only once. He also complained that he made too little money. "They paid off in peanuts," he once said.

Lee was also mighty tired of hustling work. As a runaway, he came to Saratoga with "no experience, no name, no connections," sports journalist John P. Carmichael observed. Despite some fine rides and his work for a respected horsewoman like Mrs. Clark, Lee rarely convinced other top stable owners to hire him. "By the time he had made most of the half-milers around the country and had learned what it meant to be blocked off, shuffled back, and generally kicked around in a race, he was too heavy to ride," Carmichael concluded.

Lee seldom discussed another important reason for quitting: racism. In the 1920s, he was one of only a handful of black jockeys. Discrimination on and off the track made it difficult for him to find work: "My agent would go to a man and say, 'Look, how about putting Lee on your horse today?' And he would say very simply, 'I'm sorry, but you know that no colored boys can ride my horses.' And that's the way it went."

When he did ride, white jockeys, especially those from the South, singled him out for abuse. Riding up close and turning their mounts sideways, they delighted in sending devastating kicks his way. As the horses made the final turn into the backstretch, white riders pressed in from all sides, whipping and pushing, trying to squeeze Lee out. "Those jockeys on those half mile tracks—whoooeeeee, what guerrillas they were," he recalled.

Most black jockeys had already been forced out of horseracing, a sport they had dominated for its entire history in this country. "They were ridden out of the sport, and they've been sort of written out of the sport, too," notes Edward Hotaling, author of *The Great Black Jockeys*. "Their disappearance I see really as a civil rights story."

Horseracing was America's first national pastime, and for more than two centuries the majority of jockeys were black. Colonel Richard Nicolls introduced the sport to the American colonies; as the first English governor of New York, he established a track on Hempstead Plain on Long Island in 1665 and awarded a silver cup to winners twice a year.

In no time, racing fever spread south, where plantation owners assigned slaves to train their horses, as well as feed and groom them. Before long, slaves were riding for their masters as well. The few existing programs for these early races list the names of the horses, the owners and colors, but rarely mention the jockeys' names. When they are listed, names like Scipio, Cato, and Caesar indicate that most were slaves. (Many masters had a penchant for Greek or Roman classical names to show off their erudition, to humiliate the slave, or both.)

In the decades leading up to the War Between the States, stable owners above and below the Mason-Dixon line sponsored popular "North-South" races, where black jockeys may have included free men and slaves. The war shut down tracks in the South, but wily Northern entrepreneurs—particularly in New York—made racing and gambling big business. By the end of the nineteenth century, black jockeys were racing at posh new tracks and competing in celebrated races that are still run today, including the Belmont Stakes, the Preakness, and the Kentucky Derby.

At the very first Derby in 1875, all but one of the fifteen jockeys were black and a black man, Oliver Lewis, rode the winning horse. In the next twenty-seven Derbies, fourteen black jockeys rode winners, another fourteen came in second, and twelve came in third. White men had the money to buy Thoroughbreds, but black men had the talent and experience to race them.

The first Derby racing programs listed the names of owners as well as the name, sex, age, history, and colors of their horses, but failed to record the seemingly less important names of the riders. By the turn of the century, however, black jockeys had won the respect and admiration of racing fans, and a few were sports stars of their day, featured in magazine spreads, often decked out in finely tailored suits, ascots, and bowler hats. These celebrities included Isaac Murphy, who won an astounding 44 percent of his races, including three Kentucky Derbies. Willie Simms, a two-time Derby winner, became a hero in 1895 when he traveled to England and became the first American rider on an American horse to beat the Brits on their own turf. Jimmy Winkfield, a Kentucky native who won back-to-back Derbies in 1901 and 1902, moved to Europe and won some of the racing world's richest purses at its most elegant tracks.

Winkfield was the last African American to win the Derby. In 1910, journalist Buster Miller declared the black jockey all but extinct. "Take a trip out to any track in the wee hours of the morning and there you will find a veritable array of colored men and boys doing a capable job of conditioning the Thoroughbreds, but only as lowly and underpaid grooms and exercise boys," he observed in Harlem's *New York Age*. "When the afternoon bugle calls the horses to the post, the colored rider is conspicuously absent. Why?"

To this day, black jockeys remain conspicuously absent. In the past nine decades, only one has ridden in a Triple Crown race, and there are few black trainers, owners, front office employees, or managers. "About the only racetrack occupations with more than token Afro-American presence are grooms and hotwalkers," *The Backstretch* reported in 1994, bluntly asking: "Is racing racist?"

History answers yes. Racism, economics, and politics all contributed to the disappearance of black jockeys. Around 1900, young white men, many of them poor immigrants, eagerly took the lowest paying jobs at racetracks. Black jockeys often trained these men to groom, hotwalk, and exercise horses. "Soon after that, you would see one or two riding in a race," sports columnist Tom Wilson wrote in 1940. "This marked the entry of the white faces on the track, and also a costly error on the part of the Race jockeys who began to teach white boys to ride."

Opportunities for work were scarce enough for jockeys in the 1920s, thanks to anti-gambling movements that steadily reduced the number of American racecourses from more than three hundred to about twenty-five. As rivalry for jobs grew fierce, a group of white jockeys decided to eliminate some of the rivalry. Backed by white owners and trainers, they worked to keep black jockeys out of major races. The few black jockeys who did fight their way onto the track often paid a high price. Roscoe Goose, a white jockey and 1913 Derby winner, saw black riders whipped, kicked, and crushed into fences. It got so bad, Goose said, that in the 1920s, stable owners were reluctant to hire black jockeys: "They got to thinking that if they had a colored boy up, he'd have the worst of it."

What Goose saw, Lee experienced firsthand. After two years at the track, the sixteen-year-old decided he was ready to call it quits on horseracing.

He may have grown too tall and heavy. He may have known he didn't have enough talent on a horse to become a star. But he was also sick and tired of being kicked around. Lee sought honor and distinction in the field, and it was clear that a black jockey would never be allowed to become a star on the track. The other riders were too tough, he said: "They scared me right out of that business." He stuck around the stables a while longer, galloping horses at dawn and cooling them out in the morning sun, one reporter wrote, "but found no glory in training nags for others to ride."

Lee ran away to the races because he dreamed of coming home famous, dressed in leather and silk, with gold in his purse. Instead he came home with a pair of beat-up riding boots and a couple of empty pockets. He had no regrets, though. He had made his own way in a heady, exhilarating world, and he was determined to do it again, though he had no earthly idea how to go about it.

Luckily, an old friend from P.S. 5 had the answer.

THREE

LIFE CAN BE SO SWEET

THE RING

hen Lee returned to Harlem, his parents welcomed their prodigal son with open arms, but they didn't exactly trot out the fatted calf, a new robe, or a full purse. Money was always tight, and since Lee had chosen to drop out of school and be his own man, he was now expected to get a job and pay some bills if he wanted to live at home.

"I was wondering what the hell I was going to do," Lee said.

He didn't mind hard work; after all, he had already supported himself for a few years at the track. No, the trouble was, Lee yearned for a new and thrilling career, another daring escapade. As a jockey, he'd taken risks, braved dangers, and won some races. That small sip from the cup of fame burned all the way down. "I was considered a big shot among my friends," he said. "None of them had left home the way I had done or had my adventures."

Lee Canegata wasn't about to take just any job.

He thought about music—not classical this time, but jazz and blues. He knew he had some talent, but to play in Harlem you needed serious chops. Jazz fans flocked to dances, clubs, cabarets, and rent parties, where masters like Louis Armstrong, James P. Johnson, Willie "The Lion" Smith, Coleman Hawkins, and Fats Waller were inventing wild, powerful, swinging new sounds. Musicians battled each other in "cutting" contests that left no one bleeding but made plenty of greenhorns squirm with embarrassment. Lee was years out of practice. He picked up his fiddle and set to work, but he knew he had a long way to go before he'd be ready to fight for his place on the bandstand. In the meantime, he needed a job.

One day he was wandering the streets of his neighborhood, considering his options, when he bumped into an old friend from P.S. 5 by the name of Willie Powell. Willie was looking awfully sharp in a nice new suit. He gave Canada the once-over and asked what he was doing for a living these days.

Suddenly conscious of his old work clothes, Lee let it drop that he had recently retired from a successful career in horseracing. He wondered how Willie had managed to buy himself that fine-looking suit. Powell boasted that he was making good money in the ring.

Prizefighting? That got Lee's attention, and quick: "I had always licked him in school. If he could make a living as a prizefighter, what was I doing in overalls?"

In the 1920s, America went crazy over boxing as aggressive promoters and gamblers like Tex Rickard turned a once-disreputable saloon sport into big business. Top matches earned more than $1 million in gate receipts, and purses fattened to six figures. New Yorkers packed clubs and ballrooms to watch their favorite fighters, and in 1923, the man who truly ruled the ring was the great heavyweight Jack Dempsey. Beloved by the public, the "Manassa Mauler" was as famous as any movie star. "*Everyone* was Dempsey-conscious," Lee would later recall.

William Harrison Dempsey's rags-to-riches story took him from an impoverished childhood in a small Colorado town to a seven-year stint as the world's heavyweight boxing champion. He wrenched the title away from Jess Willard in 1919 by breaking the man's jaw and two of his ribs. Dempsey's match against Luis Firpo in 1923 is still considered by many to be the most violent four minutes in boxing history. In the first round, Firpo knocked Dempsey through the ropes and into a sportswriter's lap. The Mauler dived back into the ring and sent the Argentinean slugger to the canvas seven times. Finally, in round two, Dempsey knocked Firpo out cold for the win.

Young men across the nation idolized Dempsey, but boxing was a race-conscious sport. In Harlem, thousands of boys found their own hero in a heavyweight sensation named Harry Wills. A formidable fighter with a near-perfect record, Wills was repeatedly denied a shot at Dempsey's title because he was black.

Influential figures in boxing opposed a Wills-Dempsey match-up, including Tex Rickard. In 1910, Rickard had backed the infamous "Fight of the Century," when black heavyweight Jack Johnson crushed white champion James J. Jeffries. Polarizing racial tensions across the country, the match ignited riots that left twelve black men dead. New York Governor Al Smith feared that another black-white battle for the title would lead to violence and he took Rickard's side, banning a Dempsey-Wills fight in his state. Boxing officials in other areas followed suit. Some banned mixed bouts altogether on the bigoted grounds that a white boxer would always lose because, as one official put it, "the black is the nearer approach of the gorilla, most formidable of animals," a specious contention not only grossly racist but also contradicted by ring history.

Sportswriters black and white argued that Jack Johnson was the real reason Wills was denied a shot at the title. Powerful white men in the boxing world still seethed over the black champ's flagrant behavior outside the ring. Johnson had lived fast and flaunted his success—his money, big cars, flashy clothes, and most especially his white mistresses. "Why inflict the punishment coming to him on the other splendid boxers of his race?" asked Hype Igoe in *The New York World* in December 1923. "Why discriminate against ANY good man as long as he does his best? . . . Wills has been a credit to the sport, can fight like a streak, in fact is one of the world's greatest fighters."

Black and white boxing fans avidly followed Wills's quest for a chance at the crown in their local sports pages, shaking their heads in disbelief when Wills's manager reportedly offered Dempsey a king's purse of $350,000 and *still* couldn't get the match.

By the time Lee met his old friend Willie Powell on that street corner, the Wills-Dempsey controversy was the talk of the sports world. No wonder Lee immediately seized on boxing as an opportunity for the excitement and admiration he so desired.

"There's big money in fighting," Powell said, looking cool and elegant in that finely tailored suit. Willie trained young fighters over at the

Salem-Crescent Athletic Club, which happened to be located in the basement of Salem Methodist Church. "Why don't you try it?" he said. The next day, Lee signed up for a membership, put on a pair of gloves, stepped into the ring, and instantly burned with the greatest passion he had ever known. "I loved fighting," he said, "like a beautiful girl."

Powell must have been a good teacher and Lee, as always, was a quick study, becoming "one of the luminaries of the Salem-Crescent Club, one of the leading organizations of its kind in this country," the *New York Amsterdam News* reported. "He has brought added luster to his club not only by his sterling performance but by his gentlemanly conduct, which is a feature of the boys of good old Salem."

At one of Lee's early amateur bouts, the great fight announcer Joe Humphries, a little man with a famously big voice, christened the young boxer with the fighting handle he kept all his life. In the days before sophisticated sound systems, announcers stood in the center of the ring and shouted to the four corners of the arena to introduce a match. Often, they carried small cards so they could read off the competitors' names, weights, and other vital statistics. The first time the leather-lunged Humphries got ready to introduce Lee, he looked down at his notes and saw a peculiar name: "Canegata, Lee." Flummoxed by those alien syllables, Humphries tossed away the card with a snort and introduced the young fighter as "Canada Lee."

Everybody liked the transmogrification, including Lee, and it stuck.

"Canada Lee, crack colored featherweight of the Salem-Crescent A.C., chalked up his second victory in five days over his most bitter rival Mickey McCann of the Brooklyn Union Gas Co. in the best bout at the amateur boxing show staged at the Coney Island Stadium," reported the *New York Age*. "Lee out-pointed and out-boxed his adversary throughout the three rounds . . . [He] had his right to the face working in fine form and landed it almost at will."

In two years, Lee won everything but the kitchen sink, including major amateur titles: the Metropolitan, State, Inter-City, Junior National, and National Championships. This is my future, he thought. I'm doing what I love to do, what I do best. "Some people would say it's brutal and cruel and bloody, but I say 'No, it's like a dance, with a lot of poetry in it and motion and grace,'" he said.

Lee was doing some dancing outside the ring, too, courting a neighborhood beauty named Juanita Eugenia Waller. Juanita was a petite, light-skinned woman about twenty-one years of age, two years older than Lee. She was born in Manila in the Philippines to John L. and Mabel E. Waller. Graceful, well spoken, and pretty, Juanita was a sensitive and somewhat fragile person who liked to draw and paint. Canada surely wasn't making enough money to support a wife at the time, but perhaps love and desire conquered all worries. The couple married in December 1925 and moved in with the groom's family.

By his nineteenth birthday, Canada had a wife to support and soon a baby was on the way. Faced with impending fatherhood, he decided to turn professional and make some money. He boxed his last amateur bouts during the Metropolitan A.A.U. championship, a two-day tournament at Madison Square Garden. Fighting as a lightweight, he KO'd his opponent in round one of the semifinals match and then took the title by forfeit when his opponent backed out, citing an injury.

When word got around that Canada Lee intended to turn pro, "he was besieged by managers to join their stables," Irving Rudd wrote in the *Negro Digest*. A veteran named Jim Buckley finally signed him. The *New York Amsterdam News* heralded this move on October 6 with a front-page story in the sports section and a photo captioned "Here He Is: Canada Lee, The Youngster You Have Read So Much About." According to the *News*, Lee had created "a sensation in the amateurs, and as a boxer he stands with the top-notchers. Canada has bowled them over in such regular order he could not resist the importunities of many managers to hearken unto the call of the professional ranks . . . We expect to continue to grace the columns of this paper with his accomplishments all the time . . . Good luck, Canada!"

When Jim Buckley announced that Lee's first professional match would take place in the celebrated Manhattan Casino, the young boxer was thrilled. Then he found out who he was fighting, and it jolted him like a Dempsey left hook.

His opponent was none other than Willie Powell.

"I was scared," Lee later admitted. "Willie used to beat the bejesus out of us kids back at Salem-Crescent. I was even more scared when he comes up to me before the fight and says, 'Don't worry. It won't take but a minute . . . I'll just break your neck.'"

The Manhattan Casino was a ballroom and boxing venue on Eighth

Avenue at 155th Street. (By the late 1920s, it would be re-baptized as the Rockland Palace, a Harlem hotspot for jazz where thousands gathered each year at glorious, notorious integrated costume balls to see men in drag competing to be queen.)

In the final moments before the fight, Lee's manager and trainer talk strategy as the young pro wrestles with his nerves. Weighing just 135 pounds soaking wet, the slender fighter is pure muscle and speed, but his opponent has the edge in power and experience. When Canada at last enters the ballroom to make the long walk to the ring, a few loyal fans applaud. Lee gracefully ducks between the ropes, moves to his corner, takes a few deep breaths, and stares across the ring at his old teacher. Powell smiles back at him, taunting, confident, strong. The crowd hums and buzzes in anticipation. The announcer proclaims the contenders' names and weights to the four corners of the room. Canada and Willie meet in the center of the ring. The referee lays down the rules.

Then the bell rings and the shouting begins.

Willie moves in quickly, aggressively, with rapid-fire combinations and some fancy footwork. "He's got so many tricks I just stand and watch him," Lee said. Fists up, he ducks most of Willie's hooks and crosses and then, gaining confidence, begins to find his own rhythm. Points remain fairly even until the fourth round, when Canada lands several thundering body punches, pushing Powell across the ring. "He gets against the ropes and lets himself open and I *nail* him," Lee said.

Willie drops like a stone. As the referee approaches the prone figure on the canvas, Canada squares his shoulders, surveys the crowd, and sees hundreds of people on their feet, cheering. Adrenaline surges through him and explodes in pure joy. Lee turns back to the ring to look at Powell. "He watches me from the floor and tries to get up, but I rush out of my corner, very fierce, so he lies down again," Lee said. "By that time he's out, and I win."

Willie Powell lost in a knockout, a teacher outclassed by his own student.

Lee won his second professional match at the Renaissance Casino soon after, earning the young fighter favorable mentions in the local sports pages. "Everything points to a successful invasion by the gentlemanly little Salem-Crescent fighter," a Harlem scribe penned. "He is certainly one of the best two-fisted little fighting men developed in these parts in ages, and with careful handling and opportunity he should forge to the top in a short while." The same writer, clearly a veteran of boxing's color wars, also noted that Lee's "color and his unusual ability will of course play its part in denying him a fair chance . . . He will have to exhibit the patience of a Job along with his fistic ability to get to the top."

Lee continued his string of KOs on November 6 before a packed house at the Walker Athletic Club. Matched against Julio Mollano, Lee landed a haymaker on the South American fighter in the third round. "Did Canada happen to be a white boy, they would be giving him the ballyhoo which would take him into the big money in a much shorter space of time," a Harlem sportswriter pointed out.

With his bride due to give birth any day, Canada undoubtedly hoped for some of that big money, and soon. On November 20, 1926, he returned to the Walker Athletic Club to meet Juan Shifolo, a feisty fighter who vowed to put an end to Lee's knockout streak, only to find himself facedown on the canvas in the very first round.

Two days later, Juanita gave birth to a healthy boy named Carl Vincent Canegata. The new father took a few weeks off from the ring, but was back at the Walker A.C. on December 18 to meet Cliff Graham. It was a bitterly disappointing night. "Canada Lee got a taste of what it is like to win a fight, then have the decision taken away," reported the *New York Amsterdam News*. "Lee whipped Cliff Graham, scoring a clean knockdown over his white opponent." Instead of giving Canada the win, the referee declared Graham the victor based on points. The crowd was incensed and "gave the decision the razz," wrote the *News*. The newspaper didn't make an out-and-out charge of racism, but it did urge the club to set up a rematch between the two fighters.

Though Canada needed every penny to support his family, he agreed to fight two charity matches in January 1927. At the Garden Palace Arena in Passaic, New Jersey, he knocked out Freddie Herman in the first round, donating twenty-five dollars of his hundred-dollar prize to St. Mary's Hospital Fund. The other benefit bout was for Sam Langford, a famous black featherweight who had lost his sight because of injuries in the ring. The Walker A.C. sponsored the match, raising more than eight thousand dollars "so that ole Sam, almost blind, will not need to worry anymore about his bacon and eggs in the morning." Newspapers reported "Canada Lee whipped Izzy Grove after a slashing battle in the four-round opener" and then generously contributed all of his winnings to the ailing Langford.

When he wasn't boxing or training, Canada could be found at matches around town, surreptitiously analyzing the competition. Driven by his love for precision and aesthetics, he worked constantly to improve his footwork, rhythm, and speed. "I learned new methods by watching fighters," he said. "I wanted to be a perfect technician."

Word about Lee began to travel, and promoters across the river in New Jersey and on Long Island started calling. Still, most of his bouts were on his home turf in Harlem. Almost every neighborhood had a fight club, a proving ground for aspiring boxers. Purses stayed small for up-and-comers, often around fifty dollars, so Lee continued to hone his fiddling skills, supplementing his ring earnings as the leader of a scrappy little dance band dubbed "Canada Lee and His Canadian Cotton Pickers."

Just as he analyzed other boxers, Lee studied other musicians, hunting out his favorite players at speakeasies or riotous rent parties. If you lived in Harlem and found yourself a little short at the end of the month, you'd get on the horn, hire some musicians, and invite your friends over for food, drinks, and live music, charging a few dollars at the door to raise your rent money. Canada loved these parties and made fast friends with a number of Harlem's finest musicians, including Fats Waller, Count Basie, and Lionel Hampton. To Canada, his twin passions for boxing and music made perfect sense; both vocations demanded intelligence, rhythm, and artistry.

"Fighting is beautiful," he said. "Brutality doesn't appeal to me. That's for the maulers. But boxing, that's like hot music. You have to think. You feint to make the other guy do what you want him to do. That's the fun, not nailing him."

Canada and his band got better and so did their gigs, but it was in the ring that Lee became a force to be reckoned with. Now twenty years old, his muscles grew thicker and harder as he gained more power in his legs and upper body. By the fall of 1927, Lee tipped the scales at 141 pounds and moved up to the welterweight division. A handsome studio photo shows Canada poised to deliver a punch, his stance lithe and graceful as a dancer, his muscles taut and well defined. He wears monogrammed silk trunks, and his wavy hair is combed sleek against his head. Though a bit small for his new weight class, Lee made a big impression in short order. When a hot young fighter from New Orleans named Zach Blanchard came to town that October, he condescended to fight Canada Lee as a little warm-up bout before taking on Gotham's more experienced welterweights. Blanchard was in for a surprise. Lee sent the Big Easy boy to his knees three times in the first three rounds, and less than one minute into the fourth Zach was over and out. "Blanchard was little else but a punching bag all the way," a Harlem paper noted smugly.

After losing a disappointing six-round decision to Harry Felix in November, Lee racked up a series of impressive wins and celebrated New Year's Eve by defeating Jersey City's hard-hitting hero, Billy White. Unfortunately, 1928 didn't start off well as Lee lost a string of decisions to more seasoned opponents. This result is typical of the lot: "Willie Harmon, veteran east-side welterweight, won the decision over Canada Lee, Harlem Negro, last night in an unexciting six-round bout." Canada broke his losing streak in March, fighting to a dead draw against Tony Vacarelli in a sensational eight-round bout, "providing plenty of action for the customers," according to the *New York Amsterdam News*, which praised Lee's "good boxing and jabbing tactics."

"I had a good punch. I could knock them dead," Lee said. "But I got greater satisfaction slipping punches and moving gracefully out of danger . . . There is something peculiarly exciting in the knowledge that disaster can strike you at any instant."

In April, May, and June, Lee split his time between rings in Massachusetts and New York City, racking up a series of decisions and knockouts. A "prime favorite with the fans," Canada could deliver "a sock like the kick of an Army mule," according to Nat Fleischer, boxing historian and author of *Black Dynamite*. "No Negro boxer of his warrior days rated higher as an audience-pleaser."

Lee knew the importance of maintaining a fan club. Popular boxers always caught the attention of top promoters and matchmakers who put together the "boxing card," the slate of back-to-back prizefights at a venue on any given night. In the 1920s, New Yorkers could often choose from a dozen different cards in one week; sometimes four or five cards would be running on the same night in different parts of town. Across the river, Newark and other New Jersey cities ran pro cards every week. Competition was fierce, and to ensure good crowds, matchmakers liked to pit beloved local heroes against tough contenders, fights that would inspire fans to buy tickets even when times were tough and money was hard to come by.

One of Lee's biggest fans was a young man named Leonard de Paur, who avidly followed Lee's career in the sports pages. "I was a kid, and you pick up on headline names. At that time, Canada was one of the very few prominent black fighters," he later recalled. De Paur shared Lee's passion for music and would eventually become a colleague and friend to his childhood sports idol during a long and distinguished career as composer, conductor, arranger, and founder of the De Paur Chorus.

Promoters with greedy eyes on gate receipts took note of Lee's many admirers, and he started fighting bigger matches against better fighters for fatter purses. By the summer of 1928, Lee "loomed large on the pugilistic horizon as a prominent contender for the welterweight championship title," Fleischer wrote, "a natural-born fighter, the sort that sticks to the last and never quits scrapping until the power of scrapping quits him."

That summer, Lee's manager, Jim Buckley, complained to Harlem sportswriters that Canada was so feared and respected that it was "practically impossible to drag any of the important welterweights into the ring with him." Most likely, Buckley was dangling a bit of hyperbole as he fished for a title fight. On July 4, 1928, he billed Canada as a "Championship Contender" in a flashy exhibition bout against a grossly overmatched boxer named Jimmie Moore at the Lafayette Theater. Lee thrashed the poor lad and went on to win a fight nearly every week for the next two months.

As fall turned to winter, Canada battled his way through a series of exciting bouts against other title hopefuls. He added several knockouts to his résumé, but he had his disappointments, too. In Boston, he lost a heartbreaking ten-round decision to former world champion Jack Britton. Twice he took on Vince Dundee, brother to reigning world welterweight champ Joe Dundee, and both times he dueled Vince to a draw. "In the final round they stood toe-to-toe, shooting punches at each other," reported the *New York Amsterdam News* after the second matchup on December 15. "The crowd cheered loudly as the boys went to their corners after the final bell."

Sportswriters in other cities began to describe Lee as a rising welterweight star. In *The Chicago News*, John P. Carmichael called "the chocolate youngster" a fighter "of real merit." The *Boston Herald* noted Lee had "collected wins over some of the best boys in the 147-pound division." The *Holyoke Daily Transcript* called Lee "perhaps the best welterweight" in New York City. "No fighter to appear here in recent years caught the popular fancy as did Lee," wrote *The Erie Daily Times*. He was "a big hit" with fight fans, according to *The Troy Record*. Even New York's jaded scribes were impressed, including Ed Sullivan, who found Lee an "astounding chap." The legendary host of the eponymous television variety show started his career on the sports desks at the *Evening World* and the *Evening Graphic*. Sullivan befriended Lee and later helped the boxer promote his band.

Canada's prominence in the press boosted his status and his popularity. By 1929, he was earning a thousand-dollar minimum per match. "It wasn't an era when Negro fighters pulled down very large purses," Fleischer noted. "But Canada Lee fought well and often. Promoters knew him as a sterling gate attraction, knew that Harlem always turned out in full strength to see him scrap . . . His end, win or lose, was usually worthwhile."

Fleischer credits Lee with earning ninety thousand dollars during his career, which was no small change for a blue-collar kid from Harlem in the 1920s. Unfortunately, Canada never saved any of that gold for a rainy day. He preferred to make the rounds at Harlem's clubs and cabarets, where he partied with musicians, star athletes, and other celebrities. He also took a fancy to Broadway shows. "The first stage production I ever saw was *Show Boat*," he said, recalling the hit Oscar Hammerstein–Jerome Kern musical. "How I cried when the man cut Julie's wrist and said, 'One drop of Negro blood makes me a Negro, too.' A big, tough fighter, all muscle, just sobbing."

Canada generously showered money on family and friends, and he especially loved to treat his little brother to wild nights on the town. Barely in his teens, Lovey quickly learned to enjoy spending big brother's cash and decided life should be lived according to his own golden rule: "Money is meant to be spent." Partly at Lovey's instigation, Lee dropped a fair amount of change on flattering fans and some fast-living females. "I never kept any of that money," Lee admitted to reporters a decade later with a rueful grin. "I was Mr. Dog himself after one of those fights. If I liked a girl in a show I didn't take her out; I took the whole show out. I really put on the dog."

Showgirls? Clearly, things were not going so well with Juanita.

Lee may have decided he wasn't ready for marriage and parenthood after all, or perhaps Juanita got tired of staying home with the baby while Lee traveled to matches, played in his band, or partied until the wee hours. Canada "wasn't around much" in those days, his son Carl would later confide to his partner, Elaine Plenda. "Juanita was alone a lot with his family, and with Carl," Plenda said. "She was very young, and it upset her."

There may have been another reason for trouble in Canada and Juanita's marriage. Lovey's son Bill says that while Juanita was in her twenties, she began to suffer from what the family called nerves. "She had breakdowns," Canegata said. "She heard voices, like people on the street were talking about her or something. It was terrible for her, you know, for the family, too." If Canada fell out of love with Juanita, he continued to care about her; he may have behaved selfishly at times, but he was very young, and when she became ill, it was difficult to know what to do for her, how to help.

The couple separated when their son was still quite small, and Juanita eventually moved into her own apartment. Canada financially supported his wife and child, but it was his parents and sister who looked after them day in and day out. Carl grew to be a handsome boy who favored Juanita, though he had his father's darker skin as well as his restless, quick intelligence. He was often placed in the care of Canada's mother; some say Lydia Canegata virtually raised her grandson. But Juanita and Carl remained deeply devoted to each other. "Juanita really dressed him up like a proper boy, dressed him beautifully," Elaine Plenda said. "Carl was always close to his mother."

Though Lee was gone a great deal, Carl worshipped his prizefighting father and would always remember the time he was allowed to sit ringside at one of Canada's matches. "He saw his father knock someone out of the ring and he was scared stiff," Frances Lee Pearson said. "I think he was always a little fearful of that side of his father."

Another boy never forgot Canada Lee's powerful fists. Leslie Nash, Jr., was the grandson of Professor Butler, Canada's old music teacher; his mother, Celia, and uncle, Billy, had been friends with Lee since childhood. When Nash was about six years old, his family lived in a working-class neighborhood in New Jersey where packs of young toughs roamed the streets, throwing rocks and picking fights. Nash was a favorite target for ridicule because he had contracted polio as a baby and walked with a limp. His mother tried talking to the bullies' parents without success. Her husband's solution was to give his son nightly boxing lessons after dinner. One night, the boy got a big surprise as someone crept up behind him and grabbed his wrists. "It was Canada," Nash recalled. "He put his chin on top of my head, with the back of my head nestling against his neck so that he could move his head and my head would move with it . . . He feinted a couple of times, threw a jab here and a right cross there, and suddenly I began to understand more and more about the mechanics of fighting."

Soon the boy could ably defend himself, and neighborhood thugs left him alone. But when the Nash family moved to a new town, the local bully made the mistake of calling Les "cripple" and imitating his limp. Nash took the hide off him. "I was out of my mind with anger," he said, recalling that day. Celia was beside herself, and Canada stopped by to have a talk with his protégé. Fight with all your strength to defend yourself, Lee told the boy, but don't try to kill anyone. You don't want that on your conscience. "That stayed with me, and is still with me to this day," Nash said.

After a successful summer in the ring, Lee lost a ten-round decision and a sizeable purse to Arturo Shekels in Madison Square Garden on September 24, 1929. Exactly one month later, on the infamous Black Tuesday, that lost purse seemed like small potatoes. Wall Street tottered, the stock market crashed, and the Great Depression settled like a dark cloud over the entire country. The look of shock on his father's face as he read about the disaster in the daily papers was burned into Lee's memory. "My dad couldn't believe it," he would later recall. "Money in the bank was safe — like being sure of heaven! Those were bad days for everybody — but it did seem like Negroes got the worst of it."

Banks failed, businesses closed, men and women lost their jobs, and few had any idea that this was just the start of a long economic nightmare. Boxing survived, however, thanks in part to an infusion of mafia money, and Lee continued to prosper. His ring earnings now helped support his father and mother as well as his wife and son. By the end of the year, sports scribes ranked Canada as high as eighth in the world, and many acknowledged him as a leading contender for the welterweight championship. "Lee was the [Sugar] Ray Robinson of his day," according to *The Ring* magazine. Yet no matter how hard he tried, Canada couldn't get a title match. Damon Runyon, famed sportswriter and author, claimed that Lee was overrated as a fighter, that he was primarily a crowd-pleaser who didn't have the right stuff to be a world champion.

Canada sharply disagreed with Runyon's assessment of his talent. In the racially divided world of boxing, Lee said, it was his successful record in the ring that ironically prevented him from getting a shot at the title. "It wasn't the fighters themselves. It was their managers. When my manager approached them to arrange a fight for me, they would say, 'Now look here, we don't fight colored boys. They're too tough!'" he said. "When we were in the gymnasium, training for fights, the white boys were always able to find competent people to work with, but a Negro training for a fight couldn't."

Many ring aficionados in Harlem suspected that Lee's biggest stumbling block was the same obstacle that tripped up Harry Wills—the white boxing world's lingering hatred toward Jack Johnson. According to sportswriter John Lopez, the controversial black heavyweight "cost numerous other boxers . . . any chance of following him to a championship." By 1929, Wills had all but given up the quest and was about to retire. (White fighters would hold on to the heavyweight title for twenty-two years, until Joe Louis captured it in 1937.) Fight fans and sportswriters alike were convinced that white promoters were conspiring to prevent black contenders from winning titles in any weight class, not just the heavyweight division. "A great many good colored fighters never won titles because they were not given a chance," the *Evening Journal* reported.

Canada read the papers and knew the score, but he refused to give up. After a protracted struggle, he and his manager believed they were on the verge of locking in a championship bout. And then, just as Lee neared the end of his quest for a shot at the world welterweight title, his dreams came to a shattering end one night at Madison Square Garden.

Ed Sullivan had recently moved from the sports to the entertainment desk at *The New York Evening Graphic*, but he was ringside at the Garden on December 12 to see the match between Lee and Andy Divodi. Lee was predicted to be a shoo-in, but the writers were wrong. During a bruising bout, Divodi struck Lee a crushing blow above the right ear.

Canada shook it off and hammered out a decision after ten brutal rounds, but ultimately he lost big. The blow detached the retina of his right eye. Before long, he would develop blind spots, and eventually lose all sight in that eye. "Proper treatment would have saved it," Lee said a decade later. "But I don't let that get me down."

If Canada had trouble with his vision immediately after that fateful night in the Garden, he told no one, least of all his powerful new manager, Luis "Pincho" Gutierrez, a journalist-turned-boxing entrepreneur with a squad of hot young fighters. "Lee simply held his right hand higher to guard the bad eye and continued his career," a sports reporter later wrote. "Moreover, he turned in some of his best fights."

On January 3, 1930, Pincho Gutierrez rematched Lee against Arturo Shekels in Madison Square Garden. Lee had no way of knowing this would be his last fight in the famous arena that he loved so well. Patsy Haley refereed, and in the fifth round he stopped the fight and gave the win to Shekels, claiming that Canada had fouled his opponent by hitting him below the belt. "I was pretty sore at the time because I know I never landed any low punch," Lee said.

A week later, Canada knocked down Billy Algers in the fifth round at a standing-room-only match in Harlem. Algers suffered a deep gash over his left eye and once again the referee stopped the fight, this time awarding Lee a TKO. Harlem sportswriters crowed over the win, still smarting over Lee's narrow loss to Shekels the week before, a decision they suspected was racially motivated. "[Lee] is coming into his own," reported the *New York Amsterdam News*. "If boxing referees and judges would only stop taking the decision away from Lee when it is so evident to those with a knowledge of the game that he has won, he would enjoy the most prosperous year in his career."

It was certainly the most exciting year for Lee, who was about to take his first trip to the Caribbean, thanks to his manager. A native of Cuba, Gutierrez had once been sports editor at Havana's *La Noche* newspaper. He still kept a hand in the island's boxing affairs, while in New York he managed two popular Cuban-born fighters—the famed featherweight Kid Chocolate, and a fierce little flyweight known as Black Bill. Pincho set up lucrative matches in Havana for all three of his fighters. Lee was to take on the great Spanish boxing champion Ignacio Ara for a tidy thirty-five-hundred-dollar minimum.

The Cuban press knew all about Canada, thanks to Gutierrez's public relations savvy. Huge headlines heralded the boxer's arrival in Havana, and Pincho invited reporters and photographers to a special sneak-preview training session a few days before the big match with Ara. Men in finely tailored suits and light straw hats crowded into a gym, chatting noisily and smoking fragrant cigars. "Suddenly, all conversations ceased, and everyone looked toward the ring, where a world champion boxer with a great record entered," one reporter recalled. Lee put his gloves on, posed for the photographers, did some quick exercises, and finally called sparring partner Agustin Lillo into the ring. Reporters whispered to one another that Lee's trainer had ordered him to work at half speed to fool Ara's spies who were scattered among the crowd.

Showing off a bit for the press, Lillo tried to pop Canada a good one. Lee, barely moving, ducked every punch while throwing one wicked combination after another. "On two occasions, Lillo was tossed like a toy into the ropes and knocked down," a reporter wrote. "These first demonstrations are enough to judge [Lee] a true pugilist, an authentic champion."

Disaster struck when Cuba's boxing commission banned Gutierrez from attending the Ara-Lee match. The reason for Pincho's suspension is unclear, but the decision was extremely unpopular. Furious, Lee refused to box without his manager in his corner. Though it meant giving up an opportunity to win a sizeable prize, Canada told the press that he preferred to "waste his time and return to New York" rather than go along with an unfair suspension. He criticized the commission's feud with Gutierrez, suggesting that it would be better for "the public, the ones who pay, to decide" if the manager could come to the match. Sportswriters sympathized and protested the ruling, but the commission stood firm. Disappointed and frustrated, Lee left the country.

Bad luck dogged him. Two months later, he somehow suffered a serious gash on one of his legs. The cut became badly infected and he was confined to a hospital cot for weeks. In June, Gutierrez announced Lee was finally healthy and ready for action. If he had any idea that Lee was losing his sight, Pincho didn't let on to boxing officials or the press. During this period, boxers frequently hid their injuries in order to keep making good money in the ring. Famed welterweight champ Harry Greb stayed in the ring five years after being blinded in one eye; the truth came out only after the boxer died in 1926 of complications during eye surgery. Medical regulations simply weren't as stringent in those days, and if a boxer looked good and fought well, he stayed in the game. Like most experienced fighters, Lee was battle-scarred, and his smashed-up ears bore a striking resemblance to cauliflowers. But in the ring, Lee still looked every inch the champ.

At Ebbets Field, home of the Brooklyn Dodgers, Lee knocked out Willie Garafola in the ninth round, but not before Garafola smashed his head so hard that Lee suspected the blow further damaged his bad eye. On August 8, he traveled to Erie, Pennsylvania, to face local favorite Tommy Freeman before an audience of 1,650. Canada came out tough, landing one right cross after another. In the third round, he drove Freeman into a corner, sent him staggering with a short left hook to the jaw, and all but dropped him with another right cross. "Freeman was dazed," reported *The Erie Dispatch-Herald*, "but he quickly came out of it." Three fiesty rounds followed as the crowd screamed wildly for both boxers. By the last three rounds, Lee was fighting on fumes and Freeman won the decision. "The New York Negro put up a great scrap and gave evidence that he can lick most of the welterweights in the game today," *The Erie Daily Times* observed. Canada's take was reportedly $750—a respectable sum, given that the average per capita annual income in 1929 was $750, but clearly Lee was earning less than he had at the peak of his career.

One month later, Freeman won the world welterweight championship. Canada desperately wanted a rematch with the champ for the title, and Gutierrez started working the channels. Lee fought at least twice more that fall, knocking out Freddie Fitzgerald in just two rounds, but losing a ten-round decision to Jackie Brady.

In June 1931, Canada finally got his fight with Freeman, but by the time the match was arranged, the champ had already lost the title and Lee's deteriorating eyesight was diminishing his prowess in the ring. When he faced Freeman that second time before a roaring crowd, it wasn't for the championship, it was for his pride and a much needed fifteen-hundred-dollar purse.

Years later, Canada claimed that promoters for the Freeman fight offered to pay him off handsomely if he took a dive.

"I've never tossed anybody!" Canada protested. "I can't start that stuff now."

"Don't be stupid. Get yourself some dough," he was told, but he stood firm.

"All right, fight your fight," they said, warning Lee not to say a word to Freeman or his manager about it. In the first round, Canada intentionally took two machine gun lefts to his forehead. As Freeman cockily went for a third, Lee slipped under the jab and hit Freeman with a short, solid hook. Freeman hit the deck with a glorious thud. Astonished, the fighter bellowed at Canada: "What are you doin'? Crossing me up?"

If Freeman thought the fix was in, he was wrong. Spitting mad, the ex-champ picked himself up and barreled into Lee. Fists flew during ten furious rounds, each man giving as good as he got. Canada was crushed when the judges gave Freeman the decision, and the chicanery surrounding the fight left a bitter aftertaste. Did promoters think Lee was washed up? Is that why they figured he would gladly take a dive?

His career spiraled downward. Canada fought a dozen or so matches in 1931 and lost nearly all of them. A veteran of the ring at age twenty-four, Lee became a target for up-and-coming boxers looking to prove their mettle. On February 13, 1931, he traveled to Worcester, Massachusetts, to meet a hot young fighter named Lou Brouillard. The nineteen-year-old southpaw from Quebec had already racked up an impressive sixty wins, forty-five of them knockouts. Lefties posed a particular danger to Lee; with his damaged right eye, it was tougher to see and defend against left-handed punches. Brouillard battered Canada mercilessly for nine rounds before knocking him out in the tenth—perhaps the only time Lee was ever KO'd. (He would always claim that he had been "floored" three times during his boxing career but never knocked out; however, most statistics award a KO to Brouillard.) In March, Lee lost a disappointing ten-round rematch with Brouillard; seven months later, the French Canadian captured the world welterweight title.

Things only got worse for Lee. In 1933, he suffered perhaps the most humiliating defeat of his career at Canada's Maple Leaf Gardens when he lost a decision to an awkward young farm boy from Winnipeg named Schaefer. "Losing to a greenie like Schaefer—though Canada claims the verdict was stolen—and the fact that his eyes were going bad on him brought about his quitting of the ring," a reporter for Toronto's *Evening Telegram* later wrote.

Lee knew it was time to hang up the gloves. His sight continued to deteriorate and his chances at a title were next to none. Still, it was hard to let go of a dream. For the rest of the year, he barnstormed through Pennsylvania, literally boxing in barns or schools or community halls for peanuts. When he returned to New York, he made a last-gasp attempt to lure welterweight champ Jimmy McLarnin into the ring, but Jimmy turned him down. "He still thinks he could have licked Jim McLarnin the best day the Irishman lived," sportswriter John P. Carmichael later wrote. "But he never got the chance."

By 1934, the truth was out about his blind side. Pincho Gutierrez told reporters that when he discovered Lee was boxing with a damaged eye, he gave the fighter $1,500 "and told him to quit."

Canada was out of a job. He was also broke. During his years in the ring, he earned close to a hundred thousand dollars and never saved a penny. "Just threw it away," he admitted. "Had fun, though, and lots of excitement. Money just seems to go, doesn't it, especially when it comes easy!" He lived to regret this laissez-faire attitude, and years later Lee would lobby boxing commissions to oversee insurance, health care, financial advice, and retirement homes for fighters. "Most kids take up fighting at an early age," he told *The Ring* magazine a decade after he left the sport. "The average boxer possesses little education . . . If he winds up broke, he has no trade, no education and nobody to turn to."

He spoke from experience. All the same, Canada never regretted his boxing days. "I loved fighting better than I've loved anything else in my whole life," he told one reporter. "I thrilled to every minute I ever spent in the ring, in the gym, and with the fight fans.

"No one ever enjoyed boxing as much as I did, outwitting the other fellow, the roar of the crowd," he recalled with a smile. "It's the greatest game in the world."

But those days were over and now, in the depths of the Great Depression, Canada, a junior-high-school dropout, half blind, with an estranged wife and young son to support, found himself with no money, no job, no education, and no prospects.

It was time to reinvent himself again.

FOUR

NICE WORK
IF YOU CAN GET IT

THE STAGE

In the early 1930s, as America sank deeper into economic and spiritual depression, its devastated people desperately yearned for escape. Millions found it at their local movie theater, where for just twenty-five cents they could lose themselves for hours in lavish musicals and screwball comedies. Millions more found it on the radio, where a five-dollar tabletop model bought the whole family everlasting roundtrip tickets to those fantastic worlds, thrilling adventures, and hilarious households on the airwaves—from *The Lone Ranger* to *Buck Rogers in the Twenty-Fifth Century* to *The Jack Benny Show*. And in New York City, dazzling drama and heady romance beckoned from the bright lights of Broadway.

Fans thrilled vicariously to the exploits of their favorite actors. In the Big Apple, the streets fairly crawled with publicists hawking shows and stars, while nosy parkers at the newspapers sucked up every bit of fluff and tittle-tattle to tantalize readers into buying more editions. Gotham's major dailies maintained small armies of gossip columnists with a single mission: to scoop the competition by being the first to publish who would star in what, who would marry whom, who was seen with someone else, who filed for divorce and why. This pack of scandal-mongers often commanded substantial salaries and wielded enormous power.

Ed Sullivan saw his chance and seized it, abandoning the sports desk to pen a column for the *Graphic* called "Ed Sullivan Sees Broadway!" His principal rival was the perpetually gossipy and frequently malevolent Walter Winchell. In his very first column, Sullivan promised his readers that he would rise above his competition. Unlike that weasel Winchell, he would publish no malicious rumors, spy through no keyholes, propagate no divorces, and promote no phonies. To see your name in Ed Sullivan's column would be a badge of merit, a citation!

Canada Lee read those words and an idea started percolating.

He and Ed had met years before as prizefighter and sportswriter and hit it off instantly. They had a great deal in common besides their avid enthusiasm for sports. Both were from close-knit families of modest means, firm principles, and strong religious faith. Born on East 114th Street in Manhattan to a thoroughly Irish family, Sullivan spent most of his childhood in the sleepy village of Port Chester, just north of the city. He cared little for schoolwork, though he took pleasure in reading those same tales of adventure and romance that Lee had preferred as a boy. Like Canada, Ed had run away from home; he was just fifteen when he sneaked off to Chicago, hoping to bluff his way into the Marines, but he got the boot when he couldn't produce his birth certificate. After working odd jobs during a brutal Windy City winter and sleeping at the local YMCA, he finally decided to go home to Port Chester. He enrolled in high school, and his love of reading got him interested in writing. He volunteered to cover sports for the school newspaper—a natural choice, for he excelled in athletics. A fierce competitor, he lettered in baseball, basketball, football, and track. He frequently competed against top black athletes from other schools and later said this fostered an "instinctive antagonism . . . to any theory that a Negro wasn't a worthy opponent, or was an inferior person." After graduating, he landed a job as sports reporter on his hometown weekly and then worked his way up to New York City's daily papers. Sullivan considered himself politically progressive, and he ruffled some feathers by condemning racism in the sports world. But he also did plenty of insipid interviews with sports celebrities; in fact, his penchant for mixing with the rich and famous gave him an incurable taste for the high life. Just like Canada in his prizefighting heyday, Ed made good money and spent it freely on nice cars, sharp suits, pretty flappers, nightclubs, and Broadway shows.

When Sullivan got his Broadway column, Canada said he was happy and proud: "I felt as though a friend of mine was going up the ladder of success."

As for Lee, he was clutching the bottom rung of that ladder, trying not to slide off into oblivion. In the waning days of his welterweight career, he had picked up his fiddle again and organized a little dance band. But while Duke, Satchmo, Fletcher Henderson, and other jazz heavyweights played high-profile venues like the Cotton Club and the Savoy for sizeable paychecks, Canada was lucky to drum up a few gigs in little-known clubs the size of closets for coffee and doughnut money. "I figured that my popularity as a prizefighter would carry me along into a musical career," Lee said, "but it didn't work that way. The people who thought I was important in the ring knew nothing about the music racket, so here I was with a band and nowhere to take it."

He knew he would never get a crack at the big time on his own. When he read Sullivan's new column promising to eschew scandal in favor of honorable endeavors, an idea popped into his head. Rustling up paper and pen, Canada sat down and wrote Ed a letter to suggest a human interest story for his next column: Boxer Turns Bandleader.

"I was down and out, blinded in one eye . . . with an orchestra that I couldn't find work for," he said. "I wrote to [Ed] asking for help."

Sullivan gladly gave Canada a generous plug in his column and, sure enough, the band's fortunes began to improve. On Thanksgiving Day, 1930, "Canada Lee and His Harmony Eleven" played the Dunbar Palace, a ballroom often jammed with nattily dressed dancers doing the Lindy Hop. In May 1931, Lee played the Alhambra on a double bill with Sandy "Ashes" Burns. The Alhambra, at 126th Street and Seventh Avenue, advanced the careers of legendary performers such as Bessie Smith, Jelly Roll Morton, and a singing waitress named Billie Holiday.

During the Depression, the ballroom was another oasis of pleasure for people down on their luck. Men and women saved their pennies all week to afford a fleeting chance to dance away their cares, to savor the sheer physical exhilaration of mastering intricate steps that took them sailing and spinning through space.

Making the rounds of Harlem's dancehalls, Canada helped nurture a form of jazz created by bands big and small, black and white, famous and anonymous. This was swing, and within a decade it would sweep the nation, becoming the defining music for an entire generation of Americans who bought millions of records, plugged hard-earned nickels into jukeboxes, and packed their local ballrooms.

In 1933, Canada reached the peak of his career as a bandleader, headlining at Harlem's celebrated Lafayette Theater, also known as "House Beautiful," on 132nd Street and Seventh Avenue. The Lafayette seated two thousand and was probably the first New York theater to desegregate; as early as 1912, African Americans were allowed to sit in orchestra seats instead of being relegated to the highest balconies. Canada conducted his orchestra and played violin and later worked at the Lafayette as master of ceremonies for variety shows. Lee also reportedly substituted for Duke Ellington one night at the Cotton Club during Ellington's return engagement there in spring 1933.

Despite his natural gifts, Lee knew in his heart that he didn't have the magic he needed to put him on top. He heard the complex music that Ellington, Henderson, and others were scoring, and he also knew that the dazzling, acrobatic, ingenious soloists of his day were revolutionizing the very nature of jazz.

"I had to give it up," Lee said. "I played the fiddle, but I just bulldozed. When it came to the easy passages, I could play them, but not much else. I was wondering what the hell I was going to do. I couldn't stand the idea of a routine job. I just couldn't do it."

In 1934, Canada put together enough money to open a little neighborhood nightclub called The Jitterbug, likely named for a hit tune recorded by Cab Calloway in January of that year. He kept it going for six months without making a dime before he closed it, convinced he should give up on music altogether. Out of work and out of money, he nevertheless refused to go on the dole. "I never could take that home relief and the questions they asked you," he said. Eventually, he sought his mother's counsel. Lydia Canegata loved her son and believed in his talent, but she was also a practical woman trying to manage a household and keep her family together in tough times.

"You're a man," she told him. "Go get a job."

Canada wrestled with his vanity, what he called his false pride. "Because I had been a notable figure in the prizefighting world, I was afraid I would be laughed at if I got myself a job," he said. But in the end, he knew his mother was right. "Just being a big shot didn't get me any shoes," he said.

He learned that an old friend was working as a counselor at the employment bureau of the Harlem YMCA on 135th Street, somebody who might be able to help him find decent work. He was still tormented by the idea that someone would recognize Canada Lee, the prizefighter, on line for a menial job. "I thought people would laugh at me if I didn't have any dough," he said.

Walking to 135th Street on a bright, sunny day, he gave himself a good talking-to. "Other people work," he told himself. "They're not ashamed to go out and earn a living. Who are you to be any different? People work to eat and live. You've had your fling at life. It's time to settle down." He entered the Y and started climbing the crowded stairway to the employment bureau. Halfway up the steps, he stopped.

"Did you ever come home, as a kid, and know, for instance, that you're gonna get a licking?" he later said, describing that moment. "You try to put it off as long as possible by playing ball along the way, or doing things you wouldn't normally do? Well, that's the way I felt going up those stairs . . . I decided to take a walk, once around the block."

He took that walk and still couldn't make himself go up those stairs. Instead, he wandered around the Y, brooding over his troubles. He followed a different stairway to the doors of a small auditorium. He was curious, and on impulse, like Alice in Wonderland, he walked through a door marked "Enter Here."

He found himself in a darkened theater, where actor/director Frank Wilson was auditioning men and women for a production of a new play. "I was curious to see what it was all about," Lee said. "I always admired actors . . . romance, glamour, you know." He quietly dropped into a seat about three rows back and watched.

One actor after another took the stage and read a few lines. Canada recalled that "some of them were very good, but others, well . . ." Wilson called the last name on his list. Most of the other actors had already left the theater. When no one took the stage, the director looked around, spied Canada sitting in the back, and beckoned impatiently.

"All right, you, next," Wilson said. "What's your name?"

"Me? I'm just a spectator—" Lee started to say. Then his nightmare came true. Augustus Smith, a stage veteran who had started his career in black minstrel shows, recognized him and shouted: "That's Canada Lee, the fighter!"

A boxer? That was novel. Wilson made a closer inspection. He looked to be about five feet, eight or nine inches, very trim and fit. His ears were a little bashed in, and he wasn't exactly handsome, but there was something about his expression, a smile playing around his lips that seemed both merry and a bit wary at the same time.

"Come on up here and read this," Wilson said.

Canada hesitated. What did he know about acting? Nothing. On the other hand, what did he have to lose? He took the stage and read for the part. "That was fine," the director told him. "The job is yours."

Jockey turns boxer turns bandleader turns actor.

Canada's first role was Nathan in a play called *Brother Mose*. The show turned out to be part of a work-relief program for actors, begun in 1933 by New York's Civil Works Administration with encouragement from President Franklin Roosevelt. Theatrical unemployment was extremely high during the Depression, especially in New York City. To put actors back to work, the state's emergency relief bureau allocated modest funds to start a small "Drama Department." Stage and screen stars Katharine Cornell, Peggy Wood, and Katharine Hepburn raised additional money for costumes and props. The experiment was a resounding success, employing a thousand actors by the fall of 1934 and providing free entertainment for thousands of poverty-stricken city dwellers.

Frank Wilson was a well-respected actor who had starred in *Porgy* on Broadway and in London. Unfortunately, he had less success directing this particular venture. (Some believe *Brother Mose* was Wilson's own handiwork, a trimmed-down version of his 1928 Broadway play *Meek Mose*, which featured a massive cast and roles so stereotyped that white and black critics were perturbed by its distinctly "minstrel" aroma.) Canada didn't much care what people thought of *Brother Mose*. He was making his living in front of an audience again, and he liked it. When he met up with his friend Billy Butler, Lee was clearly happy with his new job as an actor. "He always felt that he could do anything he wanted to do, no matter what it was," Butler said.

As *Brother Mose* toured the boroughs, Canada performed on the backs of trucks, in city parks and community centers until the show closed for good. In the fall of 1934, he was looking for his next job.

Through Frank Wilson, he met actress Georgette Harvey, who was in a hit play called *Stevedore*. Harvey said one of her co-stars, Rex Ingram, would soon leave the show and suggested that maybe Canada could try out for the role.

Maybe? We'll see about maybe, Lee thought. Years later, Rex Ingram recounted the night he was onstage and realized that the ex-prizefighter Canada Lee was standing in the wings, watching him like a hawk.

"Why are you staring at me?" Ingram asked, a little testily.

"Because I'm going to take your part," Lee told him.

And he did. On October 1, audience members at the Civic Repertory Theater opened their playbills to find a rather unusual bio for the new actor playing Blacksnake: "Canada Lee's training for the stage has included jockeying, boxing, and directing his own band. This is his first professional part."

Stevedore is set on the levees of New Orleans. When the story opens, a white married woman has been roughly beaten by her lover. To save herself from scandal and her lover from prosecution, she accuses a black stevedore of rape. The accused just happens to be a radical who fights Jim Crow, flirts with Communism, and agitates for organized labor. A lynch mob goes after the innocent man, and when his fellow dockworkers fight to protect him, a race riot breaks out.

The play by George Sklar and Paul Peters was directed by Michael Blankfort and produced by the Theatre Union, whose mission was to "produce plays that have meaning for and bearing on the struggles and conflicts of our times." While earning praise in many quarters for producing exciting and meaningful drama, the Theatre Union was criticized by others for hanging a shabby cloak of propaganda on mediocre melodrama for a strictly partisan audience. The Civic Rep was located just off Union Square, long a gathering place for progressive firebrands, leftists, and Communists who could often be found standing on packing crates and making speeches.

Critic John Mason Brown accused *Stevedore*'s playwrights of pandering to these champions of the revolution: "They have only to give one of their Negroes such a line as, 'White man, don't you dare to talk to me that way,' and the gallery gods become ecstatic. They have only to mention the word 'strike' and every member of the party who hears it is persuaded that a great speech has been made . . . They seem to be much more interested in putting salt into old wounds than in cauterizing them."

Given the play's themes and mixed-race cast, as well as the policy of integrated seating at the show, *Stevedore* was bound to attract the attention of conservatives in Congress. The Baltimore *Afro-American* published an account of the controversy under the headline, "Congress Alarmed Over 'Stevedore' Lynch Drama."

The production didn't alarm audiences, but it certainly excited them. Blacks and whites lustily stamped their feet and cheered on the stevedores. Legendary tap dancer Bill Bojangles Robinson reportedly got so involved in one performance that he jumped out of his seat, vaulted onto the stage, and joined the dockhands in stoning the white mob.

The atmosphere outside the theater was also politically charged. At the entrance, young radicals distributed handbills advertising debates and meetings on labor questions and the "coming war." Plainclothes policeman were seen chewing gum and surveying the crowds. One night after a performance, Canada spotted a few young hoods in the back of the theater. He could tell they were spoiling for a fight, and grew alarmed when he saw a pale, dark-haired teenager in the audience angrily rise to their bait.

"He got nasty and started for them," Lee said. "One guy came at him with a big blade. I jumped up and told the guy to get the hell out of there." Lee's menacing fists went up. The hoods dispersed. The pale young man who "almost got his head cut off" was impressed by Lee's heroism. He stuck out a hand and introduced himself.

His name was Orson Welles.

This would prove an auspicious meeting, but for the moment, young Welles stepped back in the wings long enough for Lee to tour with *Stevedore* to Chicago, Detroit, and other cities. After returning to New York in spring 1935, he promptly landed a role in *Sailor, Beware!* produced by The Harlem Players. An all-black version of a bawdy Broadway comedy, *Sailor, Beware!* premiered at the newly reopened Lafayette Theater on May 6, starring Juano Hernandez and Christola Williams and featuring Canada Lee. Brooks Atkinson of *The New York Times* enjoyed the show immensely, congratulating the players on their "gleaming gusto." But the comedy fared poorly with black audiences, according to Loften Mitchell. "Harlem in the 1930s was hardly interested in a sailor's activities," he observed, and many were offended by the production's bold sexuality.

At least one Harlemite was enormously interested in the show. As a teenager, Leonard de Paur had admired Canada from afar, reading about the prizefighter in the sports pages. Now the young man eagerly bought a ticket to see his hero in *Sailor, Beware!* De Paur was amazed to see Lee totally at ease on stage, as though he had been doing this all of his life. "Nobody appreciated how hard he worked to become an actor," he later said.

Wonderful as it was to see Canada in the show, de Paur said, it was even more thrilling to be introduced to him by none other than Langston Hughes.

Hughes, the brilliant poet, playwright, and author who captured so eloquently the moods and rhythms of his adopted hometown of Harlem, was one of Canada Lee's best friends. It's not certain how or when the two met, although several accounts suggest it was at a rent party. Without a doubt, their shared passion for jazz, blues, sports, and theater cemented an enduring friendship. In the summer of 1935, Hughes was preparing his play *Mulatto* for a Broadway production. De Paur was an aspiring young composer, and he audaciously attached himself to Langston and his friend Roi Ottley, a well-known essayist and columnist at the *New York Amsterdam News*.

Langston and Roi cruised up and down Seventh Avenue on fine evenings, often with de Paur in tow. "They would somehow tolerate me as I would tag along, trying to meet all the people they knew," de Paur said. "That's when I actually met Canada."

Lee took to the earnest young lad as well. During *Sailor, Beware!* he met de Paur almost daily at the Radio Grill, a little pub just a few doors down from the theater. Canada wasn't much of a drinker, but he was a sharp dresser who liked to see and be seen. "He would stand there with his snap-brim hat on and just survey the crowd," de Paur recalled. The two men talked with the regulars about music or theater or sports. Lee still loved the fights. When an up-and-coming boxer named Cyril Joseph cheekily dubbed himself "Young Canada Lee," his forebear didn't mind at all. In fact, Canada sent his glossy press photo to Joseph and inscribed it: "Hoping he does all the things I should have done. I hope I shall someday call him 'champ.' —Canada Lee, March 14, 1936."

Oddly enough, Lee made the sports pages himself that spring when he agreed to be a sparring partner for a sensational young heavyweight named Joe Louis. Louis, the "Brown Bomber," was training for a June 25 fight with Primo Carnera and invited Lee to box a round with him. Even though Canada was smaller and lighter and hadn't fought professionally for three years, he couldn't resist. Though the sparring date was mostly a publicity stunt, Lee was taking a risk the day he stepped into the ring with Joe Louis. The future champ possessed a vicious left hook that posed a real threat to Lee's blind side.

"I was scared, of course, and when I'm scared, I'm a boxing fool," Lee told reporters. "Louis never laid a glove on me until ten seconds before the bell."

Near the end of the round, Canada's legs grew tired. Louis pinned him against the ropes and landed a crushing right to Lee's chin. "I had been making him look silly and he was sore. He put everything he had behind the blow," Canada said. "Right on the button. I thought I'd drop. Nothing happened. After I left the ring, I thought Louis stunk." (When Joe took the title a year later, he won Lee's respect and the two became great friends.)

Once his reprise as a boxer was over, the actor had urgent business to take care of. *Sailor, Beware!* had finished its short run, and the hunt for a new job turned up zilch. He needed work, fast. Thankfully, the pale young man Canada once rescued in the back of a theater was about to return the favor—Wunderkind Orson Welles was on his way to Harlem to direct Shakespeare for the Federal Theatre.

As America's Depression dragged on, millions remained jobless, hungry, humiliated. Congress allocated $4.8 billion for work relief and created agencies to administer the funds. One of these was the Works Progress Administration (WPA), which included projects to alleviate white-collar unemployment among writers, artists, and musicians. The new Federal Theatre Project (FTP) was a blessing for theater professionals; at the time, more than 90 percent of America's legitimate theaters were dark.

Regional units of the Federal Theatre were established across the country, most of them hiring white artists to serve white audiences. The

Negro Units were the brainchild of Rose McClendon, a prominent Harlem thespian. Mindful that three out of four black Americans were out of work, McClendon convinced the WPA to create sixteen Negro Units in the FTP, including one in Harlem. More than eight hundred of the eight thousand to thirteen thousand people employed by the Federal Theater each year were black. Without McClendon's efforts, the percentage would have been smaller, if not nonexistent.

Hallie Flanagan, the Federal Theatre's national director, thought an African American should head the Harlem unit. But when she consulted McClendon and other leaders in the black arts community, she found they were divided on the issue. In the end, Flanagan sided with the faction led by McClendon who believed that a white man would give the unit additional prestige and clout.

John Houseman, thirty-three, had overseen a black cast in the Broadway production of the Virgil Thomson–Gertrude Stein opera *Four Saints in Three Acts,* and Flanagan believed he had the tact and sensitivity required of a white administrator running a black company. When he took charge of the Harlem Negro Unit that fall, Houseman quickly learned that the black revues and musicals that made so many black performers popular on Broadway were regarded as demeaning by Harlem actors and audiences. With this in mind, Houseman divided his unit into two sections. One section would present "indigenous plays—black plays written by black authors, directed by black directors on subjects of contemporary black interest." The other would perform Shakespeare and other classic works "without concession or reference to color."

Black actors performing Shakespearean roles in professional productions? This was a daring if not downright revolutionary idea at the time, but Houseman got the go-ahead from Flanagan to try. Unfortunately, he found no black directors with experience in the classics—or at least that's what he said. It's also possible that Houseman knew all along who he wanted and it was Orson Welles, the "monstrous boy" who had so captivated Houseman with his 1934 Broadway debut as Tybalt in *Romeo and Juliet.* The two men had already discussed Shakespeare and their desire to work together, so "I invited Orson Welles to come up and direct," Houseman briefly states in his memoirs.

If Houseman's decision to produce the classics was a daring enterprise for a new black theater company, his choice of director was equally audacious. Welles was a white Wisconsinite barely out of his teens who had all of two directing credits: a high-school production of *Julius Caesar* and a summer stock show in Illinois. But Houseman had a fanatic's faith in Orson's talent, and he now urged Welles to choose his play.

Orson's wife, actress Virginia Nicholson Welles, suggested taking *Macbeth* out of medieval Scotland and moving it to early nineteenth-century Haiti, setting it in the court of Henri Christophe. Once a slave, Christophe had led a successful insurrection against colonial French rulers and then, in Napoleonic fashion, crowned himself emperor. His regime was cruel and his people revolted. The similarities between Christophe's rule and the storyline of *Macbeth* excited Orson to no end. Gleefully, he set about cutting and reorganizing Shakespeare's text. Downplaying the Bard's theme of a man destroyed by his ambition, Welles emphasized instead the powers of magic, transforming the play's Scottish heath-hags into voodoo priestesses and turning Hecate into a priest of the forces of darkness who ultimately controls Macbeth's fate.

Houseman thought a black stage manager could be of help to Orson, who had no experience working with actors of color. He offered the position to Thomas Anderson, an affable, industrious young actor who had made his Broadway debut in *Four Saints*. Anderson accepted the job just as auditions for *Macbeth* got underway.

Welles vowed this would be a thoroughly modern production with extraordinary visual and sound effects. No one has ever done Shakespeare the way I intend to do the old boy, he declared. As for actors, who cares if they aren't steeped in Shakespearean tradition, scansion, or iambic pentameter? Out with old ways and outdated notions.

In this case, having minimal expectations for classical training worked for the best. The FTP's goal was to hire only theater professionals, but it also had a mandate to take 90 percent of cast and crew off the work relief rolls. Of the eight hundred professionals employed by the Negro Units, only 150 or so had substantive theatrical experience, and these included stagehands, seamstresses, and elocutionists.

As auditions began, production staff tried to hide their dismay at the task before them. Would-be actors took the stage one by one, each struggling to get through the text before them. "It was really ridiculous in a couple of instances," recalled Leonard de Paur, who was the show's choral director. "There was no way possible that some of these souls were going to be able to read Shakespeare, but read they had to, because they were told to read, and that was twenty-one dollars and eight-six cents a week."

Even the most experienced actors stumbled over the language because only a handful had ever been given the opportunity to perform the Bard's plays. The first Macbeth under consideration was Juano Hernandez, veteran of many stage and radio roles, including a stint with Canada Lee in *Sailor, Beware!*

According to Anderson, "Hernandez would say *sword*, pronouncing the *w*." The harassed stage manager thought to himself, "How can you say these things and be an actor in the theater?" Fortunately, Juano landed a role in a radio show and took himself out of the running. Orson next tried out Cherokee Fonten, "who would just make up lines that weren't in any of the Shakespearean plays," Anderson said. Fonten was out, too.

Days passed in a frenetic flurry of tryouts until at last the play was fully cast with one hundred actors, dancers, and musicians. Only five performers were professionals; of these, just two had played Shakespearean roles. For the title role of the bewitched thane, Welles gambled on Jack Carter. The actor had a reputation as a difficult personality and a dangerous drunk, but he had created a sensation on Broadway in *Porgy*. The scheming Lady Macbeth was Edna Thomas, a seasoned professional who had often performed on Broadway stages, but had only one minor Shakespearean role to her credit. Welles got lucky casting Hecate, the head witch rewritten as a voodoo priest; he found Eric Burroughs, a graduate of London's Royal Academy of Dramatic Art. Maurice Ellis, a better singer than actor, won the role of Macduff. The fifth professional in the cast—albeit still a novice—was Canada Lee. Orson hadn't forgotten the actor who once leapt to his defense. He cast Canada as his cigar-smoking Banquo and assigned him to understudy Macbeth.

Chaos reigned as rehearsals began. The huge cast was a logistical nightmare. Actors struggled with lines; some never showed up. Orson often had to shout through a megaphone to be heard. The leader of his voodoo drummers, a Sierra Leonian witch doctor named Asadata Dafora Horton, demanded live goats to make fresh drum skins.

A few days into rehearsals, Orson was offered a lucrative job that he couldn't refuse, reading poetry on the Fleischman East Hour radio program. Because Welles would now have to miss some rehearsals, Houseman promoted his stage manager to assistant director. Anderson rehearsed the cast late into the evening in any spaces available, including auditoriums, hallways, fire escapes, Orson's apartment, and finally in the Lafayette Theater itself. Welles would arrive around midnight and take it all apart, changing almost everything, working until dawn if necessary, voodoo drums throbbing through the night. Neighbors were understandably annoyed, and the assistant director got a bit miffed, too. But he was also awed by Orson's creativity. "He tried so many different things," Anderson said. "He was so far ahead."

And he was so impatient. And volatile. And caustic. His notes could be merciless: "Jack, for God's sake, learn your lines!" "Get that move right, for Christ's sake." Rehearsals disintegrated into pandemonium as he barked orders and insults over a primitive public address system. "He knew what he wanted, and he was darn sure he was going to get it," de Paur said. "He cracked the whip, he abused people. He yelled and screamed. I never saw him physically assault anybody, but he always seemed capable of it." What saved Orson from wholesale revolt was a shrewd sense of timing. After taxing everyone to their collective breaking point, he suddenly broke out the charm, the jokes, and cases upon cases of beer—and they forgave him, every time.

Directors usually rehearse plays for about a month; Orson worked his cast for twelve grueling weeks. "He kept them going by the sheer force of his personality," Houseman wrote. "His energy was at all times greater than theirs; he was even more mercurial and less predictable than they were." And he did whatever was needed to get results. Welles treated Edna, a commanding figure, with the utmost respect. He raised hell and chased skirt with wicked Jack Carter after rehearsal. He bought food and drinks for hungry actors with his radio earnings, and loaned people cash when they fell behind on their rent.

Orson won Canada's respect and admiration as well—not with food and drink, nor that peculiar mix of kindness and savagery, but with his uncompromising genius and unmitigated passion for the theater. Working with Welles was a revelation. "I wanted to stay there all the time, watching and listening. I was so excited I couldn't sleep when I went home," Lee said. "I'd found something."

Before *Macbeth*, Canada had viewed his foray into acting as a happy accident, a good gig until he figured out his next move. He didn't take acting seriously until Orson introduced him to Shakespeare: "Then I knew it was the theater for me, for good."

All of the elements of the production began to come together during the final rehearsals, including evocative sets by Perry Watkins and an eerie score by Virgil Thomson, James P. Johnson, Porter Grainger, and Joe Jordan. The music was to be performed by an orchestra and by the African drummers.

Even the raw recruits in this platoon of performers sensed something phenomenal was happening. Bloodthirsty rulers, macabre witches, ghostly backdrops, authentic voodoo drumming, and spine-tingling chants together created an ominous world that was supernatural, credible, and altogether chilling. "Though Welles's interpretation was not overtly political, this nightmare vision had obvious resonance in a world menaced by fascism and the threat of world war," observes theater scholar Wendy Smith.

As opening night approached, Harlem seethed with anticipation and agitation. Welles already had his critics; not everyone was convinced that a white director could or should direct a classic play with African American actors. Some worried that his *Macbeth* would burlesque blacks and demean the cast. One night Orson and Canada were walking through the foyer of the theater when a black man with a razor taped to his wrist materialized out of the shadows and attacked Welles. Canada quickly overpowered and disarmed the man, who allegedly was put up to it by a Communist faction.

Catching wind of possible controversy, *The New York Times* sent critic Bosley Crowther to a midnight-to-dawn rehearsal just days before the opening to find out exactly why Mr. Welles had transplanted *Macbeth* from Scottish heath to Haitian jungle. "The kilt is naturally not a particularly adaptable costume for Negro actors," Orson joked. But after serious discussion with the director, the critic assured his readers that Welles "had good, sound reasons."

Nevertheless, conservatives suspected Welles of having a subversive political motive for casting blacks in a play about assassinations and insurrection. Somebody in the WPA must have gotten nervous and made certain that programs printed for opening night carried a disclaimer: "The viewpoint expressed in this play is not necessarily that of the WPA or any other agency of the Government."

On April 14, 1936, the play opened at the Lafayette Theater with great pomp and circumstance. An eighty-piece brass band from the Mitee Monarchs Lodge 45 of the Benevolent and Protective Order of Elks, magnificent in scarlet and gold uniforms, marched to the theater and serenaded the crowds. Automobile traffic on Seventh Avenue had to be diverted for more than an hour while Klieg lights beamed and camera-men shot newsreels of celebrities arriving by taxi for the premiere. Mounted police were called in to help control the excited throng. Thou-sands clogged the streets to cheer and people-watch as theatergoers arrived, wearing silk top hats, white ties, jewels, ermine, and orchids. "Harlem was dressed beyond the teeth," marveled critic John Mason Brown.

The Broadway crowd turned out in force, as did literary types includ-ing Carl Van Vechten, Edna Ferber, and Elmer Rice. Joe Louis, the young heavyweight contender, made a brief appearance. The house was sold out, and an overflow crowd crossing racial and class lines packed the lobby and spilled into the street. First-string drama critics were in atten-dance; one reportedly asked that he not be seated next to Negroes. The curtain rose nearly an hour late, but only the critics with deadlines to meet cared. For Harlem, this was an unforgettable event.

"Within five minutes, amid the thunder of drums and the orgiastic howls and squeals of our voodoo celebrants, we knew that victory was ours," Houseman writes in his memoir. The crowd lustily cheered Carter's soliloquies, gasped at the thirty weird sisters chanting voodoo, and clapped madly as the curtain rose on the glittering ball in Macbeth's castle, where soldiers wore uniforms of emerald green and canary yellow, and women danced in gowns of salmon pink and iridescent purple. "The next scene to stop the show was the Macbeths' royal reception, shimmering couples swirling with wild abandon," Houseman recalls. "Then suddenly, a wild, high, inhuman sound that froze them all in their tracks, followed by Macbeth's terrible cry as the spirit of Banquo, in the shape of a luminous death mask, suddenly appeared on the battle-ments to taunt him in the hour of his triumph."

When the final curtain descended, "the audience, white and Negro, cheered itself hoarse" for fifteen minutes, according to one report. They clamored for so many curtain calls that the stage manager finally left the curtain open, and the audience surged en masse across the footlights and onto the stage to congratulate the actors. "That was magical," Orson said in a 1982 interview. "I think it's the great success of my life."

The company dragged Welles onstage, and pretty girls handed bouquets over the footlights to Carter, Thomas, Burroughs, and Lee. A young actor named John Randolph was one of the white folks cheering: "It was my first realization that you could see a show like that, and color disappeared in the sense of the contents of the play." Harlemites, including those who had viewed a white-organized black production with some suspicion, were completely won over. "This production proved to Harlem that it could create and support a Shakespearean play of its own," one Harlem reporter noted. "It marked Harlem's cultural coming of age." Ralph Matthews wrote in the *Afro-American* that "Shakespeare himself would have been proud to receive the plaudits of the audience of 'Bravo! Bravo!'"

After the show, cast and crew mingled with theatergoers and locals at a bar and restaurant down on the corner. Speeches were made; cheers erupted. "Everybody seemed to agree that regardless what the tony big paper critics might say or not say of the show, Harlem would hail *Macbeth* as its own," Matthews said.

Reviews from those tony papers were, in fact, mixed, and even the most positive comments were often laced with unintended bigotry. The company's acting ability was the critics' most frequent target. Brooks Atkinson lamented that the Bard's lines were spoken conscientiously, but without poetry. Percy Hammond professed surprise at "the inability of so melodious a race to sing the music of Shakespeare. The actors sounded the notes with a muffled timidity that was often unintelligible." Burns Mantle said the play's poetry fell "awkwardly but with a certain defiant naturalness from the lips of Negro actors, unaccustomed to reading verse and quite satisfied not to try an imitation of their white brothers." John Mason Brown scathingly criticized Orson's "inept" direction, concluding that Welles "wastes not only an exciting idea but murders an exciting play." As for the cast, Jack Carter and Edna Thomas in the lead roles commanded the most attention, positive and negative, but

Lee earned his share of mentions. Mantle said Banquo's ghost was "ter-rifyingly active." Sylvia Taylor was less impressed: "Banquo played with a fervor that would have appalled Shakespeareans from Macready to Greet."

Despite these reservations, many critics hailed Welles's voodoo *Macbeth* as a dazzling, sometimes breathtaking, event. "It was a spectacular theatre experience," Mantle wrote. "This West Indian *Macbeth* is the most colorful, certainly the most startling, of any performance that gory tragedy has ever been given on this continent." Robert Garland said the Negro Unit made "a show out of *Macbeth* and a monkey out of any dis-senter who said they couldn't." Brooks Atkinson called the witches' scene "logical and stunning and a triumph of theatre art," adding that the banquet-turned-ball scene "fills the theatre with sensuous, black-blooded vitality." (He also noted: "Jack Carter is a fine figure of a Negro in tight-fitting trousers that do justice to his anatomy.")

While enthusiastic about the production, black critics approached it from a very different point of view. "In *Macbeth* the Negro has been given an opportunity to discard the bandana and burnt-cork casting to play a universal character," essayist Roi Ottley noted in the *New York Amsterdam News*. "We attended the *Macbeth* showing, happy in the thought that we wouldn't again be reminded, with all its vicious implications, that we were niggers."

Though *Macbeth* and Harlem's Negro Unit won endorsement by the majority of mainstream critics, black and white, the production and the Federal Theater Project were both roundly attacked by anti–New Deal conservatives. Leading the charge in the right-wing press was Percy Ham-mond of the *New York Herald Tribune*, who condemned *Macbeth* as "an exhibition of deluxe boondoggling . . . one of your benevolent Uncle Sam's experimental philanthropies," and sarcastically noted that Wash-ington spared "no expense in making it an ostentatious spectacle." His review caught the attention of conservatives in Congress who were al-ready keeping watchful, even baleful, eyes on the project. (When Ham-mond died suddenly of pneumonia a few days after penning this review, a rumor circulated that voodoo drummers in the cast had hexed the dys-peptic and disparaging critic.)

The play ran for ten weeks at the Lafayette with sixty-four sold-out shows. On "Relief Nights," seats sold for as little as five cents, a price that encouraged many to see a play for the first time in their lives. *Macbeth* moved downtown on July 6 for a run at the Adelphi Theater before touring FTP theaters in Bridgeport, Hartford, Chicago, Indianapolis, Detroit, Cleveland, and Dallas. Cincinnati was dropped from the tour because local authorities insisted on segregated audiences. Federal Theatre policy stipulated blacks could sit anywhere, not just in the balcony.

Segregation made travel conditions difficult for a troupe of one hundred black performers. They slept at YMCAs, churches, schools, private homes, boardinghouses, and a few fleabag hotels. Canada kept his sense of humor though it all. In Indianapolis, the actor playing Macbeth fell ill; out of necessity and as a bit of a lark, Lee and his fellow actors persuaded Orson to play the title role in blackface. Canada loved to recount what happened in Dallas, where the show played as part of the Texas Centennial Exposition. *Macbeth* sold out in advance, but somehow many in the audience thought they were buying tickets for a musical comedy, like the popular touring show *Blackbirds*. Lee laughingly described what happened during a dramatic scene: "When Macbeth suddenly shouted at Macduff, *And damned be he who first cries, 'Hold, enough!'* an elderly and rather deaf gentleman in the audience turned to his companion and said, 'That's what I say! When's the dancing gonna start?'"

Macbeth came home to New York City on October 6, 1936, for a triumphant two-week return engagement at Brooklyn's Majestic Theater before closing for good. The show had traveled four thousand miles and entertained one hundred fifty thousand people. It wasn't a box-office success; it couldn't be, with tickets topping out at forty cents a seat, compared to Broadway prices of up to three dollars. The original production plus the tour cost ninety-seven thousand dollars while netting just fourteen thousand dollars. Despite its status as a financial flop, Orson's voodoo production of the unlucky Scottish-play-that-must-not-be-named became a milestone in theatrical history and took its rightful place in the legend of Welles.

Macbeth marked the beginning of the historic collaboration between Orson Welles and John Houseman that would lead in 1937 to the founding of the Mercury Theatre and its landmark productions for stage and radio. *Macbeth* also spring-launched Welles's celebrated career as a director. And the production gave much-needed credibility to the much-harassed Federal Theatre Project, a program that, according to theater historian Dr. Glenda E. Gill, would go on to benefit black actors, including Canada Lee, more than any other movement in history.

Before the creation of the Negro Units, Gill writes, the black actor had been a "soul in crisis." He worked for lower pay than his white colleagues. He was rarely admitted into unions, including Actors' Equity. He was often restricted to working for a single exploitative booking agency. Very few black performers made it to Broadway or to Hollywood. The few who did usually performed stereotypical roles in plays written by whites for white audiences; black actors knew their own people would have to sit in the balcony known as "nigger heaven" to watch them play butlers, maids, or slaves. Except for a few stars, Gill notes, steady employment was a pipe dream for actors of color.

The Federal Theatre changed all of this. Blacks in the Negro Units were admitted to unions. They earned the same weekly pay as their white colleagues. Black actors on FTP stages didn't play menials; they enjoyed meaningful roles in contemporary dramas and classic plays. And when their family, friends, and neighbors came to a show, they could sit in any seat in the house instead of up in the rafters.

Langston Hughes said the Federal Theatre was more than an innovative social welfare program, it was "a gift from God," putting food on the table while also offering black artists creative opportunities they had never enjoyed before. "Negroes were able to create their own plays and musicals, act in them, and also gain experience in directing, scene designing, and other technical aspects of theatre which had hitherto been closed to them," Hughes observed. "It was the Federal Theatre that dared to cast Negro actors in non-Negro roles, not only on Broadway, but in its units elsewhere as well. The Federal Theatre broke down not only the old taboos against colored Americans as backstage technicians, but the bars against colored actors playing other than racial roles."

Unfortunately, the egalitarian nature of the Federal Theatre Project would help bring about its downfall by drawing the ire of the conservative press and Roosevelt's critics in Congress, who viewed the project as a hotbed of dangerous radicalism. Political plays and socially relevant dramas staged by the project were vilified as New Deal propaganda at best and Communist propaganda at worst. Administrative offices and employee rolls were allegedly packed with anti-American subversives and leftists. Others in Washington simply saw no reason to fund a national theater; then, as now, there were congressmen who were diametrically opposed to pouring tax dollars into the arts.

As attacks on the FTP increased, Congress threatened to cut project funds. Actors immediately organized demonstrations against the proposed reductions. Protesters may well have included Canada, who, like many blacks in the 1930s, had placed himself firmly in support of FDR and the Democratic Party. "Roosevelt's New Deal," writes historian Thomas Cripps, "gave them so many symbols of hope." Indeed, Canada's experience in the FTP was one reason the actor became such a staunch supporter of Roosevelt and the New Deal, and why he remained a socially progressive Democrat in later years.

Despite local protests, opposition to the FTP in Washington was clearly gaining strength. Congress approved drastic cuts in all Federal Arts Projects, effective July 1937, and all theater units in New York were ordered to reduce spending by 10 percent. It was a demoralizing summer. In June, nervous WPA officials banned the opening of Welles's and Houseman's final Federal Theatre collaboration, a labor opera called *The Cradle Will Rock*. Determined to go on with the show, the cast moved twenty-one blocks uptown, only to be forbidden by their union to appear on stage. Undeterred, they sang their parts from seats in the audience.

Under this growing political shadow, the beleaguered Federal Theatre opened its third season in the fall of 1937. Canada was cast in the Harlem Negro Unit's October production of Eugene O'Neill's tetralogy *S.S. Glencairn*. He appeared in two of four one-acts, *The Moon of the Caribbees* and *Bound East for Cardiff*. On opening night, the cast waited up until the wee hours so they could read the reviews, especially by Brooks Atkinson at *The New York Times*. Atkinson had perhaps the greatest clout of the New York critics, and while he often supported Negro productions, some suspected that the critic appreciated black actors mostly when they sang or danced.

Atkinson torpedoed the *S.S. Glencairn*: "Although the Harlem mummers put on a bizarre *Macbeth* two seasons ago, and have every logical right to play any dramas that interest them, they cannot light the proper fire under the melting pot of Mr. O'Neill's British tramp steamer." The cast "flattened" the dialogue, he wrote, adding that O'Neill's masterpieces deserved a more sensitive performance than Negro actors could provide.

John Mason Brown couldn't for the life of him understand why the Negro Unit chose these plays at all. O'Neill, he said, had created a polyglot crew of Irish, cockney, Russian, Swedish, and Norwegian sailors, plus one lone Yank. The dialogue and the conflict can't work without the accents, Brown argued. It was an "insult" to O'Neill. "The Federal Theatre's colored actors . . . may rip out whole rows of 'sure faiths' and 'blimeys,' yet they carry no conviction," he wrote. "When one of them accuses another of not looking like a Britisher, it is impossible not to see his point." St. Clair Bourne, critic at the *New York Amsterdam News* in Harlem, bristled a bit at this, countering that O'Neill characters were difficult to portray "even for players acquainted with the types" (meaning white actors). He did admit that the production was only fair.

Canada earned virtually the only favorable mentions in the press. "Canada Lee comes through with a good job," Bourne wrote. Richard Watts of the *New York Herald Tribune* chimed in: "Lee, as the dying Yank, gives the most effective performance of the company."

One month later, on December 3, 1937, Canada played a bit part as Henry in *Brown Sugar*, a commercial melodrama produced at the New York Biltmore by George Abbott. The cast included friends and familiar faces: Georgette Harvey (of *Stevedore*); Christola Williams and Juano Hernandez (of *Sailor, Beware!*); and Eric Burroughs (of *Macbeth*). The obscure play is best known for introducing Butterfly McQueen in the role of Lucille, "an over-genteel parlor maid in an apartment of iniquitous leanings." McQueen, later to gain immortality as Prissy who "didn't know nothin' about birthin' no babies" in *Gone With the Wind*, was the standout in this otherwise lackluster drama of the Harlem underworld. Though this play would seem to mark Canada's first appearance on the Great White Way, Lee never credited this performance as his Broadway debut; perhaps he waved it aside because the part was so small and the production so poor.

In the spring of 1938, Canada agreed to perform in a benefit for the National Negro Congress, sponsored by the Negro Cultural Committee.

The show was called *The Bourbons Get the Blues*, and many of Lee's friends had signed on, including Tommy Anderson from *Macbeth*; bandleader Duke Ellington; Frank Wilson, who directed Lee in *Brother Mose*; and actor Rex Ingram from *Stevedore*. The show's mix of monologues, music, and dance numbers proved, according to the *New Masses*, that "Uncle Tom is dead, that the Negro remembers his heroes, working-class heroes, that the Negro is organizing for his freedom." This benefit performance may have been the actor's first brush with overt political activism. The National Negro Congress was founded in 1935 "to carry forward the militant spirit" of black Americans and secure their "full citizenship rights." The NNC also worked to unite black labor organizations. Because of these activities, as well as the group's early ties to the Communist Party, the NNC was under FBI surveillance in the 1930s and '40s and was eventually cited as a Communist front. Though Canada likely sympathized with many NNC goals, his mind was mostly on acting and finding his next paying job.

Later that spring he returned to the Federal Theatre to perform in one of the Negro Unit's most popular productions. Written by William Du Bois (a journalist at *The New York Times*, not to be confused with writer and activist W.E.B. Du Bois), *Haiti* told the story of Henri Christophe, the same slave-turned-emperor who had inspired Welles's voodoo *Macbeth*. *Haiti*, however, ended with Christophe still a hero.

Directed by Maurice Clark, *Haiti* opened at the Lafayette Theater on March 2. Congenial reviews praised its rattling good melodrama and stirring score composed by Lee's friend Leonard de Paur. Canada was initially cast in a secondary role as the heroic soldier Bertram. But on August 9, after the show moved to Daly's Theater, Lee took over the lead role of Christophe from Rex Ingram, who left to star in another show. A local newspaper announced the cast change by printing a stunning photo of Lee sporting a clipped moustache and decked out in a smart uniform with prominent epaulets. The caption proclaimed him "The New Black Napoleon."

Despite its rather conventional plot, *Haiti* was invigorating theater and Harlem audiences cheered mightily as the black heroes slaughtered the French. "If it is a tale that made the hair of the French Army curl, it does the same for the toupeed theatergoer," Brooks Atkinson wrote in *The New York Times*. "Not very many historical plays turn out so well for

Harlem." Howard Barnes wrote in the *New York Herald Tribune*: "The smashing climax, with Christophe coming from the mountains to drive the French into the sea, takes on heightened intensity before a predominantly Negro audience."

Black theater historian Loften Mitchell observed that this production "was the first time many Harlemites sat in a theater and saw Negroes beating up whites and getting away with it. And all their deep-seated resentments rushed to the surface. During the course of the play, you could hear shouts from the audience: 'Hit him again! Give him a lick for me! Man, that's it! That's it!'"

After the Harlem production closed in September 1938, *Haiti's* mixed-race cast traveled with the show to Boston's marble and mahogany Copley Theater, a prestigious venue in a town not exactly known for its liberal views. Canada suffered a case of the jitters on opening night. "I was supposed to rush madly up the stairs, two at a time, to deliver a very dramatic speech," Lee recalled. "My new pants were so tight they tripped me up not once but twice, and I fell flat on my face on the stairs. That was awful. I thought the audience would laugh me right out of the theater, but they didn't seem to mind." The critics failed to mention the fall and gave respectable notices to the show, which enjoyed solid box office business throughout the run.

A popular as well as a critical success, *Haiti* was seen by more than ninety thousand people. Regrettably, the play would be Canada's final production for the WPA Negro Unit. The FTP was once again under attack on Capitol Hill and under investigation by the new House Committee on Un-American Activities. HUAC was authorized to investigate all types of subversive propaganda. Chairman Martin Dies, a cigar-chewing Texan with a mile-wide smile and exceptionally tart tongue, pioneered techniques in defamation and self-promotion that would later be perfected by Senator Joseph McCarthy. In the summer of 1939, the Dies Committee launched a highly publicized probe into the Federal Theatre Project.

Committee members focused on charges that the FTP was run by Reds and preached Communist doctrine, but race prejudice clearly informed their definition of what was subversive. When J. Parnell Thomas, a Republican committee member from New Jersey, claimed the project was "infested by radicals from top to bottom" and that virtually every play was Red propaganda, he singled out the Negro Unit's *Haiti* as a perfect example of a show with "Communistic leanings." Abram Hill, a black playwright, said he and others from the Negro Unit went to Washington in 1939 to testify before the committee "on Canada's behalf." Evidence of a direct attack on Lee has not surfaced. Hill and his group may have gone to Washington to defend *Haiti*, its cast, and the FTP, but the committee had no interest in hearing them out.

Instead, the committee interviewed friendly witnesses who happily lambasted FTP National Director Hallie Flanagan for spending precious tax dollars on plays that glorified Bolshevik principles and the left wing's radical agenda, which apparently included horrifying notions about racial tolerance and civil rights. Attacks on the Theatre Project also included absurd charges of miscegenation. A white actress testified that she was scandalized when a black actor had the audacity to ask her for a date, while a white actor swore he saw black men dancing with white women. Tabloid editors salivated over stories mixing subversive actors and taboo sex. One headline read: "Reds Urged 'Mixed Date,' Blonde Tells Dies Probers." Hallie Flanagan wasn't permitted to defend herself or her project until December 6, nearly four months into the hearings. At that point, she needn't have bothered. The committee clearly intended to ignore her defense—any defense—of the project. By funding the Federal Theatre, Congressman Thomas concluded, the government was in fact funding the Communist Party.

It is possible that some Communists did find their way onto the payrolls of the Federal Arts Projects, and, on occasion, used them to further their political agendas. Reds or no Reds, conservatives in Congress would still have condemned the FTP. The project was a community of idealistic liberals and progressives. Politically, it was doomed.

Actors and theater artists across the nation fought to save the project. In New York City, more than two hundred thousand people signed petitions to support the FTP, which were flown by charter plane to Washington. Showgirls released ninety-six carrier pigeons from Times Square, each bird bearing the message "SOS! SAVE THE WPA." Hundreds came to a rally at the Mansfield Theater, and top Broadway and Hollywood stars went on radio to urge Congress to fund the FTP.

But it was all to no avail: an Act of Congress dissolved the project on June 30, 1939. "The killing of the FTP," said Dick Campbell, last director of the Negro Unit in Harlem, "was a collective murder by bigots and bums." Actor and author Robert Vaughn said Congress managed to "wreck hundreds of lives in the postwar period as insidiously as it returned to the relief rolls more than 8,000 living-theater artists."

The Federal Theatre Project was vitally important to black actors as a source of much-needed income. In Canada Lee's case, his involvement in the project changed the course of his career and his life. "I will never forget what Roosevelt did for the Negroes in establishing the Federal Theatre," Lee said years later. "That great experiment gave us the chance to do ourselves credit, and we made the most of it."

The Negro Unit inspired in Canada a passion for theater, a taste for stylistic experimentation, a commitment to the art of acting, a desire to perform nontraditional and classical roles, and a determination to overcome the race barrier that prevented blacks from playing these roles on most American stages.

Moreover, while it is not certain that Lee signed petitions or attended rallies to save the Federal Theatre, he was certainly exposed to political activism during the controversy over the project and the subsequent fight to save it. Eight years later, when the Un-American Activities Committee would once again turn its suspicious eyes on theater and film under the leadership of Congressman Thomas, Canada did not hesitate to fight back.

It is also quite possible that the actor had his first brush with the Communist Party's efforts to win recruits in Harlem during his time with Federal Theatre. In his book *Only Victims*, Robert Vaughn concludes that the Party did take an interest in the Negro Unit, though by no means dominated it. Lee's friend Leonard de Paur, who composed, arranged, and directed music for the Negro Units, recalled certain "people who were running, or were attempting to run, the Communist Party's business up there with the Negro project." De Paur claimed that Party members lobbied Canada to join and the actor respectfully declined. "They tried to get to him, God knows," de Paur recalled. "They certainly came at him on all sides."

But the single greatest impact the Federal Theatre made in Lee's life was personal, not political. Standing in the footlights at the Lafayette Theater as thousands applauded and cheered had rekindled his determination to be somebody. As one reporter wrote: "In the theater he has found, again, what he left on the race tracks and in the ring . . . the zest for living, the uncertainty, the escape from anonymity which he dreads."

The boxer-turned-bandleader-turned-actor now turned his eyes to Broadway.

BROADWAY MELODY

BONA FIDE STAR

In December 1938, following those disastrous Dies Committee hearings, the Federal Theatre Project was presumed dead. As Houseman moved on to other projects, and Orson Welles happily winged his way to Hollywood to make a picture for RKO, the future looked mighty dim for the Negro Unit's soon-to-be-unemployed actors and technicians who were struggling to survive in a still-slumping economy. Canada wasn't worried, somehow. "I've always been like a leaf on a stream, going wherever the tide took me," he told a reporter. And sure enough, Lee soon got a lucky break, thanks to a little help from his friends.

A new Broadway show was generating plenty of buzz even before rehearsals started. *Mamba's Daughters* had an unbeatable pedigree. The production not only featured songs by the great Jerome Kern (*Show Boat*), it also boasted a script written by DuBose and Dorothy Heyward, the husband-and-wife team behind the 1927 hit *Porgy* and its spin-off Gershwin musical, *Porgy and Bess*. Two of Lee's good pals had secured plum roles in the new show. Georgette Harvey would star as Mamba, and J. Rosamond Johnson, Lee's childhood violin teacher who also enjoyed a successful career in musical theater, was cast as the Reverend Quintus Whaley. Both actors urged Lee to audition, and on Christmas Eve the *New York Post* announced that Canada was a "late addition" to the cast of *Mamba's Daughters*.

Nine days later, Lee made what he considered to be his official Broadway debut playing a trusty old field hand. While it undoubtedly irked Lee to play a stereotypical Negro role, jobs were scarce and the show was a smash thanks to sensational singing by his fellow field hand Ethel Waters, who earned seventeen curtain calls on opening night at the Empire Theater. "You couldn't have told I was in it," Canada would later say about *Mamba's Daughters*. "I was the one Miss Waters sent to town after the knifing."

Most critics loathed the play but loved Ethel Waters; only Brooks Atkinson was lukewarm on both, describing the dialogue as "lumbering" and Waters's performance as "limp" and "plodding." His *New York Times* review incensed many readers, and a group of artists including Burgess Meredith and Tallulah Bankhead took out a full page ad in the Sunday *Times* demanding that Atkinson retract his statements about Waters. Somewhat chastened, the critic claimed he had a virus on opening night, and after seeing the show again, he gave the singer a glowing review. It hardly mattered. Audiences enjoyed Waters and eagerly bought tickets. A columnist who remembered Canada's boxing days asked him how he liked his new job on Broadway. Lee liked it just fine, the writer later reported: "The ovations for Miss Waters remind him of the cheers when he beat [boxer Vince] Dundee."

Though Canada wished for a juicier role and more attention, he still had great fun backstage with the cast, which included rising star José Ferrer, blues singer Alberta Hunter, and the sultry beauty Fredi Washington. While Ethel Waters could cuss like a sailor and aggravated nearly everyone with her temper tantrums, Lee won friends with his good humor and high spirits.

During one performance, Canada walked onstage without realizing he'd forgotten the rope that held up his pants. The scene called for him to struggle with Waters, and as the actors fought, Lee's trousers started sinking to dangerous latitudes. He mugged his plight for the giggling offstage cast. He flirted with the idea of playing the scene in the altogether, but decided he'd better let Ethel go and make a grab for his descending pants. "It was stop-the-show either way," one columnist wrote. "Canada decided the audience would recover more quickly from interrupted action than offended sensibilities."

Mamba's Daughters ran for 162 performances, and when it closed in

May, producers began to book a national tour for the fall. In the meantime, Lee made a small detour into the film business that took him back to a place he purely loved: the ring.

Keep Punching starred boxer Henry Armstrong as a champion who gambles away his career. Once again, Lee won a role with a little help from Rosamond Johnson, who wrote the script. The cast also included Dooley Wilson, who later became famous for tickling the ivories as Sam in *Casablanca*. Canada's part was small, but how grand it was to be in the ring again, even on a movie set. Lee never could stay away from boxing. He still worked out at the Pioneer gymnasium in midtown Manhattan, and enjoyed enthusiastic ovations whenever he turned up ringside to watch the Saturday night fights at Rockland Palace.

Recently, he had begun to train a promising fifteen-year-old named Buddy Moore, and one day he took Buddy along to the studio where *Keep Punching* was being filmed. During the shoot, Lee talked to Buddy about the poor choices Armstrong's character made and how important it was to act with honor. "If you ever took a dive, I would have nothing to do with you," Canada told his protégé. The actor also stressed the importance of aesthetics in the ring. Every match is a performance, he said. "You have to be graceful, you have to know when to turn, when to bow," he coached. "You are the star. All eyes are on you."

Keep Punching wrapped up by September 1939, just in time for Canada to join the *Mamba's Daughters* tour to Detroit, Toronto, Chicago, St. Louis, and other cities. Lee was on the road when *Keep Punching* premiered in Harlem on December 7. Though the plot oozed with clichés and Armstrong's acting fell flat as a pancake, the picture still scored highly with black audiences. In these pretelevision days, Harlem sports fans bought tickets to the picture just to see fight footage of the only boxer ever to have held three world titles at the same time: featherweight, lightweight, and welterweight.

Canada pulled down decent notices for his first film role and before long the radio came calling. Broadcasting work was hotly sought-after, and Lee jumped at the chance. Besides paying pretty well, network radio gave actors the chance to show off their talents to millions of listeners across the nation. Nine out of ten families had at least one radio, and Americans spent an average of four hours a day tuned in to music, entertainment, and the news, now dominated by dramatic accounts of the war in Europe. A hit radio series could forklift an actor out of obscurity and elevate him to a household name.

Lee's mellow baritone voice landed the actor his first big job as the narrator of a nationally syndicated music program. Featuring John Kirby's "biggest little band in the land," *Flow Gently, Sweet Rhythm* was one of the first network showcases for an all-black ensemble. CBS premiered the show on April 7, 1940, airing it prime time on Sunday afternoons. Bass-player Kirby's elegant sextet featured Charlie Shavers on trumpet, Russell Procope on saxophone, Buster Bailey on clarinet, Billy Kyle on piano, and O'Neill Spencer on drums. Kirby's wife, the popular singer Maxine Sullivan, contributed vocals, along with the famed First Lady of Swing, Ella Fitzgerald.

According to the *New York Age*, Canada was the first black announcer employed by a major network. A critical success, Lee benefited from lively scripts by Paul Phillips, whose writing was widely praised in trade papers for its "ear music" and realistic use of "Negro talk." *Flow Gently, Sweet Rhythm* reportedly paid Canada a weekly salary of "three figures," which was good money in those days, especially for black performers.

Also in April 1940, Lee played a return engagement of *Mamba's Daughters* at the Broadway Theater. Unfortunately the revival ran just seventeen performances before union squabbles closed it. Perhaps inspired by Kirby's radio success, Lee decided to put his own band together and pitch it to the networks. On August 24, the *New York Age* wrote that the "former boxer and now a bandleader is scheduled for a new CBS spot."

His spot didn't pan out, however, and Lee turned his attention back to the theater. That fall, as the London Blitz raged and hundreds died each day in a rain of bombs, Canada played a bit part in *Cabaret TAC*, a political revue at the Manhattan Center sponsored by the Theater Arts Committee. Formed to aid Spanish loyalists in their fight against fascism and to defend civil liberties at home, this distinctly left-wing committee included Orson Welles and actor Will Geer in its membership.

Canada next won the starring role in *Big White Fog*, a play by Theodore Ward that had premiered in Chicago a few years earlier under the auspices of the late lamented Federal Theatre. Ward, together with Paul Robeson, Langston Hughes, Owen Dodson, and Loften Mitchell, had recently founded the Negro Playwrights Company at Harlem's historic but rundown Lincoln Theater. *Big White Fog* was to be the group's inaugural production. A diverse pool of donors, including Eleanor Roosevelt and Orson Welles, supported the project and helped pay for renovations at the theater on 135th Street and Lenox Avenue.

Big White Fog was based on events in the life of activist Marcus Garvey. Charismatic and controversial, Garvey galvanized an international movement calling for an autonomous, black-led nation in Africa. He also helped found a shipping fleet called the Black Star Line, transporting goods between America, Africa, and the West Indies. Company stock was aggressively marketed to working-class blacks who lost everything when Black Star went bankrupt. In 1922, Garvey and three other company officers were arrested on charges of mail fraud for allegedly sending letters to solicit more investments long after they knew the company was insolvent. Garvey protested his innocence but ultimately served more than two years in prison and was then deported to his home country, Jamaica.

In the play, Canada would portray Victor Mason, an ardent Garvey follower left destitute after sinking his life savings of $1,500 in the doomed Black Star Line. The devastated man then dies while resisting efforts to evict his family. Technically imperfect, sometimes overly didactic, *Big White Fog* was nonetheless powerful and frequently moving. The play certainly accomplished the company's aspiration to give Harlem a theater of ideas and "honest portrayals of Negro life." To raise money for the group and its first production, Ted Ward organized a benefit concert at the Golden Gate Ballroom. The twenty-five-dollar tickets were pricey for Harlem; a mostly white, left-leaning audience streamed into the ballroom that sultry Friday evening in early September 1940. The program included a brief speech by Ward and a rather ponderous talk by his friend, the celebrated novelist Richard Wright. Everyone clapped madly for swing pianist Hazel Scott, darling of Café Society, but reserved their greatest ovations for Paul Robeson in the grand finale as he sang "Old Man River," with revised and politicized lyrics, as well as "Fatherland," an anthem to the Soviet Union.

After *Big White Fog* opened on October 22, 1940, Brooks Atkinson wrote in *The New York Times*: "Canada Lee gives an excellent performance in the leading part. He is forceful and magnetically sincere." Atkinson admired Ward's work, calling it "the best serious play of Negro authorship about race problems" he had ever seen. The playwright, he said, "made no concessions to the white man's taste," specifically, there were no "spirituals and hot dancing, which are the only two things Broadway knows about Negro theater." However, the critic held the play shared weaknesses found in most race-problem plays: "monotony of tone, and the regulation Communist finish."

In the end, the play fared best with white liberal critics and their readers. According to the *Daily Worker*, of the 25,500 people who saw the play, only fifteen hundred were African Americans. Harlem's *New York Age* strongly supported the Negro Playwrights Company and gave the show a favorable review, but black audiences may have been put off by the script's treatment of Communism, Garveyism, and materialism. Some of Harlem's community leaders and intellectuals argued that the play depicted African Americans as losers and second-class citizens. After sixty-four performances, *Big White Fog* closed on December 14.

Conservative critics, who had denounced the play as Communist cant, were particularly pleased to see it shuttered. Complaints about Red taints were tossed about with increasing frequency in the press and on Capitol Hill. Congress had recently passed the Smith Act, making it illegal to advocate the overthrow of the United States government, or to belong to any group advocating such an overthrow. This law would become one of the principal weapons used to persecute suspected American Communists.

In Hollywood, Lee's friend Orson Welles was enduring his own fair share of attacks by the right-wing press, specifically the Hearst chain. Welles had completed his picture for RKO, but his masterpiece was on ice. *Citizen Kane* was the target of a now notorious assault by William Randolph Hearst, a rich, muckraking publisher who felt the film's portrayal of a rich, muckraking publisher hit too close to home. Hearst pulled out all the stops to destroy *Kane*, including whispering campaigns to besmirch Orson's name. Welles fought back by ridiculing RKO executives for letting Hearst bully them into delaying the film's release. In a matter of months, Welles managed not only to offend the Hearst mafia, but also to irritate Hollywood moguls, agents, his own studio, and the gossip-column juggernaut of Hedda Hopper and Louella Parsons. "This was clearly a good moment at which to leave Hollywood for a little while," observes Welles's biographer, Simon Callow.

Houseman had followed Orson to Hollywood to help with *Citizen Kane*, and now he urged Welles to return with him to New York. Months before, the two men had optioned a best-selling novel for a stage adaptation. Welles had promised to direct the play when *Kane* was finished. Just after New Year's, 1941, Houseman took Orson out to dinner and presented him with the script for their new project. "With the premiere of *Citizen Kane* still in abeyance, and feeling daily less comfortable in Hollywood, Welles leaped at it," Callow writes. "Back, then, to Broadway; the sooner the better."

The script Houseman handed Welles was *Native Son*.

The protagonist of Richard Wright's bleakly powerful *Native Son* is Bigger Thomas, a poor, uneducated, twenty-year-old black man who lives with his family in a cramped apartment on Chicago's South Side. In the first pages of the best-selling book, Bigger sees a huge rat skitter across the room. Seizing a skillet, he corners the creature and smashes it to death. The scene captures the intense fear, disgust, and anger that overwhelm Bigger as he struggles to survive the poverty, hopelessness, and prejudice that infest urban ghettos. In his world, white people are a nameless, faceless, tyrannical force; he believes he has no control over his life and no chance to better his lot. Hiding his despair behind a mask of rough brutality, he joins a band of thieves. When the gang plots the robbery of a white man's store, Bigger is terrified at confronting the all-powerful oppressor, and he sabotages the scheme. Bereft of options, Bigger succumbs to pressure from his mother and takes a job as a chauffeur to the wealthy Dalton family.

Mr. Dalton happens to be Bigger's landlord, one of many white real estate barons who refuse to integrate Chicago's neighborhoods, as they pad their fortunes by forcing black tenants to pay steep rents for squalid apartments in overpopulated ghettos. To assuage his guilt over exploiting blacks, Dalton styles himself as a great philanthropist by offering menial jobs to young men like Bigger. The slumlord's sham charity does nothing to ease Bigger's anxiety and self-consciousness when he reports for work at the Dalton family's luxurious mansion. Daughter Mary particularly agitates Bigger as she cozies up to him, ignoring social taboos between white women and black men. When the new chauffeur is ordered to drive Mary to an evening lecture at the university, the girl sweet-talks Bigger into taking her to meet her communist boyfriend, Jan, instead. Eager to prove their political progressivism, the couple forces Bigger to take them to a restaurant in his own neighborhood. Oblivious to Bigger's fear and embarrassment, Jan and Mary order drinks. By the end of the evening, all three are drunk, and Bigger drives around while the white lovers spoon in the backseat. When Bigger finally gets Mary back to the Dalton mansion, he has to help her upstairs to her bedroom. Intoxicated and aroused, Bigger begins to kiss Mary and fondle her breasts. Just as he puts the girl on her bed, Mary's blind mother comes in to check on her. Panicking at the thought of being discovered, Bigger holds a pillow over Mary's face to keep her quiet and accidentally smothers her to death.

To conceal his crime, Bigger burns the body in the furnace and writes a false ransom note signed "Red," hoping to divert suspicion to Jan, the communist boyfriend. By playing the role of the ignorant servant, Bigger eludes detection at first. But when Mary's remains are discovered in the furnace, he makes a run for it with his girlfriend, Bessie, and they hide in an abandoned building. Bessie is horrified by Bigger's crime. Worried she will turn against him, Bigger becomes violent; he rapes Bessie and beats her to death with a brick. After a dramatic shoot-out, police capture Bigger. The press promptly condemns him for raping Mary as well as killing her, inciting a white mob to terrorize the South Side. Shamed by his role in Bigger's downfall, Jan vows to help and persuades attorney Boris A. Max to defend the accused. Because Max treats his client as a human being, Bigger begins to see whites as individuals and blacks as their equals. The attorney tries to save Bigger from the electric chair, arguing that part of the blame for this crime rests with the racist society that shaped him. If America does not address the destitution, violence, and despair in its ghettos, Max argues, there will be more men like Bigger. His arguments do not sway the jury, however. On death row, Bigger cries: "When I killed that girl, I didn't mean to kill her, you know that. I killed her because I was scared and mad . . . I been scared and mad all my life. But right after I killed her I wasn't scared no more, for a little while . . . I was a man."

Wright's book moved, shocked, and disturbed readers. Critics found themselves peering into the chasm between black and white and the view was vertiginous, terrifying. "A blow at the white man, the novel forced him to recognize himself as an oppressor. A blow at the black man, the novel forced him to recognize the cost of his submission," wrote literary critic Irving Howe. "The day *Native Son* appeared, American culture was changed forever."

Broadway and Hollywood producers competed fiercely for stage and screen rights to the book. Wright's friend Ted Ward tossed his hat in the ring, as did Paul Robeson. But in the end, the author favored a bid by Houseman and Welles. Years earlier, while working for the Federal Theatre in Chicago, Wright made a special trip to New York to see the voodoo *Macbeth* and was purely dazzled by the show's pyrotechnics. Houseman's reputation in the industry was laudable and Welles was the wunderkind, *enfant terrible*, genius. Still, the author worried that Bigger's story would be distorted and sensationalized. Could the novel be translated into theater "in a light that presents Bigger Thomas as a *human being?*" asked Wright in a letter to Houseman and Welles dated May 1940. "We have already enough plays and movies showing Negroes in other roles, traditional roles. To screen or stage 'Native Son' in the old way means nothing to me." Houseman replied that while movie studios routinely bastardized literature, he and Welles were convinced that the theater remained "a free medium in which a serious artist can express himself directly and courageously to his audience."

Wright and Houseman struck a deal, and the novelist agreed to adapt Bigger's story for the stage. However, contrary to Houseman's wishes, Wright insisted on collaborating with Paul Green. Green had won a Pulitzer Prize in 1927 for *In Abraham's Bosom*, one of the first sympathetic treatments of Negro life in the Jim Crow South by a white playwright. Wright, thirty-one, was a novice in writing for the theater; he believed Green would bring craftsmanship to the project that he lacked. The two men set to work in the summer of 1940 at Green's home outside Chapel Hill, North Carolina.

Houseman sniffed trouble from the start. Wright's work was dark, angry, and politically subversive. Green's plays could be critical of American society, but they often squeaked with good, clean Christian morals and Old South heroic ethics. Wright prevailed in his choice of writing partners, but Houseman's instinct proved correct. Though both writers agreed to tone down the story's sexual content, it was Green who insisted on softening the protagonist's character. He reduced Bigger's crimes from two murders to one and transformed the white victim, Mary Dalton, into a hussy, implying that a bored little rich girl who flirted with communists deserved what she got. Green was determined to make Bigger more sympathetic and appealing—a sensitive tragic hero instead of a frustrated, enraged murderer. Wright deferred to Green, and on August 12 they delivered their first draft to Houseman. He hated it.

Wright was now busy in Brooklyn with a new novel and a new wife, so Green did most of the rewriting. By January 1941, the playwright was still tinkering, the script was a mess, and Houseman was fuming. Orson had finished shooting *Kane* and would soon be free to work on *Native Son*—if he had a script to work with. Houseman was in New York City. He called Wright and laid down the law. The two men spent mornings together at Houseman's apartment on West Ninth Street working on the script, restoring much of Wright's dialogue, plot, and characterizations. This was the script that Houseman gave Welles at dinner in Los Angeles.

With *Citizen Kane*'s premiere on indefinite hold, Orson seethed with frustration. *Native Son* released that stormy, pent-up energy and the director "hurled himself at it with ferocious intensity," Callow writes. On February 11, Orson blew into New York City like a tornado and launched an immediate search for actors. The entire production process, from the first audition to opening night, would take just six weeks.

With Houseman producing and Welles directing, *Native Son* was to be a Mercury Theatre production. Faithful alumni from Mercury radio shows and *Citizen Kane* came aboard, including Ray Collins, Paul Stewart, Everett Sloane, John Berry, and Erskine Sanford. The crucial role of Bigger's murder victim, Mary Dalton, was initially awarded to Doris Dudley. Days later, the actress resigned under pressure from friends who feared the part was too controversial and could harm her career. Lurid newspaper stories about a black butler in Connecticut on trial for raping his white female employer may have fueled her anxiety.

Several other actresses turned down the role. Finally, at an open casting call, Orson found what he was seeking. Boston-born Anne Burr, twenty-two, was a John Robert Powers model with more fashion than theater credits. Welles cast her, she said, "strictly because in those days I had very pale and naturally blonde hair and very, very white skin and it was visually effective. With lights, I was almost like an albino."

But the biggest casting decision Welles and Houseman faced was the obvious one: who would play Bigger Thomas?

Even before Orson came to town, that very question had generated a steady buzz in Harlem "comparable to that which surrounded the casting of the screen's *Gone With the Wind*," according to St. Clair Bourne of the *New York Amsterdam News*: "In *Native Son*, Wright created more than a mere individual. He wrought and conceived a human soul, fettered by doubts, fears, and ignorance, fighting blindly to escape the maelstrom which life can become. In the play, that soul must take material form, be clothed in human habiliments. Who can best house such a soul?"

The names of half a dozen actors were bandied about in the black press at the dinner table, and over countless cups of coffee. Rex Ingram? Too classy to be a tortured, ghetto everyman. Paul Robeson? A physique too big for a streetwise urchin. What about Robert Earl Jones (father of James Earl Jones)? "Alas, Jones is about as big as Paul Robeson," Bourne opined, "and somehow that seems too big."

The best choice was Canada Lee, Bourne concluded. "Physically, he presents the appearance of the typical, healthy-looking, ruggedly built young fellow we envision as Bigger. His acting ability is unquestioned, successes ranging back to the historic *Stevedore* bearing eloquent testimony to that."

But talk was only talk, and as 1940 drew to a close, Lee needed a steady paycheck. He lost his job as announcer on *Flow Gently, Sweet Rhythm* when the stars, Sullivan and Kirby, called it quits on their marriage and on the show. Taking the last of his money out of the bank, the thirty-three-year-old actor decided to try out his entrepreneurial skills. On November 23, 1940, Bill Chase wrote in his *New York Amsterdam News* column: "Canada, who was once a pretty good fighter, will go into the restaurant business Saturday nite with the gala opening of his Chicken Coop at 102 West 136th Street." Fine dining would be accompanied by "intimate entertainment," Chase added. "It really oughta be somethin' different."

Lee wasn't content to open any old chicken restaurant. The Coop had to be a joint with *style*, the 21 Club of Harlem, a mecca for music lovers. Canada built a small stage and purchased the best upright piano money could buy. Perry Watkins, the brilliant set designer for *Haiti*,

Mamba's Daughters, and *Big White Fog*, painted brilliant murals on the walls including a row of comically big roosters. And Lee searched every corner of Harlem until he found a chef that could make Southern-style chicken, collard greens, and sweet potatoes comparable to his mother Lydia's legendary South Carolina cuisine.

On opening night, winds gusted fiercely and rain fell in buckets, but nothing could keep the crowds away from the Chicken Coop. "A blaze of glittery glory," wrote Dan Burley in his column, *Backdoor Stuff*. "Celebs? A dime a dozen. I lamped Dooley Wilson, Rex Ingram, Maurice Ellis . . . the voluptuous Katherine Dunham . . . [All] paid homage to one of showlife's most colorful characters, the former contender for a world welterweight championship . . . the most affable of guys . . . Canada Lee!"

After the opening bash, business was slower than molasses in January. The Coop needed a competitive edge, something no one else had. Lee started hosting invitation-only jam sessions on Sunday mornings. Normally liquor wasn't served at the restaurant, but at these private parties, the highballs started flowing at 10:00 or 11:00 a.m., cigarette smoke hung thick in the air, and food was an afterthought. At Lee's invitation, painter Anton Refregier turned up at one of these sessions with a young artist in tow named Harold Lehman.

That Sunday morning at the Coop, Lehman sketched boogie-woogie legend Pete Johnson at the piano and blues singer Big Joe Turner belting a tune, dressed in a tuxedo. "Big Joe Turner was all the rage at that time," Lehman recalled. "These were real jam sessions, everything was improvised, and everybody had a hell of a good time, I can tell you. Imagine drinking highballs in the middle of the day! People drank, I guess they ate chicken, but I can't recall whether it was boiled, or fried, or barbecued. I'm not sure I ate anything at all."

Canada showcased jazz and blues stars, tossing work to musician friends who needed the cash and offering young players a chance to strut their stuff. At fifteen, Earl "Bud" Powell dropped out of DeWitt Clinton High School to play jazz. Canada took a shining to the lad and offered him a "residency." After his gigs at the Coop, Bud usually made his way into after-hours sessions around Harlem, where the great Thelonious Monk eventually discovered him. That was the end of Bud's tenure at the Coop and the rest is jazz history. But the Coop's bandstand never lacked for talent. Lee paid musicians well, perhaps a bit too well. The restaurant ran steadily in the red, despite Canada's indefatigable efforts to promote it. In short, he was making chicken feed and desperately seeking an infusion of cash.

When Houseman and Welles called him downtown to read for the lead in *Native Son*, Canada was thrilled, and nervous. He later confessed to a reporter "he spent more sleepless nights worrying over his chances of securing this plum than he did over all the opponents of his ring days put together." On the day before Valentine's Day, 1941, he took his boxing protégé Buddy Moore to the audition for some much-needed moral support. Buddy waited outside, and when Lee returned, he was beaming. "I made it!" he exalted.

When reporters later asked how he landed the starring role in *Native Son*, Canada modestly chalked it up to luck. He recalled the night he was playing in *Stevedore* and rescued Orson from a gang of thugs. "Welles and I have been friends since," he told the press. "When he got ready to cast *Native Son*, there was nobody else but me, and there never has been anybody else. That was just crazy luck."

His cast now complete, Welles immersed himself in production design. The director envisioned a grimy, desolate vision of inner-city hell, and told set designer James Morcom he wanted "to be surrounded by brick. Yellow brick." Everything on stage had to be *real*. Props included a white Persian cat and a cage of live canaries for the Dalton mansion. (When the cat attacked the canaries and got booted from the show, the cast cheered because rumor had it the feline made more money than they did.) During a breakfast scene, actors ate cornflakes, canned peaches, and milk. But the fire department put the kibosh on one element of Orson's stage vérité by refusing to let him have a working furnace onstage to burn Mary's corpse.

From the start, rehearsals were hectic and intense. Welles had given himself a brutally short time frame to prepare a Broadway show. Anne Burr had barely introduced herself to Canada before the two of them were called onstage to block the climactic murder scene. Within minutes, Burr realized that Lee was nervous about picking her up, "afraid that it would look as though he was getting fresh in some way," she said. "He was shaking."

Canada had good reason to be nervous. In 1941, black men who touched white women like that could be jailed or lynched. And Anne was so *very* white. Houseman and Welles might have sidestepped the issue by hiring a light-skinned black actress in the role, but they were determined to cast an interracial couple. They weren't the first to break this particular color barrier. In 1924, Paul Robeson defied threats from the Ku Klux Klan by appearing on Broadway in Eugene O'Neill's play about a mixed-race marriage, *All God's Chillun Got Wings*. Since then, a handful of black actors had appeared on stage with white casts, "but never in a comparable situation," the *Pittsburgh Courier* noted. A black man was going to murder a white woman in a contemporary drama on a Broadway stage. This play was a much bigger risk.

Native Son was meant to be revolutionary: no comfortable stereotypes, not a coon, mammy, or Uncle Tom to be found. Bigger Thomas was a murderer, but he was also a man, complex and compelling, not a caricature. A test case for Broadway, this role could open new doors to black actors, or it could slam those doors in their faces.

Hoping to get the press behind this show, Houseman and Welles invited reporters to sit in on rehearsals, which turned out to be a masterstroke in public relations. Orson had learned a few lessons from his sojourn in Hollywood. He could charm the pants off the media when he wished, and now he wished. As flashbulbs popped, he did his dance. "When Orson Welles directs a play he is a show in himself," gushed a reporter for a popular entertainment magazine. "His great vitality keeps him running all over the stage, waving his arms, mugging, and telling stories. But Welles has confidence in his actors. He does not tell them how to say their lines; he explains the effect he wants produced and gets results. Orson calls everyone 'lover' and 'love boat' and his actors respect him."

Winning over Harlem's leadership and the black press proved a tougher challenge Some opposed the play because they disliked the novel and viewed Bigger as an abomination. Others who had admired the book feared that Bigger would be watered down for Broadway, where black stereotypes predominated. *PM* reported that the Negro Actors' Guild asked Welles to "go easy on scenes . . . in which Negroes do anti-social things, for fear of race incitement." Richard Wright assured reporters that due care was being taken of his story and his protagonist: "Never in my life have I been associated with a more serious, young, spirited, and talented theatrical group." The public relations effort secured support from key players in the black media. "It is more than a whisper that Messrs. Wright and Green have skillfully made use of subtle symbolism and that everyone—the reactionaries and left-wingers alike—are going to be pleased with the result," the *New York Amsterdam News* wrote.

One week into rehearsals, Canada collapsed in his bed at 3:00 a.m. After spending a long day at the theater, he had rushed up to Harlem to oversee business at the Coop. Utterly exhausted, he poured out his triumphs and troubles in a letter to his lover. Legally, Canada was still married to Juanita, mother of his son Carl, but the couple had lived apart for years now. Lee kept company with several women, but his steady flame was a white socialite some fifteen years his senior. Caresse Crosby, neé Mary Phelps Jacob, had a fascinating life story. As a gorgeous debutante, she patented the first modern brassiere, a little backless number she invented to better impress young beaux while wearing a gossamer gown. After dumping her first husband, she married Harry Crosby, godson of J. P. Morgan and poster child for the Roaring Twenties. Harry gave her the nickname Caresse and carried her off to Paris to lead the wild, wanton life of the lost generation. Between hedonistic parties and extramarital affairs, the couple founded the Black Sun Press, which published James Joyce, T. S. Eliot, Ezra Pound, and D. H. Lawrence, among others. In December 1929, Harry made tabloid headlines when he shot his mistress, the recent bride of another man, and himself. Now a wealthy widow, Caresse persevered with her publishing business and took up residence on a capacious estate in Virginia. She traveled frequently to New York to do business, visit friends, and see Canada. "Dearest My Sweet," Lee wrote Caresse:

> First! I am "Bigger Thomas" (So congratulations are in order) and I've been rehearsing day and night like mad. Orson Welles is directing and he calls rehearsals at 9 a.m. each morning—8:30 tomorrow, because I took time out to negotiate a loan today (which I didn't get) to keep the restaurant alive . . . We were nearer going under last week than at any other time. We didn't receive any gas and light bill since we opened, and last week the collector came with a bill of $141 and demanded payment or else. So you see what a spot I was in . . . Between trying to keep this place open

now that it has definitely hit, and getting up in the greatest role in my life, I am fast becoming a shadow of my former self . . . I tried to hock my soul, but nobody wanted my soul at any price. I, my sweet, am known as a man in a dilemma. The only sunshine and softness about my life is you—and "Native Son" . . . Write me soon, and pray God I keep both things, restaurant and play, for I shall die if I lose either.

Despite the intense pressure on Orson and Canada, director and leading man worked well together until the day they rehearsed the rat scene. The script called for Bigger to kill a rat and pick it up. Canada expected the usual kind of prop, a bit of fur pulled across the stage with a string, but he was in for a surprise. Welles, in his zest for realism, demanded a real rat, so the props master managed to find someone who "shot the big fat devil out on the wharf somewhere," the actor later learned.

Nobody told Canada about the rat. At rehearsal, Welles kept the stuffed rodent hidden under his coat until the actors reached the fateful moment. Then the former prestidigitator whisked the corpse from under his cloak. "I've been a tough boxer and don't scare much," Canada said, "but when he took this rat out and waved it in front of my face, I almost vomited."

Lee backed right off the stage, averting his head, refusing to go anywhere near the rat. Orson guffawed, thinking Canada was putting him on. When Welles finally realized the thing genuinely disgusted Lee, he was dumbfounded.

"You've got to pick it up, Canada," he said. "Go ahead, it's stuffed."

"To hell with it, I'll quit first," Lee shot back. Cast and crew tried to soothe the actor, but he remained adamant. The battle continued most of the week. "To me, rats signify dirt, squalor, and nastiness," Lee said. Why couldn't Orson use a fake? But Welles wouldn't budge, either. One afternoon, a little boy on the set squeezed the rat. Girls in the cast and crew started to squeeze the rat, too. Pretty soon everybody was giggling and squeezing the rat. "What the hell, I'm a dope," Canada told himself. He insisted on wearing gloves the first time he touched the thing, but after a few days, he held it barehanded. "Now we've got *two* rats," he told a reporter, laughing.

✿   ✿   ✿

At some point during rehearsals, Welles decided the ten scenes should be played without an intermission, an unusual move in those days. He hated the idea of breaking the action and dissolving tension just so people could smoke cigarettes, make phone calls, or powder their noses. Canada was in nearly every scene, and Welles's decision meant that he would have to sustain an intense energy for two hours straight.

On March 3, Canada celebrated his thirty-fourth birthday. Though he felt entirely worn down, he couldn't miss this chance to throw a party and invited cast and crew to the Chicken Coop to celebrate. A picture of Canada, dapper in a crisp white apron and chef's hat, cooking chicken for the cast, appeared in the *Pittsburgh Courier.*

A few days later he wrote Caresse: "Every day I come home late from rehearsals with just enough energy to take off my clothes and go to bed. I can't even study. I just open my book and start reading and fall asleep . . . Orson brought some of the Hollywood tricks back with him so we have to get up early in the morning to make rehearsal, then work like a dog all day . . . It's grueling but I don't mind . . . I just hope that I can be as successful as I want to be."

As he moved ever closer to *Native Son's* opening night, Welles still had *Kane* on the brain. The film was no closer to being released and he was agitated. One day he walked into rehearsal with a sled inscribed ROSEBUD and stuck it in a corner of the set for the first scene. (The *Kane* icon is clearly visible in a *Life* magazine photo spread published after the play opened.) Maybe Rosebud brought Orson some luck. Two weeks before *Native Son's* premiere, publishing baron Henry Luce, owner of *Time* and *Life* magazines and a rival of Hearst, launched a crusade for the liberation of *Citizen Kane.* Encouraged, Orson took time out from rehearsals to call a press conference, where he threatened to sue RKO and Hearst.

Native Son's premiere, originally scheduled for March 17, was pushed back to the 22nd and then to the 24th. Apparently thirty-five stagehands couldn't change sets fast enough for Orson. It's also likely that Welles needed time to polish the play's final scenes because of his unorthodox rehearsal method. Orson always started with Scene One and worked as far into the play as he could before time ran out. *PM* reported that he didn't start work on the last four scenes of the play until the final week of rehearsal. The director declined to comment. "Mr. Welles wants everything to be absolutely perfect," the front office told the press. Backstage, people joked that the title of the play was changing to "Native Grandson."

In search of some good PR, Houseman invited Bill Chase, writer and illustrator at the *New York Amsterdam News*, and reporter Marvel Cooke to a dress rehearsal. They were treated to "four hours of the amazing Mr. Orson Welles in action—dramatic, noisy, purposeful and thrilling action," Cooke wrote. "Believe me, it was an experience."

Rehearsal had been called for eight o'clock. Orson strolled in late, swathed in a huge overcoat and red knitted scarf, pipe hanging from the corner of his mouth. He took a seat (orchestra, right) and fumbled in his pockets for his perpetually missing tobacco pouch. He seemed in no hurry to start. He bellowed out greetings and orders and in between he somehow convinced the two Harlem journalists that he understood "the problems the Negro faces in these United States of America. He is sympathetic with the conditions which create a Bigger Thomas and he is out to expose those conditions—subtly, convincingly."

"This is the best play I've ever read," Orson proclaimed, "and I'm working with the best cast I've ever seen."

Canada, stretched thinner and thinner between his concerns for the show and for his restaurant, anxiously awaited the premiere. He wrote Caresse:

> I don't have time to do anything but work and sleep. They won't even let me come to the Coop. I'm staying on W. 48th Street with the asst. director Dick Wilson. I'm sorry you couldn't get me at the Coop but the phone has been turned off for want of $66. I don't know when it will be turned on again. I've spent my salary 3 weeks in advance and put it into the Coop. I'm crazy but I've got to make a success of this place. Darling, I'm stupid. The real opening (after several postponements) is now 24th. After the show everybody is coming to the Coop and celebrate. I want you among them. You're the most thrilling person in the world . . . Love, C.L.

Final dress rehearsals proved disastrous. Orson grew edgy and impatient; tempers frazzled and snapped. When Anne Burr and Lee rehearsed the scene where Bigger strangles Mary, the actress said things got so tense "I thought I was really going to get it!" One night Orson started with Scene One; three hours later, they were still on Scene One. Actors camped in the theater four straight days, going home only to shower and change. Burr sometimes curled up in her coat and slept in the aisle, while Canada catnapped on his dressing room floor.

One day before the show's first preview performance, Ed Sullivan predicted in the *Daily News* that *Native Son* would be a hit. Tickets sold well, partly due to good press, partly out of curiosity, and partly because Houseman hit on a clever strategy. He marketed the show to cultural, political, and social welfare organizations, encouraging groups to buy blocks of seats to resell at higher prices as fund-raisers. "Benefit previews" were organized for the National Association for the Advancement of Colored People, the Veterans of the Abraham Lincoln Brigade, and the *New Masses*, a left-wing magazine. Newspapers soon reported that *Native Son* tickets were selling up to three months in advance.

Though the show was already in previews, Orson demanded that daytime rehearsals continue and on the very day of the premiere he worked them until four o'clock. The actors had just three hours of free time before they had to report backstage for the all-important opening night performance with critics in the audience. Excited, nervous, and bone-tired, the cast trudged out of the theater. Some ate, while others tried to rest. Paul Stewart, who played a detective in the show, walked through the stage door of the St. James just before seven o'clock and heard shots being fired: "Here was Canada on stage, and Jack Berry and the other policemen in the gallery shooting across the audience! I came in and said, 'What is this? You're not putting this in *tonight!*' And [Welles] said 'Yes!' That was the daring of Orson."

Canada sent Orson a telegram on opening night that the director kept all his life: "Thanks for my big chance Orson. I shall live up to your confidence in me. I'll be in there punching till the curtain comes down. Canada Lee." Orson wired Canada: "You are doing a very important thing tonight and I am very proud of you. Orson Welles."

As Canada dressed and applied his makeup, more telegrams poured into his dressing room. "You will wow them in a terrific part. It's great," wired Paul Robeson. Other well-wishers included actor Lee J. Cobb; agent Edith Van Cleve, whose clients later included Marlon Brando and Grace Kelly; and poet and novelist Stephen Vincent Benét.

Artists, writers, society matrons, politicians, social activists, and celebrities streamed into the St. James. Orson made a Hollywood entrance with his glamorous girlfriend, the Mexican actress Dolores del Rio, draped over his arm. At Caresse Crosby's side was an exotic-looking woman, boyishly slim with a heart-shaped face, dressed in a dark wine velvet suit with matching hat, a frilled gray blouse, a cape cut from a dilapidated fur coat, and mended stockings. Caresse and her friend sauntered to their seats. They were the kind of women who knew how to make you watch.

Many in the audience were surprised and a little irritated to discover that there would be no intermission, although it had been announced in *The New York Times* that morning. And many were further annoyed that ushers had been forbidden to hand out programs until the show was over. Orson didn't want people spoiling his dramatic blackouts by lighting matches to read their playbills.

At 8:30, Ed Sullivan fidgeted in his Row M seat. He wasn't alone in his restless agitation. "The audience is as rude as only a first-nite audience can be, expressing its pique when the curtain fails to rise until 9 p.m.," Sullivan noted. At last, the houselights dimmed and the curtain rose, revealing that tenement nightmare of yellow brick. When the star took the stage as Bigger Thomas, the house fell silent with keen anticipation.

Canada Lee was electrifying, and so was the show. Applause thundered after the first scene, after *every* scene. Welles's staging put the audience in the middle of the action, riding thrilling currents of drama through ten scenes stitched tightly together with a symphony of city sounds ranging from merely menacing to downright demonic.

In the play's spine-tingling climax, Bigger is on the run, hiding from the police in a warehouse with his girlfriend. A neon sign blinks on. Snow falls on a skylight above them. Suddenly, sirens scream. The neon blinks off. A beam of light sweeps the room. The skylight crashes. Shots ring out and the girl dies in crossfire. Policemen slowly advance from the back of the theater through the aisles: "Come out, you black bastard!" Bigger scrambles across a narrow ramp over the orchestra pit. Cowering, he fires a gun straight into the audience. Answering shots explode from the back of the house. Several viewers scream and duck. Blackout.

For many in the audience that night, the play's final moments are the most disturbing. In his cell in death row, Bigger tells his lawyer, Mr. Max: "I reckon I had it comin'. I hated her. And I ain't sorry she's dead . . . She made me feel like a dog. Yeah, yeah, that's the way all of 'em made me feel. In their big house I was always tremblin' and scared."

Bigger realizes that killing Mary gave him the sense of control over his own destiny he had always craved. "Maybe it's 'cause they were after my life then, and I was fightin'. Made me feel high, and powerful. And free," Bigger says. "I'm more alive now than I was ever in my whole life. I'm alive now, and they're gonna kill me!" As Canada delivers his lines, he flings himself against the bars of his cell, arms outstretched. Orson had explained to Paul Green: "I want the play to end with Bigger Thomas behind the bars standing there with his arms reaching out and out, his hands clinging to the bars—yes, yes, the crucified one, crucified by the Jim Crow world in which he lived."

When the final curtain fell, people leapt to their feet, applauding, roaring, cheering. They clamored for fifteen curtain calls and might have demanded more, but Lee and his fellow cast members at last begged off. The opening night crowd clearly deemed *Native Son* a theatrical triumph. But what would the critics say?

Canada hosted the opening night bash at the Chicken Coop, partly because the producers were paying and Lee desperately needed some cash flow at the club. The first reviews wouldn't hit the streets until 1:00 a.m. or later, so his guests settled in to party. Orson and Dolores del Rio found a dark corner. Caresse swept in and introduced her friend in the wine-colored suit. It was Anaïs Nin, famed diarist and author of literary erotica. Even as Caresse purred over Canada, sparks flickered between her lover and her friend. Nin gave Canada one of her enigmatic smiles. The jukebox played hot jazz and slow blues, chicken sizzled, drinks flowed. Suddenly, someone shouted the reviews were in.

"They were unbelievable," Anne Burr said. "It was astounding."

The critics were unanimous: Orson was a genius and Canada a bona fide Broadway star. Welles was hailed as "the greatest theatrical director of the modern stage." The *Daily News* gave the play four stars, the paper's highest accolade and deemed Lee perfect. "Here is a sepian Spencer Tracy and his sustained performance in the difficult role never loses authenticity or power," columnist Ed Sullivan opined. "Canada Lee is the first top-flight athlete since Paul Robeson (Rutgers' All-American end) to make the grade with the drama critics . . . The colored race indeed is remarkable, with Canada Lee as current Exhibit A."

The nation's most influential drama critics lined up to pay their compliments to the star. "Mr. Lee's performance is, in fact, the best I have ever seen in New York from a Negro player," wrote Stark Young in the *New Republic*. Brooks Atkinson of *The New York Times* called Lee "superb" and added that "the authors and producers have an actor for whom they should be devoutly thankful. As Bigger Thomas, he gives a clean, honest, driving performance of remarkable versatility." Wolcott Gibbs, writing for *The New Yorker*, said Lee did a "magnificent job" playing a complex role "with remarkable reticence and power." *Daily News* critic Burns Mantle said Lee was "modest, simple-minded, fumbling, yet fired with a fixed conviction and eloquently pathetic." *The Wall Street Journal* praised Canada as "a master of the interplay of inward fear and force." *Time* magazine said the show was "the strongest drama of the season" and that Canada was an "actor of the order of Robeson." Richard Watts, Jr., said Lee gave "one of the season's best performances." John Mason Brown wrote that the production, which he disliked, was "fortunate in its Bigger" and "no one could ask for a more satisfactory physical or vocal representation of all that is tortured, harried, and understandably resentful in the Negro who is Mr. Wright's tragic hero." William E. Clark noted in the *New York Age* that it was Lee's "highly emotional performance from the very first scene . . . that sustains the play." The *Daily Worker* said Lee "dominates the stage like the star he is." Stage and screen star Paul Muni wired Canada: "Thank you for the most wonderful evening I ever spent in a theater." Rosamond Gilder would pen perhaps the highest praise in *Theatre Arts Monthly*: "Canada Lee has added a figure of heroic dimensions and tremendous implications to the theatre's gallery of great portraits."

Those implications, however, were chilling to white theatergoers and critics alike. "To most people, as to this department, the hero is inhuman," Brooks Atkinson observed. "Although the drama flames with violence, the authors give a cold, unyielding conclusion to the most biting drama ever written about a Negro in America." *Daily News* critic Burns Mantle said Bigger Thomas was a victim of "selfish humanity's sins, and a few that can be traced directly to the American way of life." Surely Mantle was talking about white America when he described those "who force the Bigger Thomases on relief, and into alleys, and one-room tenements," and others "who give them the same chance the Daltons gave this hero, only to find that by that time they are so afraid to trust the best of us that they go on taking their developed fear and hatreds out on the rest of us."

Black critics and audiences also mulled over the implications of *Native Son*. Billy Rowe, theater editor at the *Pittsburgh Courier*, viewed the play with mixed emotions. "As it is bad, it is good, and as it lies, it tells the truth," he wrote. Though Bigger embodies part of the reality of Negro life, Rowe said, was it right to create such a mean and loathsome character "to shoulder the pent-up emotions of a race . . . to convey to the masses the deep emotions, the intense passions and the tragic prejudices confronting a man born black?"

Edward T. Rouzeau found the play to be a superb dramatization of critical social issues. After the show was over, he stood for a moment on the sidewalk in front of the St. James, wondering what white patrons were thinking as they left the theater. He saw a rich man leave in a chauffeur-driven Cadillac. Would the man feel moved to endow a Negro school? Or would he worry about leaving his wife home alone with Negro servants? Rouzeau saw middle-class whites leave by subway. Would they show more tolerance, or be the first to cry, "The Negro did it!" the next time a crime was committed in their neighborhood?

"I can only hope that the potential benefits to the race will outweigh the potential harm," Rouzeau wrote in the Pittsburgh *Journal and Guide*, adding that as a black man watching *Native Son*, "you are haunted by a feeling that some day, somewhere, a white man is going to confuse you for a Bigger Thomas."

Ed Sullivan set off a fascinating exchange between New York's black and white media when he mused that the play might have been stronger if the main character was an "average, decent" Negro boy instead of a blasphemer and petty thief with a "background of reform school" who hates whites and blacks alike. "The case of the colored race is not represented fairly, because I doubt gravely that Harlem would concede that Bigger Thomas is typical of the race," Sullivan wrote. "Certainly he is not typical of the thousands of colored men I've known, just as a dangerous bull elephant is not typical of the herd. To present the case adequately, an author would have to build his story around, say, a colored

college graduate, decent, competent, self-respecting, and then enumer-
ate the hurdles which unjustly are placed in his path . . . The greatest
line of dialogue in 'Native Son' is not Bigger Thomas's line; it is the
line that is uttered by his sister, when she laments her brother's shiftless-
ness . . . 'I've tried so hard to amount to something.' That is heart wrench-
ing, but she accuses not the whites, but her brother for defeating that
ambition."

Though he considered himself politically progressive when it came
to race relations, Sullivan felt uncomfortable sympathizing with an angry, fearful black protagonist who can only feel empowered by taking a
white woman's life. Like Paul Green, he wanted to rewrite Bigger as a
tragic figure who strived hard and meant well but got tripped up by a few
pesky injustices. Sullivan avoided the major themes of Wright's novel, as
black critics were quick to point out, including a writer for the *New York
Amsterdam News*: "What Mr. Sullivan did not take into consideration . . . is that Bigger Thomas is the result of economic and social oppression."

Another squabble erupted in the press when drama critics for both
Hearst papers, the *Daily Mirror* and *The New York Journal and American*,
accused *Native Son* of twisting racial issues into Communist propaganda. (They also somehow failed to mention the name of Orson Welles
even once in their reviews.) Colleagues took Hearst critics to task for
ganging up on the play solely because of the Hearst-Welles feud. When
the *Mirror's* review of the play was conspicuously tardy in its publication,
the *Daily News* noted sardonically that "the only explanation leaking out
of the *Mirror* office was that a slight confusion resulted in mistaking *Native Son* for *Citizen Kane*, and so [theater critic] Robert Coleman's report
was banned." Hearst scribes defended themselves by casting aspersions
on the political motives of their critics.

Meanwhile, the Communist paper, the *Daily Worker*, extolled the
play's message: "The economic and social ostracism of fifteen million
native-born Americans of colored skin is a rotting sore in the national
organism. Jim Crow, lynchings, hunger, disease, crime are bred by the
callous disregard for Negroes by their white oppressors."

While most liberals supported the play, the Urban League picketed,
claiming the drama's tragic ending was counterproductive to progressivism. Some conservatives protested the script's leftist sympathies; others

condemned the undercurrent of sexuality between Bigger and Mary Dalton. Anonymous threats were made against the theater owners, producers, Orson, and Canada. The show's star shrugged these off, telling one reporter that the play "made a lot of people squirm and of course, that made them mad. Well, if you can make people mad because they know they're in the wrong, you're achieving something."

Controversy sold tickets, and the box office did steady business at $14,500 a week. Shows rarely sold out, but even the top-priced $4.40 seats moved fairly briskly. Orson predicted *Native Son* would run at least three years, and no one was happier than Broadway's newest celebrity. Friends would long remember the day Canada Lee's name replaced Orson's on the theater marquee in the prime spot above the title of the play. When Canada saw that, he borrowed one of Bigger's signature lines and hollered: "GODDAMN!"

Shortly after opening night, Canada dropped by the Pioneer gym and found himself surrounded by a crowd of backslapping well-wishers from his boxing days. "I can't believe it," he told them. "I just can't believe it." Ted Carroll, a reporter for *The Ring*, tagged along as Lee headed down West Forty-fourth Street to his dressing room at the St. James Theater.

"I'm still in a kind of a daze," Canada said, sipping a glass of orange juice. "I can't believe it's all turned out this way."

"You're a national figure now, and we're all proud of you," Carroll told him.

"That's what they say, Ted, but it all sort of overwhelms me—radio talks, autograph hunters, guest appearances. Sometimes I wonder if there isn't some mistake somewhere, if all this is really meant for Canada Lee," the actor said. "I've been trying so hard and so long."

During the second week of the run, producers Bern Bernard and Lionel Stander gave Canada a brand new Pontiac. The car was emblazoned with four stars in honor of the *Daily News* rating, and inside was a silver plaque with a quote from *The New York Times* review: "Canada Lee is superb." It was a generous gift, as well as a rolling advertisement for the show. But there was a catch. According to the *Philadelphia Record*, Bernard and Stander feared Lee might sell the car to help bail out his floundering Chicken Coop. To avoid this, "the producers bought that car on the installment plan, made the first payment, and then raised

Canada Lee's salary by a sum sufficient to pay the additional install-
ments."

For the first time since his prizefighting career, Lee found himself
earning a fair amount of money. Newspapers reported he would earn
$250 a week for the first six weeks; $350 a week the next four weeks; and
$500 a week thereafter. White cast members suspected that Lee earned
far less than that, and less than they did. Whatever the case, Lee was
happy to have it and happy to spend it. Feeling the need for a swankier
pad, he took a suite at Harlem's prestigious Hotel Theresa, billed as the
"most famous Negro hotel in the nation."

Reporters were either ignorant or diplomatic about the state of his
marriage to Juanita. "His wife and son, whom he sees afternoons, live in
an apartment in New York's Williamsbridge," one paper said. A magazine
published a photo of Canada pouring Carl a glass of lemonade in his
kitchenette at the Theresa. Lee is elegantly turned out in cuffed trousers,
spats, and an apron. Carl, slim and handsome, stands behind him. The
caption reads: "Canada is fond of his 14-year-old son, has great plans for
him. Son attempted to run away to Saratoga, as his father had, but
Canada brought him back."

Carl loved and admired his father, and Canada enjoyed spending
time with him as well, but they had a complicated relationship. Visits
were sporadic now that Lee was performing six or eight shows a week in
addition to running his restaurant. Canada supported Carl and his
mother, allowing Juanita to raise their son in prosperous middle-class
neighborhoods that were largely white, where Carl could attend good
public schools. But while Carl enjoyed certain comforts and privileges
by not growing up in a suffocating ghetto, he also endured "rejection and
isolation" living in white neighborhoods. When his father became a
Broadway star, Carl suddenly found himself in "double isolation."

"In Hollywood, at least the children of stars had each other," he later
told a reporter. "Here in New York, there wasn't anybody."

Besides looking after Carl and Juanita, Lee was always glad to help
his parents, his sister, Claudia, and his brother, Lovey. Claudia had married, but the union was unhappy and she often sought Lee's advice. As
for little brother Lovey, after his expulsion from DeWitt Clinton High
School (on unfair grounds, he always maintained), Lovey married his
high school sweetheart Evadney, known to all as Pheta. Lovey, now

twenty-eight, worked at the local post office and Pheta looked after their three-year-old son, Billy.

Lovey harbored dreams of becoming a star in his own right. "My father was a talented man," recalls Bill Canegata. "He could sing. He was a great comic. You would always find him emceeing at big dances and parties. He had the ability. His problem, he always said, was that he had a family too young. I think my mother put pressure on him after she had me. When he went into the post office, it was all over. He lost his chances."

Once again in the long shadow of his older brother, Lovey found he didn't mind basking in Canada's glory or spending his cash. "The man was what I would call an opportunity seeker," Bill recalls fondly. "He was always on the 'do now, pay later' plan. He had the gift of gab, I'm telling you. He could con anybody into anything."

Including Canada. As the two brothers hit Lee's favorite hot spots—especially Café Society, Barney Josephson's integrated left-wing boogie-woogie mecca in Greenwich Village—Lovey got a reputation among some of Canada's friends for being the first to order and last to pay. Lee just laughed and covered his brother's tab. "I never could understand it," actor Thomas Anderson said. "He loved Lovey so much, and it seemed that Lovey took advantage of him at every step . . . Lovey would just take everything."

Lee was generous to Pheta and Billy as well, leaving a bit of money or little presents on their kitchen table each time he visited. When someone gave Canada an Irish setter named "Bigger," the actor decided to give the dog to his little nephew. "I remember him coming up to the house and hiding out so he could surprise me," Bill says. "I was only three or four, but I never forgot that."

Canada was just as bighearted and openhanded with his friends and, in at least one case, a total stranger.

Jack Geiger was a bright, troubled kid of fourteen who had finished high school early but was still too young for college. Restless, unhappy, he fought with his parents constantly. One night Jack went to see *Native Son*. The play moved him so much that after the show, he brashly barged into Canada's dressing room and struck up a conversation. The actor didn't seem to mind his company, and soon the boy was hanging out backstage on a regular basis.

"We started out talking about the play and Richard Wright and the main character, Bigger Thomas, and race relations in the United States," Geiger says. During the second or third conversation, the actor talked a little about his childhood. Geiger suddenly unburdened his heart, confiding to Canada his troubles, his anger and frustration with his life at home. "He learned a lot more about me than I did about him," Geiger recalls.

Jack's situation at home didn't improve, and finally he decided he'd had enough. *Native Son* was dark on Sundays, so one Sunday night when his parents were out, he packed a bag, took the A-train to Harlem's exclusive Sugar Hill district, and walked right up to 555 Edgecombe Avenue where Canada had just purchased a penthouse. Jack got past the doorman, took the elevator up, and knocked smartly. Canada opened his door to find that scrawny kid from backstage standing on his doorstep, suitcase in hand.

"Lee, this stuff at home is just getting too much," Jack said, adding hesitantly, "I thought maybe I could stay here for a while."

Lee looked around, pointed to a couch in the living room and said, "Well, I guess you can sleep over there."

After Jack fell asleep, Canada called the boy's parents and assured them that their son was safe and sound at his place. "I'll send him back in the morning," Canada told them. "But why don't you let him stay here, because I'm not sure where he's going to land the next time." Thoroughly relieved, and probably exhausted, the Geigers said yes. One or two nights turned into a week, then several weeks, and in the end, Geiger lived with Lee for the better part of a year. The experience had a profound effect on the boy, who one day would become a prominent civil and human rights activist.

"He was kind of an informal, surrogate father," Geiger said. "Canada Lee himself had grown up in a pretty strict, middle-class, West Indian family and he had, he told me, the same kind of dissatisfactions and mixed-up feelings that I had about his relationship with his family and what he wanted to do. And he ran away. And I think that experience may have had something to do with *his* kindness in taking this strange kid in and making a sort of second home for him."

While Canada was generous with his family and friends, he didn't stint himself, either. Sometimes it got him into trouble, as with the case of the four-star car.

Canada decided to trade in the Pontiac. "I never felt comfortable driving that car," he later told a reporter. "Those four stars made me feel as though I was wearing shiny yellow shoes—yellow shoes that squeaked." Another columnist hinted that Lee was also a bit miffed that one of those stars fell off the very first time he took a girl for a ride. When Lee traded the car for a black Cadillac coupe, he told the dealer the Pontiac was paid for and the title clear. Somehow Lee didn't realize that he and the producers still owed $789.36 on the car and the police ended up charging him with grand larceny. To Lee's great chagrin, the story made the papers and he would have to go to court over this fiasco in the summer.

Still, Lee kept his Caddy, and also indulged his passion for fine clothes and beautiful women. The suave star dated a bevy of females, earning the good-natured envy of his friends. "Canada had the pick of the crop," recalled Dr. John Moseley, Lee's friend since childhood. "Park Avenue women, Southampton women ... They certainly loved Canada."

Now and then, the actor asked his young pal Leslie Nash, Jr., to go to a certain bar or restaurant. "There is a girl there," Canada would say. "Talk to her for a while and keep her company until I can get there." Nash would do so. When Canada arrived, he'd take the youth aside and say "Now you have to go over to this restaurant ... and see someone else." Some nights Canada sent Nash to three different places to talk to three different girls. Though he may have been Harlem's most successful Don Juan, Lee refused to brag about his conquests: "He never told me the results of these meetings," Nash said. "Whatever he did with a woman was private. He kept it that way."

Between flings, Canada came back to Caresse Crosby. After Caresse and Anaïs Nin stopped by the Chicken Coop one night, Nin described the scene in her diary. "We talked. Drank. Listened to jazz," she wrote. "Canada Lee, with his warm, orange-toned voice, his one unclouded eye glowing with tenderness and joy, his stance loose-limbed, natural; in life, relaxed, in music and acting tense, alert, swift, and as accurate as a hunter ... Caresse and Canada have been friends for a long time ... the jazz, and the soft voices, and the constant sense of touch between them."

Despite the easy intimacy Nin describes, Caresse was losing confidence in her charms. She was nearly fifty, and she confessed to Anaïs her fear that Canada would soon find her too old to love. Nin comforted Caresse, but she may not have put her whole heart into it. Anaïs was newly infatuated with jazz and blues, with Harlem and Negroes, and with Canada Lee. She, too, was older than the actor, but only by four years or so. She proudly noted in her diary that she looked much younger and weighed just 113 pounds, her waist "still pronouncedly indented. My breasts are dainty, the tops roseate." When Caresse returned to her palatial estate in Virginia, Anaïs and Canada began an affair.

In one of the actor's *Native Son* scrapbooks, there is a single-spaced typed sheet, no date, no attribution, but given the style, it is possible that Nin wrote this impressionistic sketch of Canada: "He is kindness and warmth, bringing those about him a greater joy in being . . . He is high excitement and a rushing wind . . . He is cruelty and sadism, crushing even the things he loves . . . He is mercury, a compact ball of silver fire bursting into a thousand tiny pieces at the touch of an exploring hand . . . He is greatness . . . He is birth and living and death. He is Canada Lee. And that is enough."

Though he clearly enjoyed a rich array of clandestine liaisons, Canada also loved to throw raucous parties at his new penthouse at 555 Edgecombe Avenue. This building was one of Harlem's most prestigious addresses in Sugar Hill, a block of buildings perched on a rocky promontory whose residents had arrived, socially and economically, at the summit of success. Paul Robeson, Duke Ellington, Count Basie, W.E.B. Du Bois, and a host of other celebrities lived side by side on the Hill with judges, lawyers, doctors, and entrepreneurs, as well as a few racketeers and gamblers. (*Ebony* reported that the pricey monthly rent at 555 Edgecombe ranged from sixty-six dollars for three rooms to eighty-seven dollars for five rooms.) A lovely building with marble décor and garden courtyard, 555 featured liveried doormen and a full-time concierge. Lee's terrace delivered spectacular views, especially at night, when one could see the lights of the new George Washington Bridge strung like diamonds across the sky and the carnival colors of the rides at Palisades Park just across the Hudson River. If the night was quiet, Lee could hear the rattle of the roller coaster, calliope music, and shouts of laughter.

During the run of *Native Son*, Canada's penthouse was party central in Harlem, and everybody who was anybody in New York stopped by, including Carl Van Vechten, Marlon Brando, Lana Turner, and Tallulah Bankhead, as well as Paul Robeson, who owned the penthouse next door. During the day, people sunbathed on the terrace. On hot summer nights, they sat outside, enjoying iced drinks and cool breezes. Langston Hughes, a regular at Lee's place, penned a poem called "The Heart of Harlem," a sweet valentine to his friends:

> It's Dorothy Maynor and it's Billie Holiday,
> The lectures at the Schomburg and the Apollo down the way.
> It's Father Shelton Bishop and shouting Mother Horne.
> It's the Rennie and the Savoy where new dances are born.
> It's Canada Lee's penthouse at Five-Fifty-Five.
> It's Small's Paradise and Jimmy's little dive.
> It's 409 Edgecombe or a cold-water walk-up flat—
> But it's where I live and it's where my love is at
> Deep in the Heart of Harlem.

During the months that he stayed with Canada, young Jack Geiger got to meet "the cream of the Harlem theatrical, sporting, civil rights, political, and intellectual world," he later recalled, adding that it was "the educational experience of my life.

"I had the chance to sit around, evening after evening, many weekends, listening to Langston Hughes, William Saroyan, Adam Clayton Powell, Billy Strayhorne . . . Richard Wright, who came back once from exile and stopped in," Geiger said. "What I remember most was listening to people, listening to the conversations about World War II and race and democracy, segregation in the armed forces, what was happening in the South, what was happening in New York City."

One night Canada invited Geiger's parents to a party. That evening, the middle-class Jewish couple made their first trip to the heart of black Harlem with great trepidation. When they arrived, looking a bit nervous, Canada turned to Jack's mother and said, "Hey, I'm a bachelor. Do you think you could help us out in the kitchen?" It was the perfect thing to say to Mrs. Geiger. Off she went, and while she worked, she chatted happily with guests.

"Next day, I talked to my mother on the phone and she said she had had the most wonderful time," Geiger said. She'd spent hours in Canada's kitchen enjoying lively conversation with a most interesting man, but never managed to ask his name. When Jack asked her for a description "she discovered that she had spent two hours chatting with Langston

Hughes and was mortified that she had never realized it," Geiger said. "He was as comfortable as an old shoe. And I'm sure they talked about cooking and whatever else my mother wanted to talk about . . . She never quite got over it."

The guests were glamorous, intelligent, witty, and famous, but the main attraction was always Canada. Warm and welcoming, quick with a joke or story, Lee was also a good listener and never monopolized the conversation. "He wasn't the kind of person who strutted around or showed off," Leslie Nash recalled.

Canada luxuriated in at least one moment of sheer pride and delight. After a day of hard partying, Nash was sitting on the terrace enjoying the breeze and the view while Canada took a shower. He heard a noise and looked up to find Canada, buck naked on the terrace. Standing there in the altogether, pelvis thrust forward, he beat his fists on his chest.

"GODDAMN!" Canada hollered, borrowing Bigger's line. Nash must have looked startled. Canada grinned. "You know what I just did?"

"What?" Nash said.

"I just fucked the whole world!" The two men stood together on the terrace of that fabulous penthouse, looking at the city, laughing hysterically.

Canada never lorded his success over anyone. Instead, he shared his riches with the same easy generosity that got him in financial trouble all his life. His close friend from childhood, Billy Butler, saw how freely Lee spent his money—buying friends tickets to the show, picking up all the tabs all the time. Butler told Lee he needed to be more careful, and Canada finally agreed to let Billy open a bank account for him. They made a deal. Every payday, the actor would give some money to Butler to deposit in the bank. Lee would leave the money alone for a few days "and then take it out," Butler said. "But at least I had tried my best."

Canada's biggest money problem was still the Chicken Coop, although thanks to his newfound fame, the restaurant did better business than before. "On the nights when he isn't too tired, Canada comes uptown with a party of friends and amuses himself by playing the piano for his customers, singing, or clowning like a big kid," one reporter noted. "He greets patrons, makes them welcome to the restaurant. He receives the unknowns as enthusiastically as he does the celebrities who are making his place a rendezvous these days." Nevertheless, the Coop was still a losing proposition, and it was partly Lee's own fault.

"Canada was having such fun with his own restaurant. He would invite a whole group of us up there every night," his co-star Anne Burr said. "It was always on the house . . . On many occasions he would just lock the door so no customers could come in!"

Lee gave free meals to hungry young actors, out-of-work musicians, down-and-out boxers. A hopeless pushover, he was forever feeding people. "All you had to do was come in and look sad," Thomas Anderson recalled.

To save Canada's beloved restaurant from bankruptcy, the *Native Son* cast paid off creditors now and then, and once they all chipped in to buy chickens. But Lee's troubles were never over. One night, a pair of policemen rousted the Coop and cited Canada for running an unlicensed cabaret. When the actor went to court one mild April day, reporters tagged along to watch. The judge asked Canada what happened.

"Judge, everything is going along nice and quiet at my place, the Chicken Coop, when this diner gets a little exuberated, gets up with his girl and starts to whirl around between the tables," Lee explained. He swore he wasn't trying to run a club illegally. "We set out the best Southern fried chicken and French fried sweet potatoes you ever ate, but no one ever comes there to eat," he sighed, "only to cut up, and get me called a cabaret runner."

Won over by the actor's candor and charm, the judge let him off. One headline the next day read, "Bigger Finds a Judge Who Understands."

Whatever the occasion, Canada made great copy. During *Native Son*, reporters lined up outside his dressing room door. He gave dozens of interviews before and after shows, often robed in a rich purple dressing gown, sipping his orange juice and chain-smoking Chesterfields. Feature stories appeared in top newspapers and magazines; *Life* and *The New York Times* both ran three-page spreads on the actor. Nearly every profile makes much of Canada's rags-to-riches journey from poor Harlem rapscallion to violin prodigy to jockey to prizefighter to Broadway star. The press ate it up, and Canada was happy to dish it out in quantity. He knew the score from his prizefighting days: if you want to see your name in the headlines, you've got to fork over juicy quotes and anecdotes.

He was often asked about his move from the ring to the stage. "Fighting gave me stage presence," he said. "In the ring I learned balance and fluidity of movement. There I learned that when I made a false move I had to correct it in a hurry. Without that knowledge I'd be lost now." He often spoke of how much he loved the sport, that the ring would always claim his heart. "I would give my life's blood if all this praise was for me winning the title instead of making a hit on the stage," he told one reporter. "There's no thrill in all this world like the roar of the crowd when the referee counts to ten over a tough opponent. You can't compare the polite applause of a theater audience with the lusty sweep of a fight mob's voice in Madison Square Garden." He told countless reporters: "If I had my life to live over, I'd go back to the ring."

Writers sometimes waxed rhapsodic over Canada in florid prose that would never make it past the politically conscious editing desk these days. The animal, the sensual, and the sexual often creeps into these descriptions, as does fascination, fear, admiration, and condescension. While Lee approached reporters with warmth, humor, eloquence, and self-confidence, his magnetism and charisma proved so alluring it was disturbing. When reading these descriptions, it seems as though writers felt compelled to undermine the actor's innate, captivating charm with anecdotes of stereotypical, often comic, behavior and "nigger dialect."

"Canada Lee is a Negro, and in his dark, muscled body there flows a restless torrent of strength," wrote one reporter. "He moves with an unpredictable and animal grace, loose and powerful. And now and then his body will jerk rhythmically as if way back in his mind he were listening to boogie-woogie music, as when he reaches for his new shoes in dressing room 2A at the St. James and he says loudly: 'Ho-ot damn! Look at those shoes. Daggone! Look at those big feet!'"

But there are genuine and moving moments of reflection in these stories, too. When Canada talks about his drive to be somebody, his desire is so naked, his ambition so innocent, his dreams so vulnerable, it can take the breath away. "All my life, see, I've been on the verge of something," he confided to one writer. "I'm almost becoming a concert violinist and I run away to the races. I'm almost a good jockey and I go overweight. I'm almost a champion prizefighter and my eyes go bad. Now I've got it, now I've got what I'm going to be."

Later, in the same interview, the writer asked Canada what he and Bigger had in common. "I don't know," Lee said. "But always I've got to have excitement. I have to fight, get on a horse, see lots of people, even try to write songs. It's all there pushing out of me somehow and I don't know why, got to do something, got to be somebody. I've got it over Bigger because I know how to handle myself, but I know how he feels inside. And sometimes I think of all the Bigger Thomases I've known in my life and grown up with and I think to myself, kind of scared: There, but for God, that could be me."

The most startling element in many of these articles, however, is the nascent political awareness that Canada demonstrates. In several interviews, he criticizes the limitations placed on black actors: "I never studied acting once . . . Hell, you don't have to study. What can a Negro fellow study anyway? 'How yuh boss, no suh boss, yas suh boss.'"

When critics questioned him about playing a murderer, Lee was never apologetic or defensive. He insisted on viewing Bigger as a person rather than a political symbol. "You can see, in Bigger Thomas, the worry and the fear of what other people will think," Canada said. "I like him because he's life. He's real. He's all around us."

Convinced that *Native Son* had political, social, and artistic significance, he proclaimed "We're making history in this theater," adding that "the Negro has never been given the scope that I'm given in this play. Now things are going to happen. Now they'll think of the Negro as an actor, and not as some butler-valet type."

Though he urged playwrights to create more plays on the subject of race relations, Canada was a realist and he understood the firm hold Jim Crow had over American theater. "I don't kid myself," he said. "The public can stand only so much drama from a Negro, and a classic like *Native Son* comes along only once in a generation. After that, the public wants the Negro to get back into character where they believe he belongs, dishing out that minstrel-like 'Yessuh, boss' and 'Hot diggety yeah man, boss!'"

Producers looking to hire Canada Lee to play servants and slaves would be sent packing, the actor said, vowing to fight for more meaningful roles as well as greater respect for black actors and black audiences. "If I've done nothing else than to aid my people by my acting, I believe I have accomplished [much]," Lee said. "If I have done something to change these wrong ideas, I feel that my life is worthwhile."

The boy from Harlem who decided in the first grade that he wanted to be somebody famous, somebody important, got what he had always wanted. He wasn't on the verge of anything anymore. Canada Lee was a star. And still . . . it wasn't enough. As one writer noted, Canada "has a voice now, and he'll raise it above the roar of prejudice and hate . . . even if it's alone, it will be loud and strong."

Boxer-turned-bandleader-turned-actor was turning political.

SIX

WHY DON'T YOU DO RIGHT

ON THE ROAD WITH JIM CROW

During the run of *Native Son*, friends noticed that Lee was making pointedly political remarks in the papers, something he had not done before. One of these friends was composer Leonard de Paur, who was often backstage at the St. James Theater, chatting with Canada and other actors he knew from the old Federal Theatre Project.

"What impressed me most about him at that time," de Paur said, "was a growing political awareness. I honestly can't say whether it was the play itself, the role itself, the contact with Richard Wright, or the various people around him . . . but I remember that for the first time he was becoming, at least psychologically, a politically active person."

The play, the character, the words and ideas of Richard Wright made a powerful impression on Lee. During the courtroom scene, night after night, the actor heard speeches demanding the execution of Bigger Thomas, "some half-human, black ape . . . climbing through the windows of our homes to rape and murder our daughters." He listened to equally passionate speeches in Bigger's defense: "Bigger Thomas is an organism which our social system has bred . . . You cannot kill Bigger Thomas! He is already dead! He was born dead . . . amid the rank and choking vegetation of our slums, in the Jim Crow corners of our buses and trains, in our Jim Crow army, in our Jim Crow navy, even in the trenches when we send him to war," argues Bigger's attorney. "Night and day, millions of souls, the souls of our black people, are crying out: This is our country, too. We helped to build it. Give us a part in it, a part free and hopeful and wide as the everlasting horizon . . . Give us our freedom, our chance, and our hope to be men." And finally there were Bigger's own words, inarticulate, angry, and desperate, words that gave voice to pain and rage Canada understood but rarely unleashed: "Why the folks who sent me here hate me so? Long before I ever did anything, they hated me. How come they hate me so?"

Lee's performance was one of the most celebrated of the period. He grasped completely the depths of Bigger's confused rage because he had confronted it. "I've known guys like Bigger Thomas all my life," he said. "I saw them at the racetracks . . . ex-convicts, thieves, and all kinds of cutthroats. I saw some in school and I grew up with some pretty tough guys. Some of them are in jail now, and some of them went to the electric chair."

He understood Bigger, won sympathy for Bigger, and yet the reason he found such universal favor was because he was so very different than Bigger. He was a self-made man who had worked hard, accomplished much, and deserved respect—and he quickly learned how to play that in the press. "I knew guys who said being colored was a bar to everything they hoped to be, but it wasn't so with me. I never had a break," Lee said, somewhat disingenuously. As the popular star of a tough-minded, groundbreaking political play, Lee was in a unique position; as Native Son deepened his political consciousness, it also honed his skills at charming the public and impressing the media.

Famous, photogenic, and quotable, Canada was soon recruited to speak on behalf of a number of organizations. Weeks after Native Son opened, Lee's name began popping up all over as a speaker, master of ceremonies, or featured performer at benefits, banquets, and rallies. Columnist Dan Burley saw Lee at one of his first engagements and wrote: "The Native Son sensation didn't seem to understand why he's the man of the hour." Nonetheless, that's what he was. Requests and invitations, proposals and pleas, came fast and furious. Nell Dodson, an aspiring young journalist, hit on the idea of working as a "Girl Friday" for Canada; she then wrote a syndicated column for black newspapers about what it was like to be secretary to the star. Hectic, was how she described it: "Lee is being sought for radio programs, benefits and personal appearances . . . He gets a dozen propositions a day."

As one of a mere handful of black Broadway stars, Lee was often tapped to promote better opportunities for black performers, such as a landmark radio broadcast on Sunday, March 30, 1941. "Congrats to the National Urban League and the star-studded program over the nationwide hookup on CBS Sunday," wrote the *New York Age*. "This was the first full-hour, all-colored radio program, with the most outstanding Negro stars of the country participating, and should long be remembered." Lee was a featured performer, along with Duke Ellington and his orchestra, Louis Armstrong, Ethel Waters, John Kirby, Eddie "Rochester" Anderson, Bill Bojangles Robinson, Joe Louis, and Marian Anderson.

But Canada cared about the world outside of theater and radio as well. He had come of age during the Depression and the New Deal, he read the daily papers, he educated himself on social and political issues, and his liberal views were becoming well known outside artistic circles. Weeks later, on April 4, Lee appeared at a banquet sponsored by International Labor Defense. The ILD was the Communist Party's legal aid society, famous for its courtroom battles on behalf of black American prisoners, including the Scottsboro boys, perhaps the most important civil rights case of the 1930s.

While Lee knew how to sway his audience, he could be manipulated, too, according to his co-star Anne Burr. She and Canada frequently received invitations to appear together on behalf of political or social causes, and Burr sometimes suspected the two were being used. If this is something that you believe in, that's fine, she told Lee, but let's make sure we know where we stand. "Canada was conned quite frequently at that time," the actress recalled. "I wasn't old enough, smart enough, or experienced enough to know much more than . . . it wasn't quite the way it looked. I think Canada got taken lots of ways because he was basically very generous and very concerned and very trusting."

That spring, Lee was a guest of honor at the Negro Actors Guild Tea. He also emceed fund-raisers for the National Urban League and the Greater New York Fund. Actors Eddie Cantor and George Jessel invited him to appear at a Jewish Theatrical Guild benefit. At a gala to support the Harlem branch of the Children's Aid Society, Lee performed along with co-stars Lena Horne, Hazel Scott, Art Tatum, and Boris Karloff. He raised money for the Harlem Children's Camp fund in another all-star affair with Paul Robeson, Ed Sullivan, and fifty top entertainers. Anne

Burr and Canada threw a party for two hundred youngsters at the Colored Orphan Asylum in Riverdale, paying for ice cream, cake, and lemonade out of their own pockets. Lee also agreed to judge a costume contest at a school fund-raiser along with his old friends Georgette Harvey and Eric Burroughs. He helped raise money for the Lou Gehrig Memorial Fund in honor of the baseball legend who died that year of amyotrophic lateral sclerosis (ALS). And he played in a celebrity basketball game to benefit Spanish civil war refugees.

One wonders how he squeezed in eight Broadway shows a week.

Progressive radio also had a boon to beg in the spring of 1941. *The Free Company* was a remarkable CBS radio series showcasing some of the best-known writers of the period: Maxwell Anderson, Sherwood Anderson, Stephen Vincent Benét, Marc Connelly, Paul Green, Archibald MacLeish, William Saroyan, Robert F. Sherwood, and Orson Welles. The series was initiated by U.S. Solicitor General Francis Biddle at the behest of President Roosevelt. "The goal was to alert Americans to the threat from the Nazis and to combat foreign propaganda," according to Howard Blue, author of *Words at War*, a comprehensive study of World War II radio drama. *The Free Company* asked actors who were sympathetic to the goals of the project to perform pro bono. Canada agreed, and on April 13, he starred in Paul Green's radio play "A Start in Life," poignantly dramatizing the daily indignities experienced by an African American family. *The Free Company* later drew fire from Hearst critics who condemned an Orson Welles script as "Communistic," and from conservative watchdogs including the American Legion. A spokesman for a Brooklyn Legion post said that even the name *Free Company* sounded Communist. In recognition of his stardom and charitable work, Canada was profiled on the first episode of WNYC's "Those Who Made Good," a weekly radio program sponsored by the NAACP to showcase "the most outstanding race figures in contemporary life, from all fields of endeavor." *Variety* wrote that while the show was "obviously inclined to appeal most strongly to Negroes," it also attracted general audiences. On the show, broadcast in May, Canada described his careers as violinist, jockey, boxer, and actor. "Lee revealed that he may play the title part in a production of *Othello* planned by Welles," *Variety* said, noting the show would have an interracial cast. The following month, Lee returned to WNYC to star in a dramatization of Booker T. Washington's life.

While Canada was in demand in many quarters, he was snubbed in others. Rumor had it that two Hollywood studios wanted to make a movie version of *Native Son*, but they both intended to cast a white actor in the lead role. In those days, producers avoided controversy over interracial casting by routinely hiring white actors to play black, Asian, Hispanic, and Native American roles—a practice requiring creative license by makeup artists and a sturdy suspension of disbelief by audiences. Irked by the idea of a white Bigger Thomas, Orson Welles proposed shooting the picture in Mexico where a mixed cast wouldn't be an issue, but financial backers didn't bite. Then Metro-Goldwyn-Mayer offered Richard Wright twenty-five thousand dollars for rights to film *Native Son* with white characters. According to the studio, the film would be an indictment of poor housing conditions, devoid of any reference to racial prejudice. "The film executives interested in the play are sure that everything that happened to Bigger Thomas could and has happened to white men corroded and destroyed by the slums and underprivileged life," drily noted the *Pittsburgh Courier*, an influential black newspaper.

MGM's bid to bleach *Native Son* didn't surprise the black press. What did shock them was a report that Wright was seriously considering the studio's offer. A *New York Post* columnist reported that the author had no objections because Bigger's story was "just a case history," and he agreed with the studio that it "could have happened to a white man, as well as to a Negro." Harlem was stunned. Was Wright selling out? A committee rapidly formed to oppose any such deal, and the *New Masses* supported the group's efforts. "If this plan goes through, over three or four dead bodies, we shall witness a degrading contrast to the fighting play which Orson Welles has put on at the St. James Theater," Samuel Sillen wrote. "Any subsequent Hollywood whitewash will be hooted out of existence." Wright's biographer, Hazel Rowley, holds that Wright was in fact "horrified" by MGM's proposal. The film would not be made until a decade later on a minuscule budget in Argentina, with Richard Wright in the lead.

While Hollywood cheated Canada out of playing Bigger on screen, the black press angrily charged, the white media was about to cheat *Native Son* out of winning the prestigious New York Drama Critics' Circle Award. Each May, influential critics gathered at the Algonquin Hotel to pick the year's best play. The prize bestowed more than literary honor—

it infused box-office business with new life, helping a show survive the doldrums of summer just ahead. The *New York Amsterdam News* editorialized: "What is going to be the fate of *Native Son* when the boys get in a huddle to name the prize-winning play of 1941? Although there are those of us who believe that so far it has no competition, we'd be willing to take bets that it won't get it. That's democracy for you."

Perhaps this was one snub too many for Canada. Columnists hinted that the actor was thinking about going back into the music business. "Lee, Negro star of *Native Son*, plans to organize a jazz band. Is a good violinist," Ed Sullivan announced. *Variety* heard the same rumor. On May 15, *Downbeat* magazine reported that Lee hoped to debut his new band at the Savoy Ballroom in Harlem: "Nothing definite set yet but Lee, one of the most talented Negroes to appear in years in legit circles, believes he could click as a wand-wielder." Another columnist confirmed that the actor was keen to lead his own swing orchestra, but assured readers that Lee would "wait out the run of *Son*."

Canada soon learned he might not have long to wait. Lillian Hellman's indictment of Nazism, *Watch on the Rhine*, copped the critics' prize, while Robert F. Sherwood's anti-Soviet play, *There Shall Be No Night*, took the Pulitzer. Ticket sales for *Native Son* slumped.

Lee paid little attention to box office woes at first; he had problems of his own. "The star of *Native Son* is worried about his son who has been missing the past few days," reported the *New York Post*. Canada was, in fact, frantic. Weeks before, Carl had run off to Saratoga, perhaps hoping to be a jockey like his father. Bill Canegata doesn't remember why his cousin Carl ran away this time, but adds, "He was a teenager. Maybe he was in some trouble." Whatever transpired, Carl finally returned home safe and sound, much to Canada's relief. Now that his family crisis was over, he could start worrying about his job.

By early June, gross box-office receipts at *Native Son* had plummeted to $8,500 a week, barely enough to cover expenses. Perhaps to boost the show, or just by happy coincidence, the Mutual Network on June 9 broadcast a half-hour radio program called "Salute to Canada Lee." Paul Robeson emceed the tribute, which featured music from Duke Ellington's forthcoming show *Jump for Joy*, a comedy scene by Hattie McDaniel and Rochester, and a scene from *Native Son*. Other guests included W. C. Handy and Erskine Butterfield.

Despite this star-spangled promotion, *Native Son* remained in financial peril. Wright, who had once worked as a theater publicist, typed out a three-page "Blueprint for an Emergency" outlining grassroots marketing strategies. Both playwrights agreed to cut 40 percent of their royalties to keep the show going. Houseman and Welles gave up their salaries indefinitely and asked the cast to voluntarily take pay cuts.

This request set off a dispute between Orson and Canada. Beset by money troubles, including his failing restaurant, Lee actually pleaded for a raise. On June 13 at 9:58 p.m., Welles sent a telegram from Los Angeles to Lee in care of the St. James Theater. I am unable to give you $150 more a week, he said, when others are taking cuts. Welles added icily that Canada was getting more out of this show than Orson ever would.

The cuts, reductions, and marketing strategies were to no avail, and on June 28, *Native Son* closed after 114 performances. Normally a respectable run, it was disappointing for a play that opened to near-unanimous critical acclaim. On July 2, *Variety* reported that the show was thirty-six thousand dollars in the red, noting that the delayed opening and extra rehearsals drove it eleven thousand dollars over budget from the start. The play also had trouble finding its market, *Variety* said. People who read the book passed on the stage version; conservatives and women also stayed away. And while investors assumed the show would attract steady trade from Harlem, the ticket prices were too high. "Not more than 15 percent of the average audience was colored," the trade paper stated. *The Pittsburgh Courier* argued that black audiences didn't buy into the play because they believed *Native Son* "showed the race in an unfavorable light, and could come to no good flaunting its fingers in the face of the racial caste system by bringing about the close association of a white woman and a colored man."

Sorry as he was to see the show end, Lee was never one to let grass grow under his feet and money was a great motivator. Earlier that spring, Orson had announced bold plans for a fall production of *Othello* by an interracial cast. With Lee as the first black actor playing Shakespeare's Moor opposite a white Desdemona, the production would have been a first on Broadway. (Though Paul Robeson had played *Othello* opposite a white actress on the London stage, that production had not yet traveled to America.) Lee was keen on pursuing *Othello*, but now Welles had other irons in the fire and the project fizzled. A publicity agent told columnist Wilella Waldorf, "Lee has no definite plans. He is reading a play about a famous Negro pirate by a young unknown Negro author. He may accept one of a number of movie offers."

Translating truth from public-relations-speak: Canada the Broadway sensation was at loose ends with no work in sight. Fortunately, things started looking up.

"Canada Lee is proving these days that you just can't keep a good man down!" boasted the New York Amsterdam News. "He's living up to the vote of confidence given him by the metropolitan critics and audiences by continuing his dramatic career . . . but not on the stage. The new success there will come perhaps this fall. It is through another medium entirely that Mr. Lee has been achieving new honors of late — radio."

In July 1941, Canada played three juicy roles on the airwaves, starring as Toussaint L'Ouverture on WNYC; Saint Moses on WMCA; and legendary boogie-woogie pianist Pinetop Smith on NBC. "Scores of fan letters are still pouring in," noted the New York Age. Lee had three more major radio projects in the hopper. One was a War Department special with music by the Leonard de Paur Chorus, scheduled for broadcast in August on NBC. The second was a pilot for a variety show on CBS, starring Lee in dramatic sketches and featuring music by Lena Horne and Margaret Bonds. His third and final project was the most ambitious, aesthetically and politically. He was seeking a sponsor to back "The Canada Lee Radio Drama Company," which would present a weekly series of half-hour dramas on Negro life.

"Realizing that colored writers heretofore haven't been given an opportunity to display their talents in the radio field, Canada Lee is launching a drive to encourage them by using suitable material submitted to him," wrote the New York Age on July 3.

The actor was soliciting stories about theater, sports, love, comedy, or adventure. "I will waste no time on scripts portraying the Negro as an individual with a persecution complex, or a fast-stepping night-lifer," he told reporters at a press conference. "That type of Negro has been played to death. I want to portray him as a human with normal ambitions and inhibitions."

But Canada's innovative ideas had to be put on hold; it seemed his relationship with Bigger Thomas and Native Son wasn't over yet. Harlem's famed Apollo Theater hired him to perform two scenes from the play as part of a variety show running one week in early July. *Variety's* review noted that the Apollo "shrewdly" included an aw-shucks interview with the star "to build up Lee as an unassuming thespian" in front of his hometown crowd. Theaters in Washington and Baltimore immediately booked him to do similar gigs. Next, the up-and-coming producer Cheryl Crawford arranged to take Canada and *Native Son* to Maplewood, New Jersey, for a limited run that sold out almost immediately.

Still another production company arranged for *Native Son* to tour New York City's outer boroughs in July and August and Lee stayed on board. The first stop on this tour was the Bronx. Despite a suffocating heat wave, the show broke box-office records at the 1,600-seat Windsor Theater. The crowd was standing room only every night and hundreds had to be turned away. The *New York Age* credited modest ticket prices (topping out at $1.10) for the show's success, as well as Canada's increasing fame. Ever generous, Lee bought matinee tickets for fifty underprivileged boys from the Harlem YMCA. Photographers snapped away as the actor talked to the starstruck teens after the show.

"He is now rapidly becoming a box-office attraction in his own right," reported the *Age*. "Each curtain call of Mr. Lee was the signal for an outburst reminiscent of a baseball game. After performances, all paths leading to his dressing room were blocked by hordes of well-wishers and autograph-hunters."

Sellout crowds followed Canada to the Flatbush Theater in Brooklyn, where his triumph was marred by the final chapter of the infamous four-star car story. On August 15, Canada shamefacedly went to court on West Forty-seventh Street to defend himself against larceny charges for trying to sell a car that wasn't paid for. Lee explained to the judge that he had a misunderstanding with the producers who gave him the car. During the hearing, "two things stood out like sore thumbs," according to the *New York Amsterdam News*:

No. 1 — Canada Lee received only $75 a week for his efforts and not $250 which was commonly believed to have been his salary.
No. 2 — The producers did not give him the car outright as newspaper stories about the presentation went, but merely made an initial payment on the car.

The whole episode was miserable and embarrassing. Thankfully, one of the producers of the *Native Son* borough tour came to Lee's rescue. Jules Leventhal appeared in court, checkbook in hand, and offered to settle the debt—not out of the goodness of his heart, but rather to make a quick end to bad press for his star. "He needed the Negro actor no less than the Dodgers need Pete Reiser," one reporter quipped. "The show had to go on, but it couldn't draw flies without Canada Lee." The famously frugal Leventhal said he would deduct the sum gradually from the actor's paychecks. Having learned a thing or two in this mess, Lee agreed—but only after renegotiating a higher salary.

Between the four-star fiasco and the floundering Chicken Coop, Canada was in money trouble yet again. Thankfully, *Native Son* began to move out to regional theaters and everyone wanted Canada to star. In mid-August, tickets for a production at Atlantic City's Garden Pier Theater sold out so quickly that the producers had to add several matinees. During the Atlantic City run, producer Bern Bernard offered Canada the lead in a national tour of *Native Son* during the fall and winter of 1941 to 1942. Lee was thrilled. The tour would play some of America's best and biggest theaters, bringing him national exposure and a string of substantial paychecks to help pull him out of debt.

Native Son would soon be on its way to more than a dozen cities on a long and demanding touring schedule. Before leaving town, Canada spent extra time with his fifteen-year-old son. Carl was growing up. Like his father, he enjoyed sports, especially football. He also shared Lee's passion for jazz and had begun to fool around a bit on the guitar. He was a handsome boy and popular with girls, a chip off the old block. Lee told a reporter proudly that Carl "thinks I'm a pretty hot guy." While Canada was away, Carl would stay with his mother, Juanita, and make regular visits to his grandmother Canegata's house.

Juanita's nervous condition had abated, and she was able to work in her father's shop and later in various office jobs, sometimes as a bookkeeper. Bart Lanier Stafford III, who worked with Juanita at the Department of Welfare for many years, liked her very much. "She was a super lady, in the conventional sense of the word, meek and mild and obliging," he said. "I can imagine her now in hat and gloves and starched little white collar and cuffs on her rather sedate dress . . . soft-spoken and cultured." Juanita and Canada maintained a cordial relationship when they saw each other or spoke by telephone to sort out money matters or discuss plans for Carl's education.

Many of the original Broadway cast members went on the road with *Native Son*. With Orson's blessing, Jack Berry had been promoted out of a minor part to serve as director for the touring production and to play the key role of Bigger's defense attorney. Some of the new faces in the group were actually old pals, including Thomas Anderson from *Macbeth* days. Lee made new friends, too, especially actor John Randolph.

Native Son was booked at venues in Boston, Pittsburgh, Baltimore, Toronto, Detroit, Milwaukee, Chicago, St. Louis, and various points in between. The tour was, by turns, an exciting challenge, a massive party, and a terrifying nightmare. No one connected with the production expected the play to generate as much controversy as it did. There were harrowing incidents in several towns, ugly confrontations, intimidation, vandalism, even death threats. "It was like being at war!" John Randolph recalled. "The Jim Crow in this country was something I never thought I would see quite that way."

The tour began innocuously enough in mid-September with a two-week run at Boston's Majestic Theater. Perhaps all went well because the producers had carefully cut all profanity from the script to avoid trouble with the city's censor. The *Boston Herald* called Lee's performance "little short of perfect." While in Boston, Canada maintained a whirlwind schedule of radio broadcasts, cocktail parties, receptions, and benefits for groups ranging from the Eastern New England Congress for Equal Opportunity to the United American Spanish Aid Committee, assisting anti-Fascist refugees from the Franco regime. Somehow Lee found time to return to New York City to play Uncle Tom in The Invisible Theater's production of *Uncle Tom's Cabin*, broadcast on WINS on September 21. The *New York Daily Mirror* noted it was "the first time a colored man has played this immortal role on the radio." That same day, Lee and his *Native Son* co-stars Anne Burr and Jack Berry appeared at Christ's Church to wish fifteen hundred striking Gimbel's workers good luck in their efforts to win a five-day, forty-hour work week.

Lee admitted to a reporter that he sometimes wearied of making public appearances, but found it hard to say no, especially to charities and social welfare organizations. "Now that I have had some success, my own people expect me to be a noble character and set a good example," he said. "I'm a Negro who has made good, and they expect me always to live up to my reputation. Sometimes I want to tell them to go jump in the lake: I'm no hero, I'm just an ordinary guy who's been lucky and who likes to have a good time."

Native Son traveled next to Pittsburgh. Mrs. Florence Fisher Parry, local columnist, was amused to learn that the producers had cut the play's profanity to spare the sensibilities of genteel Boston ladies. "If they know their Pittsburgh audiences, they will retain all the shock and gore of the original," Parry wrote. The standing-room-only crowd at the Nixon Theater cheered lustily at the final curtain. While the *Sun-Telegraph* critic found fault with the play's "melodramatic frenzy," he complimented Canada for "one of the most beautifully sustained performances in the history of the modern theater."

On October 4, Harlem's *New York Amsterdam Star-News* updated its readers on the tour's progress: "Although there were many who thought that *Native Son* was a little too much for the 'sticks,' the show is doing all right for itself on the road." The paper noted that five white *Native Son* stars had signed with movie studios but "Lee, who actually made the show, hasn't been approached by Hollywood bigwigs. Ah, well! The price of democracy!"

The price of democracy on the road was in everyday frustrations, like Jim Crow hotels and restaurants, which began to take their toll on the black cast and crew. Canada got a break from it all when the show hit Detroit, hometown to his friend Joe Louis, reigning heavyweight champion of the world. The "Brown Bomber" owned a ranch outside Detroit and he invited both Canada and Thomas Anderson to stay there. Lee, the ex-jockey, was eager to get back in the saddle. "Canada always wanted to go out there to ride. He bought me boots," Anderson said. "He would laugh and say, Andy, there is one thing I can beat you doing . . . I can beat you riding. And I said, 'You sure as hell can!'"

Canada bought his mother a train ticket to Detroit so she could visit him. Lydia Canegata stayed with Joe Louis's mother, Mrs. Barrow, out at the ranch, and Lee moved into Joe's apartment downtown. This arrangement may have suited the actor especially well because he happened to have another visitor in Detroit at the very same time. "There was a girl that was very much in love with him," Anderson said. Though he couldn't recall her name, Anderson remembered that she was a singer who made the song "Walkin' By the River" famous. "She was a thin girl. It wasn't Billie Holiday, but of that type," he said.

The woman in question was likely jazz pianist Una Mae Carlisle, who was certainly slender and quite a looker. As a teenager in Cincinnati, Una Mae had been Fats Waller's protégée. When she turned twenty-one, she moved to Europe. For three years, she played clubs in England and France, including the famed *Boeuf sur le Toit* in Paris. After returning to New York in 1939, she joined Fats, her old mentor, in the studio at Bluebird Records to record the hit "I Can't Give You Anything But Love." But Una Mae was determined to make her own way as a musician, singer, and composer. She wrote "Walkin' By the River" with Robert Sour and recorded it on the Bluebird label with Benny Carter on trumpet, Everett Barksdale on guitar, Slam Stewart on bass, and Zutty Singleton on drums. The record hit the Top Ten in 1941 and was still on the charts when she visited Canada that fall in Detroit. The lyrics are tender, the tune hauntingly romantic as the singer wends her solitary way through the dewy grass to the water's edge, waiting for a lover

> *Soft as the breeze that blows through the trees,*
> *Way down by the river at night.*

It's not certain whether Canada went on any riverside strolls with Una Mae, but his attention certainly did some wandering. According to Anderson, Lee had yet another female admirer in Detroit, a schoolteacher who invented her own version of new math. The teacher bought Canada a leather-covered cigarette case and lighter for twenty-seven dollars and then asked him to buy "something nice" for her in return. She showed the actor four pieces of jewelry and said, "I like this one," pointing to a little trinket that cost seventy-five dollars. Anderson threw a fit, furious at this unscrupulous dame for taking advantage of his pal. After much haranguing, he convinced Lee to just say no. "I became the S.O.B.," Anderson said. The teacher didn't get her trinket—and she took back the cigarette box.

Anderson tried to get Lee, the notorious big spender, to be more careful with his cash. Canada's parents also worried about their son's spending habits. "I were not so blessed, or else you would have had every-thing," his father wrote. "You must keep Carl in mind . . . Think of his fu-ture and save for old age." James and Lydia were worried about their own golden years. Lydia's heart was weakening, and the Conegatas hoped Lee might be able to help them buy a house without stairs. Please send a little money home each week, his mother pleaded.

Canada was worrying about the immediate future and his own health as *Native Son* traveled below the Mason-Dixon line to St. Louis, Mis-souri. The cast heard that a race riot had recently threatened to break out in the city, and when the company arrived at the end of October, they found a battalion of police officers surrounding the square in front of the theater. "That town was terrifying," Randolph said.

The American Theater was a Jim Crow house, and segregated seat-ing became an explosive issue for *Native Son*. A black newspaper, *The St. Louis Call*, was boycotting the venue because of its Jim Crow policies. Canada and the rest of the cast desperately wanted the *Call's* readers to see the play, so they organized a meeting with the editor. He agreed to suspend the boycott and to see the show along with the paper's drama critic, though it meant the two men would be forced to sit in the highest balcony, known as nigger heaven.

On opening night, an anonymous caller threatened to stop the per-formance—with a gun, if necessary. Canada convinced everyone the show must go on. When the curtain went up, the actors noticed police officers stationed throughout the theater. John Randolph was playing a policeman, and he was costumed in the same uniform as the St. Louis police. He suddenly realized he was in a whole new ballgame. "You're no longer dealing with just make-believe theater," he said. "You're deal-ing with an actual experience that is frightening. You realize how deeply the black question affects whites, because that police force was out there and they were ready to close the theater."

The house stayed eerily quiet during the opening scenes. "I really ex-pected the gun to go off during the bedroom scene," Lee later told a re-porter. Sweat stood out on his face as he acted out the murder of Mary Dalton. No shots rang out, and the play progressed through the scenes of Bigger's desperate bid to elude police and his capture.

"I'll get it in the jail scene, sure," Canada told himself.

Jack Berry, playing the attorney Mr. Max, began to deliver his defense of Bigger Thomas. The audience remained absolutely still until Max damned Jim Crow on the streets, in buses, in trains. Suddenly, nigger heaven exploded. Black audience members rose up, shouting and stamping their feet. "There was a roar that went on and on, and pounding on the floor from the second balcony," Randolph said. "It was really stunning."

The atmosphere grew increasingly tense as small groups of white patrons walked out, clearly upset. Without breaking character, Canada frantically looked around for the phantom gunman. "By the time that finale came, my eyes were rattling around like peas in a pod, hunting for a spot where the shot would come from," he said.

No shot was ever fired. As the curtain fell, applause was strong in some quarters, merely polite in others. Randolph, still in his police costume, found himself in a huddle of real St. Louis police. He remembered two officers threatening to "get that son-of-a-bitch." Who were they talking about, Randolph wondered. The anonymous caller? Canada? Others said: "Those goddamned jigs, they don't want to work anyway. What is this shit? We'll get them and we'll beat them up." *That* was clear enough. Randolph, fearing a fight and worried that he'd be mistaken for a real policeman, made his way backstage. "When I finally got there, Canada was crying. Everybody backstage was in tears," he said. "I know that I was crying."

While the performance was described as "tense" and "harrowing," the city's white critics gave little, if any, indication of hostility or friction offstage. The *St. Louis Star-Time* even sent a reporter to interview Lee for a fluffy celebrity profile. Canada refused to stay on safe ground during the interview, though he clearly was taking a risk in this racially polarized city. The actor said that he and the rest of the cast considered themselves roving ambassadors for equal rights for Negroes. "The only thing I want," he said, "is to be the kind of person my people can be proud of. I'd like to be to them what Joe Louis and Paul Robeson have been, men that the whole race could fall behind and anyone could respect. I don't want to be the sort who scrapes and bows to his public, but lords it over his own."

After a week in St. Louis, the troupe traveled to Cleveland, where performances at the Hanna Theater were well-received by critics. A reviewer for the local black newspaper, *The Cleveland Call and Post*, said he went to the play rather skeptical about how the subject would be handled. "I came away exhilarated," he wrote. "This is a play that every Negro should see, and most certainly every white person, if they would care to learn the truth. Bigger Thomas is a replica of many Bigger Thomases who stifle at the unfair treatment of the Negro in America. Canada Lee feels the part. He knows like all Negro men, that placed in a compromising position with a white woman, whether it is his fault or not, he is always the guilty party . . . [Lee] is a fine example of the young, new Negro. He wears no bandanna on his head. He wants something better for his race."

On November 10, *Native Son* opened at Chicago's Studebaker Theater to a standing-room-only house, "a good half of which was made up of well-dressed and decorous Negroes who gave the propaganda speeches enthusiastic applause," according to the *Chicago Daily News*. The city's eminent drama critics were somewhat less decorous during the play's magnificent action scene where Bigger, cornered by the police, fires into the audience.

"At the moment he began shooting, I thought my number was up," confessed *Chicago Daily News* critic Lloyd Lewis. "My colleagues were similarly swayed. Miss Cassidy and Mr. Smith, I saw from the tail of my wide eye, were racing up the aisles for the lobby, preferring to risk being shot in the back. Mr. Pollak was on his knees between the rows of seats, hiding and probably praying. I hastily put on my wife's hat while Mr. Stevens, trapped and helpless in his front-row seat, gave up hope and bravely tried to look like Lincoln . . . A few seconds later, the curtain fell and the lights came up. We critics counted our dead and, finding none, tried to laugh off the whole thing . . . but our laughter sounded a little hollow." Lee earned standing ovations and unanimous raves. "The Negro race discovers another genius in its midst," the *Chicago Daily Times* gushed.

Canada didn't feel much like a genius that first week. He had been in town just three days when he got himself in hot water with the local black community over politics. He was invited to speak at a mass meeting sponsored by the National Negro Stop-Hitler-and-Hitlerism Committee on November 12 at DuSable High School. Predictably, Lee opened his remarks by reviling Hitler's racist regime and condemning "Hitlerism" at home. But instead of attacking the usual targets—Jim

Crow, segregation, lynching—Lee's speech took an unanticipated turn. He used Booker T. Washington as an example of bigotry, denouncing him for appeasing whites and advocating a racial caste system rather than fighting for civil rights. This drew warning grumbles from some conservative blacks in the crowd. Then, while speaking of American history and slavery, Canada held that President Abraham Lincoln should not be considered an abolitionist hero by Negroes; Lincoln, he argued, was primarily interested in preserving the Union, not freeing the slaves. Upon hearing those words, J. Finley Wilson, the Grand Exalted Ruler of the Improved Benevolent Protective Order of the Elks of the World, shot to his feet, incensed.

"Abraham Lincoln took the fetters off my mother's knees!" he cried.

That set off a bona fide fracas among several black Chicago political luminaries in attendance, including Earl Dickerson, a city alderman from the second ward and a progressive attorney who fought discriminatory real-estate covenants. The local press picked up the story, and the next day, instead of STOP HITLER IN EUROPE, one headline read, STOP CANADA LEE IN CHICAGO. Thomas Anderson had accompanied Lee to the meeting. It was the first time he heard his friend deliver a political speech and he fervently hoped it would be the last. "Canada," he said, "why in the hell don't you just go on and be an actor and quit saying all those other things?"

Lee's father concurred vigorously. James Canegata, pillar of the Salem Methodist Church, a proud, sober, hardworking man who worried what the neighbors might think, penned a cautionary letter: "For the good of your profession, I would refrain from speeches affecting the race because sometimes you have to harness your candid opinion for the good of all concerned. You must be a good diplomat. Be very careful, Lee."

James loved his son and he was proud of him. A community activist himself, he had helped A. Philip Randolph organize Pullman Porters and supported campaigns against poll taxes, lynching, and the Ku Klux Klan. But James was also pragmatic, and the not-so-subtle subtext to this letter was, "Son, don't screw up a career that's making you good money."

Money was the subject of many letters from home during the tour: money for his mother, money for Carl, money for a new charity his father had organized in Harlem (the Mayfield Home for Wayward Girls and Boys), money for a fur coat for his ex-wife Juanita. ("I am enclosing a picture of the type of coat I like," she wrote to Canada. "If you select it, be sure it is not dyed skunk.")

"He took care of that family," recalled Beulah Bullock, friend to Lee and his sister Claudia. "He tried to give them the best of everything."

Canada gave them all the money and presents they wanted, or at least all he could afford, but to his father's chagrin, he flatly refused to tone down his politics. On the road with Jim Crow, Lee's commitment to political activism was intensifying. While he didn't wish to hurt his family, his career, or the show, he didn't intend to betray his beliefs, either.

Thankfully, the controversy over his speech faded quickly. *Native Son* was now Chicago's hottest ticket. Producers extended the run from four weeks to nine, and the cast happily settled in for the holidays. White actors and crew were booked at the Sherman Hotel downtown, while the black actors stayed at the DuSable Hotel in Chicago's South Side, the neighborhood that had inspired Wright to create *Native Son* in the first place. Jim Crow frustrated everyone, but Canada held cast and crew together. His sense of humor, generosity, and a seemingly endless capacity to party went a long way to curing the blues and easing the strain.

Lee had penchant for practical jokes, like tossing cold water down your back or tying an alarm clock under your bed and setting it to ring at 2 a.m. He had his sweet side, too. If an actor ran through his per diem a little too quickly, Canada paid his bills. Whenever there was a piano around, he played and everybody sang along. He once surprised Tommy Anderson with an expensive piece of luggage the young actor couldn't afford to buy himself. And when Canada decided to purchase a new blue Harris Tweed suit lined with silk, he bought two and gave Tommy one.

"Oh my God, for Christmas! I think he gave me about $350 and told me to purchase perfume, et cetera, for everybody," Anderson said. "I got liquor for all the stage hands." Lee spent more than a week's pay on presents for cast, crew, and friends.

That Christmas in Chicago was one of the most memorable in actress Sarah Cunningham's life. Raised in South Carolina, Sarah was a young drama student when she met actor John Randolph for the first time. The two were deeply in love when Randolph left to tour with *Native Son*. He asked her to meet him in the Windy City for the holidays. Sarah had already purchased her ticket when, on December 7, 1941, the Japanese bombed Pearl Harbor.

In the wake of a national tragedy, facing the fearsome drama of war, a show in Chicago could have seemed inconsequential. But the cast of *Native Son* didn't feel that way. That night, John Randolph and Jack Berry wired Richard Wright asking for changes to the script. They wanted to remind audiences that young black men were about to fight a war against racism while serving in our own segregated military. The next day, four hours before the performance, Wright wired changes to Berry, including new lines for Mr. Max; Bigger's attorney would now remind the jury that in war "there are no Jim Crow bullets."

Emotions ran high that night as the cast took the stage, and the audience was particularly attentive. Randolph later wrote a passionate description of this performance for the *Daily Worker*, noting that blacks and whites had a tremendous stake "in this war to the death against Fascism." Days later, the actor enlisted.

That changed Christmas plans a little bit for Sarah Cunningham.

"John decided that we must get married," Cunningham recalled. Like many a girl in those complicated times, she told the soldier yes and then got cold feet. She had promised her Episcopalian mother that she would never elope, and here she was, agreeing to do just that. What was she thinking? Maybe she could invite her mother to Chicago for the wedding. "But she didn't know that John was Jewish . . . let alone that we were in a company of black people," Cunningham said.

Her mother was left temporarily in the dark as plans for the wedding went ahead. The ceremony took place in Sarah's hotel room between the matinee and evening show so the entire cast could be present. After the sweethearts were pronounced man and wife, Canada announced he would host the wedding dinner in the hotel dining room. John Randolph called down to reserve a table. The cast, in great high spirits, trouped into the dining room to find the maitre d' looking quite stricken. "Oh! I'm sorry," he said. "We don't admit Negroes." When the company threatened to pull out of the hotel and call a press conference, the manager seated the party at his best table. The service—from black waitstaff—was impeccable. The bride sat next to Canada, who charmed her off her feet.

The wedding party next went to an integrated nightclub, where Canada asked the bride for a dance. "I've never danced with a black man in my life," she recalled. "There's Canada, courtly, charming, as courtly and charming as any southern gentleman I had ever met in my life. And we went up to dance . . . I said to myself, 'Shit! He's a good dancer. I'm having a good time, and who in the hell am I worrying about?' And we had a wonderful time, and that changed my life . . . I loved him very much."

Lee won the hearts of nearly everybody he met, including those tough-as-nails Chicagoans. "Every place you'd go, they loved Canada," Anderson said. The actor's appeal posed a bit of a problem for Eddie Flagg, manager of the DuSable Hotel. Once a whites-only establishment, the DuSable had just reopened as a first-class hotel catering to black clientele. The actor was quite content in his swanky suite, except for one thing. "We didn't have telephones in the hotel rooms," Flagg recalled. "Canada Lee was one of our first guests and was very popular at that time. He lived on the fifth or sixth floor and received a lot of phone calls. Each time he had a call, an old intercom system rang in his room. Since we didn't have phones in the hall either, he had to get up and go downstairs to take his call. One day he said he was moving because of the phone inconvenience—so immediately phones were installed in the rooms."

Admiring women placed more than a few of those calls; as usual, Lee had no shortage of love interests. His scrapbook contains a bit of anonymous doggerel written during his stay in Chicago, quite possibly by his friend Langston Hughes, who was also in town at the time. Handwritten on a single sheet, the poem is titled "Canada Lee."

> He had so many women that he couldn't count 'em all,
> Oh, some were fair, and some were dark, some tiny, others tall.
> Rotating 'em, he saw each one but seven times a year,
> And this infrequence, he said, made every one a dear.
> "Have lots of women," he advised, "and see each now and then,
> And you'll adore 'em all and be the happiest of men."
> Yes, Canada knew his stuff; he handled women well.
> It was another type of sin that plunged him into hell.
> Required to state his avocation,
> The evil one cried, "Defloration."

It was in Chicago that Canada finally decided it was time to be a free man, officially. One day in the lobby of the DuSable, Lee and Tommy Anderson were introduced to the hotel owner's brother, who happened to be a judge. "You know, I need a divorce," Canada told His Honor. Anderson piped up that he needed one, too. The judge instructed the two men to get letters from their wives agreeing not to contest the divorce actions. Canada wrote to Juanita at once, asking her consent. She thanked him for his "lovely letter," and gave it quite willingly. "As to whether I shall ever marry again, that remains to be seen," Juanita wrote. "No prospects yet anyway. I am not too anxious to do anything that I might later regret. Anyway, lots of luck to you, and call me once in a while."

Lee's divorce was arranged in short order, and suddenly Canada was legally single and free to do as he liked. Pictures of this now most eligible of bachelors routinely appeared in local newspapers—squiring lovely ladies to nightclubs, practicing violin in his hotel suite, or relaxing backstage in his dressing gown of blue patterned silk, a handkerchief tucked neatly in the pocket. Columnists noted where he went, with whom, and what he was wearing; the dapper actor was known to have fifty-two suits hanging in his hotel closet.

Clearly, Lee had his share of avid admirers. One of his greatest fans was Sylvester "Two-Gun Pete" Washington, a legend in the city's South Side. This tough plainclothes cop carried a pair of pearl-handled pistols, and if Pete was on your street, the street was *safe*. Two-Gun Pete took pride in looking after celebrities who visited his turf, and he had taken a particular shining to Canada Lee.

One night, Canada and Tommy took their dates to a local cabaret. A couple of thugs recognized the actors and began to harass them: "You half-assed niggers from New York. This is our place. This is Chicago!" Just when it looked like things were going to get rough, Two-Gun Pete suddenly materialized.

"Don't nobody move!" Two-Gun Pete ordered. The room fell dead quiet. "Mr. Lee, what's wrong? I understand you're having some trouble."

"These guys started to give us a hard time," Canada said, quietly.

"*Who's* bothering you, Mr. Lee?" Two-Gun Pete demanded. The thugs were surely sweating by now.

"Well, these two fellows," Canada said, pointing them out.

Two-Gun Pete slammed down his massive fist—or perhaps the butt of one of his pearl-handled guns—with a *BANG*. Tommy recalled more bangs as Two-Gun Pete punctuated his speech to the thugs: "You two think you can come in here and spoil things for this man who is an artist?" *BANG.* "If you move, I'll kill you!" *BANG.* He turned to address everyone in the club.

"Now Mr. Lee is here with his friends," Two-Gun Pete announced. "You can go any place you want, Mr. Lee. No one is going to bother you." Glaring at the thugs, he added, "If I hear of you doing anything to Mr. Lee, I will kill you!"

After that performance, no one dared glance askance at Canada Lee.

Two-Gun Pete came to the rescue again on New Year's Eve. Canada was hosting a party in his hotel room and the place was jammed. The actor bought five cases of whiskey for his guests, though he rarely touched alcohol himself. At some point during the party, Tommy heard a man on the telephone ordering three more cases. Anderson knew Canada didn't have enough money to pay for it. He angrily canceled the order and confronted the man, who turned out to be a local gangster known as "St. Louis Kelly." The next thing Anderson knew, he was being shoved into the bathroom by "a tall guy in a long black coat with his hands in his pockets." But Two-Gun Pete arrived in the nick of time and set St. Louis straight.

Lee did more than party in Chicago. Though somewhat chastened by the early flap over his Lincoln speech, he continued to support progressive political and social causes. "Unspoiled by his current success as an actor, Canada insists on appearing at every sort of charitable benefit where he feels his services can help," reported *The Chicago Sun.* "He is a press agent's dream of a star, for no hour is too early, no task too onerous, nor anything too difficult for him to do, if it will help his show, his race, or his country."

By all accounts, the man never sat down. He sponsored a "Salute to Negro Troops"; appeared with jazz maestro Fletcher Henderson at a benefit for needy South Side families; gave talks to social-work students and aspiring thespians; visited inner-city nurseries and community centers; collected "Smokes for Yanks" backstage; and raised money for the Red Cross. He was guest of honor at teas, dinners, performances, balls, and banquets. One night Louis Armstrong and his band feted Lee at the Black Spider Club; another evening, actors and jazzers threw him a party at the Plantation Café. He was honored by the Chicago Association of Negro Clubs as well as the South Chicago Players, and the Neological Foundation awarded him a fellowship for "furthering the ideals of Americanism."

Somehow, he also found time to do a favor for his pal Langston Hughes and poet Arna Bontemps. Lang and Arna had written a radio script about the Bill of Rights called "Salute to Freedom." They recruited Lee to perform poetic monologues about composer W. C. Handy and scientist George Washington Carver, accompanied by blues music. The program, broadcast on WBBM, ended with remarks by Illinois Governor Dwight H. Greene, who autographed Lee's script, as did Arna ("A good performance, Canada") and Langston ("Swell reading, Canada!"). The Elmhurst College Men's Glee Club performed on the show as well, and later that week the school newspaper reported: "Perhaps the outstanding experience of the day to most of the fellows was the thrill of talking with Canada Lee, a remarkably democratic fellow. He was friendly to all and never refused giving the different fellows an autograph, each time addressing it personally and adding a personal comment."

On January 10, 1942, *Native Son* finally ended its wildly successful Chicago run. Producers leased three seventy-foot baggage cars from the American Circus Corporation of Peru, Indiana, to move the show quickly and efficiently through short dates in Minneapolis, St. Paul, Madison, and Milwaukee. At every stop, local reporters eagerly lined up to write stories on the nation's newest stage star. In one interview by a columnist named "Inquisitive Sal," Canada was asked his marital status. "I'm single, footloose, and fancy free," he said, smiling broadly. He confided he was attracted to women with "divine eyes," and insisted that a man could only love one woman at a time. A sports reporter claimed that the boxer-turned-actor "reminds you of the smiling Negro boy that shines your shoes in the barber shop, and who's willing to wager a month's free shines that Louis will win his next fight by a knockout."

In Madison, Wisconsin, a reporter sitting in the coffee shop at the Loraine Hotel was startled to find Canada Lee and two other black actors sitting at a table and eating lunch. "I was surprised because it has been the traditional practice of first-class hotels and restaurants to deny service to members of the Negro race," he wrote. "We also understand that the hotel housed Negro members of the cast while they were in Madison. *The Capital Times* believes that the management of the Loraine Hotel is entitled to the highest commendation for this courageous gesture."

In Madison, Canada enjoyed a happy reunion with his young protégé, Jack Geiger. His erstwhile roommate, that mixed-up teenage runaway, had managed at last to find a college that would accept him, though he was still just sixteen. (Jack couldn't pay his tuition at first and refused to ask his parents for it. Canada loaned him the money.) Now a student at the University of Wisconsin, Geiger was writing socially and politically progressive articles for the school newspaper. After Lee's visit, the teenager wrote a thank-you letter to his mentor, noting that he was working on a series of articles about Jim Crow: "I'm going through the colored section of town with a camera and a notebook. Wait 'til you see the article I write then."

Days later, Canada sat in his hotel room in Milwaukee after the show, relaxed and elegant in his silk dressing gown, swinging his leg over the arm of an upholstered chair. He was speaking with a journalist about America's segregated army, "pleading softly and with unconscious dramatic power for a chance for his black brothers and sisters."

"No Negro has ever been disloyal to these United States," he said. "Why do the army and navy discriminate against them? . . . When the government allows Negro soldiers in southern training camps to be beaten up by whites, the government is not showing much consideration for men who are willing to give their lives for America . . . Give them a chance. They'll prove that they have great qualities, which will make America even greater."

Canada was making headlines with his fight against discrimination and Jim Crow laws. After the Milwaukee speech, Lee received a letter from his father, James. Though just a few months earlier, Pop had urged his son to tone down his rhetoric, fearing it could cost Canada his job, this letter glows with pride and encouragement. "I enjoyed your statement and showed it to all my friends, and everyone praised you for the stand you are taking," James wrote. "I am hoping that you would some-day prove yourself a champion of the race. Somebody will rise up some day to relieve this damnable condition, and that person may be Canada. 'All glory to you.'"

James, so often stern and reserved, writes in an entirely new way in this letter, more man-to-man than father-to-son. He seems to seek ac-knowledgment of their shared passion for social justice, and appreciation of his own good works: "It's peculiar how we link up. I am trying to help in the same way. From my boyhood days, I have always been interested in our problems and have tried to do something in a small way."

After making a quick stop at Detroit's Lafayette Theater, *Native Son* crossed the border to Toronto, where the show's star, black actors, and crew members went from hotel to hotel trying to find rooms. It took the better part of a day to find places that would house them all. Lee had looked forward to his stay in Canada, believing it to be a country where "there are no prejudices and a Negro can feel like somebody," he said. "I was very sad to find out that I was mistaken."

When he learned that relations between Toronto's black and Jewish residents were strained at best, Canada decided to do something about it. He, John Randolph, and other actors met with leaders of both communities to discuss the troupe's strategies for coping with racism. "We were sharing our own experiences," Randolph said, "and it was this that Canada was great at." After the meeting, the *Evening Telegram* reported that a rabbi at Holy Blossom Temple planned to deliver a sermon that weekend on *Native Son* as a symbol "of all the hunted and hated peoples of the earth."

Canada and Jack Berry also accepted an invitation to speak at the University of Toronto. At the Hart House Theater, Lee paced up and down the stage, speaking slowly, pausing often, as though under great emotional strain. "He started off very apologetic for being such a poor speaker and then went on to hold everybody speechless," one of his listeners wrote. "You could tell he was really talking from the heart."

Don't merely tolerate us, Canada told the crowd. Don't endure us, grudgingly acknowledging that we exist. We are as you are. Why should we suffer insults and injustices because of the color of our skin? "I feel so unhappy about it all," he said, so disappointed that racism thrived in Canada, "a place I used to call God's country."

Despite these stern criticisms, Lee charmed Toronto, and, once again, critics raved over his performance while reporters clamored for interviews. Harry "Red" Foster invited Lee to appear on his *Crown Brand Sports Club* radio show, and the actor agreed to play himself in a series of vignettes about his life. One re-created a horserace he'd run as a teenaged jockey in Toronto's Dufferin Park. Red Foster, famous for pioneering live play-by-play coverage on radio, decided to inject a lively bit of action into the scene. Pretending to be the announcer, he called the race as though it were live. Canada lost "by a neck."

When *Native Son* traveled on to Rochester, New York, Lee spent an evening at a club on Joseph Avenue, where he bumped into an old friend from Harlem, George "Twistmouth" Ganaway, who was celebrated for creating the Lindy Hop at the Savoy Ballroom. The next night Lee found himself in the town of Syracuse, where he traded soft punches with a local stagehand on the set while giving interviews to local reporters. He reminisced about matches he fought against two rivals from the area, Bucky Lawless and Jackie Brady. "Someone mentioned that Jackie Brady had a gymnasium a few blocks away," a reporter wrote. "Lee hot-footed it to renew his acquaintance with an old foe and to get another sniff of the resin."

When Canada returned to the theater that night to get ready for the show, he found yet another friend from his pugilistic past. Jimmy Stanton, former boxer and now a police officer, was backstage with a pal from his precinct, Sergeant Mickey Roessner. The three men chatted until show time. Watching the action from the back of the house, Officer Stanton must have been awfully absorbed in the play. When an actor in uniform put Bigger under arrest, Stanton nearly punched him. Thankfully, his sergeant stepped in and blocked the blow.

Native Son once again crossed the Mason-Dixon line, this time to play one week at the Baltimore's Ford Theater. Of all the battles Canada fought against Jim Crow on the road, this was perhaps the bitterest. When the actors arrived at the theater, they found it unusually barren. Baltimore's chief of police had ordered that all cast pictures and posters be removed from the theater lobby because they showed Negroes and whites together.

Management at the Ford flatly refused to suspend their Jim Crow seating policy. A committee of Quaker women who fought local segregation battles tried to buy a block of fifty seats in the first balcony, notifying management that tickets would be distributed to blacks and whites. They were told that Negroes would not be permitted to sit in those seats, and committee member Wilma Ludlow later said she was reprimanded for wanting to "entertain colored." Ludlow then told the Ford that her group would be willing to sit in a roped-off section. Management refused. She made several other suggestions; all were refused. At last she offered to buy every single seat in the first balcony "provided colored persons would be allowed to sit there with any whites." Management refused.

One of the women on the committee pointed out that America was fighting Hitler and racism was a Nazi weapon. "Hitler has done some excellent things," management reportedly told her. "We have no business in this war. Pearl Harbor was only an incident."

It was a little tough to find a polite comeback for that one.

"We've always taken care of our colored patrons in the balcony. And we certainly can't afford to change that policy for this show," theater manager John Little told *The Afro-American*. "Our white patrons, the persons who keep this house going, would object to colored being seated anywhere else. Sometimes the whites come out of the balcony because some colored people are up there and we have to refund their money. You know, Baltimore is still the South and not New York."

It was Canada's leadership, Randolph said, that kept the cast calm and united. "He never, ever let down a performance," Randolph said. "Every performance became really a fight for dignity, a fight for us."

When the curtain rose on opening night, the second gallery—the Ford's designated nigger heaven—was packed, though Negro patrons had been charged eighty-three cents a seat, twenty-five cents more than at any previous show. Eight policemen leaned on the orchestra balustrade at the rear of the hall. "Every reference to race hatred and violence sounded like hot lead being dripped on a cold surface," Randolph recalled. When Jack Berry delivered his line about the segregated military and Jim Crow bullets, the second gallery crowd whistled and cheered, and so did a surprising number of people sitting in the first balcony and the orchestra. "My heart jumped about three inches," Randolph said. A handful of people walked out after that scene, but at the end of the show, Canada and the cast got an ovation.

Life took a calmer turn in Philadelphia, where tickets to the show at the Walnut Theater sold so quickly that the run was immediately extended. Lee took time out for some fun, visiting with his friend Baron Lee, a blues musician, and Troy Brown, a three-hundred-pound comic. Canada happily agreed to help out local charities and causes and spoke to boys and girls at schools all over town. When he visited the Philadelphia Society for Crippled Children, he took one child after another into his lap and bought armfuls of Easter Seals.

When the curtain came down on the last show in Philly, the cast threw a party backstage to celebrate a full year's run of *Native Son*, dat-

ing back to the show's Broadway opening. Orson sent them a congratulatory cable from Brazil, where he was shooting a quasi-documentary
called *It's All True* in support of the war effort.

The *Native Son* odyssey was nearly over; the final stop was Pittsburgh.
Canada was backstage in his dressing room when Western Union
knocked on the door with a telegram: "Here is hoping you knock them
dead. Duke Ellington." As always, he did.

On April 18, 1942, the *New York Age* reported that Canada had returned to Harlem after nine long months on the road. Lee was glad to be
back home at 555 Edgecombe, but there was no rest for the weary actor.
The Chicken Coop still floundered aimlessly as Lee tried desperately to
refinance it. At the same time, his father was pressuring him to help out
with the Mayfield Home for Wayward Girls and Boys. Canada's sister,
Claudia, had been working at the home since its grand opening in December. "Claudia spent a lot of time there," recalled Beulah Bullock,
who lived across the street from the Mayfield Home. "She worked very
hard. I would make her lunches. Canada came a few times, too. Canada
Lee was like my very own brother. But he was away so much. The man
was working all the time."

Was he ever. Lee had barely unpacked his bags when Noble Sissle,
famed composer and entertainer, invited him to help organize a national
Negro Day Show in June for the USO. Canada agreed; he also signed on
as entertainment coordinator for a membership campaign at the Harlem
YMCA. Later, he headlined an all-star benefit for the Harlem Children's
Camp Fund, featuring Paul Robeson, Erskine Hawkins, and Cab Cal-
loway. Lee's friend Ed Sullivan, host of a new CBS radio program called
Ed Sullivan Entertains, emceed the show.

Canada also turned up at a Democracy in Action "Cavern Party" so
boisterous it made the gossip column of the *New York Amsterdam Star-
News*. He arrived with his friends John and Louise Moseley; other guests
included Evelyn Vaughn, Rex Ingram, and Leonard Feather. Lee took
some good-natured ribbing about the many beautiful women who flocked
around him. According to the gossip column, the actor "couldn't make
up his mind and drove off alone."

Or perhaps he had a date elsewhere. Rumor had it that Canada was
seeing several women that summer, including his old flame Anaïs Nin,
who was simultaneously enjoying an affair with a twenty-six-year-old

Haitian architect named Albert Mangones. "I feel a real love for the Negro world," Nin wrote in her diary. "I feel close to them, to their emotional sensitiveness, their sensory awareness, their beauty, the soft velvet of their eyes, the warmth of their smile, the purity of their violence. They are human." Her language betrays the mythology of the virile black male, the stereotypic buck. Nin deliberately sought out the exotic, the illicit, the taboo, and later wrote about these affairs in her diaries, her erotica, and her fiction. Though Nin obviously admired Canada, enjoyed talking with him and sharing his company, the thrill of the forbidden runs through her text like a seismic tremor.

In July, Lee received a lucrative offer to play *Native Son* for two weeks in New Jersey theaters, including Newark's Mosque and Passaic's Central. In Passaic, more than two thousand people "chilled and thrilled" to his performance, according to the local press, which also noted that the last time Lee visited their fair city, he knocked out Freddie Herman in the first round: "Thus, Canada Lee's record in Passaic to date is perfect. He has scored two knockouts—one as a fighter and one as an actor."

Perhaps a bit weary of playing Bigger night after night, Canada tried something entirely new. On July 20, he agreed to play the lead in a pair of one-act plays written and directed by the enfant terrible of modern theater, William Saroyan, at the new "Saroyan Theater" (known to everyone but Saroyan as Broadway's Belasco Theater).

The plays were *Across the Board on Tomorrow Morning* and *Talking to You*, and they were studiously experimental in text, staging, and casting. Saroyan hired Maxwell Bodenheim, the free verse poet, to jump up in the middle of a scene and wildly recite a love poem. He cast two Filipino bus boys as Filipino bus boys. Canada played a waiter who delivers a baby in the first one-act and a prizefighter called Blackstone Boulevard in the second.

In the middle of a summer heat wave, Lee reported for rehearsals in a white T-shirt, neatly pressed slacks, white socks, and leather loafers. A rehearsal photo shows the cast sitting in chairs, visibly wilting, staring with bemused expressions at Saroyan as the director energetically waves his arms. A reporter described the mayhem in the murderously hot theater, noting that Lee was usually "reading the *Daily News*, and paying no attention to the rehearsal except when he was called upon to speak his lines."

If this was the exciting avant-garde, Canada was underwhelmed.

Lee took a short break from Saroyan's rehearsals on August 12 to star opposite Juano Hernandez in an episode of the critically acclaimed radio series *Green Valley U.S.A.*, broadcast by CBS. For fifteen minutes, five days a week, *Green Valley* told stories of national importance through a community of characters—the grocer, the postman, the schoolteacher, the police officer. Each episode opened: "Hello, neighbor! Welcome back to Green Valley. I've got a story for you, about some people you probably know . . . people just like you . . . important people, whose story is the life story of America."

Canada played a college student aspiring to be a newspaperman like his father. On campus, a mysterious man named Thatcher offers the young journalist big money to write pamphlets arguing "Negroes have no part in this war. The Negro's place is with the colored people—the Japanese, for instance." The boy's father, shocked by what his son has written, investigates and learns that Thatcher is in fact a "Negro fascist" and enemy agent. The abashed student tells his father that "neither Hitlerism nor the Rising Sun offers any solution" to the problems of his race.

The People's Voice in Harlem called the episode "revolutionary" because the black characters used pure English instead of stereotypical black dialect; the script quoted black heroes like Frederick Douglass; and the protagonist was "a normal college boy." The *Voice* praised the cast "for excellent performances and a real service to the Negro race." The Communist press gave the show a glowing review. "With no 'Oohs!' and 'Aha!' about the wonder of it, the program presented a Negro newspaper editor and his son," noted a columnist at the *Daily Worker*. "I liked that right away. White people too often have a way of being offensively patronizing toward Negro intellectuals—'Oh, look! An educated Negro!!!'—as if he or she were a freak of nature."

The Saroyan plays finally opened August 17 and limped through eight shows before perishing in the pitiless glare of merciless reviews. One critic wrote that Saroyan was "the author of some of the most vacant nonsense written in our time," with these particular plays "very close to the top of the class." Another claimed Saroyan had committed "artistic hari-kiri," a bit of overstatement given that the Pulitzer Prize–winning author wrote over two hundred plays, and these were relatively minor works.

Broadway's pundits singled out Canada's performances as the only bright spots in an otherwise irredeemable evening of theater. John Anderson said his "superb" acting outshined Saroyan's "banal allegory." Wolcott Gibbs of *The New Yorker* and John Mason Brown agreed that Lee was the only reason to see the play. "He is an admirable actor, possessed of a versatility which his fine performance in *Native Son* did not suggest," Mason wrote. "Canada Lee's poise and apparent understanding of both these Saroyan tasks was exceptional, and his acting entirely convincing in its simple directness," wrote Burns Mantle in the *Daily News*. Brooks Atkinson at *The New York Times* concurred. "Canada Lee is honest and forceful. You instinctively believe everything a man like that says," he wrote, praising Lee's "personal magnetism and forthright style."

Two weeks later, Canada put that poise and magnetism to work as he delivered his first formal address in New York City. On August 31, two thousand people heard his short speech during a meeting sponsored by the Negro Labor Victory Committee at the Golden Gate Ballroom in Harlem. The Reverend Adam Clayton Powell, Jr., was also at the podium that day. "All speakers generally referred to discrimination against Negroes and exhorted listeners to do something about it," according to *The FBI's RACON: Racial Conditions in the United States During World War II*.

Early in September, Hollywood flirted with Canada once again. *The New York Times* reported that MGM cameramen were in New York City to test Lee for roles in a pair of scripts the studio had recently optioned. One was called *Refugee Smith* and the other was *Liberty Ships*, which the *Times* described as "a screen yarn about Pacific Coast shipbuilding." Nothing came of the test.

Jilted by the big screen, Lee was still beloved by the stage, and his relationship with Bigger Thomas wasn't over yet. Producers Louis and George M. Brandt had booked *Native Son* into their theaters in the Bronx and Brooklyn and offered the lead to Canada. Jack Berry was assigned to direct what the producers were calling a revival of Welles's production, though its magnificent staging and sets were stripped to bare bones. Still, tickets were cheap and the two-week run sold out. In fact, the streamlined production proved so successful that Messrs. Brandt decided to revive the play at the Majestic Theater on Broadway at "popular prices," selling matinee tickets for as little as twenty-five cents.

When *Native Son* returned to the Great White Way on October 23, 1942, Brooks Atkinson of *The New York Times* called Canada's performance "triumphant" and devoted his review almost entirely to the star:

"He is a superbly imaginative player. When he is on the stage he inhabits it—knows where all the doors lead, what the windows look out on, knows where he can be seen or not seen from other parts of the room; he is aware of what is going on all through the house where the play is set. When he darts one way or another he is accordingly sure of just where he is going and what he is doing, and the theatrical world of illusion becomes vividly realistic. The quality of life Mr. Lee imparts to a scene is overwhelming—partly physical, partly magnetic . . . Mr. Lee is certainly the best Negro actor of his time, as well as one of the best actors in this country. His headlong portrait of Bigger Thomas is the most vital piece of acting on the current stage."

A review like this from one of America's most powerful theater critics usually guarantees a healthy run for a revival as long as the star remains in the cast. But another influential critic, Burns Mantle of the *Daily News*, argued the Brandts' revival was but a pale shadow of Welles's blockbuster production; he reduced his rating from four stars to three. And with the nation now at war, conservative critics felt empowered to take overt political exception to the script. "At the time it opened I felt that the play was faulty and distinctly left wing in its thinking, if not definitely communist propaganda," George Freedley wrote. "I can't see that the play has changed its point of view in any way despite the fact that the script has been revised in light of the war."

Despite these damaging volleys, bargain ticket prices and Canada's name on the marquee kept the revival afloat. Lee's popularity soared uptown and downtown. In Harlem, he regularly entertained the troops at the local USO. At Carnegie Hall, he joined a dazzling list of sponsors for a rally by the Artists Front to Win the War, chaired by international film star Charles Chaplin and powerhouse talent agent Sam Jaffe.

A certified celebrity, Canada now mixed in heady circles, inspired items in the gossip columns, and sauntered into the best parties thrown by the city's progressives and glitterati. On November 11, he brought down the house at a testimonial dinner for Carl Van Vechten, the white socialite, journalist, author, and photographer who promoted many black artists. Lee performed a comic poem written by Langston Hughes for the occasion, where guests included Alain Locke, W. C. Handy, Margaret Walker, Walter White, and Grace Nail Johnson. Van Vechten later wrote to Hughes: "When Canada Lee read your poem, it was like all Christmases everywhere from the beginning of time coming to me at once."

But Canada's fame and high-society connections couldn't keep *Native Son* alive forever. Ticket sales fell steadily, and the Brandts started talking about a closing date. Then, on December 5, 1942, *Native Son* was among five shows lambasted by *The Catholic News* as "wholly objectionable" to the conservative Catholic Theater Movement. (The other shows included *Star and Garter*, *Strip for Action*, and *Wine, Women and Song*.)

This pronouncement spelled big trouble for Lee Shubert. The Broadway mogul owned several theaters including the Ambassador, which had been home to *Wine, Women and Song*. Coincidentally, a few days before *The Catholic News* appeared on newsstands, *Wine, Women and Song* had been abruptly shut down by court order as part of a cleanup drive by the city administration; the Ambassador promptly lost its license to do business.

Shubert also owned the Majestic Theater where *Native Son* was playing. The day that *Native Son*'s "wholly objectionable" rating appeared in *The Catholic News*, Shubert walked over to the Majestic and posted a notice that he was closing the show. According to *The New York Times*, Shubert said he "wanted to avoid trouble." Fifty people, including thirty actors, would be out of work as a result of Shubert's decision, the newspaper reported.

It was a pivotal moment for Canada Lee.

As a novice actor, he had seen the U.S. government close down the Federal Theatre and the Harlem Negro Unit, stifling a wellspring of work for him and his fellow performers. He had spent more than a year touring with *Native Son*, organizing cast and crew to fight racial prejudice and to advocate an end to Jim Crow in theaters across the nation. Now, in his hometown, he believed *Native Son* was about to fall victim to thinly veiled racism and a city administration eager to please rabid conservatives. Canada had a choice to make. He could walk away and avoid controversy, or ignore the risks and take a stand.

Without hesitation, Lee decided to fight. From boyhood scraps on the streets of Harlem, to bloody battles in the ring, to his struggle on the road against Jim Crow, he had never walked away from a challenge, and he wasn't about to throw in the towel now.

Every strategy he had learned for galvanizing public support he put to use. He called emergency meetings in Harlem to mobilize his neighborhood and asked Councilman Adam Clayton Powell, Jr.—a political ally as well as childhood friend—to preside. He secured the backing of prominent civil rights leaders, including Walter A. White, executive secretary of the NAACP; A. Philip Randolph, president of the Brotherhood of Sleeping Car Porters and the March on Washington movement; and Lester Granger, president of the Urban League.

Angry letters and telephone calls supporting *Native Son* and denouncing this flagrant example of censorship went out to the Shubert organization and to Mayor Fiorello La Guardia's office. Walter White wired the mayor and urged him to intervene. La Guardia was already deeply entangled in censorship issues, but only regarding obscenity—he had banned the striptease, closed burlesque shows, and threatened to take licenses away from venues presenting prurient entertainment. However, La Guardia wanted no part of any dispute that involved race prejudice. He fired off a telegram to White, grousing: "I get blamed for everything . . . I did not know anything about the closing of *Native Son*."

With help from the Theater League, the Dramatists Guild, and the Actors' Equity union, Lee led a rally to fight censorship and save *Native Son* on December 7. Questioned about the Catholic ban on the play, Lee and the show's producers were "flatly defiant," according to the press; they called the play "an important human document which is in no sense offensive." Facing down an agitated crowd, Shubert gave a brief statement saying he had been misquoted about closing the show, and that he would do so only if faced with a court order. *Native Son*, he promised, would run at the Majestic "as long as business warrants." The *New York Age* declared victory: "The attempt to stab democracy in this city last week failed because the power of the voice of the people was too great."

Native Son enjoyed a very brief stay of execution. Public interest flagged during the holiday season, ticket sales dwindled, and on January 2, 1943, the show closed at last. Theatergoers were ready for the next big thing. So was Canada Lee.

Deep in this man burned a hunger beyond ambition, a driving desire, an intellectual restlessness. All his life he wanted fame; here it was, he was famous, and it wasn't enough. Being famous was only a state of being. He needed to *do* something. Canada was on the verge of making the final and most audacious transformation of his chameleon career: the athlete-turned-actor was turning political activist.

He had no idea of the risk he was taking.

Nineteen months earlier, the Special House Committee on Un-American Activities had opened a file on Canada Lee. Later known by the acronym HUAC, the committee was charged with investigating subversives, and Lee was under suspicion.

The first entry in Lee's file was typed on a white three-by-five-inch card just a few days after the actor made his provocative debut as Bigger Thomas in *Native Son*. It read: "Photo. *Daily Worker*. March 27, 1941, p. 7." Months passed with only sporadic notations. Someone dropped a *Daily Worker* article in the file that favorably compared Canada to actor and activist Paul Robeson, a man also under suspicion at HUAC. "Canada Lee bursts with energy to achieve the things he wants for his people and all people," the article enthused. The most recent entry in Lee's file was dated December 31, 1942. The *Daily Worker* had published the actor's photo along with a short article headlined: "Canada Lee to Act at Lenin Rally Revue." Featuring some two hundred performers, this pageant actually honored the entire Allied Forces, but HUAC had obviously noted that the show paid tribute to Lenin and was sponsored by the New York State Communist Party.

HUAC clearly suspected that Lee was a Party member or, at the very least, a Communist sympathizer. The committee wasn't alone in its suspicions. The Federal Bureau of Investigation had also opened a file on the actor, prompted by a tip from an informant about an allegedly un-American speech Canada made in December 1942 at City College. According to the informant, Lee told students: "I would not fight in an army in which there exists racial segregation." The FBI classified its file on Canada under an ominous heading, "Custodial Detention—C Sedition." J. Edgar Hoover, the agency's director, had established a "Custodial Detention Index" of suspected radicals and Communist sympathizers;

the FBI was prepared to put these people in prison in the event of war or a national emergency. The informant's quote from Lee's speech, accurate or not, led the FBI to categorize Canada as a possible traitor to his country.

The FBI and HUAC files on Lee were still rather thin. They would get thicker.

In his new role as political activist, Canada was determined to fight for those who did not enjoy the full benefits of democracy, the rights and freedoms guaranteed them as American citizens. His first battles had been fought against Jim Crow in the theater, and he vowed to continue his campaign beyond the footlights.

Canada Lee was about to take his crusade to Hollywood. Secretly, silently, the FBI and HUAC would follow him.

CALIFORNIA, HERE I COME

HOLLYWOOD, WAR, ROMANCE

I n the fall of 1942, while American soldiers were fighting in Europe and the Pacific, Canada Lee was asked to narrate a victory film called *Henry Browne, Farmer*.

Generally running about twenty minutes, victory films tried to boost wartime morale. They also showed civilians how to do their bit here at home. One such short, titled *Frying Pan to Firing Line*, called for conservation and recycling; *Farmer at War* praised those men and women toiling in American fields to supply food to the front lines. Sometimes victory films mixed education and propaganda to enlighten Joe Public about the intricacies of wartime policy. *Japanese Relocation* attempted to explain why the government forced 110,000 Japanese-Americans out of their homes and into camps.

Victory films were quick to make and circulate—just eighteen to twenty-four weeks from film shoot to movie theater, compared to eighteen to twenty-four months for many commercial movies. Millions of people saw victory films in their neighborhood cinemas; by 1942, 94 percent of American theaters were showing them before or after features.

Canada undoubtedly got the call to do *Henry Browne* because of his color. The government hoped to unite African Americans behind the war effort with victory films about black soldiers and their communities. In a nation where Jim Crow was custom in the North and law in the

South, race was a potentially explosive issue in wartime. Soldiers of color were fighting a racist regime in a segregated military, and that painful irony was lost on no one in uniform, nor family and friends back home. To address this issue, the *Pittsburgh Courier* introduced the popular "Double-V" campaign, demanding a double victory against racism at home and fascism abroad. Worried that domestic struggles over race discrimination would hamper the war effort, FDR's media-savvy administration launched a public-relations campaign that generated posters, pamphlets, and victory shorts about black soldiers and families, including *Henry Browne*.

The black-and-white film, beautifully shot in rural Georgia, draws a parallel in patriotism between Farmer Browne's efforts to increase crop production and his son's service in the 99th Pursuit Squadron of the Army Air Force. Canada's narration is one of the strongest elements of the film. Instead of speaking in the tediously didactic or bleating propagandist tones heard in many wartime shorts, Lee tells the farm family's story in a simple, warm, direct style, as though visiting with neighbors at a kitchen table. The film ends at the airfield, where the Browne family has traveled by horse-drawn wagon to visit the eldest boy, a pilot. The juxtapositions of wagon and fighter plane, of father in overalls and son in cadet's uniform, are evocative and poignant.

"Farmer Browne and his wife are mighty proud of their son, and so are we," says Canada in his resonant baritone. "But we're also proud of Farmer Browne, proud of him because he's doing his job . . . an important job. And proud of him for being an American that we can count on, at a time when every American has an important job to do." There is an unmistakable ring of sincerity in Lee's voice; he *was* proud of the contributions that black Americans were making to the war effort. When he criticized the Pentagon for segregating soldiers and denying black men and women equal opportunities for training and service, he did so because he opposed discrimination, not the war itself.

Henry Browne, Farmer was released November 15, 1942, and in the spring of 1943 it was nominated for an Academy Award for Best Documentary. However rewarding that nomination may have been for Lee, these ten minutes of propaganda weren't, by any stretch of the imagination, his big break in film. But it did give the actor a fresh taste for the movie business. While the stage would always be the actor's first love, he craved the bigger audiences—and bigger paychecks—that movies offered.

Trouble was, Canada wasn't a singer, hoofer, or comedian, and he had made it patently clear that he wasn't interested in playing servants, slaves, or jungle natives. These were serious obstacles for a black actor hoping to make his way to Hollywood, where servants, slaves, and natives merrily sang, danced, and joked their way across the screen, delighting white audiences and attracting big box-office numbers. Old South stereotypes prevailed in dramas as well; the first Oscar awarded to a black actor went to Hattie McDaniel in 1939 for playing Scarlett's servant, Mammy, in *Gone With the Wind*.

But change was coming to Tinseltown, thanks to mounting pressure from black activists, the media, and the White House. That change, and a dash of luck, would finally pave Lee's way to Hollywood.

In 1942, while Canada was still touring with *Native Son*, the NAACP had begun to lobby the movie industry in earnest about eradicating racist stereotypes. Walter White, secretary and chief executive, traveled from New York to Los Angeles to meet with various studio executives. After noticing that power brokers curiously kept forgetting their appointments with him, White enlisted the help of Wendell Wilkie, counsel to the NAACP, who had run unsuccessfully for president in 1940 and now chaired the board of Twentieth Century Fox. Together, the two men lobbied producers and studio heads. Their message? That Hollywood's stock Negro, with his "rolling eyes, chattering teeth, always scared of ghosts," as White put it, "perpetuates a stereotype which is doing the Negro infinite harm." Hollywood must create more dignified roles for both ethical *and* financial reasons, he argued. Black Americans were fed up with racist stereotypes, and this audience represented a relatively untapped market of some 15 million ticket buyers who were earning better wages in a wartime economy. Savvy studio heads suddenly sat up and paid attention, seeing dollar signs in those demographics.

Making more and better race films wasn't the answer, White and Wilkie insisted; this would create a sort of "separate but equal" policy for the silver screen, and that's not what black ticket buyers wanted. They longed to see their favorite actors in mainstream movies doing more than serving tea and dancing jigs. The ultimate goal, according to the NAACP's monthly magazine, *The Crisis*, was to incorporate black actors "naturally and easily" into roles free of stereotypes.

The NAACP's first big victory came in March 1942 during a power luncheon at the Twentieth Century Fox lot, where top producers promised to eliminate the Old South brand of stereotyping. That story made front-page news in *Variety* under the banner headline: "Better Breaks for Negroes in H'wood." The black media and liberal white press began to use the March agreement as a means of evaluating racism in movies, asking themselves: does this picture fulfill Hollywood's promise to depict Negroes as an integral part of American life? The answers to this question generated more headlines. "No Bandanas in *Stormy Weather*," the *New York Amsterdam Star-News* proclaimed.

"The agreement became a standard against which studios, Negroes, and even the white press gauged Hollywood's sincerity, if not its art," writes film historian Thomas Cripps. "March 1942 became a date by which to measure the future against the past."

In the summer of 1942, a Harlem newspaper announced to Hollywood: *"Here Is Some Worthwhile Movie Material."* Lee was pictured prominently among other actors. The caption read "Talents Aplenty: With the discussion about competent Negro performers for important roles in motion pictures, we thought we'd present just a few topnotch stars."

Canada waited for offers. None came. In the meantime, many of his friends and colleagues—including Rex Ingram, Ethel Waters, and Hazel Scott—headed off to Hollywood to make pictures like *Cabin in the Sky* and *Something to Shout About*. Why was Lee left behind? Most of these films were musicals; only singers and dancers need apply. Though Hollywood had promised better opportunities for black actors, only a handful of dramatic roles were available, and those went to veterans like Ingram who already had several film credits.

Lee had to wait for a final change to take effect in Hollywood studios, spurred by a message direct from the White House: make war movies, and make sure they appeal to *all* Americans. To galvanize support for the war effort, Uncle Sam wanted to see movies that celebrated heroism in the field, harmony at home, and unity against the racist enemy.

The Office of War Information recognized that Hollywood's demeaning stereotypes undermined morale in the nation's black communities and damaged America's image abroad. An analysis of the depiction of blacks in wartime films by the OWI's Bureau of Motion Pictures would conclude that in general, "Negroes are presented as basically dif ferent from other people, as taking no relevant part in the life of the nation, as offering nothing, contributing nothing, expecting nothing."

President Roosevelt understood the power movies had in shaping public perception and opinion. He created the OWI, in part, to spur change in the motion picture business. Though FDR publicly insisted that "the motion picture industry must remain free . . . I want no censorship," the OWI did assume de facto censorship powers, and eventually extended its authority beyond war films to all films by assessing how they depicted war aims, the Allies, the enemy, and life on the home front. By the end of 1942, the OWI had also become an arbiter of racial content in films, a move supported by the NAACP and other groups. The agency issued a guidebook on the subject and published a motivational column in *Variety* reminding studio heads that our enemy was racist, and therefore "we must emphasize that this country is a melting pot, a nation of many races and creeds, who have demonstrated that they can live together and progress."

Patriotic war films and progressive racial pluralism: this was the script the OWI wanted Hollywood to write. It was also the kind of script Hollywood had promised black actors and activists. At that very moment, a rather unlikely team was working on just such a script—the script that would finally give Canada Lee his ticket to Tinseltown.

The movie was *Lifeboat*. Director Alfred Hitchcock, temporarily on assignment in Hollywood, wanted to make a film about the U.S. Merchant Marine. These seamen braved frequent attacks by U-boats in order to move critical supplies; by the war's end, mariners would suffer the highest casualty rates of all the armed services. The Merchant Marine aided Britain, Hitchcock's native land, in staving off the Nazis.

Hitchcock got Twentieth Century Fox behind the idea and immediately asked Ernest Hemingway to write the script. When Hemingway declined, Hitchcock offered the project to John Steinbeck. It was, from the start, an odd collaboration—Steinbeck, gritty realist, chronicled exploitation of the working class, and Hitchcock, witty escapist, sprinkled mayhem amongst the champagne set. But Steinbeck liked the idea of writing a screenplay about tough men who braved treacherous seas and submarines, and he took Hitchcock up on his offer. In January 1943, writer and director began work on the script.

Lifeboat was unusual for a war film. Steinbeck's story strands eight

Americans on a battered lifeboat in the middle of the Atlantic after Germans torpedo their Merchant Marine ship. They take on one more passenger—a German, whom they soon suspect is the captain of the U-boat, also destroyed in the battle. The survivors are forced to grapple with questions of leadership, democracy, fascism, class, ethnicity, and violence. As film historian Thomas Doherty notes, *Lifeboat* "casts adrift a microcosm of mankind . . . to float the family of man in the same boat." This microcosm included the racist German *übermensch*, a worldly journalist, a pompous tycoon, a mother with her dead baby, a frustrated nurse, a cheerful (but doomed) lumpenprole sailor, a timid radio operator, a leftist labor-organizing Lothario, and a reformed pickpocket turned ship's steward.

In spring 1943, rumors started circulating that Hitchcock was going to offer Canada Lee a role in his new film. Every time the telephone rang, Lee jumped. Finally, he got the call he had been waiting for—a part in a big studio film by a major director—only to discover that he was being offered the steward's role, the marine equivalent of a servant.

What a frustrating anticlimax it was.

Lee was diplomatic, but he let Hitchcock's production team know he wasn't eager to launch his Hollywood career by playing a menial. Black actors continued to battle discrimination, and Canada's friend Paul Robeson had decided to quit the film business altogether because roles for black actors remained so demeaning. Lee needed time to carefully consider the nature of the role and of the film itself. He asked to see the script. Hitchcock was reportedly making changes, so the actor agreed to read a copy of the film treatment instead.

Racial stereotyping wasn't the only thing on Lee's mind as he considered Hitchcock's offer. *Lifeboat* was a war movie, and the war was a complex issue for the actor. Because of his blind eye, he was compelled to stay at home while many of his friends, including prizefighter Joe Louis, risked their lives overseas. A feeling of impotence tormented Canada. He was a patriot, a fervent believer in democratic principles, and he longed to serve his country. "Man, how I'd love to be in there fighting!" he told *Yank* magazine.

At the same time, Lee vehemently opposed segregation in the U.S.

military. He spoke out so frequently on this subject that an informant told the FBI that Canada was "head of an unofficial organization of Negroes for the purpose of gaining equality for the Negro in the Army." According to the informant, Lee "openly and publicly stated the time is not far distant when the United States Army will give the Negro what he is entitled to, or face mutiny on the part of all Negro troops." These reports prompted FBI Director J. Edgar Hoover to write a memo to the Criminal Division of the Department of Justice inquiring if Lee could be prosecuted for violating sedition statutes. (Little evidence supports Hoover's suspicion that Lee was conspiring to incite a revolt among black soldiers, and Attorney General Tom Clark declined to pursue a case against Lee.)

In an effort to resolve his conflicted feelings about the war, Canada had embraced wholeheartedly the Double-V concept. He threw himself into countless projects, large and small, to fight racism at home by improving living and working conditions for people of color. At the same time, he rallied Harlem families to buy war bonds and delivered a stirring address at the first graduation exercises for black cadets at Camp Kilmer, New Jersey. "Your stake in this war is literally a stake for existence," he told the young soldiers. "Exert all of your energies to achieve the total destruction of the Axis."

Throughout the spring of 1943, as Lee had waited for that call from Hitchcock, he carried out his twin campaigns to support the war and fight racism. As a Broadway star, Lee was asked to appear at dozens of war-related events. He rarely turned down an invitation. At Manhattan's Town Hall, he starred in a "Negro Salute to the Fighting Jews of Europe" as well as "A New Birth of Freedom." The latter featured a live BBC broadcast of remarks by Earl of Lytton, the poet and novelist who coined the phrase "the pen is mightier than the sword." Canada delivered a lecture on "American Theatre in Wartime" at the New School, and read a poem by Stephen Vincent Benét at a program honoring the efforts of America's foreign-born to support the war.

The actor was also tapped to perform in patriotic radio plays, including *Courage*, broadcast on WINS to raise funds for polio research, and *A Tribute to Gallantry* by Ben Hecht, about the soldiers who gave their lives for their country. Hecht's poetic play gave Lee a beautiful monologue: "I speak for all the dead. They ask a reward. They ask for the sound of victory. They ask that you pour out your energy, your talent, and your valor, as they have poured out their blood. They ask that you rush forward with all you have, not to their rescue, for they are dead, but to the rescue of the world, for which they died. To the rescue of human heights. To the rescue of tomorrow. These are the dead, but their song is in your heart."

Canada's poignant rendering of these words touched the hearts of listeners across the nation; thirteen years later, a recording of the program lifted the spirits of a soldier critically injured after serving in Korea and Japan. "My head and eyes were swaddled in bandages," Donald Gillies recalled. "I was in a very depressed state, expecting that my fate was to be blind in at least one eye." As he lay there, confined to his bed, his world utterly dark, a Red Cross volunteer played a recording of Lee's monologue. "I had never heard anything like it," Gillies said. "Hearing that rich, resonant voice reciting those dramatic lines . . . opened a whole new world of possibility and understanding to me."

Passionate in his patriotism, Lee was equally ardent in his battle against racism, including pervasive stereotyping in arts and entertainment. At a Newspaper Guild Forum in April, he attacked the crap-shooting, eye-rolling characterizations of Negroes on stage and screen and boldly condemned Broadway producers and Hollywood studios. "They are guilty of perpetuating the 'yassah-boss' . . . type of Negro," he said. "The war is giving the Negro the chance to fight for his rights when the peace comes and should pave the way to a truer conception of the Negro." All I want, he said, is the chance to act like a man, but I cannot find "anything approximating the semblance of a man." A Harlem columnist noted with pride that Canada Lee was "constantly battling for the rights of minority people to experience democracy in action" and "refuses to accept Uncle Tom roles, attacks those who do with a reckless frankness which is key to his absolute sincerity."

No wonder Canada looked askance at the role of Joe the steward.

Hitchcock's team put forward persuasive arguments. Black sailors are treated as equals in the Merchant Marine, he was told, and your character will enjoy that same equal treatment in the film. African American mariners did in fact hold every type of rank aboard ship, from the lowliest deck-swabber to engineer to captain, while in the navy, black men could only serve as messmen. The actor knew this very well. By pure coincidence, he was rehearsing a monologue about black mariners written by Langston Hughes. *Sailor Ashore* was to be part of Hughes's grand pageant, "For This We Fight," performed in June with a cast of five hundred at the anti–Jim Crow "Negro Freedom Rally" in Madison Square Garden.

Canada wanted to make a movie, and here at long last was an offer. He had been promised that his character, a black mariner, would be dealt with respectfully. The story had thoughtful, political themes. And the chance to make a film written by John Steinbeck and directed by Alfred Hitchcock was certainly nothing to sneeze at. He thought it over, called Hollywood back, and took the role.

"They told me it was going to be tremendous, a great step forward as far as Negroes were concerned, which excited me no end," Canada said.

The excitement didn't last very long.

By the time Canada arrived at the studio lot in July 1943, the script was a mess. Steinbeck, who thought Hitchcock's insistence on a single set weakened the drama, had left the project after outlining a few scenes and would eventually disown the film altogether. MacKinlay Kantor was hired to finish the job, but Hitchcock was dissatisfied with his work and asked producer Kenneth Macgowan to fire him. Next in the batter's box was Jo Swerling, a screenwriter with two dozen credits under his belt including *The Whole Town's Talking*, in which he penned the immortal line, "A woman is only a woman, but a good cigar is a smoke." Swerling toiled away until mid-July, but just before shooting began, Hitchcock decided to take the script home and rewrite much of the dialogue himself. The director then asked veteran script doctor Ben Hecht to review the final scenes and make suggestions as he had done for *Foreign Correspondents*. (Hecht would later write screenplays for Hitchcock's *Spellbound* and *Notorious*.)

Hitchcock's rewritten script had its problems, and Canada definitely had problems with the script. Robert E. Morseberger, writing in *Film Quarterly*, called it "an uneven conglomeration of Hitchcock suspense, Steinbeck philosophy, and Swerling situation and dialogue." Screenplays often go through so much slicing, dicing, writing, and rewriting that who wrote what is debatable if not laughable. But for Canada, one thing was certain and it was no joke—the dialogue made Joe the steward look like Uncle Tom.

"When they first handed me the part of Joe I read it over and found 'yessir, yessir, yessir,' about every other word. I'd rather dig ditches for a living than act some foolish parody," Canada said. What about the much-vaunted equal treatment between black and white mariners? he angrily demanded. "Joe would hardly address his shipmates like that all the time," he said. "They let me revise the part and I cut them all out."

Darryl Zanuck, head of Twentieth Century Fox, was also concerned about the script's characterization of Joe the steward, perhaps spurred by Canada's objections, or by the OWI's toughening standards on the way Negroes were depicted on film. Zanuck questioned the decision to make Joe an "assistant" steward who recites psalms, "boogies up" a song, and admits to being a former pickpocket, but didn't insist on major changes.

More trouble bubbled to the surface when the cast waded into ice-cold water to film the opening scene. As the torpedoed freighter sinks, the camera pans over floating debris and an occasional body, coming to rest on the lifeboat that will be the setting for the rest of the film. The boat's sole occupant is the tough, sexy journalist Connie Porter, played by Tallulah Bankhead. One by one, other survivors drag themselves aboard. When Joe the steward swims up, Connie greets him with "It's Charcoal." Lee wasn't thrilled with the line. He accepted it because Connie later discovers that Charcoal saved the life of a drowning white woman and her child; from then on, she calls him "Joe" with a measure of respect.

"Charcoal" was also a little easier to take because it came from Bankhead. Canada and the tart-tongued Tallulah were great pals. Outrageous, flamboyant, and foul-mouthed, the actress who once said "I'm pure as the driven slush" often rubbed people the wrong way, but nothing she did or said could put Canada off. During the first week of shooting, he laughed when the crew complained that Tallulah never wore underwear and flashed them every time she got in and out of the boat. (When the production manager told the director that somebody had to say *something* to the actress, Hitchcock quipped that it wasn't his department, but rather "the makeup man's, or perhaps the hair dresser's.")

Lee befriended everyone in the cast except for Walter Slezak, who played the U-boat captain. According to Canada, Slezak made many racist comments and once professed regret "that he didn't live in the old South where he could own slaves." Lee also said that Slezak told him: "I don't like the new nigger. I like the old nigger who worked in the fields and drank out of a bottle. The new nigger you have to respect. You can't call him Uncle." Weeks later, Canada described this offensive behavior during an interview, but without mentioning Slezak by name. Though other cast members urged him to fight back, Lee told the reporter, he maintained his reserve.

"One day John Hodiak asked me why I stood for it," Canada recalled. "Well, I could have punched that guy in the eye, but I was in a tough position. I was a Negro who had come to Hollywood to make his first picture. And I was determined, come hell or high water, that when I left there, the only thing they were going to say about me was, 'He's a fine actor, and a gentleman.' I never touched him."

Canada's frustration escalated as shooting progressed. In the script, after the German is pulled into the lifeboat, the erstwhile enemy proves himself an able leader and is tentatively accepted by the group as they forage for food, kill time, and drink Tallulah's hooch.

At least, the *white* survivors were drinking hooch. Where was Joe the steward?

"The script . . . kept the Negro in a corner away from the others, while the Nazi got in and became an integral part of the group," Canada said. "I went to the writer—who had been telling me what a progressive guy he was—and I asked how about that.

" 'It's nothing,' he said. 'He just wants to be alone.'"

Alone and offscreen, from the looks of it. Canada was beginning to understand just how isolated he was. Promises had been made about this character and this script. Now those promises were being broken, and he wasn't sure how to handle it. Tallulah supported him, most cast members were sympathetic, but this was his battle to fight, his career and principles at stake. He was new to Hollywood, new to movies, new to this kind of power politics. He needed advice. He needed a friend.

He found one. And he promptly fell in love with her.

The fateful meeting took place at a party. Hollywood adored parties. Somebody somewhere was always having one; you just drove around until you smelled the martinis. Some were glamour bashes for stars and starlets designed exclusively for drinking and flirting. Canada didn't drink, but he did love to flirt—in fact, he was reportedly enjoying flirtations with a number of actresses, including Ilona Massey, who was likely filming *Frankenstein Meets the Wolf Man* around this time.

Other parties mixed movie people with political people, most of them progressives, some of them Communists. Here the talk could get interesting. This fateful party was one of the interesting ones. Canada was standing in a circle of people talking politics when he spotted actor Darby Jones waving him over. Darby was a ten-year veteran of Hollywood and had played his share of jungle natives in Tarzan pictures. He and his wife, Evelyn, had a friend with them, and Canada suddenly found himself face-to-face with a stunning young woman who had flashing eyes and some very dangerous curves. Her name was Frances Pollock.

Frances had movie-star looks, but she was no scatterbrained starlet. The only daughter of solidly middle-class Jewish parents, with brothers studying to be doctors and lawyers, Frances had discovered politics at a precocious age. She started fund-raising for liberal causes at age fourteen, and during college she took a leave of absence to work for the Democrats on the 1938 election campaign. At the moment, she was the Executive Secretary of the Federation for Civic Betterment, a coalition of labor, business, and religious leaders working to expose and clean up corruption at City Hall in Los Angeles. She was twenty-four years old.

Canada didn't know any of this, but Frances knew plenty about him. "Darby and Evelyn were always telling me about the shenanigans Canada got up to," Frances recalled. "I was a very serious young woman. The last person I wanted to meet was a playboy like Canada Lee. If I knew he was going to a party, I stayed away."

Despite Frances's objections that she had no interest in meeting Lee, Darby and his wife conspired to set them up. "It was Darby who insisted I drop by that party," Frances said. "I can remember that night very well. The hostess introduced me and took me around, and suddenly I heard this magnificent laugh. I got tingles when I heard it."

It was Canada. Introductions were made. He took one look at that face, those curves, and that was it, the party was over. "I saw that look in his eyes, and I got away from him as quick as I could," Frances said. "Within half an hour he was trailing me."

He asked for her telephone number. She demurred. He asked again. She refused. He asked for a date instead. She made her excuses and left. "That night when I got home, he was calling me," Frances said. "He'd wheedled my number out of somebody. I was furious. He started calling me every day and night."

During those first telephone conversations, Frances didn't talk much.

She didn't want to encourage him. So Canada talked. He told her all about his family back home, especially his mother, who was coming soon to visit him. Before long, he was confiding in her about his troubles on the set of *Lifeboat*. Canada was upset over the direction the script and his character were going, and Slezak's behavior irritated him mightily. "He takes great delight in undermining everything I try to do, and no one says anything," Canada complained. "Tallulah is the only one who fights for me."

Frances understood power and politics; she was a good listener, and when she offered advice, it was always sound. Their conversations grew longer. Every night, before Canada said good-bye, he asked her for a date. Each time, she turned him down.

"There is no reason you can't go out with me, Frances," Canada said.

"I don't need a reason," Frances said.

Canada couldn't believe the woman could be so stubborn, that she wouldn't even give him a chance. He wasn't used to being turned down, and it bothered him. A lot.

One evening, after several irritating episodes with Slezak, Lee called Frances, his voice quivering with anger and frustration. He had important script work to do this evening, but he found it impossible to concentrate. "I've got to get this guy's face out of my mind. It takes every bit of my energy not to haul off and slug him," he said. Frances murmured sympathetically, she wished she could help . . .

Ah, but she *could* help. "I'd like to come over," Lee boldly suggested, "and go over some lines."

After weeks of fending him off, Frances finally relented. Yes, he could come over to her place. It didn't seem so bad—after all, she was helping him work, it wasn't a date. Canada bolted out of his house, hopped in a cab, and rushed to her apartment. When Frances opened the door, her dog, Alaska, stood at her side. This formidable pooch was a volatile mix of malamute and German shepherd. Alaska gave Canada the old once-over and grudgingly let him come in.

Lee kept a wary eye on the dog as the couple set to work. "He and I were sitting on the couch," Frances said. "The script was between us. Alaska was sitting in a chair over there, like a real person, watching us."

They started reading lines, working on one scene after another. As the evening wore on, the two gradually slid closer together on the couch as they leaned over the script. Suddenly, Alaska executed a flying leap and landed with a crash between them, right on the script. Her ears slid back menacingly.

"That put an end to that evening," Frances recalled with a laugh. But it didn't put an end to Canada's pursuit. The man was relentless, and she was intrigued in spite of herself. "He was absolutely a perfect gentleman—very careful what he said and how he said it," she said. "It was genuine. It was Canada. But it was also his way to get to me."

When his mother came to town, Lee invited Frances to have dinner with them at his house. To his complete surprise, she said yes. "I guess I was curious," Frances said. "You can learn a lot about a person by meeting his mother."

At the age of sixty-one, Lydia Canegata was weakened by illness and showing her age, but she was still an imposing woman, strong-willed and plainspoken. (A photo taken on the *Lifeboat* set shows Lydia sitting comfortably, even a bit regally, with Hitchcock, Tallulah, and Canada.) If she liked you, she was generous and kind. If she didn't like you, you knew it. Frances may have been intimidated, but she never let on. From the very start, she and Canada's mother got along famously. Lydia cooked a second dinner, and a third. The two women found they had something in common. They didn't like fakes, they didn't like sponges, they didn't like shallow talk or shallow people, and that meant they really didn't like a lot of the people who were eating, partying, and frequently flopping for a night or three at Canada's house.

"He had a lot of hangers-on," Frances said. "That bothered me. But his mother held things in tow. She was very outspoken on people she didn't care for, people he shouldn't invite . . . You can tolerate such individuals if you only see them from time to time, but when they are living off you—she obviously resented that deeply."

If Lydia had any qualms about her son's desire to date a white woman more than ten years his junior, she didn't let on. Sister Canegata was sharp and she knew her son. Frances wasn't the first white woman Lee had dated, and at least she was intelligent, honest, and hardworking, not to mention fun. "We had a good time," Frances recalled. "We talked, we told stories, we laughed together. I really liked Canada's mother. I was lucky to have met her."

Frances seemed to be the only one still harboring doubts about the relationship. Canada was everything she had always tried to avoid in a man. He was famous, he was an actor, he was a playboy, he ran with a flashy crowd. There were also some unspoken issues: he was older, he was divorced, he had a teenaged son, and he was black.

"We were at opposite ends of the world," she said.

And yet she felt she knew him so well. He had talked to her for hours about his life and his dreams, his struggle to win respect for himself and dignity for black actors. She had watched him work, seen the creativity and energy and devotion and perfectionism. She had been touched by the deep affection and abiding respect he had for his mother. All of these things had chipped away at her carefully constructed defenses. Canada Lee was a gentleman, he made her laugh, and he sure wasn't hard to look at.

Frances had to admit it. She was smitten.

"There's no reason you can't go out with me," Canada told her.

"Maybe not," she said.

There was definitely good reason for being discreet, however. There weren't many mixed-race couples walking the streets of Los Angeles in 1943, and dating could be complicated. "We loved to go to Griffith Park," Frances recalls. In this four-thousand-acre expanse of hills and forest, couples in search of romantic solitude wandered the shady pine-scented trails, hiked up the Beacon, waded in the Los Angeles River, watched sunlight play on the fountain, or savored deliciously cool darkness and brilliant artificial stars in the planetarium show at the copper-domed Griffith Observatory. "We'd sit down, and he'd recite poetry for me. He loved Omar Khayyam," Frances says. "We rode horses a few times. Most of the time, we'd just sit together and talk." The couple never spoke about themselves in terms of race: "It wasn't an issue for us," she insists. "It was an issue to work on, a political issue. That's all."

It was an issue for other people, however. One day, Frances was driving Canada somewhere in her car when a policeman pulled up beside them, took a good long look, and signaled them to pull over.

"You didn't do anything," Canada said, instantly furious. Frances was a careful driver, particularly when he was in the car.

"Cool down. This is no time for you to lose your temper," Frances whispered.

After scrutinizing her identification and registration, the policeman sent them on their way without any explanation, let alone an apology. "I'm sure we were stopped just because we were a black man and a white woman," Frances said. "There were a lot of bigoted people in Los Angeles. And that situation wasn't going away any time soon."

Canada's troubles with bigotry on the set and in the script weren't going away, either. The cast was filming a scene in which an infant has died and the survivors are trying to conduct a proper burial service at sea, but they get stuck when no one can remember the words to the Twenty-third Psalm. The script called for Joe to rise up and recite the psalm in Negro dialect: "De Lawd is mah shepherd Ah shall not want. He done maketh me t' lie down in green pastures."

Canada flatly refused. Tallulah chimed in on his behalf. "No, no, no, no, no, dahlings," she said. "Canada Lee will not speak in dialect. It was *agreed*."

But it's just an *accent*, Lee was told. The German man has an authentic German accent, right? The Englishwoman has an authentic English accent, and Joe has an authentic *Negro* accent. Canada clenched his fists and seethed in silence.

"Places," came the call. Lee sat down opposite the rest of the passengers. And "Action." Waves lap against the lifeboat. The grieving mother gives a tiny hushed sob.

"Does anyone know the service for a burial at sea?" the blue-collar leftist, Kovac, says a bit sheepishly.

"Well, I suppose any prayer would do," says Ritt, the tycoon. "Hmmm, let me see now . . . The Lord is my Shepherd, uh, I shall not want . . . He maketh me to lie down in green pastures. . . . he, uh . . . he, uh . . ."

"He leadeth me beside still waters," said Canada, and in his deep, rich, polished-mahogany voice, he said the words the way they were meant to be said, not in some buffoon's idea of black dialect, but the way he heard them spoken in the Salem Methodist Church where his father was still deacon. "He restoreth my soul. He leadeth me in the paths of righteousness for his name's sake. Yea, though I walk through the valley of the shadow of death, I will fear no evil, for Thou art with me . . ."

When he finished the prayer and the scene was over, cast and crew gave him a standing ovation. Hitchcock printed it, and in the film the Twenty-third Psalm remains a quietly beautiful scene, perhaps the first in movie history in which a black person reads a Bible verse in standard English.

Canada had won his first battle, but he was far from winning the war.

Offscreen, his campaign to win Frances was faring far better as their friendship blossomed into full-fledged romance. Officially an item, they spent every free minute together, meeting for picnics and long walks, showing his mother the sights, cooking dinner together at home and then dancing to Canada's blues records. "He was an excellent dancer, very fast on his feet," Frances said. The couple appeared together in public a few carefully chosen times, including a *Lifeboat* cast party on the beach. "I have an image of Canada sitting in a beach chair," Frances recalled. She stood in front of him, trying to pull him out of the chair to join her for a swim: "I can remember the way he looked at me: *I want you.*"

Frances loved Canada's sensuality, his strength, his generosity, his wicked sense of humor. She admired his curiosity, his appetite for learning. The actor carried word puzzles everywhere he went and commanded the astonishing vocabulary of a true crossword addict. He read Shakespeare most nights before he went to sleep. In the morning, he often brought Frances coffee and English muffins while she was still in bed, a stack of newspapers tucked under his arm so they could read them together. "He was self-educated. He never stopped studying," she said. "He had an incredible mind."

The couple shared a keen interest in progressive politics and humanitarian causes and went to many meetings, rallies, committees, and parties together, including the famous Saturday-night gatherings at Gene Kelly's and Betsy Blair's house. According to Betsy, guests played charades and sang around the piano "like we were Ethel Merman, shouting and screaming and laughing." Although there weren't political objectives to these evenings, she said, "sometimes there were petitions to sign." And Canada, Betsy, Orson Welles, and screenwriter John Howard Lawson all worked on the Sleepy Lagoon Defense Committee, which was seeking to overturn assault and murder convictions for seventeen Mexican-American youths whom the committee believed to be unjustly imprisoned because of anti-Mexican prejudice in California.

According to Frances, she and Canada had a number of acquaintances in the Communist Party. "During the war, there were always Communists around. We didn't think anything of it, really. We were allied with Russia, so of course, they were at parties, they were at benefits and rallies and fund-raisers." Lee may well have been approached to join the Communist Party in Hollywood, Frances said, but he had no interest in doing so.

The FBI believed otherwise. Records in the bureau's Los Angeles office indicated that Lee initially joined the "Sunset Branch" of the local party's "Northwest Section," otherwise known as the Motion Picture Industry. Lee later transferred to the "Actors Branch" according to an FBI informant identified only as "Source A." The same informant said he had overheard two Communists discussing Canada; the actor had allegedly complained that people "would invite [him] to their homes, but that they would not invite him out in public . . . Lee resented this attitude." The actor's FBI file also summarized his connections to Orson Welles, a purported Communist, and noted that the actor had been "active in a number of functions which reportedly are under Communist control." These functions included a panel sponsored by the Hollywood Writers Mobilization for Defense, a suspected Communist front. The topic for this discussion was "History and Scientific Background of Minority Problems—the Negro." According to Agent Robert W. Hollman, Lee "emphasized the problems the negro [sic] in America has had to undergo in order to survive as a group." Dalton Trumbo, a prominent screenwriter and alleged Red, served on the panel, as did Carlotta Bass, outspoken editor and publisher of the *California Eagle*, a black newspaper with suspected ties to the Communist Party.

Any connections between Lee and Party members were simply social or purely inadvertent, Frances maintains. Canada did make a number of left-leaning speeches while he was in California, and she recalls asking him to speak at a rally for Senator Dennis Chavez, a Democrat from New Mexico who championed the rights of Hispanic and Native Americans. "If you made speeches like that, Communists were probably going to come around to make contact with you," Frances said. But she insists the actor never joined: "Canada was a Democrat, he was a liberal, he was a progressive, he was never a Communist."

Despite Lee's progressive politics and liberal views, in his private life he could be very conservative. "He never used four-letter words. He never swore in front of me," Frances said. "And God forbid I should swear in front of him!" Women's roles in mainstream society remained highly conventional, and Lee definitely preferred his paramours to be traditionally feminine. He told Frances he would never allow his wife to work; it was his job to pay the bills. At the same time, he was attracted to independent women who had their own opinions and knew how to defend them. Frances saw the contradiction there, but Lee was still more supportive of women and women's rights than most men she knew in 1943. "He respected intelligence. He wanted to know what you cared about, what was important to you," Frances said.

What did Frances care about? She wanted the world to be better—for women, for the poor, for the disenfranchised. She worked tenaciously raising money and lobbying for the causes she believed in. She was smart, she was determined, she was idealistic, she was pragmatic, and, above all, she was passionate. To Canada, she was perfect. And she felt the same way about him.

"He was my first real love," Frances said. "No question in my mind."

Lee was equally certain he had found his girl, and three thousand miles away, his friend Les Nash knew something serious was going on.

Every week or so, Nash telephoned from New York so Canada could catch up on all the doings at home. Not all of the news was good that summer. On Sunday, August 1, a black U.S. Army private named Robert Bandy saw a white officer arresting a woman in a Harlem hotel. He tried to intervene, a scuffle broke out, and the policeman shot him. A story quickly hit the streets that a white cop killed a black soldier. In fact, Bandy suffered a minor wound, but it didn't matter; a long history of white intolerance, harassment, and brutality had driven Harlem to the boiling point. Blacks took to the streets, smashing the store windows of white merchants, looting and rioting through the day and into the night. Touring the streets in sound trucks, community leaders refuted the rumor that set off the destruction and pleaded for calm. When the violence ended at daybreak on August 2, five blacks and one white were dead. Five hundred were injured, another five hundred arrested, and fifteen hundred businesses were vandalized or completely destroyed at a loss of five million dollars in property damage. People continued milling in the streets; to settle down the crowds, Lawrence D. Reddick, curator of the Schomburg Collection arranged special screenings of Lee's patriotic victory film, *Henry Browne, Farmer*.

After Nash relayed all the news from Harlem, Lee talked about his adventures in Hollywood. Conversations always ended with a quick up-date on Canada's busy love life.

"How are you doing with the starlets?" Nash always kidded him.

"There are a lot of pretty girls out here," Canada teased right back.

"How many maidens have you deflowered?"

Canada would only laugh. Then came the day when Nash asked about the starlets and got no reply. After a minute or so, he heard his friend quietly say:

"I'm not running around."

"What do you mean, you're not running around?"

"I met someone who is really very nice."

Peppered with questions, Lee refused to say any more about the mystery woman. Nash knew something was up: "I would talk to him from time to time, and it always was the same thing. I would ask him how his love life was going on, and he would say, 'I met this girl.' And that's all he would say."

Canada might have been keeping mum, but Lydia must have spilled the beans to the family back home. Sister Claudia inquired after his love life. Lee's father fretted over what a relationship with Frances might do to Canada's career. Lovey told him to find a rich woman, possibly because Lovey's wife had left him and he was in money trouble himself. Only Carl, not quite seventeen and starting his senior year in high school, appeared to be in the dark about Frances. "From reports in the papers, I hear you are going great guns. After seeing in the movies some of the parts taken by Negroes in some of these movies nowadays, it really in all sincerity makes me glad that my Pop is one of the new Negroes," he wrote. "I know you are knocking yourself out in California. In your letter you never once mentioned the fact of how you are doing."

Canada was doing as well as could be expected for a man utterly bliss-ful in love and utterly miserable at work.

Near the end of *Lifeboat*, the survivors amputate the gangrenous leg of the cheerful, doomed lumpenprole in an effort to save his life. The journalist, played by Talullah, gives him her last drop of liquor. The sailors hold him down, the rich man makes the bandages, the nurse at-tends the German, and the German cuts off the leg.

What was Joe the steward's contribution?

"I was supposed to cast my eyes to heaven and 'wordlessly pray,'"

Canada said. "Nobody else prayed." The actor was livid. Once again, his character—whom everyone swore would be treated as an equal—was instead being treated to one of Hollywood's favorite stereotypes: the Negro in crisis, falling to his knees, palms pressed, eyes rolling, teeth chattering, crying "Lawd, save us!"

Canada considered his options. He could forsake his principles, do the scene as written, and play the stereotype. Or he could refuse to do the scene, denounce the stereotype, and risk his future in Hollywood. "Places," came the call.

Lights flashed on, cameras whirred to life, and the makeshift surgery began. But when the camera panned to Joe in the back of the boat, there was no eye-rolling genuflecting going on. Sitting quietly by himself, the steward looked steadily out to sea.

"*What are you doing?*" someone hissed.

"I'm praying," Canada retorted.

This small moment in *Lifeboat* is rarely noted, but Lee fought for that bit of dignity for his character and himself. Film historian Donald Bogle has described how black performers were often faced with stereotypes, and how the very best actors fought to transcend them. "The history of blacks in films remains one in which individual actors and actresses have often had to direct themselves," Bogle writes. "Rather than *playing* characters, they have had to play *against their roles*, digging deep within themselves to come up with unexpected and provocative points of view."

The film's climactic scene held special significance for Lee. The German, revealed at last as the Nazi U-boat captain, murders the poor sailor whose leg was amputated. Sickened and enraged, the survivors turn on the German and kill him. While their fury is understandable, the execution is carried out with shocking brutality. Only one person refuses to participate in what amounts to mob violence and lynching—the film's sole black character, Joe.

Canada finished *Lifeboat* without sacrificing his principles. He had been promised equal treatment for his character, and, though that promise was broken, his performance in the film remains a testament to his determination to create a more complex character than he found in the pages of his script. It was a small victory, but a victory nonetheless. Canada was happy in his work once more, and now Broadway was calling him home.

Director Lee Strasberg telephoned Los Angeles to offer Canada the lead in *South Pacific*. In the play (no relation to the musical of the same name), a black sailor goes AWOL rather than fight the white man's war. The role was potentially controversial and the script had its share of problems, but the subject was timely and Canada was eager to return to the stage. Rehearsals were scheduled to start in a few weeks and the show would open in December. The actor and his mother set about the business of packing and returning to New York. Canada was about to purchase their train tickets when he suddenly got cold feet.

"He was supposed to go back in October," Frances said. "He didn't. They were waiting for him to start rehearsals for *South Pacific*. He delayed and delayed. He didn't want to leave Los Angeles. He didn't want to leave me."

Lee asked Frances to come to New York with him, but she couldn't. Her mother had died some years before; now her father was critically ill, and Frances nursed him by herself because her brothers were in the military. Canada put Strasberg off a little longer, spending time with Frances and supporting his various causes. In November, he chaired a discussion of the Sleepy Lagoon case sponsored by the *People's World*, a Communist paper.

Finally, Strasberg's patience reached its limit. In danger of losing his role in *South Pacific*, Canada bought train tickets back to New York. Miserable knowing they soon must part, Frances and Canada talked, hesitantly at first, about marriage. Race had never mattered to them, but it would matter to some studios and producers. "I didn't want to do anything to jeopardize his career," Frances said.

She didn't say yes to the idea of marriage, but she didn't say no, either. Frances knew little about Lee's social scene in New York, and she wondered what she might be getting into. She asked him point-blank if there were women waiting for him back in Manhattan. He had to admit there was at least one.

He may have meant Anaïs Nin, whose diaries indicate she was still seeing Canada before he left for Hollywood. Then again, their affair was never terribly serious. Nin wrote that when she threw a party at her apartment, "Canada Lee was enamored of all the women at once." When she went to a dinner at Lee's penthouse, a young red-haired actress was hostile to her. "I suddenly realized she was jealous," Nin wrote in her diary.

"Every time Canada put his arm around me, she watched him." When Anaïs announced she was leaving, the actress snapped, "No! *I'm* leaving!" and stomped out. Lee laughed. A little later, as Nin chatted with Lee in his bedroom, she looked up to find the red-haired actress spying on them from the terrace. This time, Nin did leave.

Frances was no prude, but the idea that Canada may not have terminated his various love affairs nagged at her. Things between the couple began to unravel a bit and the future was still unsettled on the day Canada and his mother boarded the express train for New York. Frances came to see them off. "We had quite a farewell scene at the train station, not knowing when we would see each other again," she said. "When he and his mother got on that train to go back to New York, he was still arguing with me."

Frances stood on the platform. Canada and his mother were leaning out of train windows, talking to her. The final whistle blew.

"Marry me, Frances," Canada said.

She gave him a long, level look and then turned to his mother.

"Tell you what," Frances said. "You tell your son this: When he goes back to New York, if he cleans up all of his dirty linen, then I might listen to him."

Lydia shot a glance at Canada and smiled at Frances.

"You're right!" she said.

By the time the train left the station, the couple was more or less engaged. And by the time Canada arrived in New York, he had a plan. As soon as he finished *South Pacific*, he would move to Los Angeles with his mother and Carl and make his living in film.

That winter was a busy, bittersweet time for Frances. Her father died not long after Canada left, and it was a terrible loss. At the same time, she was happily planning a new life with her husband-to-be. In November, she sent him a beautiful photograph of herself with her hair swept up. On the back she wrote, "Dearest Darling, I'm sorry this is the only picture you can have at the moment. I promise to get you others before we get married. I love you. Your Fran." Canada sent Frances money with instructions to rent a home for them to share as soon as he was free to move to California. Soon Frances was redecorating a little house on the south side of Los Angeles. "We were young, we were in love, we were so happy. It was beautiful," Frances said.

Lonely for his sweetheart, Canada threw himself into *South Pacific*.

He was keen to work with Strasberg, best remembered today for teaching the quintessential American acting technique known as the Method. Lee and Strasberg clicked fairly well, but the script remained problematic, which was nerve-wracking for the star. A flimsy comedy or romance could succeed despite its faults. But a flimsy play on race, war, and patriotism — touchy subjects ripped from the morning headlines — was asking for big trouble.

Ironically, Lee once again played a black merchant mariner who takes refuge on a lifeboat after his ship is torpedoed. But this time the sailor, named Sam Johnson, and his white commanding officer are both shipwrecked on an island in the South Pacific that has been occupied by Japanese troops. Pushed around most of his life, Sam refuses to fight the white man's war anymore and settles down among the natives instead. He impresses the locals with his tall tales, and woos a pretty missionary girl away from her less virile boyfriend. But when the Japanese kill an island boy who befriended him, Sam at least realizes that no man stands alone. Putting aside his past grievances, he does his patriotic duty by attacking the Japanese, his true enemy.

The playwrights managed to nibble on a handful of interesting ideas, but the plot was pedestrian, the dialogue wooden, and the characters agonizingly synthetic. *South Pacific* limped through a miserable three-day tryout in New Haven. One critic reported that the play dragged so badly it made "the Toonerville trolley look like the 20th Century Limited." The show earned less than three thousand dollars. Chortling at this pathetic box office, the trade press wickedly announced that Broadway critics were manning the torpedoes.

Clouds of theatrical doom gathered over *South Pacific*. In an interview published three days before the premiere, Lee's remarks telegraphed his anxiety. "It's not one of those nice, pat little war melodramas that are all sweetness and light," he warned. "*South Pacific* is a very tough play. That is, it doesn't pull any punches." The actor tried to win a little advance sympathy for his character. "For the first time in his life he is the right color. He doesn't have to hide," Lee said. "He doesn't want to go back to a war which he doesn't think is his." The role of Sam, he insisted, was "a great thing for a Negro actor."

"It means an awful lot to me," he said. "I'll be in there fighting for my life."

On opening night at the Cort Theater, Canada's name appeared over the title of the play on the marquee, a measure of the actor's box-office appeal and how heavily producer David Loew was banking on it. The star was under tremendous pressure to save his sinking ship. Unfortunately, everyone's worst fears were realized. While most critics were generous to the cast, they were utterly merciless to the playwrights and director.

Writing for *The New York Times*, Lewis Nichols found himself irritated by "the garden-variety plot" and directorial "mumbo-jumbo." He was thankful, however, that the producers cast "one of the best Negro actors" in the starring role, noting that Canada "gives a performance which always holds the interest." Lewis Kronenberger tried to be kind to the playwrights in *PM*: "Howard Rigsby and Dorothy Heyward have had something to say, and they have tried to say it as honestly as possible. That they have said it clumsily and confusedly at times is to their disadvantage but not their discredit."

Critic Frank Gill never doubted the sincerity of the playwrights' efforts either, but didn't hesitate to call their play "trite and tedious." Director Strasberg heaped insult on injury with his "leaden pace." Canada delivered "the sole outstanding performance of the evening," Gill concluded.

Burton Rascoe concurred. "Lee has a vivid and vibrant personality, and he is one of the most proficient actors in the profession," he wrote. "I don't know what a cast for *South Pacific* would be like without Canada Lee, because its appeal is pretty elementary even with him." The play he condemned as "amateurish." The plot in particular seemed "confusing, and often ridiculous." As for the play's blatant message that black Americans should forget any bitterness toward whites and join wholeheartedly in the war, Rascoe, writing for the *New York World Telegram*, called it an "insult to hundreds of thousands of Negroes now in uniform, and to other hundreds of thousands of Negroes who are loyal and patriotic American citizens."

The play, Rascoe suggested, could be put to one good purpose. "Communist agitators in recent years have been busily fomenting hatreds and dissensions among the Negroes against their 'white capitalist exploiters,'" he wrote. Perhaps if *South Pacific* were performed in black communities, the play's loud-and-clear message might offset "the vicious work of Communist agitators in convincing some malcontents among the Negroes that their enemies are not the Germans or the Japs, but white Americans."

Lee had worked hard on the play and felt battered by the reviews. As predicted, *South Pacific* was a giant flop, closing January 1, 1944, after five performances. Canada's bio in the show's *Playbill* noted that the actor still hoped to be a successful bandleader; he must have wondered sometimes if music might have been an easier life.

Controversy continued to shadow Canada. Days after *South Pacific* opened, John Steinbeck watched an advance screening of the soon-to-open *Lifeboat*. The author blew a gasket over the treatment of Joe the steward, which he found grossly racist. He blamed Hitchcock and Swerling. Just two days before the film opened in theaters across the country, Steinbeck wrote a diplomatic but stern letter to the Twentieth Century Fox Film Corporation and demanded that his name be removed from the film credits.

Dear Sirs:

I have just seen the film *Lifeboat*, directed by Alfred Hitchcock and billed as written by me. While in many ways the film is excellent there are only one or two complaints I would like to make. While it is certainly true that I wrote a script for *Lifeboat*, it is not true that in the script, as in the film, there were any slurs against organized labor, nor was there a stock comedy Negro. On the contrary there was an intelligent and thoughtful seaman who knew realistically what he was about. And instead of the usual colored travesty of the half comic and half pathetic Negro there was a Negro of dignity, purpose and personality. Since this film occurs over my name, it is painful to me that these strange, sly obliquities should be ascribed to me.

John Steinbeck

Unless Joe radically changed, Steinbeck wanted his name off the picture. Twentieth Century Fox declined to honor the author's wishes. Instead, the studio launched a huge advertising campaign for the film, and every trailer, poster, and handbill proudly credited Steinbeck as the screenwriter. Most of those same posters and handbills featured a dramatic illustration of the cast—with Canada Lee at the back of the boat.

On January 11, 1944, the studio hosted a gala invitation-only preview of *Lifeboat* at the Astor Theater in Manhattan. The VIP section included Sir Cedric and Lady Hardwicke, singer Kate Smith, producer Kenneth

Mcgowan, and Canada. As he watched the film, Lee was not as shocked as Steinbeck. Still, he realized Joe had ended up a minor, though hopefully memorable, character. Compared to the way the role was originally pitched to the actor, Joe had lost any real power or significance. Though in public Lee maintained his poise and charm, in private he was crestfallen.

Perhaps Steinbeck was right to blame Hitchcock and Swerling for gutting his character in favor of a racist stereotype; perhaps it was a case of good scenes left on the cutting-room floor; or perhaps good scenes never got shot. The picture's original budget of $1 million doubled, and so did the shooting schedule. Darryl Zanuck had fired off several memos complaining that the script was too long. "Drastic eliminations are necessary," he had written in August. "You are not going to get your eliminations by cutting out a few lines here and there . . . You are going to have to be prepared to drop some element in its entirety." Hitchcock fought Zanuck over cuts, arguing they would harm the integrity of the film. Still, cuts may have reduced Lee's screen time and diminished his character.

When *Lifeboat* opened in New York City, it appeared at first to be in safe waters. Howard Barnes of the *New York Herald Tribune* called the film "one of the most pertinent and disturbing war pictures that has come out of Hollywood." Archer Winston admired Hitchcock's prowess in creating a suspense film on a lifeboat in the middle of the ocean where "there's no place to hide." The *New York Post* critic only had one major complaint in his review of *Lifeboat*. "The Negro role, played by Canada Lee, is a strange creation," he mused, "almost a study in unintentional segregation. It is almost as if, someone having decided to avoid the grosser movie stereotypes of Negroes, no one was prepared to substitute anything vital in its place. Mr. Lee completes a Psalm splendidly during a burial service, and he performs a few acts of special skill when called upon. The rest of the time he is more the passenger than the participant, giving a performance of dignity to a role of dubious significance."

It was a particularly discerning observation. Black critics also found Joe's character vague at best. "Joe stands aside and does nothing," wrote Rowe in the *Pittsburgh Courier*. Measuring the film by the March 1942 yardstick, Lee's character was deemed far removed from White's and

Wilkie's goal to see a "vital and realistic interpretation of the Negroes' part in Americana."

When the rest of the reviews came in, *Lifeboat* suddenly found itself precariously adrift in an underwater minefield. Major publications accused *Lifeboat* of extolling Nazi virtues and promoting the German cause by making the captive U-boat captain a hero. One critic threatened darkly that *Lifeboat* had "ten days to get out of town." Bosley Crowther wrote a scathing column in *The New York Times* condemning the film as dangerous propaganda: "Its final, insidious implication is that the democratic peoples are weak—not only weak but vacillating—and that the Nazi is resourceful and resolved." He continued: "Unless we had seen it with our own eyes, we would never in this world have believed that a film could have been made in this country in the year 1943 which sold out the democratic ideal and elevated the Nazi 'superman.' Certainly we would never have imagined that such a picture could have been made by the estimable director, Alfred Hitchcock, from a story by John Steinbeck . . . This writer sits here in consternation at the appalling folly which it represents. What in the name of heaven has happened to the judgment of men in Hollywood?"

Kenneth Macgowan, a producer of the film, replied with a milquetoast defense: "If we have failed in making our theme completely clear, at least we may defend ourselves by saying that we didn't set out to make a symbolic film and we never let the possibilities of the theme divert us from our first object—the shaping of a film with as much excitement and reality as we could summon."

The *Times*'s condemnation had exacerbated the grudge Steinbeck was nursing against the studio. Macgowan's defense was the last straw. On February 19, the author wired Annie Laurie Williams at his literary agency: "Please convey the following to 20th Century Fox: In view of the fact that my script for the picture *Lifeboat* was distorted in production so that its line and intention has been changed, and because the picture seems to me to be dangerous to the American war effort, I request my name be removed from any connection with any showing of this film."

Much to his continuing consternation, Fox declined.

As the press continued to debate whether the film was anti-Negro, anti-American, or anti-democracy, Canada agreed to give interviews about his experiences on the set—what he had been promised, how the promises were broken, and how he had worked to salvage dignity for his character. "I don't honestly believe that pictures are made better by all the clichés you find in them about Negroes," he told reporters. "I don't see why they should always put forth a single conception of a Negro any more than of any other group, especially since this conception is usually undignified." But Canada was careful not to come on too strong; after all, he had plans to marry Frances, move out west, and build a career in film. He emphasized how much he enjoyed making his first movie, adding diplomatically: "I found that the powers that be in Hollywood are always anxious to listen to decent criticism of what should and shouldn't be."

Controversy over *Lifeboat* lingered into the spring. Alfred Hitchcock earned an Oscar nomination for Best Director, but the nomination did little to boost the film's reputation, nor its mediocre box-office receipts. On a Saturday night in early March, Lee was interviewed yet again about the picture, this time on the airwaves by Malcolm Child, film commentator on WABF. The actor had tried for weeks to remain positive, hoping to be remembered as a trailblazer for other Negro actors, not a bridge-burner. But his composure cracked a bit on this occasion.

"If the Negro is to be treated with equality," he told Child, "it is necessarily up to those who hold the power to mold public opinion (and that certainly includes those who make motion pictures) to see that the Negro is presented with justice . . . It may be a cliché at this stage of the game, but it is worth saying: If a man is good enough to die for his country, he is good enough to live in his country on full terms of equality."

And as he spoke, HUAC and the FBI were listening—and taking notes.

EIGHT

STORMY WEATHER

BOY GETS GIRL, GIRL DISAPPEARS

As of Valentine's Day, 1944, Canada and Frances were living and working on opposite coasts, struggling to maintain their long-distance romance by telephone.

"We wanted to be together, but there was nothing we could do . . . We had to make the best of it," Frances said. "We had our good days and bad days. It wasn't easy. When you are apart like that, never seeing each other, the bad days can be *really* bad."

Friends did their best to comfort Lee; they could tell how much he missed his girl. Canada had yet another reason to feel blue that Valentine's Day. The draft board had ordered him to report for a physical, so at 7:30 on a bone-chilling winter morning, Lee traveled up to the Bronx to do his duty. Hours later he was handed a paper signed by Captain John C. Shell certifying that "Lionel Cornelius Canegata" was "rejected, physically unfit." While this was no surprise, it was still humiliating. Like thousands of men incapable of military service, Lee felt frustration, guilt, even shame about his 4-F status. He dreamed of being a soldier, fantasized about flying for the Air Force or charging with the cavalry. "Man, how I'd love to be in there fightin'!" he told *Yank* magazine. "Body 'gainst body, my life or his. Blood and thunder—let me have it!"

But Lee would never see action on the front, never have the chance to test his courage in the heat of battle, nor risk his life for his fellow soldiers, his loved ones, his country. "He saw himself as a fighter," Frances said. "He always felt terrible that he wasn't able to go into the war."

Lonesome for Frances and frustrated at his impotence, Canada threw himself into his work. If he couldn't serve abroad, he would be a hero on the home front, the "champion of his race" that his father encouraged him to be. With a heightened sense of mission and purpose, he intensified his campaign against racism and segregation. While he had long been a warrior in the cause, he now began to envision himself as a general spearheading the attack. The *Yank* article concluded with a stirring call to arms: "Here is a message from the actor to all fighting Americans on all fronts: 'We're fighting this war for a land we all call our own. Let's throw aside stupid prejudices. Now is the time for unity and tolerance of each other.'"

Canada pursued his mission as artist-activist with more energy than ever before, and those who watched him stepped up their quiet surveillance.

In February, Lee starred in several war-related radio projects designed to promote racial tolerance, including a biography of George Washington Carver. This program was part of NBC's *Words At War*, an anthology of war stories that often addressed racism, anti-Semitism, and social injustice. *Variety* praised the series "for dramatizing some of the finest words that have come out of the war dealing with the vital issues that confront the country today." Lee was also featured in a radio pageant written by Langston Hughes called *The Ballad of the Man Who Went to War*. Commissioned by the BBC, the program was recorded in New York as a morale booster for the war-ravaged British from their "Negro allies in the U.S.A. — by Americans, in other words, Americans of color." Paul Robeson and Ethel Waters both contributed songs to the show, which emphasized the black community's loyalty to the Allied cause. "I should like to congratulate you on the outstanding performance you gave," BBC Deputy Director John Salt wrote in a thank-you letter to Lee dated February 22. "It will win the deepest appreciation on the part of the British people."

On March 5, Canada debuted as the narrator of a new series on WMCA. *New World A-Comin'* was revolutionary radio, and Lee's role was his most provocative to date over the airwaves. Created by black artists and activists, the series showcased black performers and explored issues important to black audiences. Nathan Straus, president of WMCA, was determined to show "the contributions of the Negro race to American life, 'his country and ours.'" Adapted from a book of essays by journalist Roi Ottley, *New World A-Comin'* heralded the emergence of a new generation of African Americans, a generation determined to fight for civil rights, to overcome obstacles, and enjoy a better life. Duke Ellington composed the program's theme song, a suite for piano and jazz orchestra. "I visualized this new world as a place in the distant future, where there would be no war, no greed, no categorization," Ellington said.

New World A-Comin' held a prime-time spot on Sundays at three minutes past 3:00 p.m., and instantly delighted audiences with its incisive, moving, witty vignettes about controversial political and social issues. A *New York Times* critic called it "a public invitation to decent thinking," adding that "Mr. Lee, one of Broadway's better actors, is extremely effective as narrator precisely because he is not an actor giving a performance, but an intelligent man saying, calmly and patiently, 'This is how it is.'" From 1944 to 1945, Canada appeared in thirty-four episodes of *New World A-Comin'*. Recordings clearly show the craftsmanship he brought to the series, as well as genuine feeling for its themes. "The whip of intolerance has been felt by the Jew and the Catholic, the immigrant, and by the humble seeker after truth," he intones serenely before threading his voice with darker intensity: "But it's the Negro who feels the hand of intolerance most heavily."

Several episodes dramatized Jim Crow efforts to turn away would-be black voters by means of poll taxes and literary tests. Others exposed the prejudice black Americans faced in everyday life, including the satirical "White Folks Do Some Funny Things." *New World A-Comin'* could afford to be outspoken because it targeted a Northern, urban, liberal black audience; it boldly voiced some of the most candid views about the war from the black community's point of view. "This is the white man's war," one character says flatly. "Let them kill each other." At a time when 40 million people, black and white, tuned in each week to hear two white men playing two black buffoons in *Amos 'n' Andy*, *New World A-Comin'* was downright radical in its content and approach.

In March 1944, Canada took his activism off the air and on the road to Washington, D.C., joining a delegation of artists in lobbying support for President Roosevelt's efforts to allow 11 million servicemen and women stationed overseas to vote by special absentee ballot. Lee's goal was to ensure that African Americans in the military had a voice in the next election. When he returned to New York, he sat on a planning committee for a "Racial and National Unity" dinner at the Roosevelt Hotel, sponsored by the National Federation for Constitutional Liberties (NFCL). A newspaper photograph showed the actor having tea with other event organizers, including Mrs. J. Borden Harriman, former U.S. Ambassador to Norway; sculptor Jo Davidson; and Samuel L. M. Barlow, composer. Lee may not have realized it, but he was sipping tea with suspected Reds. HUAC condemned the NFCL for its left-wing positions, including its demand to put an end to HUAC. The Attorney General later listed the group as a Communist front.

Canada the activist was still an artist, and he did manage to squeeze some theater work into his busy schedule. In April, he did an eight-minute act at the Apollo consisting of a comedy routine with Happy Felton followed by a patriotic monologue. "Canada Lee is more at home in the drama purlieus than in vaudeville, where his gifts and range are more or less limited," *Variety* reported. "Lee has undoubted audience appeal and both his entrance and exit were well accorded. He requires more suitable material, however."

Thankfully, Lee found more substance in his next role, a part he had long desired to play. The noted critic John Gassner was presenting "March of Drama" lectures on Shakespeare at the New School for Social Research in Manhattan. To illustrate these lectures, actors performed scenes from the Bard's tragedies under the aegis of The Dramatic Workshop. Famed for its experimental and politically committed theater, the workshop was the brainchild of distinguished German director Erwin Piscator, who came to New York as a refugee in 1939. His project attracted many distinguished artists, including Stella Adler, Lee Strasberg, and Harold Clurman.

The role Piscator offered Canada was Othello.

Though he would only appear in selected scenes, this was still a risky gambit for Lee. At that very moment, his friend Paul Robeson was making history as the first black actor to play Othello on Broadway. For more than a century, Shakespeare's Moor had been played by white actors in blackface. Robeson had shattered the color barrier, earning rave reviews in the process. *Variety* declared his performance "of such a stature that no white man should ever dare to presume to play it again."

Aware that he would undoubtedly face comparison to Robeson, Lee nevertheless eagerly accepted Piscator's offer. The chosen excerpt was the famous "jealousy scene," Act III, Scene iii, in which the scheming Iago convinces Othello that Desdemona has been untrue. ("All my fond love thus do I blow to heaven: 'Tis gone./Arise, black vengeance, from the hollow hell!") John Ireland, an alumnus of *Native Son*, was cast as the villainous Iago, and Elena Karam played Desdemona.

On April 2, the Studio Theater at the New School was packed with students, actors, directors, theater buffs, and critics. Conversation hummed until the houselights dimmed. The curtain rose, revealing a stage littered with props but void of a set; the castle garden was left wholly to the imagination. It didn't matter, for all eyes were on the star. Earle Hyman, destined to become a renowned Shakespearean actor himself, never forgot Lee's performance. "His Othello was the greatest Othello I've ever seen, the most moving," Hyman recalled some forty years later. "Paul Robeson's was unforgettable in its majesty, but Canada tore my guts out in those jealousy scenes. When I play it, I always think of the things he did that moved me so much."

When the scene ended, audience members leapt to their feet, boisterous applause punctuated by calls of "Bravo, bravo!" Lee and the cast took their bows, and the star was called back for more. For a single scene, it was an amazingly emotional response. Critic Wilella Waldorf was a bit more reserved in her *New York Times* review, noting that Lee had trouble with a few of Shakespeare's lines, "a tendency to spit them out in too much of a rush when overcome with emotion." Even so, she wrote, "he is a good enough actor to move his audience whether it could always understand him or not." Canada lacked "the towering stature and the organ-like tones of Mr. Robeson," the critic continued, "and he has a good deal to learn about speaking blank verse, but there was a dignity, a sympathetic understanding of the dramatic aspects of the role, and a strong emotional quality in his characterization."

Critic Bob Francis had no reservations whatsoever. "It was Canada Lee's evening," he wrote in *Billboard*, adding that if any producer happened to be "looking for another Othello, there he is."

As much as Canada liked and admired Paul Robeson, he surely enjoyed reading that review. As for Robeson, he smiled benevolently on Lee's small foray into his dramatic territory and sent along his congratulations.

Lee's and Robeson's paths first crossed when the two men were both acting on New York stages in the 1930s. In those days, Robeson was already an international star, while Canada was still working his way up. By 1944, Lee and Robeson were friends and colleagues, fellow activists and frequent collaborators, not to mention former neighbors at that exclusive Sugar Hill address in Harlem, 555 Edgecombe.

"Canada had great respect for Paul Robeson," Frances said. "Paul was a sort of senior statesman, someone who had been out there fighting for his people, fighting against racism and Jim Crow, for years. And Canada admired that, tremendously."

Two weeks after he played Othello, Canada spoke at an all-star event celebrating Robeson's forty-sixth birthday. The party also honored the Council on African Affairs, a pioneering organization cofounded by Robeson to combat apartheid and colonialism in Africa. More than twelve thousand crowded into the Armory on Thirty-fourth Street, gazing in awe at the giant six-tier cake donated by Local 1 of the bakers' union. Count Basie, Jimmy Durante, W. C. Handy, Mary Lou Williams, and Duke Ellington performed during a five-hour program of entertainment and oratory. Canada was one among the many celebrities who came to praise Robeson's contributions to the community; Mary McLeod Bethune's greeting famously hailed Robeson as "the tallest tree in our forest." When Robeson took the podium, he urged his audience to support self-government for African countries: "It is impossible to keep 150 million Africans in slavery and think we can be free here."

The Council on African Affairs would soon be cited by the U.S. Attorney General as a Communist front.

Canada never stopped waging his Double-V campaign, rallying the war effort while condemning racism at home. On April 25, he starred in a tribute to Dorie Miller, an African American hero at Pearl Harbor. The

A ring announcer struggling to pronounce "Lee Canegata" gave Canada Lee the fighting handle he kept all his life. (Private collection)

(*below left*) Lee played Banquo in Orson Welles's legendary voodoo *Macbeth* production for the WPA Federal Theatre in 1936. (Library of Congress, Prints and Photographs Division)

(*below right*) When Canada took over the lead role of Christophe, hero of the revolution in the Federal Theatre's production of *Haiti*, a local newspaper announced the cast change by printing this photo of Lee with a caption proclaiming him "The New Black Napoleon." (Bettmann/CORBIS)

A rehearsal photograph of the opening scene of *Native Son*: Canada Lee as Bigger Thomas with his family in Chicago's South Side ghetto (Courtesy of the Lilly Library, Indiana University, Bloomington, Indiana)

During rehearsals for *Native Son*, Lee was extremely nervous about picking up co-star Anne Burr. In 1941, black men in America were jailed or lynched for less. (Courtesy of the Lilly Library, Indiana University, Bloomington, Indiana)

Director Orson Welles created a
sensation on Broadway with
Native Son, based on Richard
Wright's best-selling novel.
(Courtesy of the Lilly Library, Indiana
University, Bloomington, Indiana)

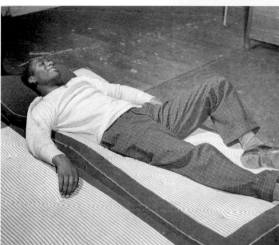

Canada catches a catnap in the
theater between long rehearsals.
(Courtesy of the Lilly Library, Indiana
University, Bloomington, Indiana)

Richard Wright couldn't stay
away from rehearsals, and paid
high compliments to the cast,
including Anne Burr. (Courtesy of
the Lilly Library, Indiana University,
Bloomington, Indiana)

Bigger stokes a fiery furnace before burning the body of a young white woman he has accidentally murdered. Such images from *Native Son* disturbed white conservatives; both at home and on the road, Canada was the target of death threats, pickets, verbal abuse, and vandalism. (Museum of the City of New York, The Theatre Collections—Gift of Frances Lee Pearson)

At the end of the play, Orson Welles wanted to see Bigger clinging to the bars of his cell, arms outstretched, "crucified" by Jim Crow. (Museum of the City of New York, The Theatre Collections—Gift of Frances Lee Pearson)

Native Son made Lee a bona fide Broadway star; columnist Ed Sullivan called the actor a "sepian Spencer Tracy." (Museum of the City of New York, The Theatre Collections)

(*below*) Lee backstage at the St. James Theater by a wall of good-luck and congratulatory telegrams from actor and activist Paul Robeson, actors Lee J. Cobb and Paul Muni, and poet and novelist Stephen Vincent Benét, among many others (AP/Wide World Photos)

In 1940, Canada opened his Harlem restaurant, the Chicken Coop, to showcase his favorite jazz and blues artists. Singer Big Joe Turner and boogie-woogie pianist Pete Johnson entertained at one of Lee's private Sunday morning jam sessions there. (Sketches by Harold Lehman, courtesy of Konrad Nowakowski)

Lee's mellow baritone voice was perfect for the airwaves. His radio career began to take off in the early 1940s and flourished during the war, when he starred in dozens of patriotic programs as well as innovative dramas about issues crucial to the black community—including segregation, poll taxes, and lynching. Pictured at WOR's studio in New York City: (*left to right*) author Richard Wright; jazz pianist Erskine Butterfield; dancer Bill Bojangles Robinson; Canada Lee; singer Paul Robeson; pianist/composer W. C. Handy; radio show host Roger Bower (Library of American Broadcasting, University of Maryland)

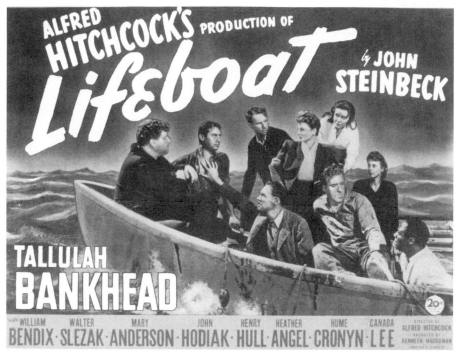

Confronted with racism in the script and on the set of Alfred Hitchcock's 1944 film *Lifeboat*, Lee tried to rise above his stereotyped role. A publicity poster depicts him as the film did: in the back of the boat, behind his white co-stars, including his pal Tallulah Bankhead. Several posters neglected to include Lee at all. (CinemaPhoto/CORBIS)

Five of the characters set adrift in *Lifeboat*: (*left to right*) Willy (Walter Slezak); Alice MacKenzie (Mary Anderson); Constance Porter (Tallulah Bankhead); George "Joe" Spencer (Canada Lee), and John Kovac (John Hodiak) (John Springer Collection/CORBIS)

Lee faced down criticism over his decision to play Caliban in Margaret Webster's 1945 Broadway production of *The Tempest*. While the actor hoped to encourage multiracial casting in classical plays, his critics believed he only aided and abetted racial stereotyping by playing Shakespeare's monstrous slave. (Wisconsin Center for Film and Theater Research)

Actor Raymond Massey and Canada record "Two Men on a Raft" at NBC studios in April 1945 as part of a national USO-YMCA race-relations program. Lee once said that the domination of white culture in the arts and media made black Americans virtually invisible—as though they were a people without a past, without problems. (Library of Congress, Prints and Photographs Division)

program "Dorie Got a Medal" also featured actors Earle Hyman, Rosetta Lenoir, and Jim Backus (later famous as Mr. Magoo and Thurston Howell III on TV's *Gilligan's Island*). Miller was a black Navy messman serving on the *U.S.S. Arizona* when Japanese forces attacked. In the segregated Navy, black sailors were forbidden to use weapons. When the bombs began to fall, Miller grabbed a machine gun and shot down two enemy airplanes. Though he was awarded the Navy Cross, Miller remained a messman until he died in action in 1944. "Dorie Got a Medal" was praised in many quarters, but the black press was less than enthused. One columnist decried "the absence of even 'a single note of protest' in the entire thing." In the radio play, he continued, Dorie "didn't seem to be particularly angry or disturbed that he had to get his training in machine guns in a penny arcade . . . if he had any inner tension or resentments, they didn't come out in that radio program."

Lee also took his Double-V campaign to the local cinemas, delivering passionate appeals between screenings. William Marshall was a young art student in New York at the time. When he heard that Canada was speaking at the Criterion Theater, he headed off to the movies. The actor spoke in blunt terms about race relations in America "so that those who should feel guilt would really feel guilty," Marshall said. "It was a very exciting experience. I know that my stomach was in knots."

Text from a speech Canada made about this time provides an idea of what Marshall heard. "There is no such thing as a good race or a bad race, or an inferior race or a superior race," he said. "The day we stop judging a man by his religion or his race and judge him instead by his thoughts and his deeds, the day we stop looking at a man's skin and look into his eyes instead . . . on that day, we'll know that Hitler and his gang are dead here, dead for good." Marshall saw people in the audience grimacing and sighing with relief at the end as they applauded, but he was enthralled by Lee's oratory: "I must have seen him do that at least four times that day."

One of the most informal and touchingly personal speeches Canada ever made about racism was delivered May 4 at an 11:00 a.m. school assembly at P.S. 37 on East Eighty-seventh Street in Manhattan. When he took the stage, he saw children fidgeting, staring, giggling, squirming. This was a tough audience. "I don't know what I am going to say, and I am a little afraid to say anything at all," Lee said. He looked around him,

at the school and the children, and he thought about himself as a school-
boy in Harlem. The last time he sat in a classroom as a student, he was
fourteen years old. Lee had just turned thirty-seven.

Canada told the children about his life—how as a teenager he had to
fight against prejudice and discrimination at the racetrack, how he continued that fight as a boxer and an actor. He looked into those small
faces, those shining eyes, and told the children that they had to be fighters just like him. All of them, black and white, must play together, eat
together, work together—now, and when they were all grown up.

"I only hope to God that you kids never in your whole life, as long as
you live, give up the fight," he said. "It is most important for the future of
the world, for the world that you want to live in, that your children shall
live in, and it's worth every ounce of strength and everything else that you
can put into it."

Days later, Lee made a much higher-profile speech at the "Celebra-
tion and Rally to End Jim Crow in New York City." He shared the
podium with the Reverend Adam Clayton Powell, Jr.; City Councilman
Benjamin Davis, Jr.; and Earl Browder. Davis and Browder were prominent members of the Communist Party, and both men were closely
monitored by HUAC and the FBI. Canada's presence at this event in-
evitably attracted the note-takers' attention.

As spring turned to summer, Frances was still far away, the war raged on,
and Lee filled his date book with more speeches, rallies, and fund-raisers.

He appeared in a "Negro Salute to the Fighting Jews of Europe"; a
dance at the Savoy Ballroom to support a Harlem youth center; a benefit concert for the United Negro College Fund; and the annual Negro
Freedom Rally at Madison Square Garden. The latter featured a dramatic pageant titled Carry on, America—Victory Is What You Make It.
Lee's friend Langston Hughes wrote scenes for the spectacle, which also
featured Paul Robeson.

Coincidentally, Lee, Robeson, and Hughes had just joined a new
consortium of black leaders and white trade unionists called the National Citizens Political Action Committee (NCPAC). Newspapers ran a
photo of Canada and Langston at an NCPAC rally, holding a sign that
read: "For Full Employment After the War: Register. Vote."

Almost immediately, HUAC began investigating NCPAC and its members, including Canada Lee, seeking evidence of Party membership and subversive activities.

At the FBI, Lee had already been pegged as a Communist, thanks to the ongoing investigation in Hollywood nicknamed COMPIC: Communist Infiltration of the Motion Picture Industry. In June 1944, J. Edgar Hoover received a three-page dossier on Canada. Based on press clippings, anonymous informants, and inquiries at Twentieth Century Fox, Agent Robert W. Hollman found that the actor "strongly resents the concept of the negro [sic] which the motion picture industry has so widely publicized . . . Lee wants to portray and to see portrayed a strong, alert, intelligent negro rather than the ignorant, indolent negro which is usually seen on the American screen." Since Lee was presumed a Communist, perhaps these goals were considered suspect, even perfidious.

Hollywood didn't offer Lee any roles that summer, ignorant, indolent, or otherwise.

"Of course we hoped for a film role," Frances said. "He wanted to come back to Hollywood. Nothing would have made us happier."

Instead, Canada picked up a number of radio jobs in New York—some for the war effort, some to fight Jim Crow, and some just for fun. In June, he narrated a WMCA program called "Negro Music" featuring singer Billie Holiday and an all-star jazz band with Roy Eldridge, Ben Webster, and Art Tatum. He also piloted "The Canada Lee Show," broadcasting live jazz and blues. During the July 4 edition, Canada patriotically urged listeners to buy war bonds, and then sat back and enjoyed himself as Bud Powell and Cootie Williams scorched their way through an old Louis Armstrong hit called "West End Blues." Keeping those airwaves humming, Lee starred in a program called "Tolerance Through Music" and recorded a show for NBC showcasing contributions by black Americans to the war effort.

Art and activism intertwined ever more tightly for Canada, and it was his political agenda that led him back to the stage that summer.

Lee sat on the board of the American Negro Theater, founded in Harlem by playwright Abram Hill and actor Frederick O'Neal. ANT's mission was to provide work for black artists and entertainment for black audiences. Earlier that summer, the company had presented a play called *Anna Lucasta* in the basement of the Schomburg Library. Originally a salty drama about a Polish prostitute and her avaricious family, ANT set the story in a black household instead.

Every show sold out, and the buzz lured Broadway producers uptown for a look. No chance, the money-boys said. "It's all right up in Harlem," was the general consensus, "but Broadway won't go for a Negro drama." One month after the show closed, John Wildberg decided to take a flyer. He had a hand in two big hits, *Porgy and Bess* and *One Touch of Venus*. He was on a roll, and he decided to move *Anna Lucasta* to Broadway.

Director Harry Wagstaff Gribble kept many actors from the original cast. The ravishing Hilda Simms played Anna, the fallen woman; Frederick O'Neal was her greedy brother-in-law; Rosetta Lenoir her sister; and Earle Hyman, the country bumpkin who makes an honest woman out of Anna in the end. Good as they were, none of these actors had star power. Wildberg wanted at least one big name on the marquee.

He called Canada Lee.

The role on offer was Danny, a sailor from Brooklyn who admires Anna but just isn't the marrying kind. It was a bit part but a good cause, as Lee obviously felt the need to explain in his *Playbill* bio: "It was his great interest in the American Negro Theater and in *Anna Lucasta* that caused him to volunteer to play the comparatively small role."

The show opened August 30, 1944, at the Mansfield Theater before a mixed-race audience. They laughed, they cried, and by curtain time *Anna Lucasta* was a certified hit. "What a night that was!" recalled actress Hilda Haynes, who was in the audience. "It took Broadway by storm. They had never seen this kind of serious work done. It was really a monumental opening. I sat there and counted fourteen curtain calls. Fourteen!"

Critic Burton Rascoe called it "the most important event in our native American drama in twenty years . . . the first American play, designed for an all-Negro cast, to treat Negro life without a certain amused condescension." Howard Barnes dismissed the show as a "tedious charade," though he added: "Lee, as a Brooklyn roustabout, and Earle Hyman, as the hayseed, bring warmth and conviction to the passages."

Audiences paid no attention to the critics and throngs of ticket-buyers besieged the box office. "Broadway needed a lift, needed a laugh, needed to try to forget the war in Europe," actress Ruby Dee said. "*Anna Lucasta* was just the ticket." Two weeks after the opening, the *Brooklyn Daily Eagle* said the show was "a hit that's turning away the customers. And one of the reasons, of course, is Canada Lee. He's done it again. Short or long, he's made his part another standout."

Anna Lucasta ran for 957 performances. Those sage and cynical producers who said a "Negro drama" would never play on Broadway surely kicked themselves when trade papers reported a minimum seventy-five thousand dollars return for every five thousand dollars invested. The show spawned six touring companies over several years; handbills in every city proclaimed *Anna Lucasta* "the longest-running Negro drama in the history of the theater."

A triumph for the ANT, *Anna* was a career boost and steady income for the actors. "They were a happy crew," theater historian Loften Mitchell wrote. "You could see them leaving the theatre after a performance, patting each other on the back, stopping for coffee and planning their next venture. Some were writing plays; some were going into directing; some into other acting ventures. All were committed to the theater and all expected brighter things for the Negro artist."

Earle Hyman, not much out of his teens when the show opened, would remember his experiences in *Anna Lucasta* all of his life, especially the opportunity to work with Canada Lee. "He was the greatest black actor I ever saw—that includes James Earl Jones, Moses Gunn, Morgan Freeman, you name 'em."

Canada agreed to stay on for six weeks, partly because he had negotiated a rather lucrative contract for such a small role. Lee earned $400 a week plus 5 percent of the gross profit over $8,000. By contrast, Fred O'Neal earned a flat $450 a week; nearly everyone else made $150 or less. Still, Lee proved a worthwhile investment. His star power helped make the show a success, and that in turn benefited other black actors, according to actor Ossie Davis, who toured the show with his wife Ruby Dee. *Anna Lucasta* paved the way for more and better productions about African Americans. "Broadway producers saw how much money they could make showing this brand-new, broad, uproarious version of Negro life in America—something that appealed to both white and black audiences," Davis observes in his memoirs. "Broadway seemed anxious to welcome us . . . both on stage and in the audience."

🐾   🐾   🐾

That September, Lee spent his nights playing to full audiences and his days stumping for the Democrats as the 1944 election campaigns heated up. Jumping into the fray on FDR's behalf, Canada joined the Independent Voters' Committee of the Arts and Sciences for Roosevelt. The committee hired James Montgomery Flagg to design its poster, a spin-off of the artist's legendary finger-pointing Uncle Sam over the caption I WANT YOU FOR THE U.S. ARMY; this time, a stern Uncle Sam pointed at the President and said: I WANT YOU F.D.R. — STAY AND FINISH THE JOB!

Lee campaigned for Democrats in New York, New Jersey, Connecticut, Pennsylvania, and Maryland. In his speeches, he demanded an end to discrimination and racism. He criticized Republican officials, declaring that the only government jobs they offered to Negroes in city halls and state capitols were sweeping floors and running elevators. He called for improved housing, especially for black veterans and their families. He lobbied for blacks to be appointed to the Board of Education. He reminded his listeners that voting was a privilege denied to tens of thousands of blacks in the Jim Crow, poll-taxing South.

In Philadelphia, Canada condemned a strike by white transit workers who were protesting a ruling that blacks could no longer be denied employment as motormen and conductors in streetcars. The strike brought work to a near standstill at the Navy Shipyard and locals feared a race riot. President Roosevelt sent federal troops to run the transit system; for the first time since Reconstruction, the U.S. government used the military to enforce a civil rights law. Lee backed the President, of course, placing blame for the strike "on well developed, well planned, and well recognized Fascist ideology . . . ideology we have long identified with the tactics of the Ku Klux Klan."

Fearlessly critical of white politicians and labor leaders, Lee was equally bold in attacking prominent blacks when he disagreed with them. He denounced Ralph Matthews of *The Afro-American* in Baltimore, and Clelan Bethan Powell, editor of the *New York Amsterdam News* in Manhattan, for backing New York Governor Thomas Dewey, the Republican candidate for President. Canada was certain that both men had been bribed, noting that Dewey had given Powell a lucrative job as Boxing Commissioner.

"Even today we have our handkerchief-heads who are willing to sell us Negroes down the river to get into the good graces of their Massa, Governor Dewey," he lamented during a speech to maritime workers in Baltimore. He upbraided Matthews and Powell: "By spreading the Dewey gospel among the Negro masses through the influence of your newspapers, you are preaching race suicide for us Negroes. Therefore, I proclaim you two men the Judases of our race."

The actor-activist headed home to Harlem to deliver another speech, this time a memorial tribute to Wendell L. Wilkie. Lee greatly admired the late statesman, who had defended the Federal Theatre from the Dies Committee and lobbied Hollywood to give more dignified roles to black actors. Near the end of his life, Wilkie had vigorously promoted human rights and civil liberties at home and abroad, especially in Africa. "The best way to mourn Wilkie is to champion those things he stood for," Canada told his audience. Later in the speech, Lee spoke passionately of his interest in the future of Africa.

"I am an American of African descent," he proclaimed with pride. "Some Negroes say that they have been far removed from Africa, that they have lost all connections . . . In a few years hence, these same people will echo me — 'I, too, am African,' for they will find it, the land, from which to draw inspiration, and they will also learn to draw strength from it when the overmastering struggles of this life become too difficult for them. I say therefore, without apology or hesitation, that it is through Africa that the American Negroes can revive their pride and then be proud of their heritage. This recovery of pride is a forerunner to a total freedom."

Canada's speech was a resounding success, according to K. Ozuomba Mbadiwe, president of the African Academy of Arts and Research, which sponsored the event. "I trust you will apply yourself to take matters pertaining to this race which we belong to very seriously," Mbadiwe wrote in a letter dated November 3. "You have a chance through the stage, screen, and now in the forum, to bring your message across to the people of the world." Weeks later, the actor joined the board of the academy, which promoted the history and culture of people of African descent and supported their struggle for civil rights at home and abroad.

Now the world was Canada's stage.

As his sphere of influence widened, so did his circle of friends, colleagues, and acquaintances. At his penthouse apartment, Lee now entertained politicians, reformers, and activists, as well as writers, artists, and celebrities. Friends describe the hush of anticipation that would come over a room as soon as Canada entered, the magnetism and charisma and authority he radiated. And yet he never called attention to himself. "He knew who he was and he knew his worth as a person, but he had modesty and he had humility," recalled Lee's friend, Leslie Nash. "This was unusual in someone who had reached the heights that he did, because back in those days, he was *it*. He was one of the most famous Negroes, or black Americans, around in those days. And yet it never went to his head. He was just himself—and that was enough."

But in fact it was not quite enough to be just himself. He missed Frances terribly. He began to pressure his fiancée to join him in New York, but her father had died and she was still handling his estate. They argued sometimes on the telephone, and at one point Frances suggested they break off the engagement. Some family members and friends urged Canada to say yes. They worried about his career, about Carl. Lee told them, politely, to go to hell. "The only selfish thing Canada ever did was to have me in his life," Frances said. Slowly but surely, the couple moved forward with their wedding plans. Frances sent Canada more photos. On one of them she wrote, "Let's compromise . . . I'll say 'Yes' if you will agree to eliminate 'Obey' !! I will cherish."

Lee was lonely, but he soon had three exciting women in his life. Frances had no cause to worry, however. These ladies were not after romance.

They had Shakespeare on their minds.

Cheryl Crawford, Eva Le Gallienne, and Margaret Webster were fast becoming powerhouses in the theater world. Crawford had worked her way up through the Theater Guild before launching the Group Theater with Harold Clurman and Lee Strasberg. As a producer, her Broadway credits included *One Touch of Venus* and *Porgy and Bess*. At forty-two, Crawford cut an imposing figure—slim and smartly dressed, she wore her auburn hair short and combed back, framing a strong face with a pensive expression.

As a dazzling eighteen-year-old ingénue, Eva Le Gallienne toured with Ethel Barrymore; at twenty-one, she was a Broadway sensation in *Liliom*. Five years later, she founded the Civic Repertory Theater, where she produced, directed, and starred in forty plays. Civic Rep was America's first nonprofit theater, a model for the Off-Broadway theaters that flourish today. As complex as she was gifted, Le Gallienne was a savvy producer, a respected Ibsen scholar and translator, a hard drinker, and a forthright lesbian.

Daughter to English actors, Margaret Webster spent twelve years onstage in London and New York. She then carved a niche for herself directing Shakespeare on both sides of the Atlantic, including that groundbreaking 1943 production of *Othello* starring Paul Robeson opposite Uta Hagen. What Orson Welles and Canada had once hoped to do, Webster and Robeson accomplished; as the first black actor to play a classical role on Broadway, Robeson was now touring the show across the country to great acclaim.

Crawford, La Gallienne, and Webster decided to unleash *The Tempest* on Broadway, where the play hadn't been seen in thirty years. La Gallienne conceived a set that would put Prospero's island on a revolving stage. Webster took the director's chair and Crawford raised the necessary cash. It was time to start casting. Director and producer found themselves at cross-purposes at first. Webster believed *Tempest* would work best with an ensemble cast rather than showy stars, but Crawford worried they wouldn't sell tickets without a few big names.

They balanced their proclivities, choosing the world-famous diva ballerina Vera Zorina to play Ariel and two brilliant but relatively unknown Czech comic actors as the Stephano-Trinculo team. Casting the principal male roles proved the most challenging— many of the best classical actors, British and American, were fighting in the war. They eventually secured Brooklyn-born Arnold Moss as Prospero.

That left Caliban. Mavericks all, the three women firmly believed in casting actors of color in classical plays and were determined "not to let the Robeson-Othello precedent wither for lack of successors," Webster recalled. Canada's name immediately came up. Crawford had been following his career and likely saw his New School *Othello* that spring. "He seemed an inevitable Caliban," she later wrote.

After playing his bit part in *Anna Lucasta* for six long weeks, Lee was more than ready to move on. "Shakespeare!" he told a reporter. "That's what I've wanted since I met Orson Welles." Robeson had made theater history in *Othello*, and Lee was eager to become the second black actor to play a classical role on Broadway. Crawford offered him Caliban and without hesitation he accepted.

Then the trouble started.

"Plenty of people didn't want him to play Caliban, and they let him know about it," Frances said. "That was very upsetting to him."

Two influential black newspapers, the *New York Amsterdam News* and the *Pittsburgh Courier*, said Canada would demean his race by playing the monster, the slave. Some of Lee's closest friends concurred. Shakespeare's "savage and deformed Slave" had frequently been played by white actors in dark makeup, a choice that seemed to equate black skin with monstrosity, inferiority, and evil. Canada was urged not to perpetuate such ideas by playing Caliban.

Margaret Webster told the press that she chose Lee because of his intensity and his ability to create powerful characters, not because she had decided that a black man should play Prospero's slave. "I do not intend," she said, "to make Caliban a parable of the current state of the American Negro." She admitted, however, that she chose the play in part because it dealt with power and the misuse of power, major preoccupations of the day. In her heart, she believed Canada could ignite anger and ambition and desire in Caliban, bringing the character to full and furious life.

And in his own heart, Lee knew this to be true, but he was torn. Classical roles had long been awarded to white players only, and he wanted to help shatter that barrier, as Robeson had. But perhaps it was wrong to play a slave, when he had spent the last decade arguing that black actors deserved roles other than Uncle Toms and mammies. If only La Gallienne, Webster, and Crawford had offered him Prospero . . . but they hadn't.

The three women took a risk by casting him. They invested their hopes and dreams in him. And at the last minute, they almost lost him.

But Webster refused to give up without a fight. Part of Shakespeare's genius is that people can look at his characters and plays and see the same conflicts in themselves and their times, she told Lee. But it would be wrong to view Shakespeare through a narrow social or political lens, the director argued; he was too great an artist and too good a showman to shove sermons down our throats. What Shakespeare offers in *The Tempest* are difficult, complicated characters that are neither wholly bad nor wholly good. His monstrous slave is a creation of subtle beauty. "Caliban yearns for power to destroy," she said, "and finds freedom to grow."

You can bring that subtlety, that complexity, that longing for freedom to this role, she told Canada. Those people who insist that a black actor shouldn't play Caliban are themselves exhibiting an insidious type of racism, something you have never espoused. And in the end, Canada agreed.

Now the production team was assembled. Two of the famous trio of designers known as "Motley" agreed to do the show: Elizabeth Montgomery took on the costumes, and Margaret Harris got the job of making a workable, rotating set out of La Galliene's cardboard model. She divided the circular island into triangular sections of disparate heights representing different locations called for in the script, creating distinct playing areas that would rotate past the audience as the actors moved from scene to scene.

The set design was ingenious, but it put Webster in a bind. The island would be the last thing built for the production, which meant the director had to keep the complex levels in her mind while blocking all of the scenes on the flat floor of her rehearsal space. "I covered the floor with a big circular ground cloth, the same size as the revolving stage and marked off in triangular segments for the sets," Webster told a reporter. "We'd do a scene in one segment, and then hop over into the next for the next scene." A rehearsal photo shows the director crouching with Canada on this makeshift set; Lee is nattily turned out in a crisp white shirt, white suspenders, and neatly pressed trousers.

Webster commanded tremendous respect in rehearsal, and most of the cast regarded her with something approaching awe. Lee wasn't afraid to speak his mind, however. "He was terribly hard to work with," Arnold Moss later recalled. "He and I were good friends, but he was hard to budge if he thought he was right."

In late December, the show's tryout in Philadelphia garnered good reviews, and on New Year's Eve, Lee got a nice little end-of-the-year bonus from Ed Sullivan. As the columnist looked back at the Broadway shows of 1944, he typed the heading "They Were Tops" and followed it with: "Hilda Simms, Canada Lee, and the cast of *Anna Lucasta*."

When *The Tempest* traveled to Boston, Mother Nature played a naughty little joke by unleashing a tempestuous blizzard in the North-east. The show almost didn't make it to opening night. Although some scenery got lost on the way, the play fared well despite the weather. "The Boston matrons seemed to like it," Webster noted. In fact, *The Tempest* did better box-office business in its second week than the director's famed production of *Othello* had done. The director took that as a good sign; her show was ready for Broadway.

The Tempest premiered at the Alvin Theater on January 25, 1945. Canada and the rest of the cast were nervous, excited, and exhausted—a dangerous mix that nearly caused a calamity. In the play, Caliban doesn't enter until the end of the first scene. Webster's staging called for the monster to appear suddenly over the top of a high rock. Because the island was in the middle of an otherwise bare stage, Canada couldn't simply enter from the wings; the audience would see him, spoiling the effect. Instead, he had to hide behind the rock for the entire scene, frozen in place, until his surprise entrance.

After weeks on the road with the show, Lee had this routine down pat. Still, just to be on the safe side, the stage manager peeked out from the wings a minute or two before Lee's entrance to make sure he was all right. "He was," Webster recalled. "He was lying peacefully behind the rock, fast asleep."

The stage manager panicked. She couldn't creep over and shake him without being seen. Frantically, she hissed at him, but the actor slept blissfully on. At the last possible second, she spotted a stage brace—a long thin pole used to hold up scenery. She slid it along the floor and gave Canada a ferocious jab.

That woke him up.

"What ho! Slave! Caliban! Thou earth, thou, speak!" called Prospero.

"There's wood enough within," Caliban muttered sleepily.

Thankfully, Canada managed to shake himself awake and pull himself together. Five lines later, he clambered up his rock and made his appearance—and nearly gave Crawford and Webster a heart attack, not to mention the Motley crew. "He was dressed—or rather undressed—in a costume none of us had ever seen before," according to Webster. Lee was wearing the fish-like headpiece they'd given him, but "the rest of his body was stuck over with bits of fur, feather, spangles and so forth, which gradually came unstuck as the evening wore on."

It turned out that Vera Zorina had invited her husband, the renowned

ballet choreographer George Balanchine, to dress rehearsal the day before. The impresario had decided on the spot that Caliban's costume
wasn't fanciful enough and somehow he contrived to alter it in time for
the premiere. Balanchine alone was pleased with his alterations. "We
thanked him," Webster said, "and asked Canada *never* to repeat them."
The rest of the show went along without mishap, although "the audience
were beastly," Webster said, "hard and granite-faced, not wanting to like it."

Fortunately, most critics enjoyed it. John Kieran said Canada was
"certainly one of the stars of the season." John Chapman wrote that
"Lee's portrayal of the monster, Caliban, is one by which I shall measure
all other readings in the years that are left. It is most beautifully spoken—
it is at once fearsome and touching." The *New York Times Magazine*
published a three-page photo spread on the show, though *Times* critic
Lewis Nichols noted some flaws on opening night: "Mr. Lee, in costume, is a dangerous-appearing Caliban; he has the air of a snarling dog,
but he also at times is a little indistinct. He is a Caliban built to invite
shudders, and in that he succeeds; some of the lines, however, are lost."

Comparison to a menacing canine is rarely something an actor rel-
ishes, and Lee was in for other disturbing descriptions, several of them in-
sulting, even if unintentionally so. Otis L. Guernsey, Jr., said Lee played
his part "with uncouth power." *Newsweek* called Lee "both articulate and
monstrous, which is probably all that one could demand of the grotesque
role." Burton Rascoe compared Canada's Caliban to a famous circus gorilla that was currently thrilling audiences under the big top. "I suspect
Mr. Lee stood before the cage of Gargantua in Ringling Brothers' Circus, studying Gargantua's postures and grunts and breathing sounds, in
preparation for his role as Caliban, for, in wondrous costume, he was
very like Gargantua last night—an articulate Gargantua to be sure." Lee
may have heard a few "I-told-you-so's" from those friends and colleagues
who had warned him against taking the role.

Aside from monstrous similes, *Tempest* got good press and word-of-
mouth, tickets sold well, and the production settled into a comfortable
eight-week run. Canada's Caliban was less controversial than Robeson's
Othello, since Caliban neither kisses nor kills a white woman onstage,
and yet audiences still found it a curiosity to see a black man playing a
classical role, especially an ex-prizefighter. *Variety* persisted in calling
Lee "the only Shakespearean actor with a cauliflower ear."

Lee's boxing history never ceased to intrigue the press. One day Canada was sitting at a table with a group of friends, black and white, in the Fifty-seventh Street Cafeteria. Jack Harris, reporter for *The Hobo News*, a small underground paper, was drinking coffee and reading his paper at the next table. He thought Lee looked familiar, but couldn't place him. "One eye was slightly defective and an ear slightly cauliflowered," Harris wrote. "His nose appeared to have stopped punches at one time. I tried to recall old time fighters of days gone by. No go."

Canada was watching another customer, an elderly man at the next table who was fishing in his pockets, looking perplexed. After a minute or two, Lee joined the man at his table. "If it's a cigarette you want, here," the actor said with a friendly smile, pulling a pack from his pocket and handing it to the old man.

"Whoever this guy is, he's pretty regular," Harris thought to himself. The next day Harris's publisher assigned him to interview an actor who always made for "good copy." To Harris's surprise, it was that "pretty regular" guy in the cafeteria: Canada Lee.

The actor was putting on his makeup backstage just before a show when Harris stopped by. They shot the breeze, talking about Canada's life in sports and music, and how he finally tumbled into acting. "What do you think of the opportunity for Negroes on the stage today?" Harris asked. Lee's expression grew serious, contemplative.

"Never in the history of the theater has there been so much opportunity for Negroes as today," he told the reporter. Just then a small boy knocked on the door. "Five more minutes, Mr. Lee," he announced. The show was about to start. Harris asked the actor if he had a special message for the paper's Negro readers. "My credo is the message," Canada replied. "I promised myself never to do anything low . . . or cause my people to be held in contempt." Heading off to make his entrance onstage, Lee remembered his Double-V campaign and hurriedly added a final word: "If you eliminate this master race idea," he said, "you'd eliminate all wars."

Once *The Tempest* settled in, Canada resumed his politicking. Like so many celebrities, he frequently agreed to loan his name to liberal organizations, often based upon quick conversations on the train, in the neighborhood, or on the phone. And, like so many celebrities, he never imagined that supporting a good cause could be perceived as a bad thing, let alone traitorous, even treasonable. But the note-takers in Washington had been busy, and Lee's files at the FBI and HUAC had grown steadily thicker with more reports and three-by-five cards.

A number of Canada's activities during the 1944 campaign season were recorded. For example, the actor had cosponsored a dinner in honor of Ferdinand C. Smith, a prominent black labor leader campaigning coast to coast for Roosevelt; Smith was a suspected Communist. Lee had also penned an essay for the *Daily Worker* titled "Why Theater People Support FDR," recalling how New Deal programs like the Federal Theatre gave a living wage to thousands desperate for work and food. He called the President "a towering figure of hope for justice and peace for all men." This article was dropped into Canada's HUAC dossier without comment. Was it good because Lee supported Roosevelt, or bad because he mentioned the subversive Federal Theatre? Canada's appearance at a "Register-to-Vote" dance in Harlem also got a mention in the actor's HUAC file, probably because it was written up in the *Daily Worker*.

In October, Lee's ties to Communist groups came up during a HUAC hearing. The committee's research director, J. B. Matthews, vehemently denounced the National Citizens Political Action Committee as "the leading Communist front organization in the United States," with a membership "virtually determined by the Communist Party." In fact, NCPAC members included a broad spectrum of political progressives, including newspaper and magazine editors, judges, screenwriters, and a Catholic bishop. Many were liberal Democrats who, like Canada, joined primarily to support FDR's reelection.

At the hearing, Matthews presented charts and diagrams linking the 141 members of NCPAC to twenty-five organizations designated as "subversive and Communist" by the U.S. Attorney General. Canada reportedly had links to three such organizations. But Matthews solemnly warned the committee not to judge a Commie by the number of his links. "A halfway Communist or a 75-percent Communist may be affiliated with twenty-five Communist-front organizations," he intoned, "whereas an out-and-out Communist may be affiliated with only one or two or three Communist-front organizations."

Right-wing columnist George E. Sokolsky trumpeted Matthews's byzantine report, arguing that the vast numbers of "interlocking fronts" clearly demonstrated "the organizational genius of the Communist Party." However, the columnist had to admit that members of these suspect groups were not all card-carrying Communists. "Many are innocents who always go along—maybe because they like the society of the Reds. Whatever may be the reason, their names keep reappearing on the lists." Sokolsky concluded his diatribe by advising the Attorney General to beef up his official list of 90 Communist fronts, pointing out that HUAC's list already totaled 245.

The secret FBI and HUAC files on Canada attempted to document any link to Communists, no matter how tenuous. When he entertained revelers during the Spring Hop at the Jefferson School of Social Science, HUAC put it in his file; the school was a suspected Communist front. And when the actor's name turned up on the letterhead of the "Joint Anti-Fascist Refugee Committee," which raised funds to aid victims of the Spanish Civil War, the FBI took note; this group was also cited as a front. The bureau's file stated that Lee sponsored a "race meeting" of the Hollywood Democratic Committee, another front. An FBI informant spotted Lee's name on a souvenir program distributed at a *New Masses* awards banquet cochaired by Paul Robeson; the *New York World-Telegram* had denounced the prizes as Commie Pulitzers. Lee's friendship and frequent collaborations with Robeson, a suspected subversive, were repeatedly cited in his files.

No action was beneath notice. An open letter published in the *New York Sun* asked Governor Dewey to release professor Morris U. Schappes from prison. During an investigation of subversive activity on college campuses, Schappes was convicted of perjury because he said he knew only three other Communists at City College. He had served eleven months, and any more would be "political persecution," according to the letter. Lee's name was spied among two hundred signatories listed in fine print; the letter was promptly clipped and added to his file.

Someone at HUAC was reading the papers very, very carefully.

On a chill and gloomy Wednesday in 1945, Canada found himself spending Valentine's Day alone, again. Frances was still in California, still sorting out family business. No matter how often they spoke on the phone, the sound of her voice could never quite erase the loneliness in Lee's heart.

He wanted to be with her; he wanted her to be his wife.

Every now and then, Canada sweetly addressed a card or letter to "Mrs. Canada Lee." Someone in Los Angeles spotted one of those cards and blew the whistle. Walter Winchell broke the story of their engagement in spring 1945, according to Frances, and other columnists picked up the item. "Then some people in the industry started saying that Canada was not actually divorced. And they raised the race question," she said.

At first, Frances was merely annoyed at the invasion of their privacy. Then her lawyer called. There had been some difficulties in settling her father's estate; now there was talk of a lawsuit, and this story about her engagement to a Negro was going to make matters worse. The implication seemed clear: get rid of the black boyfriend.

Frances became frightened for herself, her future, her own hopes and dreams and ambitions. "I knew he was going to take me over lock, stock and barrel," she said. "I didn't want any man to take me over. No man was going to be responsible for me. The fact that I was not going to be able to do what I wanted to do . . . I just couldn't accept it."

She began to question the relationship. Frances had questions about herself, too. "I was very independent," she said. "In the political arena, as a woman, I was ahead of my time. Men would say, 'Stop talking like a man!' or, 'Are you a man or a woman?'

"I had to come to terms with myself: What am I? Do I like it or not?"

One day that spring, while talking on the phone, Canada and Frances had a fight. An icy, angry silence followed. "Canada could not reach me after the argument," Frances said. Apparently, she wasn't taking his calls.

After settling her business affairs, Frances packed a suitcase. She told her brothers she was leaving. She told Canada nothing at all.

And then she disappeared.

NINE

NO BUSINESS LIKE SHOW BUSINESS

WHITE WAY AND WHITEFACE

Frances had simply vanished into thin air.

Canada called her brothers first. They were worried, too. She told us she was leaving, they said. They hadn't seen or heard from her since.

Do you have any idea where she might be? Canada fought down the panic that crept into his voice.

No, said her brothers. They had already called everyone in the family, people she worked with, the friends they knew. No one had a clue where she was. They told Canada not to worry. Frances was headstrong, she needed some time. She would get over whatever it was that was bothering her. She would come back.

But she didn't. Days, then weeks went by. Nothing. She was just gone.

Canada knew in his heart that he was the reason. One day they argued on the phone. The next day, she packed up and left. He went over and over the things that were said, things he had done. He never meant to hurt her, never meant to frighten her away. He loved her. He wanted to marry her.

Where was she? Was she safe? Would she ever come back to him?

Time crawled by without any word from Frances. Night after night he played Caliban, and filled the rest of his waking hours with one benefit, ball, or banquet after another.

Lee's first major speech of 1945 was in the national political arena. In February, Congress broke out in a scuffle over Henry A. Wallace's nomination for U.S. Secretary of Commerce. A major player in the New Deal, Wallace had been vice president during Roosevelt's third term. Now Harry Truman sat in the VP seat, and Roosevelt wanted Wallace in his cabinet. When conservatives balked, Canada rallied support for Wallace. "We will win because we have a mighty army," he proclaimed. "We will rout selfish, bigoted, and shortsighted men who do not serve the interests of the *whole* American people."

The Senate confirmed Wallace's appointment on March 1. Six weeks later, Franklin Delano Roosevelt was dead and Truman succeeded to the presidency.

For Canada and many other African Americans of his generation, political life without Roosevelt seemed unfathomable. FDR and the New Deal had helped shape the way black progressives thought about government and social policy. With Roosevelt's support, they believed they had a chance at improving conditions for black Americans in the postwar world. Now they had a Southerner in the White House. How far could Truman be trusted? Not very far, many suspected, but only time would tell. For now, Lee faithfully supported Henry Wallace and other New Dealers. That loyalty would land him in trouble as the nation's political balance began to tip to the right.

The Tempest's eight-week run at the Alvin was nearly over, but box-office sales were still going strong. Producer Cheryl Crawford booked another theater, the Broadway, and cast and crew happily moved house. Although Lee performed eight shows a week, he still found time and energy for countless speeches and causes. After one show in March, he hurried out of his Caliban costume and into a tux before dashing off to Harlem to headline a "Parade of Stars," supporting more government jobs for black workers. Another night, Lee hustled uptown after a Sunday performance to entertain guests at a gala benefit ball for the American Negro Theater. Photos show Lee beautifully attired in a sleek suit and snowy white shirt, taking a few turns on the dance floor. His petite partner is prettily anonymous, her back to the camera.

As much as Canada grieved over Frances, he wasn't a man content with his own company for very long. Columnists began to spot Lee and his dates-of-the-week at the best jazz and blues clubs in town, especially Café Society. "Sunday night, everybody in show business would come in—Billy Strayhorn, Paul Robeson, Lena Horne, Joe Louis, Canada Lee," said trumpeter Adolphus "Doc" Cheatham, who played in the house band.

Lee loved the Café. Everyone talked jazz and politics, and no one batted an eye when mixed couples turned up—a special attraction for Canada, who dated both black and white women. One night, Lee escorted a drop-dead gorgeous blonde to the dance floor. Sitting at a ringside table were three white sailors on shore leave without dates. Every time Lee and his girl danced by their table, the sailors glowered at them, muttering angrily.

"They went crazy," club owner Barney Josephson recalled. "They started making remarks and I saw Canada stop dancing and start telling them off. One of the sailors stood up and raised his hand and Canada gave it to him right in the mouth and knocked out two teeth. He knocked the second guy down, too. By the time the third guy got up I was at the table with my headwaiter and we broke it up." Shore patrol arrived and demanded Canada's arrest, but a white naval officer quickly intervened. Insisting that Lee had clearly been provoked, the officer filed charges against the three sailors instead.

Rumor had it that Lee was entertaining a variety of paramours. One wrote children's books, while another lived in New Rochelle near his parents. A third was a well-known Harlem actress. Canada was generally discreet, but one of his affairs was bound to be noticed. Kitty Lehman was wealthy, white, and definitely high society. Her grandfather, William Jennings Bryan, was a famous statesman. Her mother, Ruth Bryan Owen, was the first woman to serve as a U.S. Ambassador (to Denmark, 1933–36).

A lovely, fascinating, slightly eccentric creature, Kitty had a knack for marrying well. Her second husband, Robert Lehman, of the Lehman Brothers banking family, was one of the richest men in the country. The divorcée had marriage on her mind again, and though Lee gracefully demurred, the lady lingered in the picture. The two were involved off and on for months, often hosting elaborate parties at her Park Avenue apartment.

Every day Lee hoped for a letter or a call from the one he truly loved. The other women in his life were merely there to help pass the time.

After a successful twelve-week run, *The Tempest* closed on April 21, 1945, just as dramatic events unfolded in the European theater, commanding the world's attention.

Allied forces were marching on Berlin. On April 25, Russian and U.S. troops met on the Elbe just south of the city and celebrated together all night by drinking whiskey and vodka and dancing to accordion music. Heinrich Himmler, Minister of the Interior for the Third Reich, began negotiating Germany's surrender. Three days later, Benito Mussolini and twelve of his former cabinet officers were executed at Lake Como. On April 30, Adolf Hitler committed suicide in the Reich Chancellery in Berlin as Soviet troops converged on the city. After six devastating years, the war in Europe was over.

On May 7, as Germany surrendered unconditionally, Lee traveled north through the Hudson Valley to the ivy halls of Vassar College, bastion of female education, to address the graduating class of 1945 on "What the Negro Wants and Hopes For in the Post-War World." The Negro's hopes, he told them, "may be summed up in a phrase: full equality and the end of Jim Crow. In this, the race is united as never before. Indeed the attainment of that goal is today more than a mere hope. It is now . . . grim determination."

There was a new undercurrent of urgency, frustration, and impatience in this speech. For those of us striving to make democracy a reality, Lee said, the present pace is far too slow. President Roosevelt made "a sound beginning" in the struggle for civil rights, but black Americans were now watching "with some trepidation the road which the new administration under President Truman will take."

They had reason to worry. Still consumed with the war against Japan, Truman made little headway in continuing, let alone expanding, New Deal reforms. Conservatives in Congress seized upon any opportunity to weaken or kill FDR's social programs, and one of their first targets was the Fair Employment Practices Committee.

When Roosevelt created the FEPC in 1941 by executive order, he effectively banned racial discrimination by defense industries receiving federal contracts. Congress had recently voted to eliminate funding for the FEPC by June 1946. Truman wanted to make the committee permanent, but conservatives were fighting tooth and nail to block any such legislation. Canada headlined a rally to save the FEPC at Manhattan's Town Hall on June 19. Black veterans will need employment, he said, and shame on this democracy if it discriminates against them in the workplace after the sacrifices they made on the battlefield. He lashed out against conservatives who were attacking the FEPC in particular and civil rights in general, including Congressman John Rankin and Senator Theodore Bilbo, both of Mississippi, the latter a white supremacist. If black Americans don't have equal access to jobs, Lee warned, beware "disunity of the most dangerous proportions."

Later that month, Canada took the FEPC fight to Washington, delivering one of his most impassioned speeches in ringing tones: "As Negroes have died on foreign soil for the liberties of other peoples, I propose to die here, with my blood running red on the cobblestones of America for the principles that I have believed in, in spite of having those principles denied me . . . the principles of democracy and justice." Paul Robeson joined Lee in his urgent appeal to save the FEPC at the annual Negro Freedom Rally in Madison Square Garden on June 25. Thousands cheered as the two great orators shared the podium, calling for an end to all practices that discriminated against black Americans.

Though he was an activist and orator of great stature, Canada never neglected humbler causes and community groups. On July 2, he spoke to thirty-five Girl Scouts during the grand opening of a play center in Harlem. Scouting, he told the girls, will teach you to "want to belong to America." And in turn, you must teach other Americans the important role we have played in this nation's history, and demand respect for the sacrifices black Americans have made. This country was built "largely on the backs, sweat, tears, and broken bones of the Negro," he declared. "America is ours as much as it is anybody's."

It was pretty strong rhetoric for the Girl Scouts.

Lee's tone grew more ominous in a speech delivered at a war bond rally on Independence Day. Canada pointed out the irony of celebrating the signing of a document that declares that all men are created equal

when the American Red Cross blood bank still segregated white and Negro blood; when the military segregated its soldiers; and when a Negro
soldier returning home could be lynched in uniform. These were surprisingly harsh words to deliver at an event designed to encourage people
to buy bonds to support the war. An early draft of the speech was bitterer
still, but someone convinced him to tone down his language. A note attached to an extant copy, signed only "Your Girl Friday," argues: "You
can't tell Negro parents whose boys are fighting not to buy bonds—not to
send help to their boys. Please! . . . Save your Sunday punches for the
times and places they will be effective."

A week later, Canada took a Sunday punch himself. His mother Lydia died suddenly of a heart ailment in the house he had purchased for
his parents in New Rochelle. She was sixty-three. Lee would miss the
wise, strong, and determined woman who had raised him and helped to
raise his son. He was devastated by the loss, as were all who knew Lydia
and admired her. The church was full to the rafters for the services that
bid Sister Canegata good-bye. As Canada sat with his family in Salem
Methodist, his thoughts surely turned to Frances, who had won Lydia's
respect and friendship, and her blessing.

He missed his true love still. Time passed, but the pain in his heart
persisted.

In the weeks following the funeral, Lee often visited his father in New
Rochelle, and he was there on August 6 rehearsing a little "Parade of
Stars" benefit for the local boys' club when the news came over the radio
that the United States had dropped an atomic bomb on Hiroshima,
Japan. Days later, a bomb exploded in Nagasaki. Newspapers reported
inconceivable destruction; 175,000 died in an instant, and an equal
number would die of radiation sickness and burns. Japan sued for peace
on August 10. World war had ended; survivors mourned 55 million dead.

Canada, a disabled man unable to serve as a soldier, had done his patriotic best for his country. His scrapbook was full of certificates of appreciation from the U.S. Treasury, the United Seamen's Service, the USO,
the Newspaper Guild Canteen, the U.S. Maritime Service Center, and
countless other wartime organizations. He was proud of what he had
done, and proud of his son Carl, nineteen, who was now in the army and
stationed at Fort McClellan, Alabama. He also quietly rejoiced that his
only son had been spared any harm.

Proud and relieved as he was, this was a blue period for Lee. The disappearance of Frances, the death of his mother, the absence of his son, and the frightening implications of the atomic bomb infused the actor with a deep melancholy. He tried to focus his attention on finding work and furthering his causes. He felt irritated and impatient.

As the summer of 1945 drew to an end, New York City began gearing up for local elections. Despite rampant Red-baiting, Canada stuck his neck out for two left-wing candidates running for City Council: the incumbent Benjamin J. Davis, a Communist, and Eugene Connolly of the American Labor Party, a suspected Communist.

Lee also lobbied Congress to support passage of the Full Employment Bill of 1945. Many Americans were worried about the economy and unemployment, fearing the country would slide back into a depression now that the wartime boom was over. Both parties had promised a job to every able worker during the 1944 Presidential campaign, and now it was time to ante up. Democrats in both houses proposed legislation guaranteeing full employment and making the federal government ultimately responsible. Republicans and big business initially backed the bill, but now support was crumbling. Truman's foes in Congress decided it gave the executive branch too much control over the federal budget. Capitalist barons were reluctant to give government a permanent hand in the workings of the free market. Conservatives ominously noted that the Soviet Union ensured full employment, too—through totalitarianism. And the extreme right wing hinted that full employment should only be guaranteed to whites.

On Labor Day, Lee traveled to Baltimore to address union workers at a mass demonstration for full peacetime employment. He fired off the names of legislators, including the white supremacist Senator Bilbo, who opposed equal job opportunities for workers of color. Canada's great fist slammed the podium. "Who will permit our nation's law-making chambers to be defiled by the filthy, insidious rantings of Bilbo?" he demanded. "Who in this country will tolerate this spewing of Hitlerite hate and insult into the faces of the very people who helped destroy Hitler?" Lee glared fiercely at the crowd, gone utterly silent as they watched this electric performance. "No one," he said.

💀   💀   💀

In October, Lee happily accepted an offer to reprise his role as Caliban in Chicago at the palatial Studebaker Theater. The show played to full houses and great acclaim; the *Chicago Times* called Lee's Caliban "a first-class job."

William Branch eagerly bought a ticket to a matinee performance. He had seen Lee on Broadway in *Anna Lucasta*, and it was even more thrilling to see him play Caliban. After the show, he wished very much to talk to the actor, "but who was I, a little freshman at Northwestern, to go backstage and ask for Canada Lee?" He walked to the train station. "Just before I put my coin in the slot I thought, 'What the hell? All they can say is no.'" He rushed back to the theater. The guard at the stage door said Canada was upstairs with friends, but the young man could wait for him if he liked. Minutes later, there was the star.

"I stammered out that I enjoyed the performance and just wanted to shake his hand," Branch said. Lee could have left it at that, but he didn't. He asked the young man what he was doing in Chicago, and Branch told him he was studying theater.

"Oh!" Canada said, perking up. "How would you like a job?"

Anna Lucasta was on its way to Chicago, he said, and local actors were needed to understudy roles. Lee told the young man exactly when and where he could audition for the director. "Be sure to tell him Canada Lee sent you," he said. Branch did exactly that and got the job of his dreams, working with the great stars of the black theater as well as a certain "greenhorn" named Sidney Poitier. "I've stayed with the theater all my life," says Branch, an accomplished playwright and academic. "I'm not sure that would have been the case had I not spoken to Canada Lee."

While Canada was in the Windy City, he visited friends he'd made during the *Native Son* tour and enjoyed a set or two at most of the city's jazz clubs. He made a couple of speeches, including one that encouraged Chicagoans to impeach their mayor if he didn't support equal education for black students. He saw a few women, but no one important. He got a letter from his son, Carl, who was tired of basic training at Fort McClellan and homesick for his family, his friends, his girl, Rhoda, and the bright lights of New York. "By the way, Mr. Lee," Carl asked his father, "just when in the hell are you expecting to do that little thing yourself (marriage)?"

There were women, yes. But there was no word from the one who mattered most.

Canada and *The Tempest* returned to New York on November 12, 1945, for a quick holiday revival of twenty-four performances. The day before it opened, Lee starred opposite film star Boris Karloff in a Theater Guild presentation of Eugene O'Neill's *Emperor Jones*, broadcasting live on WABC from Broadway's Belasco Theater. Playing Emperor Jones was a royal treat, but the ever-ambitious actor was looking for the next big step up in his career. Serendipitously, he got a call from playwright Maxine Wood.

A white journalist hailing from Detroit, Wood wrote plays on the side and was hoping to break into Broadway. Her newest work, *On Whitman Avenue*, had been gathering dust in Lee's apartment for weeks. He hadn't cracked it. "I felt guilty, and so I started reading," Canada later told a reporter. "The next thing I knew, I was crying. Me, a hard guy!"

In the play, a white liberal coed from Detroit named Toni Tilden sublets a second-floor flat in her parents' house to black veteran David Bennett and his family while her parents are away on vacation. Neighbors are shocked and angry. Toni's parents return to find themselves at the center of a middle-class uproar. A committee votes to "protect the neighborhood" by sending the Bennett family packing. In a climactic scene, David Bennett confronts committee members, who insist their decision to evict isn't a personal attack. "I realize that," Bennett replies. "But you have to keep the nigger in his place. Let's be honest at least. Call this meeting by its right name—a lynching bee, northern style. No bloodhounds, no tar and feathers, no shriveled flesh on a lonely tree. But the fruit is the same, ladies and gentlemen. The fruit is the same." The Bennetts eventually surrender the apartment, but the episode creates an irrevocable rift in the community.

The script needed some work, but the subject was timely and dear to Lee's heart. He was convinced he should play David Bennett on Broadway. But what producer would gamble on a play so potentially controversial? Then it came to him—*this* would be the next big step in his career. He would back the show himself and become the first black producer to present a drama on the Great White Way.

He couldn't do it on his own, of course; producing a Broadway show is rarely a one-man enterprise, so Lee invited his friend Mark Marvin to join him in the venture. Marvin had worked in film, dance, and theater, and he agreed to provide the administrative expertise Canada sorely needed. The two men immediately decided that hiring a hot new director would help them attract investors, so they signed on Margo Jones. The talented Texan had recently co-directed the Broadway premiere of Tennessee Williams's *Glass Menagerie*.

Canada and Mark announced that the show would open on Broadway in May after tryouts in Buffalo and Detroit. This gave them the entire winter to court investors. To get things rolling, Lee headed off to one of the famous Sunday afternoon salons hosted by actress Stella Adler and her husband, Harold Clurman. Richard Adler, aspiring composer and lyricist (*Pajama Game* and *Damn Yankees*), was at his sister's salon that day. As Lee worked the crowd, talking about his new play, young Adler grew very excited. "*On Whitman Avenue* was years ahead of its time . . . enormously daring," he later wrote. While serving in the navy, Adler had saved twenty-five hundred dollars. He gave it all to Canada. The show would be "as much a crusade as a production," he said. "We all believed in the play fiercely."

Canada's fierce beliefs placed him among nineteen artists and civic leaders honored for "contributions toward a democratic America" at a ceremony sponsored by the left-wing journal *New Masses* on January 14, 1946. Other honorees included Benjamin Davis, Jr. (public life); W.E.B. Du Bois (history); Duke Ellington (music); Paul Robeson (citizen); and Frank Sinatra ("for his courageous fight on behalf of all minorities").

The following night, Lee entertained at the annual Lenin Memorial in Madison Square Garden, sponsored by the New York State Communist Party. A number of unions were on strike at the time, and the meeting turned into a mass demonstration by twenty thousand workers. The next day, the *Daily Worker* quoted speeches at great length, and concluded: "The voice of Lenin, preserved on one of the few records in existence, was heard during the presentation of 'Report on the 152nd Day,' a dramatization of the events since V-J Day. Canada Lee, noted Negro actor, appeared in the sketch."

Organizers of political rallies often asked stars to appear in dramatic skits or even song-and-dance numbers to liven things up a bit and draw bigger audiences. Canada got asked, and often; one wonders if he *ever* said no. On January 24, he starred in a political piece called "How Do You Spell Democracy?" at the "Rally for a Democratic Japan." He was scheduled somewhere between the "native Japanese dancers," the "Chinese People's Chorus," and an opera singer.

The stakes were much higher for Lee's next assignment as artist-activist. In Washington, Senator Bilbo and other Dixiecrats were in the midst of a three-week filibuster against a bill to create a permanent FEPC. (Bilbo, author of *Take Your Choice: Separation or Mongrelization*, once praised Hitler on the Senate floor.) Canada got a call for help from a community group in Manhattan and rushed off to the Capitol on January 31. He arrived just as Senator Mead of New York managed to wrest control of the floor away from Bilbo and his cronies. Mead "dashed into the corridor and received a petition from Canada Lee, Negro actor," reported *The New York Times*. The petition demanded ratification of the FEPC and the expulsion of Senator Bilbo from the Senate for "conduct unbecoming a member of Congress." Canada and twenty-five thousand other New Yorkers had signed it. "The citizens of New York call upon the Senate to meet this challenge," Canada told reporters.

The challenge went unmet. Bilbo kept his seat, Congress rejected the bill, the FEPC was doomed to die in June, and Lee made new enemies for taking a bold stand against a powerful right-wing politician.

After returning to New York, Canada earned some quick and easy money narrating a film documentary called *The Roosevelt Story*. Elliot Roosevelt, a bit of a black sheep, supervised this tribute to his father, a corny mix of newsreel footage and dramatizations. In the film, FDR's life story is told by a cabdriver, representing "The Voice of the People." Ed Begley, Sr., is "The Opposition," while Canada personifies "The Depression" in cahoots with Brownie McGhee, who improvised blues music under Lee's narration.

Canada also picked up some radio work to help pay his bills, but he devoted every spare moment to raising money for *On Whitman Avenue*. He was terribly frustrated. For all his hometown popularity, he couldn't seem to find a dime in Harlem. Actress Fredi Washington chided her neighbors in a column published by the *People's Voice*: "When you see new bars being opened daily in Harlem where there are far too many already, you wonder why some of these people would not invest in projects which have the ability to make the lot of the Negro better."

In February, director Margo Jones assembled her cast, including Augustus Smith, the aging stage veteran who helped push Lee into auditioning for his very first play. Will Geer, a liberal activist famous for roles in *Waiting for Lefty* and *Of Mice and Men*, signed on as Mr. Tilden. Donald Oenslager designed the set and lights, and Paul Bowles wrote incidental music. Rehearsals were set to begin March 13.

Mark Marvin issued press releases emphasizing Canada's dual roles as star and producer. Jimmy Cannon, sports columnist at the *New York Post*, invited Lee to be on his radio show. Jimmy played up Canada's sporting history and the actor went along with his banter, claiming he liked show biz just fine, but he'd go back to prizefighting any day.

Though he was under twice as much pressure, Lee obviously took great pleasure in his double duty. George Freedley, on assignment for *Playbill*, found him tucked into a corner table at Sardi's one day, enjoying a soft drink. "Me, a producer! Me, the boss!" Canada said, as his chums laughed. He cheerfully admitted that he "sometimes forgets he's the producer . . . he has found himself joining the cast in usual backstage gripes about the management."

On April 10, the Erlanger Theater in Buffalo hosted the first tryout for *On Whitman Avenue*, and on opening night, the producers sent a telegram backstage to the playwright. "Maxine dearest, You did all this with your own little typewriter and we're proud to help a bit in presenting the American theater with an important new playwright who is not only an artist, but a people's artist who never says blotto to injustice anywhere in the world. Love, Canada Lee and Mark Marvin."

The premiere left "many a sophisticate in tears, and many a veteran playgoer impressed," according to *The Buffalo Courier-Express*. The reviewer for *The Buffalo News* was less enthusiastic: "Like many other productions with entirely worthy ideals, it has a tendency to become more of a preachment than a play . . . Canada Lee is a superb player, but he hardly has enough to do in the production to bring the part fully to life." A reviewer for *Variety* predicted that the show's chances were "decidedly limited."

After the shows, people crowded backstage to say how moved they were by the Bennett family's plight, but others were wary of the play, including the Detroit police commissioner. In 1943, race riots had erupted in Detroit, leaving thirty-four dead, most of them black. The commissioner considered stopping the show from playing his town, but in the end he allowed it to open at the Lafayette Theater.

Maxine Wood's play got a decidedly warm reception in Detroit, even though the writer had exposed race prejudice in her own hometown. "On Whitman Avenue is not a study in miscegenation, as many may have feared, but a forthright examination of white intolerance toward Negro nearness," wrote a reviewer for The Windsor Daily Star in nearby Ontario, Canada. "It is a disturbing subject, of atomic bomb proportions in its possibilities . . . There are those in Detroit—and in Windsor, too—who won't like On Whitman Avenue. It hits too close to home. Yet . . . it is a play of absorbing interest and definite power, one that should be seen."

By the end of April, On Whitman Avenue had collected enthusiastic endorsements from artists, politicians, labor leaders, and civic activists, including Henry Wallace, U.S. Secretary of Agriculture; Philip Murray, President of the CIO; playwright Elmer Rice; and former First Lady Eleanor Roosevelt. In her nationally syndicated column, Roosevelt praised Canada and Mark for their courageous production: "This play, through its portrayal of day-by-day incidents in an average community, makes one alert to the dangers that may defeat democracy and justice if we are not on our guard."

On Whitman Avenue now moved to New York to prepare for the Broadway opening. Several preview performances were organized as benefits for charities and progressive causes. Eleanor Roosevelt came to one such fund-raiser for the Southern Conference for Human Welfare and had her picture taken on the theater steps with Canada and Mark.

Just before the premiere, the beleaguered producers finally pulled together the entire fifty thousand dollars they needed. "With the exception of one backer, Canada raised all this dough among non-Negro financiers," the New York Amsterdam News reported, adding that the single black contributor was from Illinois. (Congressman William L. Dawson, D-Ill., gave a thousand dollars.) Thirty-three backers contributed between five hundred and five thousand dollars, including Canada's former lover, Caresse Crosby, who invested a thousand. The News said Lee deserved a medal "for having the doggedness to raise such coin, and for his faith in the play."

Through it all, Canada kept his sense of humor, according to his friend Lloyd Gough. While Lee was in previews for *On Whitman Avenue*, Gough was at the Fulton Theater in *Deep Are the Roots*, directed by Elia Kazan. The two actors hadn't seen each other in years, and Lee decided to stage a memorable reunion. While Gough was performing on stage, he looked through the French doors of the set and saw Canada Lee standing in the wings, looking dapper as always in a gray suit, white shirt, and necktie. Gough carried on with the scene. The next time he looked, Canada was still standing there, solemn and attentive—with his trousers dropped to his ankles.

Klieg lights flashed in front of the Cort Theater on May 8, 1946, announcing the premiere of *On Whitman Avenue*. Prestigious artists and activists, black and white, were in the audience, including opera star Muriel Rahn, theater impresario Dick Campbell, civil rights leader Lester Granger, film moguls Samuel Goldwyn and Spyros Skouras, and actresses Stella Adler and Olivia de Havilland.

Backstage, Canada sifted through dozens of good-luck telegrams. Adrenaline surged through him, jangling his nerves. He told a reporter later what it felt like that night in his dressing room: "You start to put on your shoe, and maybe you reach up and put it on your head. You try to get into your coat, but you can't find the armholes."

The houselights dimmed and the curtain rose, revealing a Rockwellian vision of Midwestern Americana: a white Victorian clapboard house with gingerbread trim, utterly realistic down to the flowers in window boxes. (The *New Masses* later sniffed: "The façade must have cost as much as a whole house, plumbing and all.")

At intermission, the chatter didn't have the electric buzz of a hit in the making. After the show, backstage well-wishers were painstakingly polite. By the time Canada and Mark got the first reviews, they knew they were in for a rough ride. Lewis Nichols wrote in *The New York Times* that he understood why Canada chose to produce the play, but "the fact remains it is just not good theater." Lee had overacted, he complained, which didn't help. "The play's aspirations are honest and sincere, but the effect grows increasingly disappointing," the critic concluded.

Howard Barnes concurred: "While it rates a high mark for sincerity, it is lean on theatrical effectiveness." He singled out Canada for praise: "The fine actor makes the role of the embittered Negro veteran rounded and resolute." Walter Winchell griped that the show's "eyes are raised toward the idealistic heavens while its feet are rooted in dramatic medi-ocrity." Hollywood's *Daily Reporter* was succinct: "The play has three producers and 34 backers, and hasn't the ghost of a chance." Louis Kro-nenberger, drama critic for the liberal *PM*, was unexpectedly harsh. The issues were "vital and immediate," he wrote, but the play was "unsatis-factory." Listing a string of faults, he was particularly disappointed that "so good an actor as Canada Lee is guilty of bad overacting."

Though critics at black newspapers agreed the play missed its mark, *PM*'s stern critique prompted them to vociferously take up the cause. The *People's Voice* claimed there was a "Broadway lynching" going on. Theater editor Fredi Washington said white critics "have become cyni-cal, lazy, tired of going to the theater, or what is worse, in the best fascist tradition, have agreed on an unwritten plot to kill plays dramatizing people's problems, especially Negroes." Her parting shot: "You've made us mad, boys."

Reviews cheerleading the play appeared in black papers across the nation. The *New York Age* declared it was "loaded with dynamite." *The Afro-American* said Canada Lee "brought tears to the eyes of those who shared his sense of frustration." In the *Chicago Defender*, Langston Hughes ranked the drama with *Uncle Tom's Cabin*, calling it "the most effective play I have ever seen dealing with the problems of Negro-white relationships in America . . . People laughed, cried, and applauded all the way through. Negroes are particularly moved by it. To us it is almost too real." Paul Robeson's wife, Eslanda, penned a glowing testimonial for the play, published in the *Daily Worker*.

Liberal and left-wing whites went to bat for the show as well. "I can understand why some of the critics gave this play bad reviews," Eleanor Roosevelt observed in her column. "We do not want to be reminded of our unpleasant shortcomings. We don't want to face up to the big prob-lems that we have." Charles Humboldt, Communist and editor of the *New Masses*, was perhaps the play's most passionate champion. "This is our play. It is a play about white and Negro people and most of the crit-ics do not like it," he wrote. "The critics were forced to look life in the face . . . This was the truth that troubled them. So they turned to a dis-cussion of 'style.' Safe ground."

Lee's friend Ed Sullivan sent the star his compliments. "Canada Lee, who just won rave notices in *On Whitman* Avenue . . . has the technique and sincerity that lifts him to the Spencer Tracy level," Sullivan wrote in his Sunday column. "Even in star-studded Broadway casts, Canada Lee more than holds his own." This was a very sweet little plug for the show; the *Daily News* circulation was about 3.5 million that day.

Buoyed by this support, Canada openly derided the play's detractors. "Critics rejected us. Do you know why?" he asked a reporter. "Because this play held themselves and their stupid prejudices up before their own eyes, and they didn't like it." *On Whitman Avenue* "hit at the conscience of America," he said.

PM stood by its review and tried to defend itself to black and liberal readers who sent dozens of angry letters to the editor. To defuse the situation, the paper sponsored a public forum on the play. A standing-room-only crowd came to hear panelists including Maxine Wood, Margo Jones, Mark Marvin, *New York Post* critic Vernon Rice, *Brooklyn Daily Eagle* critic Arthur Pollock, and Thurgood Marshall, attorney for the NAACP. *Variety* summarized the controversy in its own inimitable way: "Harlem Whets Sharp Ax Vs. 'Whitman' Nixers; Calls New York Crix 'Fascists.'"

As this stormy debate raged on in the press, scuffles occasionally broke out in the audience as well. Michael Carter, reporter for *The Afro-American*, was standing outside the theater on May 23 during intermission when he overheard a white man say he didn't like the play. Another man standing nearby took offense at this remark.

"You are an old Bilbo!" he exclaimed. "We got too damn many people like you. You ought to be ashamed."

"I'm not an old Bilbo," the first man said angrily. "I'm as sympathetic as you are. I'm as sympathetic as anybody. But I still don't like the play."

The two men squared off, glaring at each other, fists raised, until the theater's fireguard broke it up. Coincidentally, that same week Canada invited Senator Bilbo and his fellow racial demagogue Congressman John E. Rankin to the show, all expenses paid, for an education "they couldn't overlook." Predictably, Bilbo and Rankin declined Lee's offer.

Unfortunately, they weren't the only people staying away. Despite two weeks of constant media hoopla, Harlem wasn't buying many tickets. White liberal audiences were keeping *On Whitman Avenue* alive, but just barely. The box office was lucky to break even most nights. Lee refused to give up; instead, he announced that he had ordered an additional hundred thousand tickets to be printed, as a show of faith.

Behind the scenes, Mark and Canada began to cook up new marketing strategies.

While those ideas were simmering, Lee made a string of public appearances, headlining benefits for the George Washington Carver School in
Harlem (later cited as a Communist front) and the United Negro College Fund. He helped Paul Robeson rally support for anticolonial movements and famine relief in Africa at "Unity for Colonial Freedom,"
which drew sixteen thousand people to Madison Square Garden on June
16. In Jersey City, he spoke about the perils of prejudice to a standing-
room-only crowd at a local church. Those who suffer from discrimination must be careful not to discriminate themselves, Canada warned.
"We have every right to be antiwhite, but that would avail us nothing," he
said. "Intolerance is undemocratic, unmanly, and like a boomerang, returns back . . . Let all of us learn to live in peace with our fellow man.
The world is big enough for all of us if we are guided by humanity and
justice."

Lee also rekindled one of his old causes, organizing a rally to banish
Jim Crow from theaters in Washington, D.C., with help from playwright
Garson Kanin. While New York venues had ended segregation, Jim
Crow was alive and well in the nation's capital. Kanin and Canada both
spoke at the rally, along with designer Robert Edmond Jones and actor
Buddy Ebsen, urging artists to boycott the National Theater, Constitu-
tion Hall, and other performance spaces until management agreed to
suspend discriminatory policies.

It was a noble effort, but trouble lurked in the wings. "Unbeknown to
the speakers, the lobby of the theater was filled with individuals promoting what was then called 'communistic' literature," recalled Nancy Wolcott Ebsen, Buddy's wife at the time. "Everything from Karl Marx to the
latest 'cell' newsletters. This was evidently sufficient to place one on
the dark gray list." Ebsen reportedly lost jobs because of this rally.

Back on *Whitman Avenue*, tickets sales continued to plummet. The
Rocky Mountain News said "the benefit of much persuasive noise from
the leftist ranks" couldn't offset damage done by negative reviews. None

of the show's investors had recouped a dime, including Canada and Mark. They had to find a way to keep the show going through the summer. Working unbelievable hours on very little sleep, the two men now took all of their simmering ideas and organized them into a vast grassroots marketing campaign.

"We talked to teachers in schools, we called on friends and neighbors, we talked to the barbers who cut our hair, and left leaflets everywhere we went," the men later wrote in *The New York Times*. They mounted handmade signs on a horse-drawn cart that traveled up and down the streets of Harlem. The signs read: "HAVE NO PLACE TO LIVE! WHITES WON'T LET THEM STAY! Find out how to stop this kind of thing we all hate! See Canada Lee in the play that every Negro should see—*On Whitman Avenue*."

They made pitches to union weeklies and the Jewish press and jimmied their way onto every possible radio program. Radio's "lady commentators" were particularly receptive to Canada, according to the *New York World-Telegram*. Lee once spoke on five of these shows in a single week, gratis, happy for the chance to pitch his play to an aggregate audience of 3 million women in the New York area. The actor fended off questions about his unusual life story. "People know all about me," he said "What I want to talk about now is prejudice." The actor had to admit that it was hard to wake up at the crack of dawn for these interviews, "but as long as the show stays open, he's willing to get up anytime," the *World-Telegram* noted. "He's a man with a cause."

Forums about the play were sponsored by public libraries and speeches were made to a plethora of cultural organizations. "I was dispatched to churches, labor unions, and synagogues," Richard Adler recalled. "I spent long, heated evenings exhorting audiences to support this noble and, to me at that time, important play."

Employers with ethnically diverse workers, including the New York Stock Exchange and the Police Department, were persuaded to buy discount tickets to offer to their employees. Brooklyn's black liberals and artists threw a party at Club 78, raising $250 for the show. The Harlem branch of the YMCA bought five hundred tickets at full price to sell at a discount to local families. Endorsements for the play by prominent Americans were telegraphed to ministers and congregations. Schools, Sunday schools, and churches bought tickets for children, the aged, and the poor. Community groups came to Saturday matinees, and Canada often stayed to visit with them after the show.

Lee, a Broadway star, was making an extraordinarily heroic, personal effort to save his show, and Helen Ormsbee of the *New York Herald Tribune* decided to do a story about it. After a matinee, the reporter elbowed her way through a teeming, chattering crowd of visitors in Canada's dressing room. "This interview came along in snatches before and after a radio broadcast which the actor had agreed to do between performances," she later wrote. "He has inexhaustible energy, and is always superimposing assignments like this on his regular schedule . . . to crusade for *On Whitman Avenue*." Canada's pitch to Ormsbee was aimed directly at her predominantly white readers. "This isn't a play about Negroes," he said, it's about discrimination. "These people could be Jews or Roman Catholics or Poles or Italians or anybody else in a community that considers them outsiders."

The actor also agreed to an in-depth interview with Howard Cushman for a lengthy profile in *PM*. The two men met at Café Society. While sipping a Coke, Lee admitted he had received threatening letters warning him to "lay off the subject of Negro residents living where they want to," but dismissed any notion that he was in danger. Conversation turned to more pleasant subjects as Lee proudly relayed that his son, Carl, was now stationed in Nuremberg. "A corporal," Canada said, and then he slapped his forehead, smiling abashedly. "No, gosh! A sergeant now! Better change that."

At the conclusion of Cushman's generous, heartwarming profile, the writer left his readers with the impression that Canada "works at democracy twenty-four hours a day." If any hard feelings had lingered over *PM's* negative review of the show, the newspaper had just gone a long way toward making amends.

In mid-June, Canada and Mark's nonstop marketing and public relations efforts paid off. Five weeks into the run, *On Whitman Avenue* turned a profit for the very first time. "I am happy to announce that this show has weathered through the crisis," Canada stated in the *New York Age*, adding that tickets were now on sale through August 3.

Canada and Mark, now roommates as well as producing partners, were elated, exhausted, relieved. With the show finally in the black, they had a fighting chance.

HUAC, on the other hand, was infuriated. Congressmen on the Un-American Activities Committee would venomously call the campaign to save *On Whitman Avenue* "a brilliant account of how left-wing groups work."

PM exaggerated by saying Lee spent every waking minute striving for liberty and equality. He was onstage nearly every night, which left him only twenty-odd hours each day to campaign for his show's survival *and* for those innumerable causes.

Lee became expert at quick changes and fast dashes.

He hopped an early-morning train to Philadelphia to address a high-school group called the Youth Builders and made it back just before his afternoon matinee. Next, he somehow convinced the entire cast of *On Whitman Avenue* to spend their one precious day off at a rally for the doomed FEPC. Along with Paul Robeson, Canada addressed five hundred delegates at the National Convention of American Youth for Democracy. He also joined a "Committee to Win the Peace," lobbying to pull American troops out of China's escalating civil war. After a Friday-night show, Lee raced uptown to appear with Billie Holiday and Louis Jordan at a black-tie benefit for the Riverdale Children's Association. The next day, after doing two performances, Canada hustled Mark and the cast to the Upper West Side to receive an award from the Citizens Committee for "contributing to interracial understanding."

During this whirlwind of activity, Lee and Mark worked up a deal to take the play's plea for tolerance to a mass audience. Newspapers hinted that the producing partners had spoken with "a top Hollywood director." Lee said he expected to reprise his role as David Bennett in a film adaptation that would star "name" actors. Marvin planned to travel to Los Angeles in early August to cast lead roles "and negotiate a motion picture sale of *On Whitman Avenue*," the *New York World Telegram* reported on July 7.

A film deal seemed imminent, the box office reported twenty-one thousand dollars in advance sales, and Jules Leventhal was talking about a national road tour. Everything on *Whitman Avenue* seemed jake, really. There was just one problem.

It was too darned hot.

In July, temperatures soared as high as 105 degrees, and a day in the nineties was considered a break. As water levels dropped in Central Park's reservoirs and lakes, fire departments worried about water pressure because so many neighborhoods were uncapping fire hydrants, creating fountains for children to splash in. Air-cooled theaters usually attracted big crowds in sultry weather, but the summer of 1946 was so hot that people could barely drag themselves off their stoops.

Ticket sales for *On Whitman Avenue* took a dip over the Fourth of July holiday, but that was true at most Broadway shows, so no one got too excited. "The wilting summer heat has been rather cruel, but we will do our best to hold it through the summer until Broadway becomes itself again," Canada wrote in a July 11 letter to Caresse Crosby, his former lover and an investor in the show. "If we do, and I have every reason to believe we shall, *On Whitman Avenue* should become the hit of the '47 season. It has what it takes."

Lee's optimism seemed justified at first. The *New York Post* said the story of the show was one of faith and miracles: "No astute showman would have given 5-to-1 odds that a serious play would have had a chance of lasting beyond the first heat wave, A/C or no. The public is supposed not to want to think unless the thermometer registers below 80 degrees." But inexhaustible marketing efforts by cast and crew were keeping their show alive. "Even the stagehands, hardened to Broadway and to show biz, fell under the spell and were seen handing out leaflets," the *Post* observed.

Newsweek declared that *On Whitman Avenue* could justifiably thumb its nose at the critics who originally panned it. "The chief reason for its survival as Broadway entertainment is Canada Lee, a Negro, and one of Broadway's finest actors," the magazine reported, adding: "Also involved are left-wing organizations, unions, and school groups which circularized their members to buy blocks of tickets."

Lee continued to forge close ties between the show and various liberal causes. In July, the entire cast stepped to the footlights after their bows, asking audiences to support an upcoming consumers' strike for the restoration of federal price controls. That same month, the American Labor Party—which included former New Dealers—presented an award to Canada Lee and Mark Marvin for their "fight against intolerance and discrimination." Assemblyman Leo Isacson of the Bronx (later a successful ALP candidate for Congress) led a question-and-answer session after another performance.

Playing this show to a liberal crowd was preaching to the choir, however, and Canada was always eager to take *On Whitman Avenue* to new audiences. On a Monday night, which was often the cast's only free night, Lee carted everyone off to a USO in New Jersey to perform selected scenes for an audience that included hospital patients, medical staff, Red Cross workers, Army officers, and soldiers from local barracks.

During that long, hot summer, Canada's role as David Bennett grew increasingly topical as crimes against black veterans became an explosive issue in New York and across the nation.

In Freeport, Long Island, a black veteran named Charles Ferguson was shot to death by a white policeman. On the day of the shooting, four Ferguson brothers had reunited for the first time in two years. One was a soldier, one a sailor, one a veteran, the fourth a civilian. The men stopped in a lunchroom for coffee, but were refused service. As they walked back to the bus station, a policeman reportedly insulted them. Charles, the veteran, lost his temper and answered back. The officer kicked him in the groin and pulled his gun. He lined all four brothers up against a wall, swore at them, and fired off several rounds. Two brothers slumped to the ground, dead; a third was wounded. The policeman was exonerated by a grand jury. "You would think a note of protest, of shame, of sorrow, would sound," Howard Fast wrote in the *New Masses*. "The silence was deep and profound." Canada helped break that silence, and his speeches raised much-needed funds for the veteran's orphaned children and bereaved family.

Black soldiers who had survived war in Europe and the Pacific were killed that summer in Georgia, Alabama, South Carolina, and Tennessee. Maceo Snipes was lynched the day after he courageously cast his ballot in the Georgia election—the first time black Americans had been permitted to vote in that state since Reconstruction. Weeks later, news reached the nation about a horrific mass murder, also in Georgia: the shotgun lynching of two black men and two black women in Moore's Ford. George Dorsey, a twenty-eight-year-old Pacific war veteran, was among the victims. On the evening of July 25, the two couples were crossing a one-lane wooden bridge that spanned the Apalachee River when white men surrounded them. The mob fired three separate volleys totaling more than sixty shots. A neighboring farmer said the crackle of gunfire sounded like "fire in a canebrake." The white men drove off, leaving four bullet-ridden bodies bleeding in the dirt.

Mass antilynching demonstrations were organized in black communities across the nation. On July 27, five thousand people gathered at 125th Street and Seventh Avenue in Harlem. In simple but compelling language, Canada urged his audience to demand justice for lynch victims. "Each of us has strings and ties in the South," he said. "If we in the North don't fight now, we will get the same thing that those men and their wives got."

Under intense pressure from civil rights groups, President Truman ordered the FBI to investigate the Moore's Ford killings; it was the first time the bureau took interest in a lynching, which was not yet a federal offense. No one was ever convicted.

Two weeks later, Canada performed at a benefit for Isaac Woodard, another black Pacific war veteran. After Woodard was honorably discharged in Atlanta, he immediately caught a bus to Winnsboro, South Carolina, to meet his wife. When the bus stopped at a small-town drugstore, Woodard asked the driver if he could go to the washroom. The driver cussed him; the veteran cussed back. A few towns down the road, in Aiken, South Carolina, the bus driver asked police to take Woodard off the bus. Though Woodard offered no resistance, two policemen beat him severely and threw him in jail. He woke up the next morning, blind in both eyes. His wounds went untreated for two days. A judge eventually fined the veteran fifty dollars for disturbing the peace. Woodard became a cause célèbre among left-wing and black activists, and on August 16, Canada joined Billie Holiday, Count Basie, Cab Calloway, Pearl Bailey, and Joe Louis at a benefit show in Lewisohn Stadium that drew thirty-six thousand people. Woody Guthrie sang a song he had written that morning. In "The Blinding of Isaac Woodard," the veteran tells his own story. The final verse reads:

> *Now you've heard my story, there's one thing I can't see,*
> *How you could treat a human like they have treated me;*
> *I thought I fought on the islands to get rid of their kind;*
> *But I can see the fight lots plainer now that I am blind.*

Canada helped the Southern Negro Youth Congress organize an anti-lynching rally in South Carolina. He sent Orson Welles a telegram urging the director to appear with Isaac Woodward at the rally, arguing that it would strike a blow against the Ku Klux Klan and inspire liberal forces in the south.

On August 3, the cast and crew of *On Whitman Avenue* celebrated their hundredth performance, a benchmark of success for any Broadway production. But the show was teetering on the brink of ruin, and everyone on the Great White Way knew it.

The *New York Post* reported that backers had not recouped their initial investment, and many nights the box office was still lucky to break even. Producer Theresa Helburn, long associated with the Theater Guild, editorialized in *The New York Times* that "special appeal" plays like *On Whitman Avenue* would fare better in some kind of new "experimental" theater, rather than on Broadway.

Lee and Marvin wrote a joint response for the *Times*. While they both supported the idea of an experimental theater, "it is a remote hope for the present," they said. "And in the meanwhile, what? No plays with special appeal?" Socially and politically charged dramas couldn't wait around until somebody invented a new kind of theater, they argued: "Even under the hazardous conditions of Broadway production, such plays can succeed."

Or at least partially succeed. The two men had fought the good fight, they achieved victories, but they didn't win the war. "Nothing I or anybody else did could keep *On Whitman Avenue* open," Richard Adler wrote, calling the production "another daring and worthwhile experiment dead of avoidance by the public."

Canada and Mark were forced to announce that after fourteen weeks and 150 performances, *On Whitman Avenue* would be forced to shutter on September 14. Bitterly disappointed, the producers admitted to trade papers that their show would close in the red. (The final financial statement lists total income at $140,700 in gross receipts plus $60,000 raised by investors; expenses exceeded $213,000.) They mailed letters to their thirty-odd investors warning them to expect no dividends, although they hoped to make good on everyone's losses by organizing touring productions and selling film rights. This turned out to be a pipe dream. Though they sent pitches to a hundred studios and producers, legitimate offers failed to materialize.

Canada had sunk most of his savings into *On Whitman Avenue*. Never a brilliant money manager, his bank accounts were running dangerously low. As soon as the show finished its funereal march, he would need some well-paying work, and fast.

Mark Marvin floated an idea past Robert L. Joseph of United Attractions and the producer bit the hook. The two men would coproduce a road tour of *Othello* with Canada in the lead and Philip Huston as Iago. (Huston, son of actor Walter Huston, had been in *The Tempest* with Canada.) A press release said that Lee would spend eight months "on a real old-fashioned barn-storming tour of the United States, with runs in Australia and England to follow" before the show transferred to Broadway.

Lee was delighted. The tour would put much-needed money in the bank, but more importantly, it would give him a chance to shine in a role he had long wanted to play. "My reigning ambition is to play the Moor in *Othello*," he once told *Ebony*. "I know I can give the part a new interpretation and I feel it would open a new field for the Negroes who aspire to act." When asked how playing Othello could do that, he said: "I'll play Othello not like a blacked-up white man but like a genuine Negro. I'll give the part dignity and make the Moor a beautiful character. If I'm a success it will prove to the producers and public that Negroes can play roles other than old Mammies."

Emotions ran high during the final performance of *On Whitman Avenue*. After the show, Canada made the rounds, personally thanking every actor, understudy, manager, assistant, stagehand, and usher for their hard work and steadfast support. Then he changed out of his costume for the last time, packed up his belongings, including faded telegrams that had graced his dressing room since opening night, and headed back to the midtown apartment he still shared with Mark Marvin.

Minutes after he walked in the door, his phone rang. That call would lead to one of the strangest experiences of Canada's life — and an opportunity for the actor to make history on the American stage once again.

🦶   🦶   🦶

The Duchess of Malfi was in Rhode Island, desperately seeking an assassin.

Written in 1613 by John Webster, *Malfi* is a revenge drama stuffed with secrets, schemes, and bloody deeds. This production boasted impressive credentials. The famed English poet W. H. Auden had adapted the script; the striking Elisabeth Bergner starred as the Duchess opposite film legend John Carradine; and Benjamin Britten composed the show's incidental music. Director George Rylands had scored a great success with the *Duchess* in London the previous season. Producer Paul Czinner, Bergner's husband, had arranged for the play to tour Providence, Boston, Hartford, and New Haven before opening mid-October on Broadway.

A week before the play was scheduled to premiere in Providence, the actor cast in the crucial role of Daniel de Bosola, spy and assassin, abruptly announced he was quitting the show due to poor health. Czinner and Bergner wracked their brains for a feasible—and immediate—replacement. Tickets were selling well for the tour, and advance sales in New York already topped fifty thousand dollars. "If we only could get someone with real playing power—someone like Canada Lee, a white Canada Lee!" they told each other.

Then Bergner said: "Wait a minute. Why *not* ask Canada Lee?"

Czinner got the actor's number in New York and phoned to offer him the role, just hours after Lee gave his last performance in *On Whitman Avenue*.

This particular call from Providence was serendipitous indeed.

In the play, the eponymous Duchess is a widow who has inherited land, title, and money. Her two brothers urge her to stay chaste, single, wealthy, and under their complete control. They hire ex-convict Daniel de Bosola to spy on their young sister, lest she try to wed again. Bosola soon discovers that the Duchess has already secretly married a man of lower rank and (equally secretly, somehow) given birth to several children. Furious at the Duchess for defying their wishes and dishonoring the family name, the brothers order Bosola to strangle her. Bosola murders the innocent woman, and then, sick with remorse, kills the wicked brothers, but not before he, too, is mortally wounded.

Bosola was a fascinating role, but infinitely more important to Canada was the opportunity to break another color barrier. If he accepted the role, he would be the first actor of color to play a white character on an American stage.

However, stepping into the show at this late date would be a Herculean task. Czinner and Bergner wanted Lee to make his debut on opening night at Providence's Metropolitan Theater, a mere five days hence. Lee would have to memorize hundreds of lines and learn complicated staging; he wasn't at all sure he could do it. There were other problems as well. First and foremost, what would this do to *Othello*?

Canada telephoned Robert Joseph and Mark Marvin, who had already raised thousands of dollars for *Othello* and were now negotiating with theaters. Not surprisingly, they were reluctant to postpone the tour. However, the three men worked out an amicable compromise. The tour would be postponed a few weeks. When *Malfi* moved to Broadway in October, Lee would rehearse *Othello* during the day while performing Bosola at night. After *Malfi's* limited run was over, Lee would immediately hit the road with *Othello*.

One problem solved, but there was still another. Canada had agreed to make several major public appearances to support antilynching legislation in the next few weeks, and he insisted on honoring his commitments. A bit frantic at this point, Czinner agreed.

On Monday, September 16, Canada made a quick trip to Chicago to speak at an antilynching rally. More than two thousand people, mostly black, gathered on Michigan Avenue near the Loop to hear Canada speak, along with Malcolm C. Dobbs of the Southern Conference for Human Welfare. During the rally, a thirty-one-year-old white man from Tennessee reportedly snipped a wire connecting a loudspeaker to the sound truck. The man was surrounded by an angry mob demanding his arrest. A reporter on the scene wrote: "Police quickly spirited the Southerner to safety as some Negroes shouted: 'Let's lynch him—treat him the way they treat us in the South!'"

The following day, Czinner announced to the press that Canada Lee would step into the role of Daniel de Bosola in *The Duchess of Malfi*. Newspapers from coast to coast and in the West Indies reported this historic event, the "first time in theatrical history a producer had selected the man he considered the best actor for a role regardless of color."

It was also the first time a black actor would play a classical role in whiteface.

"There's nothing at all unusual about a white entertainer appearing in blackface," wrote reporter Sam Zolotow in *The New York Times*. "But a Negro performer disguised as a white actor is a rarity indeed. Such an assignment has been accepted by Canada Lee in *The Duchess of Malfi*." Zolotow drily pointed out that the show's producer no doubt "realized the publicity value of the stunt, too."

White actors had long played roles in blackface. "The practice had originated in the days of slavery, when Negroes were not permitted to appear on stage," writes film historian Donald Bogle. "White minstrels blackened themselves with burnt cork better to mock and caricature the plantation slaves they imitated." After the Civil War, when freed slaves formed minstrel companies, black performers still used cork on their faces because white audiences expected it. The legendary vaudeville comedian Bert Williams was still darkening his already dark face in the early 1900s.

Canada was prepared to flip this practice on its head to prove that black actors could and should be cast in traditionally white roles. He rushed to Providence, trying to memorize his lines on the way. He plunged into nonstop rehearsals at the theater and in his rooms at the Hotel Biltmore. Every waking minute he was practicing his lines, rehearsing the staging, or standing impatiently through costume and wig fittings.

And then, of course, there was the makeup.

"Bosola . . . is a Spaniard who has recently arrived in Italy, and these conditions call for a man of swarthy complexion," reported the *Providence Bulletin*. "For several days there had been conflicting reports as to how white Lee's makeup would appear. Company officials were careful to stress that although they were not changing the Bosola role from that of a white man to that of a Negro, the part did not call for the actor to look the way a white man would, for instance, in a drawing-room comedy."

Makeup artists experimented with different concoctions. If too thin, it dissolved in sweat under the lights. Too thick, it looked like Canada was smeared in plaster of Paris. Thankfully, specialists at a cosmetics company learned of Lee's predicament. Covermark had been founded by Lydia O'Leary, a Massachusetts woman refused a job because of the port-wine birthmark on her face. O'Leary patented a special makeup to cover birthmarks, scars, and other blemishes, and her company now came to Canada's aid with a face paint that was perspiration-proof, but still allowed his skin to breathe.

Journalists traveled from Harlem to Providence during final dress rehearsals. "Watching the make-up expert apply the specially prepared grease paint, we weren't entirely convinced the trick could be done effectively," reporter Bill Chase wrote.

In truth, makeup was the least of Lee's worries. Poised to make theater history, with the press crawling all over the story, Canada panicked. Five days hadn't given him enough time to learn all those lines. Hours before the premiere, he refused to go on.

"We journeyed up to Providence . . . for what we thought was a pretty dambig [sic] assignment, that of witnessing for the first time the almost unbelievable phenomenon of a Negro playing the role of a white man," Chase wrote. "We arrived at the theatre and Canada told us the role was such a lengthy one that he was afraid to take a chance of performing that night." Chase and many others in the audience were sorely disappointed when director George Rylands went on as Bosola in Lee's place.

Paul Czinner announced that Lee would debut the role in Boston instead. By the time *Malfi* arrived in Beantown, the show was a sellout. Canada Lee in whiteface was the talk of the town, although some of that talk was negative. Boston was a segregated city, as cast and crew learned when their fashionable hotel refused to honor Canada's reservation. "For a time it looked as if the gifted actor would have no place to sleep," *The Boston Post* reported. Elisabeth Bergner offered her suite to Lee, but the hotel nixed that idea. After a three-hour search, Lee was shown to second-class rooms in the theater district.

Some townspeople grumbled at the mixed-race cast, demanding to know why the producers didn't hire a white actor for the role. "The answer seems to be that there are no white actors now available on Broadway capable of playing it properly. It was *necessary* to hire Canada Lee," the *Post* reported. "Bosola is one of the scurviest wretches in the whole gamut of drama. Talent isn't enough for the actor who would play him: He must have the capacity to suggest utter villainy."

First Caliban, monster of evil mien, now Bosola, the contemptible villain—Canada may have wondered if he was truly breaking down barriers for black actors or pigeonholing them as nefarious characters instead. In interviews, he emphasized his artistic and political goals. Playing

Bosola, he said, "can open up vast new fields to the Negro actor whose parts previously have been limited by color."

"I hope it will be a long step toward becoming 'actor Canada Lee,' not 'Canada Lee, Negro actor,'" he told the press.

Three days before the opening, critic Elliott Norton called Lee's performance a test case. "Theoretically there is no reason why a colored actor should not play any role for which he is qualified, in the whole range of drama, regardless of color," he wrote, adding "the native hue of their skin has not prevented Caucasian players from assaying characters of every other race."

For well over a century on the American stage, white actors had appeared in black-, yellow-, and red-face, including Edwin Booth as Othello; Otis Skinner as an African beggar in *Kismet*; and Mabel Morrison as a Native American in *The Squaw Man*. Hollywood followed suit, casting Peter Lorre as the Japanese detective Mr. Moto; Luise Rainer and Paul Muni as a Chinese couple in *The Good Earth*; Rex Harrison as the Asian king in *Anna and the King of Siam*; Philip Reed as the scout Uncas in *The Last of the Mohicans*; and Dorothy Lamour as a Tahitian bombshell.

While black actors were historically "barred from playing any character of size or stature unless they did it in a company of their own fellows and probably for an audience of their own race," Norton wrote, "*Malfi* marks the first time a colored man has had the opportunity to appear as a white man, to try his ability in what is really a classic, alongside of white players." The critic wished Canada good luck, adding that he hoped the whiteface proved convincing because "democracy should be made to work in the theater."

The black press provided historical perspective as well, pointing out that while the American theater crowed over its newfound democratic casting, Europe had embraced the concept a century earlier when African American actor Ira Aldridge won fame and fortune playing Shakespearean roles on continental stages.

Four steps must be taken to emancipate African American actors, wrote Bill Chase in the *New York Amsterdam News*. The first two—eradicating minstrelsy and the eternal menial—were still in process. The third step was interracial casting in leading roles; Paul Robeson set this precedent in *All God's Chillun Got Wings* and *Othello*. Now Canada Lee was about to take the fourth and final step, "the presentation of an actor solely on his ability and without thought of his color." Chase hailed Lee as "the pioneer in a venture which may well revolutionize the plight of the talented Negro, whose traditional roles in the theater and movies have been relegated to the lot of buck-eyed buffoons and menial servants."

On September 23, Canada the pioneer was nervous as a kitten. That very night, he was expected to make his debut as Daniel de Bosola in whiteface before the Boston critics and God and everybody, and he still didn't know all of his lines.

Just a few hours before curtain time, Paul Czinner was once again forced to tell a disappointed audience that Lee was not yet ready. An understudy covered the role, and the next day newspapers throughout the country reported that Canada had delayed his momentous debut a second time. The actor knew the first two acts cold, according to *The New York Times*, but his third act was still shaky. "I don't want to mess this up by a poor performance," Lee told reporters.

Two days later, the actor found the confidence and courage he needed, and the audience watched with amazement—some with delight and pride—as Canada Lee made history by taking the stage as a seventeenth-century white man.

His long-awaited debut as Daniel de Bosola was not exactly a triumph. He fumbled some lines and forgot others entirely, and overall the show was a bit rocky. Though critics freely criticized the production, they treated Lee's flawed performance with generosity and respect. "He showed that he, too, is a versatile, able artist," *Billboard* wrote. "When he has mastered the rhythm of the verse and the feel of the play, he will be superb." The *Christian Science Monitor* was more parsimonious in its praise. "So far as his appearance was concerned, his performance may be set down as a success," the review read. "In other respects, his impersonation was less satisfactory . . . His voice was badly controlled, his readings suggested only a vague notion of the thought behind the lines, his gestures were stilted, and his facial play gave no hint of what Bosola was thinking."

Nearly every review discussed Lee's appearance, some in great detail.

"In profile, there was no hint of his race," observed Elliott Norton. "When he faced the audience squarely, the flatness of his nose was strikingly apparent. As the afternoon wore on, however, you could forget about that. Perhaps this was the most striking thing about the whole performance: There were some scenes in which you forgot entirely that he was a colored man in makeup."

The white press, the black press, wire services, and radio stations coast-to-coast filed stories, reporting that audiences were "stunned" and "astounded." There was Canada, in hundreds of magazines and newspapers, in whiteface and wig, before and after, natural and painted, in profile and full-face—a novelty photo. For many Americans, Lee's principal claim to fame was his ability to successfully impersonate a white man.

This was ironic and more than a little frustrating to Lee. He had no desire to pretend to be white. He wanted to see black actors cast in the classics *without regard* to race. Revolutionary in his time, this concept is now taken for granted on stage and on screen, though it's often given more lip service than action. Canada fervently believed he should be allowed to play any role. He only permitted himself to be painted because in 1946, that was the only way he could play a white man on stage.

Lee's courageous effort to break this color barrier was undermined by the tabloid reporters who treated it as cheap titillation or a publicity stunt. This got the actor in some hot water at home. "Canada Lee's turning 'whiteface' in *The Duchess of Malfi* angered many of the sepia intelligentsia," Lew Sheaffer noted in the *Brooklyn Eagle*.

Nevertheless, advance sales were strong on Broadway, no doubt boosted by Ed Sullivan's glowing report in his *New York Daily News* column: "You always felt that Negro star Canada Lee was greater than Spencer Tracy. Well, at Boston, he's winning raves, playing the part of a white, via a white paste makeup."

The *Duchess* swept into Broadway's Ethel Barrymore Theater for her October 15 premiere. Harry Wagstaff Gribble, who directed Canada in *Anna Lucasta*, sent the actor a good-luck telegram paraphrasing *Hamlet*: "Thou didst not have to cast thy nighted color off to be as a friend, but we hail thee with pride and affection as the new white hope."

The Duchess of Malfi had never been on Broadway before. After the beating she suffered at the hands of New York critics, it's no wonder the lady has seldom returned.

John Gassner: "It is my unpleasant duty to report that *The Duchess of Malfi* production made the old play look like a mildewed heirloom."

John Chapman: "Historians say it has never before been played on Broadway. After a rather long evening of it, I have an idea that all the generations of actors and managers who could have presented it and didn't had the right idea."

Howard Barnes: "Even the research student is likely to find *The Duchess of Malfi* a preposterous bore. Vaguely resuscitated on the stage of the Ethel Barrymore Theater, the John Webster melodrama makes a cogent plea for being left in the library."

While the play suffered a drubbing, Canada drew high praise. "His performance was vastly to his credit," Gassner wrote. "It showed how greatly he had progressed as an actor, how well he had acquired fluency, flexibility, and ease." *The London Daily Telegraph* called Lee the most interesting feature in the whole production. Brooks Atkinson of *The New York Times Theater Review* expressed "delight" over this proof that Lee "has acquired mastery of the stage."

In most reviews, however, Canada's makeup got more ink than his acting. Barnes called his face paint a "stunt" as unsuccessful as the play itself. Atkinson agreed, but more charitably: "He counterfeits a white man about as successfully as a white man in burnt cork counterfeits a Negro—which is hardly at all. But that is only an amusing detail by comparison with the intelligence, ease and scope of Mr. Lee's acting." Ward Morehouse sniped: "He presents a rather comical figure, although his lot is one of tragedy. His extraordinary make-up consists of flesh-colored grease paint, a thick wig, bushy eyebrows, a goatee and a putty nose." Richard Watts, Jr., completely disagreed, calling Canada's appearance in whiteface a "tour-de-force."

Damon Runyon, a former sportswriter and legendary chronicler of New York's underworld, was weak and sick due to a long battle with throat cancer, but he made the trip to Broadway to see a former prizefighter tread the boards in whiteface. Runyon noted offhandedly that Canada didn't merely play a villain, but a real "stinker."

Right-wing columnist Westbrook Pegler read that and worked up a fierce head of steam. A black man playing a white stinker? How dare he! "Our blackface white men," Pegler protested, always play "comedy Negroes" with "no malice or disparagement of the colored people in anything they did." He dismissed the idea that blackface was degrading, adding that all this business about discrimination was just "propaganda." Sure, those Negroes were a bit "put-upon," but Pegler argued that most talk about racism came from Communists who didn't really care about improving "the colored man's condition," they only wanted to "create friction, strike sparks, and cause commotions." Pegler implied that by agreeing to play an evil white man, Canada proved he was either a gullible idiot duped by Communists or a Commie himself. Hearst papers and other conservative journals across the country printed Pegler's column.

Poor, abused *Duchess of Malfi* limped along at the box office. Despite the abysmal reviews, curiosity over Canada sold just enough tickets to keep the show afloat.

In November, an eye-catching and obviously staged photo appeared in the *Daily Worker*. Lee was standing backstage at *Malfi*, decked out in the now-familiar whiteface and wig, smiling at three attractive young women. A caption explained that the Broadway star was sponsoring the upcoming "Boot Out Bilbo Ball," a fund-raiser supporting a campaign to remove the white supremacist from the Senate. The girls were members of the Southern Negro Youth Congress (SNYC), which was organizing the dance.

More radical than most other civil rights organizations of the period, SNYC urged black Americans to vote, organize, and actively oppose police brutality, mob violence, and segregation. Founded in the 1930s by black Communists and progressives, SNYC had long before attracted FBI attention. When the *Daily Worker* published the showy publicity photo advancing SNYC's Bilbo Ball, the FBI clipped it and put it in Lee's file.

The note-takers hadn't slackened their surveillance work in the past twenty-four months. In fact, 1946 had been a banner year as HUAC added fifteen cards to Canada's file while the FBI's dossiers fattened up with more than a dozen reports.

What were Lee's suspicious activities in 1945 and 1946?

HUAC's neatly typed cards document them succinctly. He received the *New Masses* award for greater interracial understanding, and per-

formed in the infamous "How Do You Spell Democracy?" sketch at a
"Rally for Democratic Japan." He signed a *New York Times* ad condemning U.S. support for Franco's fascist Spain, backed Communist and
left-wing candidates for City Council, and lent his name to the annual
May Day Parade. He defended the rights of a black rape victim whose
white attackers went unpunished in Alabama, and raised money for the
orphaned children of a black veteran killed in cold blood by a white policeman. He backed "Veterans Against Discrimination," which helped
returning soldiers of color find better jobs and housing. He was on a
"Committee to Win the Peace," trying to get U.S. troops out of China.
He sponsored a conference on the Far East, seeking peaceful solutions to
political conflicts through the United Nations. He supported members
of the American Labor Party for carrying on the work of FDR's New
Deal. He spoke out against mob violence and lynching.

At the FBI, reports on Lee's questionable deeds could be found in
several investigation files. He fought to save the doomed FEPC, which
would have protected jobs for black workers. He performed in a skit
about V-J Day during the annual Lenin Memorial. He helped Paul
Robeson rally support for anticolonial movements and famine relief in
Africa. Together with Robeson, he honored labor leaders who were either Communists or Red sympathizers. And, once again, his vocal opposition of mob violence and lynching raised a flag.

In mid-November, *The Duchess of Malfi* died a relatively noble death.

Before the play gave up the ghost, Lee got a backstage visit from his
old friend Leonard de Paur. Canada said he had no regrets about wearing whiteface on Broadway. "This was beyond the realm of a stunt," de
Paur said. "He felt it was important to play this role because it gave him
a chance to play it as white man—to make a breakthrough."

Lee had reason to be proud of his accomplishments during the past
year. As Caliban in *The Tempest*, he had become the second black actor
to play a classical role on Broadway. He had made a respectable run with
On Whitman Avenue, shattering a color barrier as the first black producer to present a drama on Broadway He had made history in the American theater by playing a traditionally white role in *The Duchess of Malfi*.

Canada was eager to take his ambitious campaign to desegregate the stage even further. After he finished the *Othello* tour, Lee intended to play Shakespeare on Broadway again, this time starring as King Lear, without makeup, in a mixed-race cast. It would be the first time a black actor played one of the Bard's tragic heroes on a major American stage.

A bold idea, but it was not to be. Instead, Hollywood came calling once more, this time with a part that seemed to be written expressly for him.

TEN

BODY AND SOUL

RED SCARED

Back in 1943, when Canada was out in Hollywood filming *Lifeboat*, he bumped into screenwriter Robert Rossen. Both men were native New Yorkers and almost exactly the same age. Rossen had admired Lee as a prizefighter; he confessed to Canada that he had boxed a little in his youth, and once harbored dreams of being a contender. When Rossen said he hoped to direct a fight picture someday, Lee said: "Sign me up."

Rossen wasn't able to get the project moving quite as quickly as he had hoped. He had some writing contracts to honor, including scripts for two Lewis Milestone films, *A Walk in the Sun* (1945) and *The Strange Love of Martha Ivers* (1946).

"A year went by," Lee said, "and another went by and another."

In 1946, while Canada was fighting to save *On Whitman Avenue*, Rossen was at Columbia Pictures making his directing debut with *Johnny O'Clock*, starring Dick Powell. Rossen knew the buzz on his film was very good and decided the time was ripe to pitch his pet project, the boxing picture. He took his idea to Enterprise Studios.

Enterprise was an anomaly in Hollywood: a small independent studio striving to turn out socially relevant films. Clout and money weren't lacking, however. One of the founders was David L. Loew, son of MGM founder Marcus Loew, and matinee idol John Garfield had also invested heavily in the company, along with a few other actors. Enterprise was a scrappy underdog in studio land, which may be the reason it was Rossen's first choice. As a writer, he had created sympathetic characters who battled the system, often to be destroyed by it. As fate would have it, Garfield had also been hoping to make a boxing picture about exactly that kind of man, based on the life of prizefighter Barney Ross. However, the boxer's drug addiction was considered too controversial to get past Hollywood censors. Rossen wanted to direct a boxing picture, and Garfield wanted to star in one—all they needed was a screenplay. Rossen had substantial credits, but Enterprise decided to hire another writer, possibly because Rossen still had to finish *Johnny O'Clock*. Someone at Enterprise suggested a fellow by the name of Abe Polonsky.

Another native New Yorker, Abraham Lincoln Polonsky had practiced law, taught English, scripted radio dramas for Orson Welles, and written several novels. During the war, he took a job as a screenwriter purely to serve as his cover while spying for the Office of Special Services, the forerunner of the CIA. When the war ended, the government said that as a returning GI he should get his "old job" back, and that's how he found himself in Tinseltown earning $450 a week as a screenwriter. Polonsky was working on the Paramount lot when he got the call.

"A friend of mine at Enterprise said the executives were looking for a boxing movie and they wanted me to write it," the writer recalled. "I had about an hour until I met with them." Polonsky struck out on foot to the Enterprise lot and made up a little boxing story on the way to the meeting. "I held them, enthralled them, and they were in business," he said. Enterprise offered him two thousand dollars a week to write the screenplay, and he accepted with alacrity. "It was a lot back then," Polonsky said, even after Paramount took a stiff 50 percent cut in return for loaning him out.

Body and Soul turns up on nearly every list of Hollywood's best fight films. The protagonist is Charlie Davis, a talented boxer from a poor Jewish family who falls under the sway of Roberts, an unscrupulous promoter. Roberts books Charlie into an exhibition bout against a former black champ named Ben Chaplin. Ben has a life-threatening clot in his brain, but he's desperate for money and accepts the match after Roberts promises Charlie will go easy on him. But the promoter says nothing to Charlie, and Ben nearly dies in the ring. Guilt-ridden, Charlie hires Ben as his trainer and the two become friends. When Charlie wins the title, Ben pleads with him to stay on the straight and narrow, but the champ, firmly in the clutches of Roberts, slides into drunken dissipation. Roberts orders Charlie to take a dive; Ben confronts the promoter and after a struggle, Ben dies. The loss of his friend gives Charlie the courage he needs to stand up to Roberts, redeeming himself in the eyes of his family and fans.

Casting for the film moved swiftly. Garfield, of course, would star as Charlie. Character actor Lloyd Gough took on Roberts, the evil promoter. And just before Christmas 1946, Rossen called Lee in New York to offer him the role of Ben Chaplin. "He had remembered me all that time," Canada said. "So many new things happen, so many new faces, so many new people, and he remembered. It was wonderful."

The connection between Rossen and Lee went deeper than New York and boxing. "The element common to many of my films is the desire for success, ambition, which is an important element in American life," Rossen once wrote. At the same time, he said, there are forces at work in our society that block men from achieving and the ambitious must sometimes "strike out against society" to order to "get on top."

It was a story line Canada knew all too well.

In Polonsky's script, Ben is exploited and demoralized by the system, personified by the evil Roberts. But Ben fights back and eventually emerges as the moral conscience of the film, its most sympathetic character, and the white champ's only true friend. These qualities push Ben's character dangerously close to the cliché of the faithful servant, the Uncle Tom, but Canada found Ben intelligent, courageous, and honest; the actor was convinced that the script showed the black fighter to be Charlie's equal, not his menial.

Lee was excited about the role and the film. He knew all the major players, either personally or by reputation. Nearly everyone was politically progressive. A few were in the Communist Party, including Rossen, Polonsky, and Lloyd Gough, an old friend of Canada's. This experience would be altogether different than *Lifeboat*, Lee thought: I certainly won't have to worry about nigger dialogue, and if something bothers me about a scene or my character, I can speak out and be heard.

Canada had no qualms about working with Communists, although there was plenty of Red-baiting by the conservative press in those days, particularly at the Hearst chain. Like most liberal activists, Lee often worked side-by-side with Party members on campaigns against segregation, lynching, poll taxes, and other injustices. Canada didn't care if there were Reds, pinks, or any shades in between on *Body and Soul*. He was thrilled to have an intelligent script in his hands that treated his character with respect. "For the first time in my acting career, I've found a film role which really satisfies both my artistic and social requirements," he said.

Lee made his second trip to Hollywood in January 1947. It was good luck for him that Enterprise was behind his new film. A union strike had slowed work to a standstill at mainstream studios, but Enterprise was exempt because it was partly owned by actors.

From the very beginning, *Body and Soul* was an earnestly left-wing endeavor. Rossen and the producers hired a diverse cast and crew to work on the film, including thirty black actors as extras and bit players. Rossen aimed to make black characters completely integral to the action; Southern censors who habitually lopped off "unessential" scenes with black characters would find it tough to cut anything out of this film. Canada's charm and sense of humor quickly unified the mixed-race cast and crew. The black press later reported that Lee had "an almost catalytic effect on race relations. On the *Body and Soul* set there was an unusual camaraderie between Negro and white players."

Canada forged an especially close friendship with John Garfield. Known as "Julie" to his pals, Garfield was born Julius Garfinkel on the Lower East Side in 1913. As a young actor, Garfield struggled to find work and left the stage at one point to ride freight trains as a hobo. After a stint with the Group Theater, he landed a contract with Warner Brothers and moved to Hollywood. In his first film, *Four Daughters*, he dominated the screen with his darkly sarcastic, dangerous, sexy presence. Warner Brothers knew a star when they saw one. With his unruly mop of dark hair and pugnacious grin, Garfield became one of the screen's favorite tough guys. By 1940, he was earning fifteen hundred dollars a week. Six years later, when his contract at Warner was up, Julie went over to the fledgling Enterprise, hoping to make better, more adventurous films.

As staunch liberals and committed activists, Julie and Canada immediately found much in common. On the set, Lee came to admire the film star for his generosity as an actor. "You rarely find as unassuming a guy as Julie," Lee said. "He constantly wanted to help me. We had some scenes together that he could have turned around for himself—after all, he's a big star—but he insisted they were my scenes."

Much admired for its stark beauty and realism, *Body and Soul* is best remembered for its fight footage. Cinematographer James Wong Howe expressed ring combat with unparalleled excitement and brutality. Howe used three cameras placed on cranes for overhead views, three mounted on dollies, and two held by hand. Strapped into roller skates, he took one of the hand-held cameras and told a grip to push him around the ring. "I wanted an effect where the boxer is knocked out and he looks up into a dazzle of lights," Howe later said. "With a heavy, fixed camera, you'd never get that." Circling the actors amid a flurry of punches, Howe jerked the hand-held camera slightly whenever blows landed on the champ. He let the camera go out of focus to suggest a pummeled fighter's groggy, punch-drunk point of view. This intimate, dynamic camerawork set a new standard for fight films.

Enterprise hired a technical advisor to coach Garfield and Lee through their fight scenes, and Canada had a good laugh when he found out who it was. Lee knew Johnny Indrisano all too well, having lost a match to him in Portland, Maine, back in 1932. The old pros exchanged a few jokes and a punch or two. Later, Lee told a columnist he took a lot of teasing from Julie and Johnny: "When I'm acting, they say I'm a good fighter. And when I'm fighting, they say I'm a good actor!"

Garfield was no chump in the ring; the actor had boxed in his youth and could still pack a punch. In their ring scenes, Julie and Canada "really battled it out with the gloves, and sported substantial bruises by the time the fighting sequences in *Body and Soul* were finished," the press reported. Garfield evidently suffered a mild heart attack filming one scene, and nearly knocked himself out by colliding with a camera boom in another.

Off the set, Lee and Garfield chatted and joked around, often talking about the day's news with Lloyd Gough over meals or during coffee breaks at the studio commissary. Politics made for hot topics in Hollywood canteens, and that was particularly true at their table. On any given day, conversation ranged from the implications of the union strike to the Soviet Union's annexations in Eastern Europe.

One day at lunchtime, a couple of reporters were at a table interviewing a young actress in the cast. The starlet was asked to comment on the current notion that Communists were infiltrating Hollywood. "I'm against communism, socialism, liberalism, anarchism, and all those other 'isms,'" the actress proclaimed archly.

Canada shot Gough a look across the table, his good eye twinkling mischievously, and asked, "Tell me, Mr. Gough, where do you stand on cannibal*ism*?" Gough chewed thoughtfully as Garfield and the rest of the cast giggled into their sandwiches.

Though Lee made light of Communist infiltration, the FBI had already heard from several informants that *Body and Soul* intended to espouse Communist propaganda—a charge that would dog the film and many people who collaborated on it.

Polonsky and Rossen did inject *Body and Soul* with a political context, but it would be a stretch of the imagination to call this picture Communist propaganda. The two men were particularly determined to block racist or reactionary messages from the film, which could easily be taken for subversive behavior in those days. If the FBI had a mole on the set, perhaps that's what incensed the informant.

Garfield was equally sensitive about the way race was handled. While filming one scene, he accidentally called Canada "boy" instead of "Ben." When Rossen shouted, "Cut! Print it," Garfield immediately protested, quick to point out his own mistake. At the star's insistence, Rossen shot the scene over so Julie could fix his line. "The funny thing is, I didn't notice his calling me boy," Lee later told a reporter. "When people call me boy—and I'm getting on in years—there's a deliberate condescension in it. But when he did it, it was so unlike the usual way, I passed it by. I knew what he stood for, and how he meant it, not the way the others meant it."

During the film shoot, Lee joined the board of HICCASP, the Hollywood Independent Citizens Committee on the Arts, Sciences, and Professions. The group lobbied studios to make more progressive films and to diversify their workforce, from the stars on the screen to the people behind the scenes. (Ronald Reagan had resigned from the group's board of directors in 1945 and later denounced it a Communist front.) HICCASP's agenda often found its way into Lee's press interviews about *Body and Soul.* "It's remarkable—in the whole picture you never hear the word 'Negro.' There is no differentiation made," Canada told one reporter. "I am just accepted as a character in a story. That must be the first time the movies have handled an American Negro like any other human being."

One day, when shooting was nearly finished, Rossen and Canada were talking about how the film would fare once it was released. The director predicted his picture would be banned in the South. "I don't understand that," Canada said. "My part has nothing to do with a white woman. Why do you think it's going to be banned?"

"You don't say 'Yassuh, boss,' anywhere in the film," Rossen told him. "When you talk to Garfield, you talk on the same level. He calls you Ben, you call him Charlie."

"The stupidity of it," Lee later told a reporter, clenching his fist. "All of a sudden you feel the viciousness of these people who won't accept a picture because it may affect their ideas about superiority and inferiority. You feel the futility. You wonder, you really wonder how a man can be a Negro and a good American at the same time. It calls for a lot of guts."

Canada had guts and class; it took both to deal with discrimination in Hollywood, both professional and personal. When a swank Hollywood eatery refused to serve him, sympathetic friends and colleagues organized an immediate boycott. One evening, Lee escorted a friend to a dinner-dance in place of her husband, who was sick in bed. Some of the guests were upset to see a mixed-race couple dancing. A haughty blonde made derogatory remarks as she danced past them with her date. Canada's friend was furious. "Don't say a word," Lee told her. "Calm down. It's OK." With a mischievous smile, the actor maneuvered his partner across the dance floor to a ringside table where a group of VIPs were sitting. Charlie Chaplin stood up and greeted Canada with a huge smile and hearty handshake. Lee introduced his dance partner—who was delighted to note the shocked expression of the blonde who had just insulted them.

But Lee had his fans in Hollywood, too. In March, the actor turned forty, and friends decided to fete him with a dinner party at a popular West Hollywood restaurant. They booked a private dining room, hoping to avoid any unpleasantness with white patrons, management, or staff. As it turned out, they needn't have worried. Two white waitresses recognized the actor and treated him like royalty the whole night. From his place of honor at the head of the table, Lee was absolutely radiant with delight.

That happiness evaporated days later when Canada received word that his sister, Claudia, had died suddenly of a heart ailment. The actor took a leave of absence from the film shoot and immediately traveled to New York City to attend the funeral. "He was very upset, just terribly upset," recalled Beulah Bullock, friend to both Claudia and Canada. "Claudia was the only daughter, the only girl. She was a talented person, a good woman, and the whole family loved her."

When Lee returned to the set, his spirits were noticeably low. As much as he loved working on *Body and Soul*, he was relieved when the film was done and he could head home to New York to spend time with family and friends. He left Hollywood with a deep sense of satisfaction, something he hadn't felt after completing his first film. "This picture I think, I hope, will do an awful lot towards getting me the kind of break I want out there," he told a reporter. "More important, if it's a success, it'll prove you can treat a Negro as a human being and still have a picture that'll sell. And if that is so, then we're on the way to something tremendous."

In fact, Canada was on his way into America's Red Scare nightmare.

The Red Scare began when Lee was still a boy in elementary school. Near the end of World War I, the Russian Revolution put Bolsheviks in power. Here at home, Bolshevik anarchists were accused of inciting violent labor struggles and terrorist bombings. A young up-and-comer in the Justice Department, J. Edgar Hoover, was chosen to head the new "Anti-Radical Division." He compiled membership lists of subversive organizations, collecting the names of 150,000 suspected radicals, including some 60,000 Communists. Hoover fervently believed that Communism was "the most evil, monstrous conspiracy against man since time began." Thousands of alleged anarchists, many of them innocent immigrants, were rounded up, beaten, and jailed. Super-patriotic organizations constantly watched for signs of creeping Bolshevism in our workplaces and our classrooms.

This initial Red Scare subsided in the mid-1920s, but Hoover continued to rise in stature, assuming directorship of the FBI in 1924, the same year Stalin rose to power in Russia. After the stock market crashed, Americans lost interest in the Red Menace as they struggled to find jobs, pay rent, and buy food. But anti-Soviet sentiments resurfaced when the American press described Stalin's brutal purges, the Great Terror of 1936–38. These reports confirmed the suspicions of the Red-fearing right and rocked the formerly sympathetic left. In 1938, Congress created the House Un-American Activities Committee to expose Communist plots in everything from organized labor to show business, including the Federal Theatre, Lee's first brush with Red-hunting.

Fear of Communism spiked in the fall of 1939 when Stalin and Hitler signed a nonaggression pact. Two years later, everything changed when the Nazis invaded the Soviet Union and America allied itself with its old enemy. Domestic propaganda quickly repositioned the Reds as our imperiled comrades. Americans eagerly read articles about brave Russians in *Life* magazine and flocked to movies like *Mission to Moscow*. Nazis became our new demons, and woe to anyone who depicted them as anything less, as Canada saw in the outcry against *Lifeboat*.

After the war ended, America watched uneasily as the USSR extended its political and military influence throughout Eastern Europe. The Truman Doctrine offered aid to countries threatened by Communist takeover, and Congress created the Central Intelligence Agency to spy on Soviet activites abroad. By 1947, the former allies had launched a volatile and dangerous Cold War between East and West. Domestic propaganda rekindled the Red Scare, portraying Communism as an alien and seditious movement determined to undermine democracy and destroy political freedom everywhere. Our former comrades-in-arms became a terrifying Red Menace. Members of the Communist Party here at home were suspect; party membership remained legal but was seen by many as despicable.

Hoover called for a holy war against the rising Red Tide, that "godless, truthless philosophy of life." He warned that Communists were infiltrating every aspect of American culture. He described Party members as "panderers of diabolic distrust." He started a secret Security Index of aliens and citizens whom he believed would be dangerous to national security in times of war or national crisis. In the first year alone, 10,673 names made the list, based on evidence fraught with innuendo, racism, antilabor prejudice, and partisan politics. Though he didn't know it, Canada Lee was on that list.

Conservative politicians thrived in the Red Scare's atmosphere of anxiety. Republicans had gained control over both House and Senate for the first time in sixteen years. The GOP believed the American people had given Republicans a mandate to fight Communism on all fronts. HUAC became a permanent standing committee to investigate "subversive and un-American propaganda activities." The 80th Congress set about launching twenty-two probes of Communism; in contrast, the 79th Congress had conducted only four.

Hollywood was an obvious target for Red-hunters. Liberals in show business openly expressed their political sentiments and supported controversial causes. The FBI already had Hollywood stars under surveillance as part of COMPIC, the ongoing investigation into Communism's influence over the motion picture industry. Clearly the game was afoot. More importantly, prying into the entertainment business virtually guaranteed headlines for HUAC and its chairman, J. Parnell Thomas, a Republican from New Jersey.

In May 1947, HUAC descended on Tinseltown for a series of closed hearings on alleged Communist activities in the film business. The FBI supplied HUAC staffers with information from COMPIC. The committee interviewed several "friendly witnesses," including Ronald Reagan and Walt Disney. Hollywood runs on gossip, and though the hearings were supposed to be secret, nearly everyone in town seemed to know who testified and what they said; on May 15, *The New York Times* published a front-page summary. Forty-one suspected Hollywood subversives had been named. More than a dozen were targeted for further investigation, and HUAC began compiling a witness list for October hearings in Washington, D.C.

On May 28, Congressman Karl E. Mundt, a HUAC member, presented a lengthy report on Communist activities in various fields, including show business. Reds recruited actors to add a little "dazzle" to Communist fronts, he said. Most of these stars "know little or nothing about politics," he added, "but their mere presence on committees and at rallies is certain to attract other people." He listed ten celebrities "persistently found in Communist fronts," including Canada Lee.

Though Canada probably had no idea his name had been dropped in Washington, the HUAC investigation into Hollywood subversives cannot have escaped his attention. Activists in show business were under attack, and Lee was a liberal with close friends on the far left, including Party members. He knew several who were named at the May hearings, including director Herbert Biberman and screenwriter John Howard Lawson.

Perhaps Lee thought he was safe because he had never joined the Party (or so he said; the FBI certainly believed he had). In any event, the HUAC hearings didn't put a damper on his political activities in the spring and summer of 1947. As usual, he was tapped to support a wide range of causes. He aided efforts to settle displaced Jews in Palestine and helped raise funds for an underground army led by Menachem Begin that was fighting to free Palestine from British rule. He spoke out against the Taft-Hartley bill, nicknamed the slave-labor bill by unions because it severely curtailed workers' rights to organize, bargain collectively, and strike. Lee entertained at a benefit for the Progressive Citizens of America, which promoted peaceful relations with the Soviet Union, nuclear disarmament, and a strong United Nations; that platform earned the group "subversive" status as the Cold War grew chillier. Canada also received an award for his ongoing campaigns against segregation and lynching, and he agreed to star in a movie short with Lena Horne designed "to slap race hatred and Jim Crow," the *Daily Worker* wrote. "The film reportedly tells the story of a Negro butler who changes places with his white master (in a dream), with the latter thus forced to perform the racial stereotypes to which Negro actors are limited."

Though Lee clearly remained committed to political activism, the actor spent most of his time that summer working on three new creative projects.

His first idea was to establish a fully integrated Shakespeare repertory company. He would produce *Macbeth* and *Othello* on alternating nights and play the starring roles. "In *Macbeth*, the Negro actor would do a carbon of his feat in the legiter, *The Duchess of Malfi*—that is, play whiteface," *Variety* reported. "For *Othello*, he'd reverse to the natural." Canada hoped to recruit screen stars, noted the trade paper, adding: "He's also dickering with film industry people who will probably bankroll the project."

Studio moguls? Backing a mixed-race theater company? In the middle of a Red scare targeting Hollywood's liberal left? Heads wagged. Doors slammed. Project one, admittedly idealistic, quickly fizzled.

The second project involved a whimsical attempt to rewrite the opera *Turandot* as a musical. Retitled *The Reluctant Virgin*, it featured book and lyrics by Maurice Valency and music by a virtually unknown composer named Albert Hague (who later won a Tony for scoring Bob Fosse's *Redhead* and the hearts of kids everywhere for composing the music to *How the Grinch Stole Christmas*). Canada aimed to produce the show on Broadway with choreography by his friend Bruhs Mero. After rounding up some other backers, he organized a summer tryout at an open-air theater in Cleveland's Caine Park. Locals found the title too racy, so the show opened as *The Reluctant Lady*.

The lady was indeed reluctant; she never left Cleveland, thanks to her lackluster reviews, and project two fizzled as well.

Canada's third project was *The Painted Wagon*. He and actor Philip Huston (from the not-yet-materialized but still-not-forgotten *Othello* "barnstorming" tour) were eager to do the new play, but no one else seemed interested in producing it commercially. Canada and Philip took the play to Lucille Lortel, an actress who had retired early from the stage to become a socialite after marrying a fabulously wealthy chemical engineer. "They asked if they could read it for my theater friends to get their reactions," Lortel recalled. "I said, 'Sure,' and arranged for the reading to take place in my barn."

The play was read, and to Canada's chagrin, nobody liked it. Lortel's offbeat venue was a huge success, however. The renowned "White Barn Theater" in Westport, Connecticut, has since premiered works by Tennessee Williams, Edward Albee, and Lanford Wilson, while its drama school boosted the careers of Mariette Hartley, Peter Falk, Linda Hunt, and other actors. (Lortel would later found the Lucille Lortel Theater. An anniversary present from her husband in 1955, the well-known Off-Broadway house at 121 Christopher Street remains an active theater to this day.)

When project three fizzled, it marked a disappointing end to a frustrating summer. Canada took solace in the company of friends and a few fleeting female companions.

While Canada sang the blues, the one he loved was hearing samba in the streets.

In the 1940s, most Americans imagined Brazil as a land of vast coffee plantations bordered by a mysterious rain forest and peopled by exotic, dark-skinned natives who picked the aromatic beans and danced at Carnival. In fact, Brazil was in political and economic turmoil—a nation striving to leave behind its colonial past in favor of industrialization and commerce, a land of burgeoning cities and sprawling shantytowns where the rich elite held sway over millions of illiterate, unskilled poor who struggled to survive in the new market economy.

Ruled for more than a decade by the popular dictator Getúlio Vargas, Brazil had broken its historically close ties with Germany during the war. More than twenty-five thousand Brazilian combat troops had served with the Allies, and the government provided the United States with key bases on the Atlantic. To strengthen this valuable relationship with Brazil, the U.S. State Department had created the Office of Inter-American Affairs, with Nelson Rockefeller in charge, and during the mid- to late-1940s American companies, American dollars, and American citizens poured into Brazil.

One of those citizens was a striking young woman with a head for business.

In the fall of 1945, Frances had arrived in Brazil with a couple of suitcases and a determination to start a new life with good, honest, hard work in real estate, banking, whatever she might find. She eventually settled down in Rio de Janiero, where she had befriended an American couple who worked in the U.S. Embassy. She traveled, she met interesting people; she learned to drink gin and tonics and swear a little in Portuguese when necessary. On weekends and holidays, she worked up a good tan on the beach and dated a few handsome men.

And yet . . . she still missed Canada.

"I knew the whole time I was in Brazil that I was still in love with Canada," Frances said. "I didn't know how I was going to get over him."

She came across hotels and kiosks that sold American newspapers and magazines, and found herself scanning the headlines, looking for his name or his picture. Despite her pledge to put the past behind her, to concentrate on her own dreams and ambitions, she couldn't stop herself from following Canada's career: "Not one day went by that I didn't think of him, wondering how he was, and what he was doing."

Lee was about to give her some interesting reading material.

🐾   🐾   🐾

As the summer of 1947 ended, Canada, like many show business people, turned his attention to the upcoming HUAC hearings on Communist activities in Hollywood.

On September 21, the press reported that the committee had subpoenaed forty-three producers, writers, actors, and directors, including Robert Rossen. *Body and Soul* had not been released yet, although select critics had been invited to a preview screening. (A reviewer for the *Daily Worker* had called the film "an indictment against exploitation and corruption" that "rises above the ranks of ordinary film fare.") Of those subpoenaed, nineteen, including Rossen, were defined as "unfriendly witnesses" who would not cooperate with the hearings.

The HUAC hearings were perceived as a significant threat to the film industry. Artists worried about the oppressive social and intellectual climate, while studio heads feared the HUAC attack might hurt box-office business. Editorialists in the nation's most important publications opposed the hearings that they viewed, at worst, as a violation of the First Amendment, and at best, as a tacky publicity stunt. "Don't look for any so-called corrective legislation to result from the forthcoming Un-American Activities Committee investigation of Communism in Hollywood," warned *Newsweek*. "Primarily the committee is fishing for headlines."

Fishing or not, the committee was certainly reeling them in. To fight back, the "unfriendly nineteen" took their case to the American people, positioning themselves as civil libertarians fighting for free speech. This argument found support in Hollywood, especially among liberals who believed that the HUAC hearings represented an assault on personal and artistic freedoms. This kind of talk dominated lunch conversation one day at Lucy's restaurant, across from the Paramount lot. If HUAC was going to use headlines to attack the Hollywood left, then by golly, Hollywood should fight back by making headlines of its own.

"We have to fight fire with fire!" decided the lunch group, which included directors William Wyler and John Huston, and screenwriter Philip Dunne. The three men founded the star-studded Committee for the First Amendment (CFA), whose members included Humphrey Bogart, Lauren Bacall, Danny Kaye, and Ava Gardner.

The CFA's mission, according to Dunne, was to fight four major threats: "The threat of a blacklist; the threat of censorship; official inquiry under threat of contempt of any citizen's legal political beliefs and affiliations; and the indiscriminate trial and conviction by headline of hun-

dreds of persons deprived of any legal opportunity to defend themselves."
All CFA members opposed Communism, Huston said, but they believed
that "mass hysteria was no way to fight it." The group placed ads in the
Hollywood Reporter and other trade papers criticizing HUAC's methods,
and began to work on forthcoming nationwide radio broadcasts to protest
the hearings.

While Hollywood did its bit for free speech, Broadway was also organizing.

On October 14, actor John Garfield sent mimeographed letters to a
number of politically progressive friends and colleagues, inviting them to
discuss a proposed campaign against the HUAC hearings. Writer Jerome
Chodorov and dancer Paul Draper also signed the letter. On Thursday
evening, October 16, the three organizers and thirty other theater luminaries crowded into Draper's apartment at 131 East Sixty-sixth Street.
Canada was there, along with his friend Paul Stewart (from *Native
Son*), actress Uta Hagen, writers (and twin brothers) Julius and William
Epstein, producer Oscar Serlin, and writer Irwin Shaw. William Pomerance represented the Screenwriters Guild. A reporter from *Variety* arrived and said he might write a story about the group.

Present as well was an actor and FBI informant, identity unknown,
who kept a scrupulous account of the evening.

According to the informant, Draper presided. He "outlined with sarcasm" the investigation by HUAC "and belittled the charges against
those subpoenaed." Pomerance then took the floor, arguing that HUAC
was trying to break up guilds and unions at the behest of Hollywood producers. Garfield quickly disagreed. An attorney representing some of the
subpoenaed artists "spoke brilliantly of the Bill of Rights, free speech,
civil rights, etc., and then left the meeting." "Several crackpots" spoke of
"grievances, mostly personal," but Draper cut this off and urged everyone
to focus on a viable course of action the group could take to protest the
hearings. They discussed joining forces with their Hollywood colleagues
and raising money for full-page ads in top newspapers. Just then, Draper
received a long-distance phone call from "one of the subpoenaed" who
told the group that "help for them of any sort was urgently requested—
ads, money, radio." The informant couldn't identify the caller; the FBI
thought it was screenwriter Howard Koch, but it may also have been
Robert Adrian Scott.

The following day, FBI Agent Edward Scheidt interviewed the informant at his apartment. At 10:30 p.m., Scheidt sent a coded telegram from the New York office to Hoover in Washington. The telegram, marked "Urgent," summarized his interview: "All speakers denounced the House committee and indicated that the closed hearing was a witch hunt." The agent mailed a full report the next day; at the end, Scheidt said the informant, "Mr. [*name blacked out*], requested that his contact by this office and the information he supplied the Bureau be treated as highly confidential since any publicity in this regard would greatly affect his future employment and present commitments."

Undoubtedly, it would have lost him friends as well.

Broadway's "Committee on First Amendment Defendants" named Draper its acting treasurer and affiliated itself with the Hollywood CFA. Contributions poured in. Garfield learned that the Hollywood wing was making plans to charter a plane to Washington. Soon, Garfield and Draper announced that the Broadway CFA would also fly an all-star contingent to the nation's capital to protest the hearings.

On Monday, October 20, 1947, at 10:30 a.m. in the crowded Caucus Room of the Old House Office Building in Washington, HUAC launched its inquiry, a heady blend of showbiz hoopla and partisan politics conducted amid whirring newsreel cameras and popping flashbulbs. Portly and diminutive, Chairman J. Parnell Thomas presided over the proceedings, perched on a stack of telephone books and cushions so he could be properly photographed. The press continued to exhibit cynicism toward the hearings (*Variety* called them the "Red Quiz Barnum Show") but reporters and cameramen nevertheless turned out in force in the Caucus Room day after day.

"Scores of correspondents covered the proceedings, which took place before 30 microphones, six newsreel cameras, and blazing klieg lights," relayed *The New York Times*. "Fervent applause, boos, cheers, hisses and laughter punctuated the packed session, at which Mr. Thomas presided with a rapping gavel and flourishes of rhetoric."

The Broadway CFA contingent chartered a DC-3 to Washington and on October 23, Canada boarded the plane along with John Garfield, Paul Stewart, Paul Draper, Uta Hagen, Julius and William Epstein, actress Bernice Parks, Irwin Shaw, and Oscar Serlin. After landing at National Airport, the group took taxis to the Old House Office Building.

Film fans swarmed around Garfield, pleading for autographs. The star obliged and then announced that he was here to conduct a press conference. Word spread to the press, and the cameras came clicking in a hurry. Garfield, Canada, and the rest of the Broadway CFA gathered near the Caucus Room, where the day's HUAC hearings had just concluded. Garfield climbed a set of steps so he could be seen and began to read a statement denouncing the hearings as "an outrage to human decency."

FBI Agent Guy Hottel was there. He reported that the crowd grew "voluminous and unruly." Garfield was ordered to go inside the Caucus Room and direct his remarks solely to the press but the actor refused on the grounds that "he wanted the public to hear what he had to say." Guards then "forcibly escorted him back into the Caucus Room," his fellow CFA members in tow. Only the media and Agent Hottel were allowed in. Reporters asked if the group was pro-Communist. Garfield, Lee, and others "denied vigorously that it was Communist, or anyone connected with it was a Communist or fellow traveler," Hottel stated, but in his opinion, the Broadway CFA took "the general Communist party line."

According to *New York Post* columnist Earl Wilson, Paul Draper, who had famously tap danced to music by Handel, Bach, and Beethoven, insisted that nobody in the group was Communist and that he didn't know a single Communist on Broadway.

"Not one?" a reporter asked, incredulous.

"Not one on Broadway," Draper said. Then, perhaps realizing how that sounded, he quickly added, "In fact, I don't know any Communists."

Several reporters snickered.

After the press conference, Earl Wilson placed a call to J. Edgar Hoover. This Broadway group claims to be anti-Communist, he said. What do you have on them? "I told Mr. Wilson that the Bureau files were confidential," Hoover noted in an internal memo. However, he hinted that the Bureau had nonclassified information readily available "if he knew where to look." Wilson promptly asked if he could interview an FBI spokesman on the record. Hoover agreed and told him to call back in half an hour.

In his next column, Wilson dismissed the CFA press conference as a crude publicity stunt by the Broadway stars who "swarmed down here to try to steal the circus from the big pro-committee movie stars." Though he professed ennui with the whole affair, Wilson nevertheless took care to name every prominent member and contributor of the New York CFA group, a list the FBI might well have put into his hands. Wilson dubbed it "A Broadway who's who!" He named writers Moss Hart, George S. Kaufman, Irwin Shaw, and Jerome Chodorov; producers Oscar Serlin and Cheryl Crawford; choreographer Agnes de Mille; composers Leonard Bernstein, Harold J. Rome, and Goddard Lieberson; conductor Daniel Saidenberg; music critic Olin Downes; and actors Philip Loeb, John Garfield, Paul Stewart, Uta Hagen, and Canada Lee. (Several in this group would later be blacklisted; in 1955, the unemployed and embittered Loeb committed suicide.)

The next day there were more press conferences and photo ops outside the Old House Building, and Canada attracted a fair amount of attention from conservatives, especially Southerners who thought Lee should be holding doors for them, not protesting. As always, Canada put discrimination at the top of his agenda. One morning, as the press headed inside for another day of testimony, he grabbed a reporter's arm. "How can they talk about Americanism when they still have segregation in Georgia?" Canada demanded.

"What's that got to do with these hearings?" the reporter coolly replied. After all, papers wanted sexy headlines about Reds and Pinks; segregation just didn't cut it.

Days later, the Broadway CFA drifted into the wings, upstaged by their glamorous movie star colleagues. "Humphrey Bogart, his sultry wife Lauren Bacall, Danny Kaye, and a score of other Hollywood celebrities landed in a special plane at the National Airport tonight after an all-day flight from the West Coast, fighting mad about the Congressional probe of Reds in film-land," the New York *Daily News* wrote on October 26.

Reporters flocked to the airport to interview the twenty-seven celestial beings just descended, which included actress Marsha Hunt. "We were revved up," Hunt recalled. "We were doing something new to all of us, and with a sense of mission." That same night, CBS broadcast the first segment of "Hollywood Fights Back," an anthology of ardent protests recorded by Judy Garland, Gene Kelly, Peter Lorre, Burt Lancaster, William Holden, Lucille Ball, and John Garfield, among others.

Canada couldn't stay in Washington any longer. It was campaign season, and he had agreed to lead a political rally for Congressman Adam Clayton Powell, Jr., and other Democrats at Harlem's Golden Gate Ballroom on October 27. He had also promised to appear at rallies for American Labor Party candidates and the Progressive Citizens of America that same week. Before leaving, he signed a CFA statement attacking the hearings, due to be published as an ad in major newspapers. He also told the Hollywood group that he would be happy to record a segment for their next "Hollywood Fights Back," but the bill was filled. On the next program, Vincent Price thanked a host of actors who couldn't be fitted into the broadcast, including Canada, Henry Fonda, Katharine Hepburn, Gregory Peck, and Rita Hayworth. A bit weary of Washington, Lee took the train home.

Other CFA members who stayed in Washington were in for a shock as they watched the hearings rapidly degenerate into name-calling and shouting matches. While the committee's high-handed tactics were appalling, CFA members were equally upset, even embarrassed, by the volatile and sometimes arrogant testimony given by the witnesses, whose performances at HUAC ranged from theatrical or comical to raucous and downright rude.

Writer John Howard Lawson was the first unfriendly witness to be called, and his aggressive retorts to the Chairman's hostile bullying antagonized not only the committee, but also many in the press corps and the audience. Lawson was asked the so-called $64,000 question: Are you now, or have you ever been, a member of the Communist Party of the United States? Lawson immediately accused the committee of attempting to "invade the basic rights of American citizens." As Chairman Thomas pounded his gavel, Lawson began to shout.

MR. LAWSON: You are using the old technique, which was used in Hitler Germany in order to create a scare here—
THE CHAIRMAN (*pounding gavel*): Oh—
MR. LAWSON: In order to create an entirely false atmosphere in which this hearing is conducted—
(*The Chairman pounding gavel*)

The shouting and pounding continued another minute or two, with Lawson accusing the committee of violating his rights as a U.S. citizen, and Thomas insisting that HUAC would get the answer to their question "if we have to stay here for a week." He asked Lawson again: "Have you ever been a member of the Communist Party?" Lawson replied acidly, "It is unfortunate and tragic that I have to teach this committee the basic principles of American—"

Thomas pounded his gavel. After a last bitter exchange, the Chairman cried, "Officers, take this man away from the stand." Some in the audience applauded; others booed.

Screenwriter Dalton Trumbo was next on the stand. He was, if anything, more ferocious than Lawson. When asked if he was a communist, he demanded to see any evidence the committee had to support such a question. Flustered, Chairman Thomas said, "Oh. Well, you would!"

"Yes," Trumbo said.

"Well, you will, pretty soon," Thomas snapped, and several in the audience laughed and applauded. Pounding the gavel again, the Chairman abruptly excused the witness.

"This is the beginning of an American concentration camp," Trumbo said, speaking loud enough to be heard over Thomas and his gavel.

"This is typical Communist tactics. This is typical Communist tactics," the Chairman said, and a number of people applauded.

During his testimony, writer Albert Maltz referred to the committee's chief investigator, Robert Stripling, as "Mr. Quisling," deliberately comparing him to the World War II Norwegian traitor. Adrian Scott so befuddled the Chairman with his rhetoric that Thomas finally admitted, "I must be terribly dumb, but from your answer I can't tell whether you are a member or not," to which Scott replied magnanimously, "I don't think you are." And when writer Ring W. Lardner, Jr., was asked the all-important question, he replied coyly, "It depends on the circumstances. I could answer it, but if I did I would hate myself in the morning." CFA member Marsha Hunt was perturbed at the witnesses who chose to be "so shrill and defiant in their demeanor. It hadn't helped their cause."

Chairman Thomas unexpectedly called an abrupt halt to the proceedings on October 30 after hearing testimony from only eleven of the nineteen men subpoenaed. (The final witness, playwright and screenwriter Bertolt Brecht, left the country after testifying; the rest would soon be famous as the "Hollywood Ten.") Journalist Eric Sevareid reported that negative response from the press and the public had forced Thomas to shut down early. "The most un-American activity which I have observed in connection with the hearings has been the activity of the Committee itself," studio executive Samuel Goldwyn said in a statement issued on October 30. Prominent editorial writers found it was much ado about nothing. *Variety*'s headline was derisive: "Commie Carnival Closes: An Egg is Laid."

As for the CFA, both the Broadway and Hollywood contingents claimed victory at first. They believed they had achieved their goal in securing public support for the First Amendment rights of all artists. A few committee members reportedly toasted their success at New York City's famous 21 Club. "We had won," said Henry Rogers, publicist for the CFA. "This was total victory for our side." But a number of CFA members went home feeling troubled by the behavior of the very people they had tried to help. Philip Dunne believed that "this blustering and shouting" was "getting in the gutter with the committee." He and others worried that the Hollywood Ten's antics had ultimately sabotaged CFA efforts to defend important political freedoms.

Those who were worried soon found out they had a right to be.

Moderates and liberals who had been ready to support a valiant fight by civil libertarians were put off by the defiant polemics and insolent antics of irritating political malcontents. Support for the Hollywood Ten crumbled, and the once-heroic image of Bogart, Bacall, and other CFA members tarnished overnight. "We woke up the next morning to find that the press, which had praised us so fully, had done a complete about-face," Paul Henreid recalled. "We were no longer knights in shining armor. We were 'dupes and fellow-travelers,' 'pinkos,' who were trying to undermine the country."

Ed Sullivan, one of the nation's most powerful columnists, exemplified how quickly the tide of public opinion turned. Initially, he backed the Broadway CFA's campaign, calling HUAC hearings a "star chamber" where defendants weren't permitted to face their accusers. "Broadwayites, opposed completely to Communism" had a right to be "leery" of the committee's tactics. But Sullivan was also virulently anti-Communist, and testimony at the hearings proved to him that "the Commies not only have tampered with motion pictures—the Commies also have paid more than passing interest to the Broadway theatre." He admitted he was changing his tune: the hearings showed him that certain "celebs reject the freedom of this country for the slavery of the Comintern." Sullivan knew

Canada was in the Broadway CFA. He didn't call the actor on the carpet in public, but he undoubtedly thought Lee had made a big mistake.

In the backlash against the Hollywood Ten, HUAC emerged triumphantly on the side of patriotism, a victory that would have chilling consequences. The committee had justified its mission, its importance, and its very existence; in so doing it won a mandate from the press and the public to continue the hunt for Communists, a mandate that would encourage the government, media, academia, unions, and big business—especially show business—to identify and punish suspected subversives.

The instrument of this punishment would soon reveal itself; for the moment, Canada Lee and other future victims had no inkling of the misery to come.

The month of November turned out to be a roller-coaster ride for Canada, specifically, and for the entertainment industry in general, with thrilling highs, doomsday lows, and neck-snapping plot twists.

Body and Soul hit the theaters on November 9 and critics declared it a knockout. "It is Canada Lee who brings to focus the horrible pathos of the cruelly exploited prizefighter," raved Bosley Crowther in *The New York Times Film Review*. "As a Negro ex-champion who is meanly shoved aside, until one night he finally goes berserk and dies slugging in a deserted ring, he shows through great dignity and reticence the full measure of his inarticulate scorn for the greed of shrewder men who have enslaved him, sapped his strength, and then tossed him out to die. The inclusion of this portrait is one of the finer things about this film." *Variety* said he handled his role "exceptionally well." The *Daily Worker* wrote: "Pathos and anger color his performance in a burst of excitement," noting that such a role is "seldom scene on the American screen, viz: A Negro with courage and dignity."

Great reviews generated great box office. *Body and Soul* cost just $1.8 million to make and grossed $4.7 million. The film was a triumph for Lee, Garfield, Rossen, and everyone connected with the project—until HUAC implied that everyone connected with the project was a Red. According to the committee, one look at the credit lines on *Body and Soul* demonstrated "the manner in which Commies and pinks, in the field of communication and ideas, gave employment to each other."

The FBI took a long hard look at the film as well. Agents in Los Angeles got the okay from Hoover to organize a private screening where an unidentified expert examined *Body and Soul* for Communist content. "It is not as hot as others I have seen," the expert found. "The principal form of propaganda in this picture" is "portraying the Negro in a fine light" as a "noble and sympathetic character" while white characters were shown as "unscrupulous, dishonest, heartless."

For his role in *Body and Soul* and his ongoing struggle against discrimination, Lee was honored "for contributions made to promote democracy and interracial unity" by the *New Masses* at the left-wing journal's second annual award ceremony on November 18. The next day, J. B. Matthews, HUAC investigator, called Canada a "confirmed fellow traveler" during a speech on Communist front organizations presented at an American Legion Seminar in Washington, D.C.

On November 24, the House of Representatives voted to cite the Hollywood Ten for contempt for refusing to directly answer HUAC questions. Congressman Richard Nixon, a young Republican from California, argued in favor of the citations: "Ten witnesses refused to answer pertinent questions. These questions have to be answered. Our national security demands that we protect our free American institutions from being infiltrated and dominated by those who serve the Communist cause."

On the same day, executives from Hollywood's most powerful studios, including RKO, Twentieth Century Fox, and Metro Goldwyn Mayer, met at New York's Waldorf-Astoria Hotel to frame a policy regarding Communist employees on studio lots. When the meeting was over, the producers announced their policy to the press, which came to be known as the Waldorf Statement.

Previously, many of these studio executives had sworn they would never stand for any sort of blacklist. Now, they vowed to fire the Hollywood Ten and agreed they would not rehire them until they cleared themselves of contempt and declared under oath that they were not members of the Party.

"On the broader issue of alleged subversive and disloyal elements in Hollywood," the statement continued ominously,

we will not knowingly employ a Communist or a member of any party or group which advocates the overthrow of the government of the United States by force, or by any illegal or unconstitutional method. In pursuing this policy, we are not going to be swayed by any hysteria or intimidation from any source. We are frank to recognize that such a policy involves dangers and risks. There is the danger of hurting innocent people, there is the risk of creating an atmosphere of fear. We will guard against this danger, this risk, this fear. To this end we will invite the Hollywood talent guilds to work with us to eliminate any subversives, to protect the innocent, and to safeguard free speech and a free screen.

With this pronouncement, the Hollywood blacklist officially began.

"Only Sam Goldwyn protested the decision to start a movie industry blacklist," writes historian Larry Ceplair. The rest of the studio heads feared hostile public reaction and boycotts if they didn't sweep the Reds out. Business in Hollywood had slumped after the war, a problem exacerbated by union strikes. Studios didn't want to give the public any reason to stay away from their hometown cinemas. The moguls also hoped the Waldorf Statement might appease conservatives and keep HUAC away from Hollywood.

The significance of the Waldorf Statement was noted as early as December 8, 1947, in a Newsweek article flatly stating that the Hollywood Ten had been "blacklisted" by Hollywood for defying HUAC. This action was unprecedented: never before had an industry combined to bar Communists and other subversives from employment.

The blacklist quickly spread beyond the Hollywood Ten to the other nine witnesses initially subpoenaed, as well as their most vocal supporters. The CFA was now officially smeared as a Communist front. Columnist Hedda Hopper said these Hollywood Ten lackeys ought to be summoned before HUAC. Several CFA members had their jobs threatened. "Far from being offered thanks for defending our industry, we were suddenly controversial ourselves, and under suspicion," recalled Marsha Hunt.

Westbrook Pegler singled out CFA members Canada Lee and John Garfield in a scathing column that stopped a hair short of calling the two men Reds. Noting that the actors were costarring in the hit film Body and Soul, Pegler came equally close to calling Enterprise Productions a Communist front in his December 15 syndicated column.

According to Pegler, Enterprise was suspect because the studio paid hotel and restaurant tabs for those traitorous CFA rabble-rousers when they went to Washington. Garfield was suspect because he was born Garfinkel, had praised Russia in speeches made during the war, and failed to serve his country except by entertaining troops. As for Canada Lee, Pegler said it was unfortunate that a respectable prizefighter became an actor and "developed something called a social consciousness, a common malady of actors these days. His name bobs up again and again in the company of other names often cited by the committee on un-American activities." Pegler noted that Lee's performance in *Body and Soul* earned "rapturous" reviews in the *Daily Worker*, which made Lee and the film smell fishy because everyone knew that Commie newspaper "praises only persons whom it has inspected and approved." In other words, Communists.

Columnists of all stripes jumped on the anti-CFA bandwagon. The previously moderate-to-liberal Ed Sullivan, now rabidly anti-Red, lobbied Bogart to recant his membership in the CFA. "The public is beginning to think you're a Red! Get that through your skull, Bogie," Sullivan told him. Wilting under pressure, the actor apologized to America for his "foolish" expedition and got a full FBI clearance to go back to work. Ed Sullivan and George Sokolsky, who wrote for Hearst's *New York Daily Mirror*, started hunting Reds themselves, exposing suspected subversives in their syndicated columns. Before long, the two men had plenty of competition; it seemed as though every two-bit columnist tried to be the first to name a name.

Yet the judgment of these arbiters of public opinion could be rather fluid. Even as Sullivan advised his good pal Bogie to clear his name, the columnist was pestering the FBI for any secret information the agency had on the actor. According to FBI files, "Sullivan stated he would like to know anything that we could tell him about Bogart, because he certainly is not going to let Bogart sell him a bill of goods."

Bogart may have been the first to pull out of the CFA, but he would not be the last. Many of the stars who had journeyed to Washington to fight for the cause of freedom of expression now found themselves under pressure to renounce their political stands—pressure that came from agents, studio execs, journalists, gossip columnists, financial backers, managers, family, and friends. To save their careers, they were told, they must withdraw their opposition to HUAC and obtain "clearances" from the FBI. Acting had apparently become potentially dangerous to national security.

The Hollywood CFA fell apart. Work in the movie business was never a sure thing. Even actors with studio contracts were vulnerable as most of these agreements contained morals clauses that allowed execs to summarily dump actors with bad press or shaky reputations. Many of the screen stars that had supported the Ten began backpedaling to salvage their careers. Some in the CFA grew bitter about this duck-and-cover strategy.

"Humphrey Bogart caved in the most demeaning, debasing way, saying that he was duped, didn't realize what he was doing, but he was sorry," said Larry Adler. "Then Gene Kelly reneged, and Danny Kaye reneged, and Frank Sinatra reneged, and those of us who didn't stood out like carbuncles."

Driven by fears of consumer boycotts and lost advertising revenues, the Waldorf Statement spread its chilling effect beyond Hollywood into radio and a brand new medium—television. "To be leftist was to be suspect," writes historian Richard M. Fried. "Studios began to question employees about their politics and affiliations. If the answers were unsatisfactory, work fell off or ceased."

Broadway held the blacklist at bay, becoming the last bastion of liberals in the entertainment industry. Perhaps because he was still considered a Broadway actor, rather than a film star, Canada Lee avoided immediate censure by columnists and other Red-hunters, despite his membership in the CFA and his support for the Hollywood Ten.

But his safety was short-lived. A Cold War drama of coded messages, secret surveillance, and Russian spies would soon ensnare Canada Lee in his very own Red Scare nightmare.

ELEVEN

TROUBLE, TROUBLE

RUSSIAN SPIES AND PINK PAINT

hile HUAC hunted Reds in Hollywood, U.S. Army intelligence conducted a sensitive operation to unmask spies posing a greater danger to national security than any leftist actors, directors, or screenwriters ever would.

Officially acknowledged for the first time in 1995, the Venona Project was one of the most closely guarded secrets of the Cold War. Now viewed as perhaps the greatest achievement of American counterintelligence, Venona uncovered an enormous range of Cold War espionage activities: proof that Soviet agents infiltrated the Manhattan Project and stole atomic secrets; references to espionage activities by Julius Rosenberg and Alger Hiss; evidence of spies in the highest levels of the State and Treasury Departments; corroboration for charges that the American Communist Party played an important role in Soviet espionage; and indications that more than 350 Americans were involved in the Soviet theft of industrial, military, scientific, and diplomatic secrets.

"This is the stuff of spy novels," said John M. Deutch, Director of Central Intelligence, when he unveiled Venona at a 1995 press conference.

In 1948, this super-secret project led to the arrest and conviction of a certain female spy, and in the process inadvertently ended Canada Lee's career.

🐾   🐾   🐾

During World War II, the U.S. Army began to suspect that our Russian allies might be spying on us. We wanted to know what they knew. On February 1, 1943, the Army's Signal Intelligence Service (SIS) created the Venona Project to decipher the Soviet's secret messages.

Code-breakers assigned to the project discovered they had plenty of material to work with. In 1939, the SIS had begun collecting thousands of encrypted radio and telegraph communiqués between Moscow, its foreign embassies, and other Soviet outposts. Venona's bewildered analysts shook their heads: where to start? A former schoolteacher, Miss Gene Grabeel, got the job of sorting messages based on who sent them, who received them, and the code system used to encrypt them.

Cracking the codes used in the earliest years of the war proved impossible, so the Venona team concentrated on messages sent in 1942 or later. The Soviets used five different code systems for five types of "subscribers"—diplomats, trade representatives, the navy, the military, and an intelligence agency (KGB). For three years, cryptanalysts, linguists, and mathematicians worked countless hours, making painstaking progress. Then, in the summer of 1946, analyst Meredith Gardner made a stunning breakthrough; he deciphered a two-year-old message sent to Moscow by KGB agents in New York. In the next few months, Gardner deciphered more messages. One contained the names of scientists working on the top-secret Manhattan Project to develop the atomic bomb.

By July 1947, army officials were growing alarmed at the information coming out of Venona, now hidden away in Arlington Hall, a former girls' school in northern Virginia. Decoded messages contained dozens of cover names of KGB operatives, as well as evidence that Americans in high government positions, including the State Department, had passed classified information to the Soviets.

The army decided it was time to call in the FBI.

In 1948, special agent Robert Lamphere joined the Venona Project. Gardner showed him dozens of decryptions, and before long, Lamphere was hot on the trail of Soviet spies. "We were inside the enemy's house; men were coursing down the corridors, following the leads to which our keys had opened the doors," he wrote in his memoir. "It was easy to envision that soon, very soon, there would be more keys available . . . to spies who were actually still at work among us."

Despite everything Canada had seen and heard in the HUAC hearings, despite the Waldorf Statement and the threat of blacklisting, despite right-wing paranoia and rampant Red-hunting, Lee kept right on politicking for liberal candidates and taking stands on controversial issues. He was either a brave man, or a naïve man, or both. Sometimes, it must have seemed to friends and foes alike that Lee was just asking for trouble.

For one thing, he was campaigning for Henry Wallace, a third-party candidate challenging President Truman in the upcoming 1948 election. Conservatives pegged Wallace's Progressive Party as a bunch of Reds. "Wallace is Stalin's candidate—nothing more, nothing less," notes an anonymous report submitted to Truman and the FBI.

Lee stepped in more hot water by supporting an American Labor Party candidate, Leo Isacson of the Bronx, for a seat in the House of Representatives. Descriptions of Isacson as "Henry Wallace's Man" and "a stooge for Stalin" were submitted to Truman by an informant who also named twenty members of a committee raising funds for Isacson's campaign. Canada Lee and Paul Robeson topped the list. "It would be difficult to find a better way of pinning a Communist label on any candidate than to have the above names give him their endorsement," the report concluded.

While Truman read FBI reports on Lee at the White House, HUAC added more index cards to Canada's file covering a wide spectrum of activities—from the slightly risky to the downright dangerous.

According to committee records, Lee supported more than a dozen Communist fronts, including the Civil Rights Congress, the George Washington Carver School, and the Joint Anti-Fascist Refugee Committee. HUAC staffers weren't alone in tracking these affiliations; an article in the ultraconservative journal *Plain Talk* described the actor as one of several "theatrical bigwigs who continually front" for Reds.

To the note-takers, Canada always seemed to be in the wrong place at the wrong time, backing the wrong positions and the wrong people. He opposed plans for loyalty investigations of government employees; shortly after, Truman mandated them. The actor hosted a dinner for

Dorothy Parker, the deliciously malicious wit who once graced the Communist Party as well as the Algonquin's Round Table. Lee also sponsored the annual May Day Parade, viewed as a "Commie cavalcade" by the right-wing press. In March, he spoke to a thousand artists and entertainers at the Hotel Astor, urging them to join a new "All-Arts Stop Censorship Committee." According to the *Daily Worker*, the group intended to fight Congressional "witch hunts" and combat "local censorship and intimidation of all kinds." The anticensorship, anti-HUAC coalition was yet another suspected Communist front.

Sometimes it can be difficult to make out exactly what grabbed HUAC's attention, as in the case of a card noting that Canada volunteered to judge the "maddest" costume at a Mad Arts Ball, with proceeds funding grants for young black painters and sculptors. It turns out that the ball was sponsored by the Committee for the Negro in the Arts, a group listed as subversive by the Justice Department. In another seemingly innocuous, even laudable, action, Canada presented an award to Arthur Gaeth, the only journalist to witness the executions of Nazi war criminals at Nuremberg. Once again, the problem is with the sponsor, the Voice of Freedom Committee was a media watchdog that lobbied radio to put more artists and journalists of color on the air, among other things. The California Committee on Un-American Activities denounced it as a front "whose function is the support of commentators who have received the acclaim of the Communist press." Simply finding Lee's photo in the *Daily Worker* seems to have been damning enough to justify adding a card.

But HUAC's reasoning is usually quite obvious, as in the case of a card citing a speech Lee made to twenty-five hundred people at a Progressive Party rally in Baltimore. The actor denounced Maryland's decision to have its own version of HUAC. He also vehemently condemned the Mundt-Nixon Bill, which required Communist front organizations to register with the Federal government, and made it a crime to "aid the immediate or ultimate objectives of the world Communist movement." The bill was cosponsored by Congressmen Karl Mundt and Richard Nixon, two powerful and politically ambitious members of HUAC.

Lee was indeed very brave or tragically naïve, or both.

🐾 🐾 🐾

Canada the actor did very little acting in the first half of 1948, although he was having great fun with his own weekly radio show.

On Saturdays at 8:00 p.m., he was spinning records at WNEW, and he insisted on playing music by black artists exclusively. "At a time when it seemed reasonably certain that the business of disk jockeying had been done to death, Canada Lee has proved everybody wrong," one reviewer wrote in January. "With a magic all his own, Mr. Lee relies on his well-chosen records and words to establish a mood—a mood that on the premiere was sultry, torrid, low-down, meaningful and always rhythmic. It was a vignette for the ears and not for the typewriter. Mr. Lee should be heard."

Canada also got a little recording gig narrating "Jazz Band," produced by Young Peoples Records to introduce kids to jazz. The band featured Buck Clayton on trumpet, Edmund Hall on clarinet, Teddy Wilson on piano, Sid Weiss on bass, Jimmy Crawford on drums, and Kenneth Spencer on vocals. "In music and text, you follow the story of jazz from its birth among African slaves to its fusion with New Orleans café music and its travels up the Mississippi, and eventually throughout the country," noted Saul Pett, reviewing the album for the Associated Press. Lee also starred in a couple of radio dramas, including "Toussaint L'Ouverture Liberates Haiti" on May 30, part of the CBS series *You Are There*, which re-created historical events through "interviews" by anachronistic "news correspondents."

Then in June, a dream long deferred came true: Lee took the stage as Othello.

The production was at a smallish summer stock theater in Saratoga Springs, New York, that tended to cater to the glitzy racing set, but Lee didn't care—he would have gladly performed this play for the horses in one of the local barns. Here at last was his chance to play the Noble Moor, to experience the joy and sexual passion of love, the doubt and murderous rage of jealousy, that had so moved him every time he read the play on the subway, in his dressing room, or at night before sleep. During the first week of rehearsals, other actors carried scripts as usual, but Lee had whole scenes memorized already. His gestures were graceful, tender, fearsome, effortless. Sweat streamed from his face as he unashamedly wept in some scenes and thundered through others. When he took the stage on opening night, he was simply in his element.

"Canada Lee, in restraint and passion, gives one of his finest performances as Othello," critic Pat Keasby wrote. "He makes Othello human— a man of any age."

Unfortunately, his stint as the Moor was over all too soon. With no immediate prospects for stage roles, Lee returned to the airwaves as George Washington Carver in an episode of *Lest We Forget These Great Americans*, a series of inspirational biographies broadcast on NBC. When that was over, Lee stared at his silent phone for a while.

Tired of waiting around for good roles, he began to flirt with the idea of producing on Broadway again. Oddly enough, he chose a script by William Saroyan, though their previous collaboration in 1942 had earned miserable reviews and closed in a blink (*Across the Board* and *Talking to You*). Nevertheless, Lee, along with his intrepid producing partners Mark Marvin and Robert Joseph, became enamored with a Saroyan play called *Jim Dandy, or Fat Man in Famine*. Featuring music and ballet, the play contained "no characters, no imitation of people, and no plot," Saroyan declared.

The three producers started soliciting investors, hoping to open *Jim Dandy* on Broadway in October. In August, Lucille Lortel helped organize an invitation-only reading of the play at her White Barn Theater. Canada starred opposite Zero Mostel, who played the eponymous Fat Man. According to *The Bridgeport Post*, the reading turned into quite an event as theater fans from New York City and Fairfield County jammed the barn and spilled onto the terrace. Lortel deftly arranged for loud speakers to broadcast the reading to the lively group sitting outside.

"Mr. Mostel appeared under a handicap," the *Post* noted. "Last week he fell and broke his left leg. As a result, he read his lines from wheel chair with his leg in cast. Mr. Lee only has to speak to bring home forceably [*sic*] his great talent as actor. A poetic play, this Saroyan opus listens well. The action takes place inside an eggshell."

Canada's producing team, without comment, opted not to take the show to Broadway that fall. The play has seldom been seen since, and is perhaps most notable today for originating the phrase "Yadda yadda yadda."

Instead of producing a show, Lee decided to run for office. On July 28, 1948, *The New York Times* announced that the actor had filed as a candidate for the New York Senate on the American Labor Party ticket. He was running in the 23rd District, Richmond County, which is the borough of Staten Island.

At the same time, a major spy scandal hit the front pages. Waves of anti-Communist turbulence struck the country as readers pored over startling stories of Soviet espionage on American soil. Dubbed "the Red Spy Queen," Elizabeth Bentley testified before HUAC that she had passed data from federal employees to a Soviet intelligence apparatus during the war. She implicated Whittaker Chambers, a senior editor at *Time* magazine. Chambers in turn implicated Alger Hiss, a former State Department official, who denied the charges.

On August 18, Canada condemned these HUAC hearings as a "spy scare" that substituted "trial by public inquisition for trial by a jury." He signed a statement urging a swift end to the spy inquiry issued by the National Council of the Arts, Sciences, and Professions. "Evidence and fact have no part to play in these investigations; only the desire to subvert, to smear, to divert a people in need of houses, anti-inflation legislation, and medical care," the statement said. The hearings were characterized as "attacks upon New Dealers" in an attempt to destroy FDR's record of achievement. "Although President Truman denounced these investigations, we must remind him that the atmosphere in which such anti-democratic activities are possible was created and nurtured by his Loyalty Order, the recent arrests of the leaders of the Communist Party, the activities of the FBI, and the Attorney General's so-called 'subversive' list." Other signers included Albert Maltz, one of the Hollywood Ten.

Four days later, Canada announced in *The New York Times* that he was withdrawing from the New York Senate race, citing commitments in Hollywood.

It's possible he was pressured to dropout of the race because he had censured HUAC, but his statement was corroborated in *The Afro-American*, which reported that Lee had been inked for the role of a U.S. Army chaplain in a film called *Children of Vienna*, slated for production that fall. The film was likely based on a book of the same name by Robert Neumann, an Austrian Jew who emigrated to London in 1933. But this film deal—if it indeed existed—fell through.

Perhaps a Hollywood offer was simply more tempting than a run for public office, or maybe Canada decided that he could achieve more as an activist in the trenches than as a politician in the glaring spotlight. His decision may also indicate a sudden interest in self-preservation. His bid for the state senate was on the American Labor Party ticket, and conservatives openly accused the party of having Communist ties. As the Red Scare heated up, liberal politics became a dangerous business, and links to the Communist Party were political suicide. New York City Councilman Ben Davis, along with eleven other members of the National Board of the Communist Party, had just been indicted by a grand jury on charges of conspiracy to overthrow the U. S. government.

If self-preservation was indeed a factor, it didn't run very deep. The day after he withdrew from the state senate race, Lee was back in the news for defending Ben Davis.

"President Truman and Attorney General Clark were condemned this week by 395 Negro citizens for jeopardizing rights of minority groups by the recent 'hysteria-breeding arrests of national leaders of the Communist Party,'" the *Daily Worker* wrote. Robeson and W.E.B. Du Bois orchestrated this denunciation and Canada's photo appeared as a prominent endorser. Lee and his fellow signatories said they were not defending Communist principles but rather the rights of political minorities, including Negroes. They quoted Henry Wallace: "Defense of the civil rights of Communists is the first line in the defense of the liberties of a democratic people." And they called upon the president and attorney general "to give more than lip-service to civil rights," to outlaw lynching, repeal poll taxes, abolish discrimination in the workplace and segregation in the military, and "to defend the lives and liberties of the Negro people in the South." Predictably, HUAC kept close tabs on all of this, documenting it in Lee's file.

Lee, Robeson, and Du Bois were also working together to back Wallace in a fractious presidential campaign fueled by public furor over Soviet espionage, a flagging economy, and friction over civil rights. Truman was an unpopular, never-elected president and Democrats were by no means unified behind him. Enraged by Truman's (albeit meek) support for civil rights, Governor J. Strom Thurmond of South Carolina ran under the Dixiecrat ticket on a platform of strict segregation, luring many Southern Democracts. A few politically ambitious Democrats jumped the fence to support the Republican candidate, Thomas E. Dewey. A handsome moderate famous for inanities such as "Your future is still ahead of you," Dewey was widely believed to be a shoo-in for the White House given Truman's diminishing support. Finally, splintering off at the far left, still other Democrats switched to the Progressive Party to support Henry Wallace—self-proclaimed internationalist, champion of true democracy, and America's last hope to preserve the New Deal. As Wallace made heady speeches calling for peace and denouncing the Cold War, Truman flagrantly baited him as a Red, while Dewey polished his platitudes and Thurmond promised Southerners he would keep the "nigger race" out of their homes, churches, and swimming pools.

Black Democrats were not about to vote for a white supremacist, and very few supported Dewey. The NAACP went for Truman, but Wallace won the hearts and votes of many, including Canada Lee, who put their trust in his civil rights record and his pledge to aid repudiated minorities and the disenfranchised poor. W.E.B. Du Bois, who at eighty years old was the most highly regarded black intellectual of his time, wrote in the *Chicago Defender* that Wallace was the only candidate "for whom a Negro can vote with self-respect." Though he admitted that Wallace's chances were "about nil," Du Bois believed it was "infinitely better for us to throw our votes away upon a great man who stands for real democracy than to shame ourselves, our people, our country." Three years later, the elderly statesman's distinguished career and reputation would be jeopardized by Red Scare paranoia.

In late September 1948, as the presidential campaign heated up, Canada put politics on the back burner when he got a call for help from a director in Boston who was deep in casting trouble.

Set My People Free by Dorothy Heyward was based on the true story of Denmark Vesey, leader of an abortive slave revolt in South Carolina in 1822. Envisioning himself as a Moses chosen to lead his people out of bondage, Vesey used a network of churches to organize a vast, well-disciplined conspiracy. In Heyward's play, his plans are thwarted by George Wilson, a head slave devoted to his master. While Vesey wants to destroy all plantation owners, Wilson refuses to sacrifice his kindly master to win his freedom.

Martin Ritt was directing the show for the Theatre Guild. He had chosen Canada's old friend Rex Ingram to star as the rebel Vesey, and then picked Juano Hernandez to play George. But Hernandez, a former boxer, was a short squat man with an iron will, a steely gaze, and a big, bad attitude. It turned out to be impossible for him to play a credible house slave. "That stare would wilt you," recalled one of the other actors in the cast. "That man took absolutely nothing from anyone."

Including the director, and his fellow actors, and the Guild.

Rex Ingram solved the problem by agreeing to switch parts with Juano, though it meant giving up the starring role. Ritt and the Guild breathed a collective sigh of relief, but their troubles weren't over yet. Two weeks into rehearsal, the FBI arrested Ingram on charges of transporting an underage white girl across state lines for immoral purposes, a violation of the Mann Act. The actor missed a day of rehearsal sitting in jail. When the Guild bailed him out, Ingram took it as a sign that he would be allowed to keep his job. He turned up at the theater promptly the next day, reporting for work. A sympathetic cast member broke the news that the Guild was going to fire him.

Shaken, Ingram asked if he could collect his check for the days he had already worked. He got his money. Later, the actor pled guilty and was paroled after serving ten months of an eighteen-month jail term. Ingram lost his home because of the scandal and didn't step onstage again until 1951; his career never fully recovered.

When Ritt called Canada from Boston, he asked the actor to replace Ingram as George Wilson. Though Lee was eager to return to the stage, he didn't want to play a loyal slave—he wanted to play Vesey the rebel. Ritt and the Guild explained why this just wasn't possible. Lee thought it over, and regretfully turned them down. Disappointed, the Guild hired John Marriott for the role instead. But the producers left the door open, and eventually Lee had second thoughts.

Three days after *Set My People Free* opened in Boston, cast and crew spotted Canada lurking in the wings. Word travels quickly backstage, and Marriott soon learned that Lee was going to replace him. Many actors would have quit on the spot, but Marriott had a contract for two weeks and he intended to stick it out. When his contract was up, he packed his bags. The Guild sent out a press release stating Marriott had "resigned" and would be replaced by Canada at the next tryout in Philadelphia's Forrest Theater.

While Lee proved to be a poor money manager at times, he was a consummate contract negotiator. He knew the Guild was desperate to land him, and when the dust finally settled, he had hammered out a sweetheart deal that gave him star billing in the *Playbill*, theater marquee billing equal to or better than Juano's, and exclusive rights to take the star's special bow after the curtain.

Juano, the ostensible star of the show, blew a very big fuse when he arrived in Philadelphia to find Canada's name on the marquee under his own name, but twice as big. Ditto on the *Playbill*. When he found out Lee would take the star's bow, he threatened to walk, but the Guild and its staff stood firm.

Hernandez didn't quit, but he made life hell for Canada. Shortly after the cast arrived in Philadelphia, the director called several emergency rehearsals to prepare for Lee's debut in the show. The light plot hadn't been hung yet, which meant the actors had to rehearse on a fairly dark stage. This was going to be tough on Lee because of his impaired vision. Hernandez took the stage in a Homburg hat, standing ramrod-straight. Refusing to look at his new costar, he commandeered the only part of the stage with good lighting, closest to the audience. Canada, script in hand, traveled downstage to say his lines to Juano.

"Get back! Stand back there! You are upstaging me," barked the star.

"Juano, come on, man, I'm not upstaging you," Canada said. "We don't have much light, that's the problem. I'm just trying to read my script."

"You belong in that spot," Juano scowled, pointing to the black hole upstage.

"Juano, please, I only have one eye," Canada said.

"That is your spot," Juano said.

Though he was mightily irritated with Juano, Lee never lost his temper in public. He seemed determined to keep up appearances; perhaps he still hoped he might eventually take over Juano's role.

On opening night, Juano glowered at the special bright lights over Canada's name on the marquee. Somehow, the two men put aside their differences long enough to put on a brilliant performance. The audience roared, stamped, and applauded as Canada took the star's bow. Backstage, Juano fumed. That was *his* curtain—Canada had stolen it from him! When it was time for Juano to take his bow, he turned to the stage manager and crew running the curtain. "Is this where I stand? In the center? This is where the light will be?" Juano barked. A chorus of heads nodded fearfully. "Keep the light shining," the actor told the crew. "I will not be there." Every night during the run, Juano refused to take his bow. Puzzled audiences applauded a well-lit curtain instead.

In mid-October, *Set My People Free* traveled to New York to prepare for the Broadway opening. Happy to be home again, Lee resumed his campaigns for Wallace and various causes. Almost immediately, he found himself under attack by conservative pundits. The heat was so fierce they could feel it across the Hudson River in Passaic.

The northern New Jersey town was excitedly preparing for a one-day visit from the Freedom Train. Created in 1947, this special train was a rolling history exhibit traveling across the nation to give Americans the chance to see, close-up, priceless copies of documents guaranteeing our civil liberties. Truman had recently appeared on the train to give a speech regarding his hopes for the United Nations, and Passaic decided to sponsor a "United Nations Day" when the Freedom Train arrived on October 22. When city leaders invited Canada to make a speech, the *Passaic Herald-News* was outraged: Lee was a Wallace supporter and a Communist sympathizer! Abashed, the organizing committee dropped the actor from the program. Equally outraged, the Civil Rights Congress of New Jersey immediately condemned the committee: "It is ironical and sad that the arrival of the Freedom Train, which carries the immortal documents of American history, should be the signal for an intemperate, anti-democratic outburst against a leader in the present-day fight for freedom."

Soon after this brouhaha, a young woman arrived in New York with bulging suitcases. Her brother was gravely ill, and his wife and children needed her help and support. One evening, her uncle invited her along with him to a rally for Henry Wallace. She agreed to go, but mostly out of fondness for her uncle and the promise of a nice buffet dinner afterward. (The event was likely a fund-raising dinner for Wallace at the Hotel Commodore on October 28, hosted by the National Council of Arts, Sciences, and Professions.)

When Canada Lee took the podium to speak, he spotted her in the audience and they both nearly fainted from shock.

It was Frances.

"He saw me while he was speaking," she later recalled. "I was petrified. I thought to myself, 'Run!'"

She knew he would corner her as soon as he finished his speech, and he did. Canada seemed overjoyed and upset all at the same time. "How long have you been in New York?" he asked. "Why didn't you call me?"

Frances wasn't sure how to answer. The entire time she lived in Brazil, she was proud of her new life and independence, and yet lonely and miserable without Canada. The situation was unbearable. She realized she had to cut the man out of her system for good, or go back to the States and admit to Lee that she was in love with him. "It just couldn't continue as it was," she said. While struggling with this dilemma, she received word of her brother's illness. Immediately, she packed her bags and set out for New York. By the time she arrived, she had made a decision. She wanted to be with Canada. "If the opportunity was there, I was going to grab it," she said. "I just didn't know what to do about it."

Fate and her uncle intervened, and suddenly here she was, standing next to the man she still loved.

"Are you married?" he asked.

"No," she said.

"Good," he said. And smiled.

"Are you?" she said, holding her breath.

"No," he said. "No, no, no, no, no."

This time, Frances gave Canada her telephone number when he asked. He called her the next morning before she was even out of bed. He came to visit her every day, either at the hospital or at her brother's house. "Within three or four days, we were right back where we started," Frances said. "To me, it was a miracle that he still wanted me."

They decided to live together. Though Frances says race was never an issue in their feelings for each other, couples that crossed the color line had to tread carefully. In postwar America, marriages between blacks and whites were illegal in thirty-one states; in some cases, it was a felony punishable by fines or jail time. Living together without marrying was taboo in most communities as well. White Americans overwhelmingly opposed race-mixing, and black leaders such as W.E.B. Du Bois also opposed it. Yet in the 1940s, mixed-race couples in the celebrity world often received deferential treatment in black media, including

Ebony and *Negro Digest*; the new black middle class wondered whether interracial relationships were a symbol of social equality or a loss of cultural identity. So, whereas most interracial couples remained on the edges of black and white society, Canada's fame gave him and Frances a bit of leeway.

Nevertheless, they were quiet about it at first. Frances remembers women stopping by the apartment who were obviously interested in Canada and had no idea that Frances was now living with him. Sometimes a whole flock of admirers gathered; these women would try to "out-sit" each other, Frances said—each of them waiting for the others to give up and go home, leaving one lucky lady alone with Canada. Frances fixed them every time.

"I'm tired. I'm going to bed," Frances would say, and walk back to the bedroom.

That usually ended the evening.

"I don't want to know anything about your women, and I won't tell you anything about my men," she told Lee after they got back together. But she couldn't help finding out about some of his devotees. One evening the couple went to a party with their friends Billy Butler and Beulah Bullock. A gifted designer and seamstress, Beulah had created a dreamy royal-blue velvet dress especially for Frances. "There was a lady there, a contessa, and she liked Canada, you see," Beulah recalled. "When Frances came in the room, I heard 'Aaah!' It was a little cry, it sounded so sad. I thought something terrible happened." The countess had tearfully accosted her rival. "Canada is watching every move you make!" she told Frances. "Where did you get that dress?"

Some friends tried to convince Frances that she was making a mistake. After all, Canada still had a reputation as a lothario; he had kept company with a string of women while she was in Brazil. Could she really trust him now? But Frances believed Canada when he swore to be faithful, and she promised never to leave him again. "We never got over those years we lost," she said. "Nothing would tear us apart now."

Set My People Free opened at Broadway's Hudson Theater on November 3, 1948, the day after a famously down-to-the-wire presidential election.

At home in Missouri, President Harry S Truman went to bed a loser and woke up the winner. On the train back to Washington, he smiled as he posed for a now legendary photograph, holding a *Chicago Tribune* headlined DEWEY DEFEATS TRUMAN. While the drama over the election overshadowed almost everything, critics were nevertheless front and center at the opening of *Set My People Free*.

"Mr. Lee suggests with eloquence the timeless, tragic frustrations of his role in life," wrote John Lardner in the *New York Star*. "Canada Lee as the self-tortured Wilson makes for absorbing and emotionally disturbing theater," *Newsweek* observed. Richard Watts, Jr., deemed Lee's performance the highlight of "a fresh and powerful drama about the background of racial injustice in America." Noting weaknesses in the script, Watts wondered if the playwright had been a bit timid, knowing that a race uprising of a century and a half ago "is still a dangerous topic."

Canada had his detractors, however. Several reviewers criticized Lee for looking and acting like an Uncle Tom. Lardner admitted the actor sometimes seemed "conventionally smug, and a little uncomfortable, too, in the bulldog livery the Guild has given him." Wolcott Gibbs of *The New Yorker* called Lee's performance a caricature. "The costumer," he wrote, "has rigged George up like the Frog Footman," and Canada Lee "plays him in much the same spirit." John Chapman concurred, slamming Lee for "really hamming it in a last-act soliloquy."

Brooks Atkinson came to the actor's defense in *The New York Times*. "Since Negro actors are pretty generally confined to Negro parts on Broadway, they seldom have an opportunity to show how wide their range as actors is," he said, singling out Canada's "superb" performance in a difficult role: "Mr. Lee brilliantly acts the whole character, never letting the natural power of his acting crush the content of the part."

Frances and Canada celebrated his success, never dreaming that *Set My People Free* would be Lee's final performance on a Broadway stage. The curtain was going up on the drama that would end his acting career.

In December 1948, Venona analysts gave Agent Robert Lamphere copies of recently decoded messages concerning a female KGB operative working in the U.S. Justice Department. Decrypted text described her as a valuable source, "a serious person who is politically well developed and there is no doubt of her sincere desire to help us." Her cover name was SIMA.

Other decoded material indicated that SIMA had transferred from the Justice Department's New York offices to headquarters in Washington. When Lamphere's boss, Howard Fletcher, learned the date of SIMA's transfer, he pinpointed her identity.

"There can't be any doubt," he told Lamphere. "Her name is Judith Coplon."

Coplon was a political analyst in the Foreign Agents Registration (FAR) Section of Justice who frequently worked on internal security matters, giving her easy access to secret FBI reports. While the most sensitive matters—including the Venona Project—never went near her, what she did see was damaging enough.

Agents started tailing Coplon and, with permission from the U.S. Attorney General, her phones were tapped. Meanwhile, the FBI ran a background check on the suspected spy. Coplon had studied history and Russian culture at Barnard College. A popular student, she graduated with honors in 1943 and immediately got a job in the Justice Department. Ironically, the FBI ran a check on Coplon then, noting she was active in the Young Communist League at Barnard and published pro-Soviet writings while editor of the student newspaper. But in wartime, Russia was our ally, and on many campuses, it was socially and politically acceptable—even fashionable—to be a Communist. Justice hired her, and in January 1945 she had been transferred to Washington. Coplon now had access to secret FBI reports on suspected Soviet agents—she knew just who the FBI was watching and on American counterespionage activities, information that would be invaluable to the Russians. A top-rated employee, Coplon often took work home; neighbors sometimes complained that she tapped away at her typewriter until the wee hours. She was awarded promotions and substantial raises. Off the job, she reportedly was working toward a master's degree in international relations at the American University. Her thesis was on economic planning in the USSR.

"When I had all these data in front of me, I groaned," Lamphere recalled. "Everything about her pointed to her having been a Soviet agent."

Coplon usually traveled to Brooklyn twice a month to see her parents. On January 14, 1949, FBI agents tailed her to New York City's

Pennsylvania Station. To their surprise and excitement, Coplon took an uptown subway, the opposite direction from Brooklyn. She got off in the Washington Heights section of Manhattan. On the corner of Broadway and 193rd Street, she met a short, dark-haired man, clean-cut, conservatively dressed. After dinner at an Italian restaurant, the two argued as they walked to a subway, Coplon angrily waving a rolled-up newspaper. They took the subway downtown several stops. At 125th Street, the man bolted out of the subway, losing the agents who were tailing him.

The next day, the FBI identified Coplon's companion as Valentin Gubitchev, thirty-two, Russian national, former secretary to the Soviet United Nations delegation.

"We had one hell of an espionage case in the making," Lamphere recalled.

Lamphere desperately wanted to crack a spy ring, and he was determined to arrest Coplon and Gubitchev in the act of passing and receiving secret information. But Justice was afraid to leave Coplan on the job much longer, preferring to discharge her under the Loyalty of Government Employees program. Hoover was caving under pressure. If Lamphere wanted to catch his suspects in the act, he needed to speed things up.

"I decided to bait a hook," Lamphere said. With Hoover's blessing, the agent prepared a decoy memo with enough facts to be credible and enough phony information to seem irresistible. He made sure Coplon saw the memo before February 18, the date of her next trip to New York.

But the February trip proved to be a bust. Coplon broke an ankle-strap on her shoe, making her late for her rendezvous with Gubitchev, and the Russian seemed to know he was being tailed. When the two finally made contact, FBI agents couldn't get close enough to tell if an exchange was made. Lamphere seethed with frustration. But he didn't give up.

That same month—February 1949—Canada received an unsettling letter from a friend out in Hollywood. Lee had asked this pal to get the scoop on casting plans for a new MGM film he had heard about, directed by Clarence Brown. The film was likely *Intruder in the Dust*, based on the Faulkner novel about race prejudice in small-town Mississippi.

In June 1945, Lee spoke at a rally to Save the FEPC at Town Hall in Manhattan. Conservatives in Congress killed the agency, which effectively banned racial discrimination by defense industries receiving federal contracts. (AP/Wide World Photos)

Lee and other Broadway stars joined a left-wing arts activism group called "Staged for Action," which in January 1946 entertained the pickets in front of the Western Union building: (*left to right*) Kenneth Spencer, star of *Show Boat*; actor Howard da Silva; a guitar-playing picketer; Canada Lee; and singer Jane Martin. (Bettmann/CORBIS)

With *On Whitman Avenue*, Lee became the first black producer to present a drama on Broadway. Maxine Wood's 1946 play on housing discrimination featured a Rockwellian set by designer Donald Oenslager. In the living room are (*left to right*) Ernestine Barrier, Lee, Will Geer, and Perry Wilson. Augustus Smith, who inadvertently pushed Lee into acting a decade earlier, is on the upper porch. (Wisconsin Center for Film and Theater Research)

In *On Whitman Avenue*, Lee played David Bennett, a returning war veteran whose family is evicted from a white middle-class Detroit neighborhood by a committee of neighbors. Bennett tells them they are conducting a "lynching bee, northern style." (CORBIS)

To keep *On Whitman Avenue* alive after white critics panned the show, Canada organized a grassroots marketing campaign, including this horse-drawn wagon, which rolled through the streets of Harlem with signs urging residents to support the play. (Billy Rose Theatre Collection, The New York Public Library for the Performing Arts, Astor, Lenox and Tilden Foundations)

Friends, colleagues, and prominent black activists supported Lee in his campaign to save *On Whitman Avenue*—including Paul Robeson, sitting on Lee's right, and Langston Hughes, on his left. (Billy Rose Theatre Collection, The New York Public Library for the Performing Arts, Astor, Lenox and Tilden Foundations)

Former First Lady Eleanor Roosevelt praised *On Whitman Avenue* in her nationally syndicated newspaper column, and turned up at a performance to have her photograph taken with Lee and co-producer Mark Marvin. (Photograph by Austin Hansen, courtesy of Blanche Marvin)

The busy Broadway star always took time out to support local causes. In June 1946, Canada Lee (*right*) and bandleader Louis Jordan (*left*) publicize a special screening of Jordan's new film, *Beware*, to benefit the Riverdale Children's Association. (Bettmann/CORBIS)

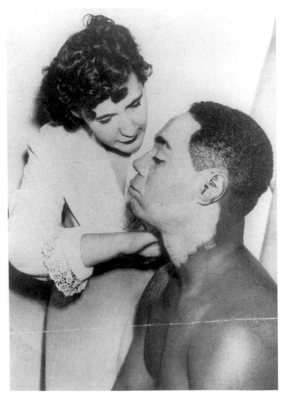

In 1946, Lee made national headlines when he took the stage in whiteface as Daniel de Bosola in *The Duchess of Malfi*. Canada permitted himself to be painted to prove that black actors could be cast in "white" roles; to tabloid readers, it appeared that he was trying (rather unsuccessfully) to impersonate a white man. (Museum of the City of New York, The Theatre Collections—Gift of Frances Lee Pearson)

(*above*) In whiteface on the
Great White Way, opposite
John Carradine (Wisconsin Center
for Film and Theater Research)

Canada Lee with actor John
Garfield on the set of the 1947
film *Body and Soul*. Many
people connected with the
film would find themselves
blacklisted as the Red Scare hit
Hollywood. (Museum of the City of
New York, The Theatre Collections—
Gift of Frances Lee Pearson)

(*above*) The Broadway contingent of the Committee for the First Amendment flies to Washington to support the Hollywood Ten during the October 1947 hearings by the House Un-American Activities Committee: (*left to right*) Julius Epstein, screenwriter; Canada Lee; Oscar Serlin, producer; unidentified woman; Irving Pichel; John Garfield; Larry Parks, actor; Uta Hagen, actress; Philip Epstein, screenwriter; Paul Draper, dancer. (Wisconsin Center for Film and Theater Research)

Actor Carl Lee followed his father's footsteps into theater and film. (Private collection)

Lost Boundaries was based on the true story of a black physician and his wife who quietly passed as white for years in a small New England town before at last telling their neighbors—and their own children—the truth. Lee played a wise and kindly policeman who helps the couple's runaway son embrace his identity. (The KOBAL Collection)

In his final film, Lee played the Rev. Stephen Kumalo in *Cry, the Beloved Country*, shot on location in South Africa. The actor was compelled to enter the country as the indentured servant of director Zoltan Korda. An eyewitness to atrocities, Lee spent the last months of his life denouncing the cruel system of apartheid. (AP/Wide World Photos)

Cry, the Beloved Country was Sidney Poitier's second film. The young actor liked and admired Lee, and would follow Lee's footsteps in breaking color barriers on screen. (AP/Wide World Photos)

Desperate for work, Lee briefly eluded the blacklist to star in a low-budget television biography of scientist George Washington Carver in 1952. (Museum of the City of New York, The Theatre Collections—Gift of Frances Lee Pearson)

(*above*) Canada, arms uplifted, c. *Native Son*
(Museum of the City of New York, The Theatre Collections)

Lee's funeral program
(Wisconsin Center for Film and Theater Research)

Funeral Services

FOR

James Lionel Canegata
"Canada Lee"

AT THE SALEM METHODIST CHURCH
129th Street and Seventh Avenue
New York City

REV. C. Y. TRIGG, Minister

TUESDAY, MAY 13th, 1952 - 1:00 P. M.

Lee's friend had dutifully chatted up the casting director, and reported back with some bad news. When Canada's name came up for a part, Brown demurred, saying Lee was a great actor, but "he did not like your political affiliations and your beliefs and your various statements."

Brown didn't elaborate on those affiliations and beliefs and statements, but it isn't hard to guess what he was talking about. After all, Lee had been Red-baited in the media for his links to alleged Communist fronts, his stands on civil rights and First Amendment issues, and his attacks on the Un-American Activities Commitee. These same activities had prompted HUAC staff to add more index cards to Lee's file. Besides documenting the actor's campaign, HUAC had followed all of these activities. Besides documenting the actor's campaign for Wallace, there were notes on the Freedom Train controversy; his opposition to HUAC spy hearings; his denunciation of the arrests of Ben Davis and other Communists; a speech at an anti-Franco demonstration; his membership in a group of artists and scientists calling for a world conference on peace and international cooperation; and his sponsorship of a rally to end segregation and discrimination.

Lee obviously wasn't going to get a role in a Clarence Brown film anytime soon. The actor now had proof that he had lost at least one role because of his activism, but it didn't stop him from speaking out. It didn't even slow him down.

Hollywood might spurn him, but theater beckoned once more.

Robert Joseph announced that the on-again, off-again Broadway production of *Othello* starring Canada Lee was on once more. Joseph posted a bond with Actors' Equity, noting his intention to raise seventy thousand dollars for the show, which would begin rehearsals July 15. While negotiating tryouts in Boston, Philadelphia, Toronto, Montreal, and Pittsburgh, Joseph planned a ten-week Broadway run followed by a transfer to London's West End.

Radio remained faithful to Canada as well. He starred in several shows, including NBC's biography of Frederick Douglass. And when the Voice of Freedom Committee began lobbying the major networks to hire black news commentators, Lee's name promptly came up. "There is not a single Negro announcer, technician, or writer on any of the networks," committee chairwoman Dorothy Parker pointed out. "The actors who are employed play only stereotypes. It's about time the Negro people, who comprise one-tenth of our population, had a spokesman of their own on the air." Parker's committee created a ballot with eighteen candidates for the job and sent it to thousands of radio professionals and listeners. Lee was a top vote-getter.

And Canada's hometown loved him still. In March, *Ebony* published a charming photo of Lee along with a fluffy feature on the actor, penned by his old friend Langston Hughes. Later that month, the *New York Age* published a celebrity profile of the actor illustrated by caricaturist Bobby Dorsey. It's a fascinating glimpse of the actor's public persona:

> BORN: Lucky Lionel Canagata [*sic*] on March 3, 1907 . . . The brawny youngster who never got beyond the eighth grade in P.S. 5, Manhattan, has done better financially and artistically than some guys with degrees enough to roast a duck. He was bouncing around a racetrack on nags when other shavers his age were doing the same thing around the block on tricycles . . . he proved his virility by taking unto himself a wife at the age of 20.
>
> BIRTHMARKS: None, but he has lots of large beautiful muscles, and with lots of large beautiful muscles, does he need birthmarks, too?
>
> IDIOSYNCRASIES: He hates to wear anything ragged or worn . . .
>
> HIS SUPRESSED DESIRE: To be identified as an actor with but one descriptive adjective—American, that is.
>
> HE LIKES: Pretty girls, silk pajamas, pretty girls, old friends, pretty girls, new adventures, pretty g— —, etc.
>
> HIS PET HOBBY: Proving that New York is the democratic, broadminded city that it is supposed to be. It has been an amusing and sometimes profitable pastime.

Under a final heading, "Little Known Facts," the article said Lee's twenty-two-year-old handsome heir was training as an actor "to carry on when Pop lets go." Carl was serious about a career in theater, and would train for seven years with a number of the most prominent acting teachers in New York, including Stella Adler, Sanford Meisner, Paul Mann, and Morris Carnovsky. The profile of Canada concluded: "Since his divorce, he has been reported betrothed (or secretly tied) to prominent beauties enough to weary a Solomon, but as yet he hasn't made that second trip to City Hall."

Apparently, Frances was still a secret. But overall, the article paints an accurate if lighthearted picture of Canada's sterling reputation in his old hometown. Lee was also popular in black communities farther afield. Later that month, Chicago radio station WMAQ broadcast a glowing profile called "Do Something! Do Something! The Story of Canada Lee." This half-hour biography was part of a series called *Destination Freedom*, in which writer/producer Richard Durham showcased African Americans who were, in his words, "rebellious, biting, scornful, angry, and cocky." Durham's program praised the actor's battle against demeaning images of black life in art and entertainment.

On March 3, 1949, Carl the actor sent his old man a telegram: "Happy Birthday to a wonderful father and a great guy." On his forty-second birthday, Canada Lee *was* happy. He had family, he had friends, he had a community that admired him, and to top it all off, the woman he truly loved.

Work was a little slow, maybe, but all in all, life was good.

In Washington, pressure to catch Coplon and Gubitchev in the act intensified, and Lamphere rebaited his hook with a stronger lure. Using classified information from the Atomic Energy Commission, he wrote another decoy memo that he believed "no Soviet spy could afford to ignore."

Coplon was planning another trip to New York City on March 4, and once again, Lamphere plotted to put his decoy memo within her reach before she left. The FBI agents who would be tailing the suspected spies didn't have a warrant, but the Attorney General's office said they could make an arrest if they saw Coplon give something resembling a document to Gubitchev, or if the agents had probable cause to believe they had witnessed a felony.

On March 4, the FBI put a fleet of radio cars on the streets of Manhattan and thirty agents in the field, ready for the chase. Coplon arrived in Pennsylvania Station. Three agents took the subway with her to 190th Street. An hour later, Gubitchev turned up and the couple immediately set off in opposite directions, perhaps realizing they were being followed.

Gubitchev ditched his tail, but an agent managed to get on a subway car with Coplon. At Forty-second Street, Coplon got off the train and boarded a downtown bus. Gubitchev was already on it. FBI cars flew down the West Side Highway to intercept the bus at Fourteenth Street, where the couple transferred to the crosstown subway. Agents now believed they had probable cause that a felony was being committed. When Coplon and Gubitchev got off the train, they were arrested.

Gubitchev had a plain white envelope holding $125 in small bills, possibly a payoff. Coplon's purse was the real prize. Inside was a copy of Lamphere's decoy memo. "She had taken the bait!" Lamphere later wrote. "The paper had been folded into a square the size of a postage stamp, then sealed with Scotch tape; an arrow was inked on one corner to indicate where to start to remove the tape." The FBI also found a sealed packet of Belle Sharmeer–brand stockings in her purse. Inside were thirty-four data slips with notes on top-secret documents in Justice Department files.

On March 5, the Soviets attempted to claim diplomatic immunity for Gubitchev. Coplon pleaded not guilty to all charges; her trial in Washington, D.C., was set for April. "Coplon's case was the first to implicate an American spying for the Soviets," writes historian Richard M. Fried. HUAC announced it was launching probes into the Justice Department, the State Department, and the United Nations regarding this scandalous infiltration by Soviet spies. Washington journalists eagerly awaited Coplon's trial. It would provide steamy copy beyond their wildest dreams.

In New York City, journalists dutifully noted the approaching espionage trial in the nation's capital, but they were far more interested in the fracas erupting in their own backyard over the Cultural and Scientific Conference for World Peace, the "most controversial meetings in recent New York history," according to The New York Times.

The peace conference was sponsored by the National Council of Arts, Sciences, and Professions (ASP). Prestigious members included scientists Linus Pauling and Albert Einstein, as well as writers Lillian Hellman and Norman Mailer. Harvard astronomer Harlow Shapley, elder statesman of science, called the meeting to discuss the need for capitalism and socialism to peacefully coexist in order to avert World War III.

ASP booked the conference into the swank Waldorf-Astoria on March 25–27. Artists and scientists from thirty nations accepted invitations, including the distinguished Russian composer Dmitri Shostakovich, who would be making his first trip to the United States Canada Lee was acknowledged as a sponsor in preconference press coverage, and other prominent black activists, including W.E.B. Du Bois and Paul Robeson, signed on as delegates, intending to advocate for the importance of civil rights for black Americans.

One week before the conference, the U.S. State Department denounced the event as Communist propaganda and refused visas to several delegates, including the painters Pablo Picasso and David Alfaro Siqueiros, as well as poet Paul Éluard. (Picasso and Éluard were members of the French Communist Party; Siqueiros, the renowned Mexican muralist, stated on his visa application that he was a Communist.) The State Department did approve seven visas for Russians, and about twenty more for delegates from Eastern Bloc countries, including Poland and Romania.

Like flies to honey New York journalists descended on the story. The right-wing *Journal-American* sounded a clarion call for right-thinking readers to protest the peace conference, and predicted that a hundred thousand pickets would demonstrate that weekend. The *Daily Mirror* reviled the event's sponsors as a "bunch of woozy Americans" putting on a "propaganda show" in cahoots with the Commies. The *Mirror* went on to name these idiot sponsors, including Canada Lee, and told its readers: "Throw the bums out . . . We don't want them. We don't like them. We intend to insult them, if it is possible to insult a gang like that . . . You are free to insult them too, if you like . . . The Constitution gives us the right to decide each one for himself who is an enemy of his country . . . This newspaper has printed their names . . . Remember them. They're free to do what they do. But we're all free to hate their intellectual innards, and to let them know it as intensively, actively, and practically as we can."

Chaos reigned at the elegant Waldorf on Manhattan's East Side as Catholic War Veterans and scores of other protesters lined up along nearby sidewalks. Members of the People's Committee for Freedom of Religion marched with flags of Iron Curtain countries draped in black crepe. In the midst of the hoopla, *The New York Times* reported that four people had withdrawn their support of the conference. One was actor

Canada Lee, who claimed "his name had been listed as a sponsor without his knowledge."

Why did Lee make this announcement? In nearly a decade of activism, he had never shied away from working with liberals, leftists, and Communists if it served his goal of drawing attention to race discrimination and other important causes. Robeson and Du Bois did exactly that at the conference. Was Canada suddenly treading more carefully?

Playwright Maxine Wood, an ASP member and Lee's friend since *On Whitman Avenue,* later said the actor did not tell the truth when he claimed he never agreed to be a sponsor. "The letter of acceptance was on file," she stated. "His resignation was a great disappointment to me." But Wood didn't hold it against Canada. She recognized that HUAC and influential columnists, including Walter Winchell, were "hysterically against the conference and put pressure on the sponsors to resign. Some did. Canada Lee was, unfortunately, one of them." Wood assumed that Lee decided the issue was too hot and the atmosphere too risky: "Perhaps because of the reign of terror in 1949 against liberals . . . Canada felt obliged to 'cleanse himself' of any so-called left leanings."

If that's true, it was definitely a first for the actor-activist.

When FBI agents filed their quarterly COMPIC report on Communist activities in the entertainment business, they included a section on the Waldorf peace conference. ASP was "in the hands of CP members," agents said, and twenty conference sponsors were "affiliated with the Communist Party," including Canada Lee. Seven of the Hollywood Ten were also on that list of sponsors; they would soon go to jail, appeals exhausted. Canada was in hazardous company.

That spring, Lee and Frances moved into a new apartment on West Fifty-seventh Street, not far from Carnegie Hall. Though few landlords would issue a lease to a mixed-race couple in those days, Canada just happened to know a man in the theater business with a liberal attitude and a vacant apartment. "It had beautiful, huge rooms," Frances said, though she recalled that the apartment suffered one rather peculiar omission: "It didn't have a kitchen. But we made do."

Pretty curtains billowed at the wide-open casement windows on the second floor and bright flowers overflowed their window boxes. Lee was eager to show off his place and his girl. Friends invited over to meet Frances found themselves smitten by those beautiful eyes and friendly smile. Her expertly tailored clothes showed off her stunning figure. Lee couldn't stop smiling. "There was a transformation in Canada," Leslie Nash recalled. "He was in love like nobody had ever seen before. He couldn't take his eyes off her. When she wasn't around, he couldn't stop talking about her."

Even those who had disapproved of Canada's decision to live with a white woman found themselves won over by Frances's warmth and keen intelligence. Lovey had never been wild about the relationship, but the brothers were close, and when Canada asked Lovey to come on over to a little party, he did, along with his wife, Pheta, and their son, Billy, now eleven. "That apartment was like a palace to me, like Versailles or something," Billy recalls. "I remember the odor of expensive cologne. Everything was so *suave*, you know? Burt Lancaster was there. I was knocked out. My family, I guess we were the normal people."

Langston Hughes was a particular favorite at Fifty-seventh Street. "Lang was always around the house," Frances said. "He was very sweet, warm. He was particularly soft and tender around Canada. They'd laugh about everything and nothing all the time." She found it fun to listen to the two men as they talked, slipping in and out of Harlem argot and "high-toned" talk: "These men lived in two separate worlds, the street and the salon. Both of them could go from one world to another, one language to another, depending on what they were talking about."

Conversations wandered from politics to literature to theater to music. "They both loved the blues," Frances said. "Canada had so many blues records, we could listen to them all day." Sometimes the two men would sit quietly, not talking, just listening to music, intent on their own thoughts. Langston might pick up paper and pen and write, sometimes for hours. "Lang's mind never stopped," Frances said. "Never."

Lee still loved to throw a party, and Frances willingly indulged him, shopping for good food and wine, cooking gourmet dishes, and introducing people to a new drink she had learned to like in Brazil called "gin and quinine." She managed to engage all of her guests in conversation, and effortlessly put everyone at ease.

Canada also loved to take Frances out on the town, and they often went to the Rooftop, a jazz and blues joint run by Victoria Spivey.

"Spivey and Canada were great pals," Frances said. Spivey started singing blues in the 1920s while still a teenager, recording with New Orleans jazzmen Louis Armstrong, Henry "Red" Allen, Zutty Singleton, and "Pops" Foster. Spivey knew everybody in the blues business, and anyone who passed through New York stopped at the Rooftop. "Canada loved to go there. He could never get enough of that music," Frances recalled.

As romantic as it was to be wined and dined, it was the small sweet things that meant the most to Frances. She loved it when Lee sang, when he read poetry and Shakespeare to her by the hour. "I have memories of mornings when Canada would bring me coffee in bed and English muffins," Frances recalls. "I relish those memories."

Lee still believed it was the man's job to support the family. Frances had her work cut out for her anyway as the household accountant—managing the money, minding the bills, and sorting out his taxes. The actor had somehow accumulated a daunting backlog of tax problems. "Canada's one and only character flaw was the way he spent money, the way he gave it away, and never kept track of anything," Frances said.

When Frances took over the books, Lee's accounts were running a little low. Thankfully, some money was coming their way as the actor headed north to Portsmouth, New Hampshire, to play a small role in the movie *Lost Boundaries*.

Louis de Rochemont was famous for his monthly "March of Time" newsreels, and now he was producing his first feature film. *Lost Boundaries* was based on the true story of Dr. Albert C. Johnston and his wife, Thyra. After finishing medical school at the University of Chicago, Johnston applied for an internship. Most hospitals would not accept him because he was black; hospitals that did accept black interns were already fully staffed. The couple had never tried to pass for white, though they were light-skinned. But when Maine General Hospital in Portland finally hired Johnston without asking his race, the doctor realized his colleagues thought he was white. He never disabused them of this notion. Later he set up a private practice in rural New Hampshire where the family lived for twelve years, quietly passing. The Johnston children had no idea they were black. In 1941, the doctor volunteered for the U.S. Navy and won a commission as a lieutenant commander. But the navy discovered his secret, and revoked his commission on the grounds that black men were not permitted to serve as officers. The doctor decided to tell his children the truth. As the story became public knowledge, a few angry neighbors thought the family should leave town, but most were undisturbed, though frankly amazed.

De Rochemont had grown up in New Hampshire, and happened to hear the Johnstons' story first-hand from the doctor's son. The filmmaker pitched the story first to *Reader's Digest*, which published a slim book, and then to MGM executives, who agreed to make the movie. But after several months of work on the script, the studio backed out over "the handling of the Negro theme," according to *Ebony*. De Rochemont decided to produce the project himself, and although he hired Alfred Werker to direct, it was still very much de Rochemont's picture. He insisted the movie be shot on location in Maine and New Hampshire, and cast two unknown white actors, Mel Ferrer and Beatrice Pearson, as Dr. and Mrs. Johnston. Canada was to play Lieutenant Joe Thompson, a police officer who befriends the couple's son when he runs away to Harlem, trying to come to terms with the fact that he is black.

De Rochemont arranged for the cast to be lodged in Portsmouth's historic Rockingham Hotel, but when Canada and other black actors walked in, the proprietor balked. The cast would have to be segregated, he said, including meetings and meals. After de Rochemont threatened to take his business elsewhere, the hotel owner changed his policy. "Economics prevailed over prejudice, and the integrated cast was welcomed," writes journalist J. Dennis Robinson. "People in Portsmouth still talk about the day (de Rochemont) broke the color barrier here."

As soon as the shoot was over, Canada collected his $750-per-day pay and made a beeline for home and Frances. He also went back on the job as activist, raising money for Spanish refugees and supporting a strike at City College. Students were calling for the dismissal of two staff members—a professor of Romance languages charged with making anti-Semitic remarks, and a dormitory supervisor accused of permitting segregation. "You are fighting for democracy," Lee told striking students on April 19. "Keep at it with good courage."

On April 25, 1949, Judith Coplon went on trial in Washington, D.C., on charges of espionage. "G-girls," the female government workers of the city, piled into the courtroom, some breathless with excitement, some scandalized to see "Judy," one of their own, lifted from obscurity to noto-riety. The press section was crammed with reporters, including someone from Tass, the Russian news agency; the FBI suspected he was taking notes for the KGB.

The cast of this courtroom drama included U.S. Attorney John M. Kelley, Jr., a well-spoken, well-dressed, by-the-book prosecutor, and Judge Albert L. Reeves, seventy-six, a mild, taciturn man recently dragged unwillingly out of retirement. The attorney for the defense was Archibald Palmer, sixty-five, a short, pear-shaped, florid and wily man who spent most of his career chasing ambulances and handling bank-ruptcy cases. Palmer immediately turned the courtroom into a circus. As *Time* magazine described the scene, Palmer "gauged the temper of mild, white-haired Federal Judge Albert L. Reeves with the eye of a mule trader sizing up a parson; after that he did everything but shoot off firecrackers under the judge's nose. He objected incessantly. He told bad jokes. He brayed, waved his arms, and quoted the Bible with enthusiastic piety. On one of those rare occasions when the judge reproved him, he replied ob-sequiously, 'Beggars mustn't be choosers and I'm happy to get what you're gonna give me . . . I subside.' Then he would continue as before. As he ranted, he stood close behind U.S. Attorney John M. Kelley, Jr.; from time to time Kelley brushed chewed fragments of Palmer's Life Savers from his hair."

Thanks in part to Archie's antics and viscous verbosity, a trial origi-nally scheduled for five days would last nearly five weeks.

The prosecution opened by calling to the stand FBI agents who described in mind-numbing detail the evasive maneuvers made by Coplon and Gubitchev the night they were arrested. When Palmer cross-examined the agents, he quizzed them on Soviet geography, trying to show they were too ignorant to know a Russian spy "if they fell over one." Coplon giggled while her mother sorrowfully dabbed at her eyes with a handkerchief. Palmer admonished the grieving woman: "Try to smile, Mrs. Coplon."

Kelley's case hinged on the fact that Coplon had extracts of classified material in her purse when she was arrested. The FBI hadn't actually caught her passing the information to Gubitchev, but the prosecution ar-gued that the documents in her purse and the pair's suspicious behavior proved that she intended to give secrets to the Russian.

The defense argued that Coplon and Gubitchev were lovers, not spies, and that the materials in Judy's handbag were research for a novel she was writing. When asked to produce this novel, Palmer said Judy had destroyed it rather than see it used in court.

Kelley, the prosecutor, said the novel was a ludicrous cover story: why would a novelist fold her notes into a tiny triangle, or hide them in a package of stockings? Palmer sensed the tide turning against him. He had to attack and discredit those damning data slips in Judy's purse. In a moment of desperation, inspiration, or sheer craftiness, Palmer demanded that the FBI produce the original secret files in their entirety.

In that instant, the feisty defense attorney turned the trial upside down, making the FBI files, and not Coplon's summaries of them, the center of attention.

Palmer argued that the FBI couldn't prove that the data slips were stolen secrets unless the original files could be examined in court. Kelley flatly refused to produce the files, arguing that disclosing the full text could jeopardize national security. What about my client's security, what about her rights? Palmer demanded to know. He raged, bullied, and badgered. Judge Reeves fined him twice for "obvious contemptuous conduct." But Palmer was tenacious. He knew Kelley was nervous. The FBI must be hiding something.

FBI Agent Robert Lamphere had seen these secret files. Some contained the names of Americans suspected of working for the Soviets. Some were utterly innocuous; some, if made public, could do real harm. Some were littered with allegations by informants that had never been confirmed and could very well be a pack of lies. Lamphere and his colleagues at the bureau were dead against airing this kind of rumor and innuendo in public. But Palmer continued to argue that his client's freedom was at stake, and that was more important than any secrets in those files. "He knew we didn't want those files in the open," Lamphere wrote. "He believed Justice would rather forego the trial than have FBI methods, informants, and targets made public."

As Kelley and Palmer argued, Lamphere watched Judge Reeves's face. The agent had a very bad feeling about this. When Judge Reeves excused the jurors for lunch, saying he would make a decision based on his own close review of the disputed files, Lamphere recalled, "The smell of disaster was in the air."

One hour later, Judge Reeves read his carefully worded opinion. "I am not charged with the responsibility of protecting the government," he

said. "I'm here to see that justice is done." He had examined the documents and found "they do not suggest danger to our national security,"
adding "they could only produce irritations and maybe endanger individual lives."

Possible loss of life obviously didn't cut the mustard with Judge
Reeves. In the interests of a fair trial, the judge held, the defense must be
allowed to have the secret FBI files that were the alleged sources for the
data slips in Coplon's handbag. "If the Government has something to
hide," he said, "the Government ought not to be here."

Lamphere assumed the trial was over and the prosecution would
drop the case. But Kelley didn't have the Attorney General's permission
to withdraw the indictment. The two men watched in dismay as the secret FBI files were brought into the courtroom.

Archie gleefully began to read the contents aloud. He started with a
fifteen-page report that named stage and screen stars as Communists and
fellow travelers. With visions of page-one stories in their heads, the press
devoured the information in a feeding frenzy. When Palmer became too
hoarse to read, a substitute took over.

The next day, the *New York World-Telegram* headline screamed: TAG
FILM STARS AS RED STOOGES IN SPY REPORTS. The headline on *The New
York Times'* front page story was more subdued: FILM "COMMUNISTS"
LISTED IN FBI FILE IN COPLON SPY CASE. The *New York Daily News* story
was typical of the lot:

> Actors Fredric March, Edward G. Robinson, and nine other top
> Hollywood and Broadway personalities were described as mem-
> bers of the Communist Party in 1947, in a top secret FBI report,
> which was sprung at Judith Coplon's espionage trial today.
>
> The sensational official report on Red infiltration of the movie
> colony after the war was one of 12 hush-hush documents men-
> tioned in data slips found in the petite, ex-government girl's purse
> when she was arrested. It was read over a storm of objections by
> government lawyers who claimed "national secrecy" was involved.
>
> In addition to March and Robinson, a confidential FBI in-
> formant named as Communist Party members Paul Robeson,
> Dorothy Parker, Donald Ogden Stewart, Ruth McKenney, Albert
> Maltz, Alvah Bessie, Dalton Trumbo, Millen Brand, and Michael

Blankfort . . . A large number of other top stars were mentioned elsewhere in the report as sponsoring, or taking part in, various Communist-front activities. Included were March's wife Florence Eldridge March, Sylvia Sidney, Paul Muni, John Garfield, and Melvyn Douglas . . .

Another source, identified only as "T-6," said in December 1947 that March and Canada Lee, Negro stage star, were two "Communist Party fellow travelers" connected with the Institute for Democratic Education in New York.

As bad luck would have it, when Canada Lee's name was named, it happened twice in the same day.

The Associated Press filed a story from Sacramento stating that anti-Communist Senator Jack Tenney had released a report listing hundreds of people who "conspicuously followed or appeased some of the Communist Party line programs over a long period of time." Once a radically left-wing politician, Tenney had reinvented himself as a racist, anti-Semitic conservative. For the past eight years, he had chaired the California Senate's "Fact Finding Committee on Un-American Activities." In the current report, Canada and Frederic March apparently came under fire for starring in a 1943 radio play about racial harmony sponsored by the YMCA. In the play, titled *Beyond the Call of Duty*, a black Navy messman from New Jersey named French risks his life to save four white sailors. That particular plot point, of course, was acceptable to conservatives: a black man should sacrifice himself in the service of whites. But when a white sailor wonders aloud whether he and French will ever swim together at the Jersey shore, it was obvious to Tenney and his cronies that Commies were present.

"Movie figures, writers and politicians today cried 'lies' and 'slanders' to the legislative committee," the AP article stated. Canada Lee was among them.

The actor thought it prudent to issue a formal refutation. On June 10, Canada told *The New York Times*: "I have by now publicly stated many times that I am not a Communist. However, I will continue to fight for the cause of the Negro people and other discriminated-against minorities, no matter with what names I am labeled."

Fighting words for a man tainted Red twice in one day.

The *Times* published an editorial urging caution on all sides. Under the headline "Freedom Comes First," it summarized the events of the Coplon trial, and how the secret FBI reports on suspected Hollywood Communists came to light. "We cannot tell how seriously the FBI took this report, which in many respects resembles the allegations so often made with a beat of drums and tooting of trumpets by the Committee on Un-American Activities," the editorial read. "Still, the names have been published and something of a sensation has been produced."

This episode, like the HUAC probes and other Red-hunting investigations, contains a warning, the *Times* said: "We are in grave danger of holding individuals guilty because of their associations, or because in some cases and on some issues they take the same positions as communists." Red-hunters could be attacking honest liberals while seeming to attack dishonest Communists, the editorial warned; furthermore, we cannot allow paranoia over Communist propaganda to have a chilling effect on freedom of thought and freedom of speech. "All we can reasonably demand of any citizen," the *Times* continued, is that "he shall not act or conspire against his own country."

As for the people named at the Coplon trial and during the California probe, "certainly many of the names mentioned have no place in any list of dangerous Americans. In every case we should reserve judgment until proof is produced," the *Times* concluded. "Meanwhile, it is of the utmost importance that the whole American institution of freedom of thought and freedom of expression be preserved. We need the free and inquiring liberal mind."

Canada may have taken this editorial in the nation's leading newspaper as a sign that he was safe from censure. And in the beginning, the egg seemed to be primarily on the FBI's face. The exposure of the secret files enraged Hoover and appalled Truman. Rumors circulated that the FBI director was going to resign. On June 13, the *Daily News* reported, "High Justice Department officials are known to regret that what are described as seemingly innocent people have been made targets of derogatory public disclosures."

Somewhat belatedly, Archie Palmer extended a helping hand to the stars whose reputations he'd helped sully. On June 14, as the attorney prepared to open the case for the defense in the never-ending Coplon trial, the *Daily News* reported that "Archibald Palmer said he already has invited actors Melvyn Douglas and Canada Lee to take the stand and debunk the FBI reports which last week charged them with being fellow travelers."

Canada declined. The actor discounted the importance of the whole episode at first—or at least, in front of Frances. "He knew that he was named," she recalls. "But we didn't think or talk about it much." Lee was at work on an episode of *The Big Story*. Ironically, it concerned a case of mistaken identity and Canada played an innocent man convicted of murder who is later exonerated. It was based on actual events.

Judith Coplon also claimed a case of mistaken identity. When the accused took the stand, she swore she was no spy but rather an aspiring novelist whose only mistake was to fall in love with the wrong man. It made great copy, but it didn't sway the jury. On June 30, the former G-girl was convicted of stealing classified documents with the intent to benefit a foreign nation and sentenced to forty months to ten years. (In March 1950, Coplon stood trial again in New York, was convicted on conspiracy charges, and sentenced to fifteen years. Both convictions were overturned on grounds of illegal arrest and illegal wiretapping; Coplon never served time. She married a lawyer, moved to Brooklyn, had a family, and vanished from public view. Only after the 1995 release of the Venona Files did it become clear that Coplon had been, in fact, SIMA, a Soviet spy.)

Despite the U.S. Government's apparent chagrin over the spilled secrets in the Coplon case, no public apology was ever made to Canada, and the allegation that he was a "Communist Party fellow traveler" was never corrected or retracted. Could the Department of Justice have in fact manipulated events in the Coplon trial to intentionally expose these files, knowing that dozens of alleged subversives, including Lee, would likely be discredited? Agent Lamphere's memoirs categorically state that this was not the case, that Kelley desperately tried every possible argument to keep those classified files closed.

In any event, the damage was done, and Canada began to worry.

The actor fired off a passionate statement of innocence and sent copies to editors of newspapers and influential news and trade magazines, including the left-wing *Daily Compass*. On June 22, the *New York Herald Tribune* ran an edited version under the headline "A Red Tint is Rubbed Off and Rights Are Defined by Canada Lee." It reads:

There comes a time in every man's life when to keep silent is to negate one's entire life. Such a time has come for me. I refer, of course, to the drivel that has come from the so-called secret files of the FBI about one Canada Lee.

As an American, as a Negro, and simply as a human being, I feel I must uphold my integrity and dignity against all accusations made in regard to my beliefs. The only way to accomplish this is to define these beliefs. I have from time to time stated that I am not a Communist. This is a simple fact.

I believe with 99 per cent of the American people, however, that a man has a right to his individual opinion. Further, I believe he has a right, outside of slanderous remarks and downright inciting of riots, to express that opinion. Actually, my beliefs can be summed up thusly: I believe in mankind, therefore I believe in democracy. Since this democracy does not completely exist for my people and other minorities, it is my duty as an American to fight under our democratic processes (freedom of speech, worship, and thought) for these freedoms of which America so proudly boasts. To fight also for that fourth freedom—freedom from fear!

My son served in the Army. I was fortunate. He returned in one piece. There, for the first time in his life, he saw and felt the American policy of "Jim Crow" at its worst, and thought that if he must die in a segregated army, why not in a segregated battlefield? After all, he said, "there are no Jim Crow bullets!" But it was there he also learned that democracy and freedom was something one had to fight to attain and retain. Of my own talents I gave freely to the war effort, despite the discrimination practiced against minorities. For I believe to the extent we contribute to democracy, to that extent can we demand our just rights.

I believe this constant screech of Communism is only a smoke screen designed to hide very unpleasant facts. These facts are that Negroes, among other minority groups, do not have full civil rights; that housing is very inadequate; that serious unemployment threatens us; that the peace of the world is indeed very shaky . . . I say, and very sincerely, let us better examine those who do most of the screeching . . . It is they who are Un-American!

Conviction by smear or accusation alone is an altogether too familiar pattern. It is the intent to frighten people into silence and submission by implying a connection with or association in a so-called subversive organization . . . "Subversive" was just as easily applied to the American revolutionaries who founded our great country. Washington, Lincoln, Jefferson, Paine were all called traitors by their enemies in their day. This pattern of terrorization is one that appeared only such a short time ago in a country we fought so determinedly against, and in which conflict so much American blood was spilled.

Shall we, too, be silenced by fear of unfounded labels:

Until minorities are not only suppressed but erased?

Until the lynch mobs increase in violence and number?

Until we no longer think as free people?

Until one day we awaken to find ourselves unable to speak?

Until our own conscience does not permit us peace? . . .

My duty, my heart, is with those in America who do not experience the full realization of the democracy we all talk about, and with them I shall always be found, no matter by what names I am unjustly labeled. I take my hat off to no man in my love for my country. I will let my acts speak for me.

On Wednesday, June 22, the same day his letter appeared in print, Canada Lee stood onstage in a Portsmouth, New Hampshire, movie theater.

Portsmouth was proudly hosting the world premiere of *Lost Boundaries*. More than three thousand people lined up, mostly locals, to watch four screenings at two cinemas, the Colonial and the Olympia. Opening night festivities were planned, and Dr. Johnston and his family were among the honored guests.

"A packed audience applauded for a full minute when the last voice and scene had died away on screen," reported *The Portsmouth Herald*. "Then the audience fell into an unembarrassed and universal wiping of eyes and snuffling to choke back the emotions aroused by the bold story of a race problem."

Just before one of the screenings, Canada had slipped into the theater, unexpectedly and unannounced, to watch the film. He saw a black doctor assume a white identity because it was the only way he could do the job he loved and was meant to do. He saw the doctor and his wife keep this secret from everyone, including their children. He saw the secret come out, saw a wrathful community turn against the family, saw the son run away from home. He saw himself, as a wise and kindly man, helping the boy understand what it means to be black. He saw a preacher ask the white townspeople to turn away from anger and prejudice; he saw white people admit they were wrong, saw them welcome the Negro family back.

Then the movie was over. After the director and other dignitaries spoke, a local pastor took the stage and announced without preamble, "Canada Lee is here."

Canada walked slowly to the center of the stage, into the spotlight. He wasn't prepared for the thunderous applause that rolled through the theater; after all, his part in the film was rather small. He twisted his big hands in front of him, waiting for silence, and when it came, he began to speak, his voice full of emotion. He said that he was proud of *Lost Boundaries*, proud of what the film was trying to say.

"It's about America," he said. "Our America that I read about in books when I was a boy. Our America that I read about in books but was not so—for me."

He wrung his hands and rubbed his head—the great orator for once at a loss, searching for words. In the days since his condemnation in the press, he had known anger, frustration, and anxiety, perhaps even fear. In those difficult days, he must have wondered if he was about to pay a high price for having the courage of his convictions.

"You see a picture like this and hear all the applause," he said, "and you begin to believe again."

But that belief was about to be sorely tested.

TWELVE

BABY, IT'S COLD OUTSIDE

FRIENDSHIPS BETRAYED

C anada knew he was in danger of being blacklisted, if he hadn't been already.

He had publicly criticized the government, and made powerful enemies in Hollywood, Washington, and New York in his battle against racism and segregation. Now he had been named as a Communist sympathizer in a federal trial and in the press.

Had he sacrificed his career for his political convictions?

"When a black artist is successful and silent, he remains a national favorite," observes historian Donald Bogle. "But when a black artist becomes important enough to want better roles . . . or when the artist makes some comment against the social-political climate of the country, he becomes a doomed man."

Lee couldn't be certain he was on the list. Officially, there was no list; the entertainment industry categorically denied its existence. Calls for work simply stopped. When Canada pursued auditions and screen tests, he was told he was "too good" for the part, "too expensive," or "just not right."

He decided he would create opportunities for himself. On June 29, *Variety* published a blurb under the headline "Canada Lee Has Own Idea For Negro Film." The actor was collaborating with screenwriter Arnold Perl on an "anti-Negro stereotyping" script and soliciting funds from New York sources to raise a modest two-hundred-thousand-dollar budget for the picture. Canada would play the lead role, "that of a Negro detective who uses stereotyped white concepts of the Negro to break a case," according to *Variety*.

He also tried to clear his name in the press, sending letters to the editors of dozens of newspapers and journals across the country. "I freely admit that my work, my art, my livelihood, is very much affected by the irresponsible, nebulous, false insinuations directed at my name," he wrote. "However, I shall continue to speak my mind. I shall continue to help my people gain their rightful place in this America . . . What I do, I do because I believe in it."

He kept swinging, but in July 1949, he suffered a dreadful blow. Ed Sullivan picked up the accusations made during the Coplon trial and condemned Canada as a Communist sympathizer.

This was a shocking and painful betrayal, given that Sullivan was not only a powerful force in shaping public opinion—he had also been a good friend. In a letter to Sullivan, Canada recalls their long relationship, dating back to the days when Lee was a prizefighter and Sullivan covered sports for the *Daily Graphic*. "I remember when I was down and out, blinded in one eye from my fighting career, with an orchestra that I couldn't find work for, and I wrote to you asking for help—and I remember that it was you that boosted me and my band," Canada said. "I can remember a lot of things, like your raves about me in several plays when I became an actor, that helped me to reach the position I find myself in now. I remember these kindnesses, Ed, and you and they are very dear to me."

I am not a Communist, he told Sullivan. I am being harassed by anti-Negro groups trying to undermine my fight for civil rights. I don't care what names they call me, he said: "Nothing or no one can force me out of the struggle my people are making in this country for democracy which only exists for some."

"Tell me, Ed. Should I stop fighting for the lives of six Negroes in Trenton who are being electrocuted for a crime they didn't commit because I'm called a fellow traveler? Should I put an end to my fight for civil rights for my people because I'm tarred with the red brush? Should I keep my mouth shut when the Ku Klux Klan and other bigots spew out their un-American venom?" he asked.

Sullivan never answered, and their friendship withered in that barren silence.

On July 6, Canada called a press conference at the Apollo Theater in Harlem. He was just about to open a two-week run playing Danny in a revival of *Anna Lucasta*; perhaps he felt he owed it to the Apollo to clear up this mess. After the press conference, *The New York Times* ran a story under the headline: "Canada Lee Explains."

Declaring that he had been disturbed by reports that he was a Communist or a "fellow traveler," Canada Lee, actor, denied yesterday that he was a member of the Communist Party . . . He said he was willing to appear at benefit performances and social conferences that were sponsored by allegedly Communist groups. He added that he was still ready to appear "anywhere" to talk against racial or religious discrimination and that a love of freedom and democracy compelled him to participate in any program that was designed to make the world a better place to live in, no matter what organization or political party was listed as a sponsor.

Explaining that a conference called for Saturday at the Theresa Hotel by the Committee for the Negro in the Arts was a case in point, Mr. Lee said that he was ready to join any group that would "expose racial discrimination in the radio and television fields."

By saying he would continue to fight for civil rights, regardless of whether the Communist Party was involved or not, Canada threw down the gauntlet to conservatives. He was either unafraid of the consequences or didn't understand them; perhaps he already suspected it was too late to salvage his career. His son believed that Lee boldly chose to defy the blacklist machine and had no intention of backing down. "If there was one important thing I remember about my father," Carl Lee later said, "it was his courage."

Lee's defiant quotes in the *Times* article were carefully recorded in the actor's HUAC file. His decision to participate in the Hotel Theresa conference was particularly significant because two of the featured speakers were Communists: William L. Patterson, founder of the Civil Rights Congress, and acclaimed author Howard Fast.

The other major speaker on the agenda was Paul Robeson.

By July 1949, it was hazardous to appear at Robeson's side for any reason. Just three months before, Robeson had made a speech at an international peace conference in Paris where he said African Americans would not go to war against anyone, including the Soviet Union, on behalf of those who had oppressed them for generations. Robeson's remarks (widely misquoted) were denounced as unpatriotic by many prominent blacks, including Reverend Adam Clayton Powell, Jr., Walter White, and baseball star Jackie Robinson. Robeson was blacklisted by the entertainment world and put under FBI surveillance.

Sharing a bill with Robeson was risky enough for a man threatened by the blacklist, but Lee went even farther with his scathingly contemptuous keynote speech at the Hotel Theresa's Skyline Room. Three hundred black and white workers in radio, television, and theater listened intently as Canada charged that the "lynch mentality" of American radio made "cannibals, dehumanized monsters, clowns, menials, thieves and liars" out of the Negro people whom it had "jailed in a concentration camp of silence where we are surrounded by indifference and our real words reach nowhere."

Each week, Americans listened to 604,800 fifteen-minute radio broadcasts. Of those segments, twelve or fewer depicted the history and culture of black Americans. Not one of those twelve were produced or directed by a black American. "The ideology of white supremacy" controlling radio and television "cast the Negro into a vacuum of non-existence," Lee said. In the studio, the only jobs we can get are menial, he said, and on the air, the only roles we get are demeaning stereotypes.

"The richness of Negro life, its humor, warmth, humanity, and fighting spirit, are not considered fit subjects for depiction on the air," he said. "Negro actors recently were asked to play the role of cannibals on a television show, to eat a white dummy before the cameras. Of course, they refused to take the role. The Negro on the air is depicted in stereotyped fashion as a minstrel or buffoon. He is restricted to characterizations like those played by 'Beulah' and 'Rochester' and 'Amos 'n' Andy.' Where is the story of our lives in terms of the Negro slums in which we must live, insecurity of life and limb, food not available, and jobs not available? The plain fact is that a virtual Iron Curtain against the entire Negro people exists as far as radio is concerned."

The New York Times summarized the speech the following day, noting that Lee concluded by urging a "militant struggle" against Jim Crow in the arts and media. In Washington, HUAC staff clipped the article and put it in Lee's file with a typed précis noting that he "made a violent attack on American radio owners for alleged efforts to distort and conceal negro [*sic*] problems."

Soon after, commercial sponsors banned Lee from forty radio and television projects. Walter Klee Associates produced several five-minute spots for television starring Canada. No one would buy them. A network executive took Klee aside and said the spots were wonderful; if Canada weren't in them, he would buy them in an instant.

If Lee wasn't blacklisted, he was certainly a hot potato that no one wanted to touch. Money and jobs were suddenly scarce. Some black-listed actors landed decent work on Broadway. Canada sweated out a lackluster two-week summer run of *Anna Lucasta* at the Apollo, followed by a demoralizing summer-stock production of *Native Son* at the Crest Theater in the seaside community of Long Beach on Long Island. Local reporter Nadia Dunkel decided to do a backstage interview with Canada about how it felt to be playing Bigger again. She found herself trailing the actor down a dark alley, picking her way over bundles of scenery, and crawling under the stage with a hand from Canada before finally arriving in his dressing room. There was no star on the door, because there wasn't a door at all. His gloomy cubbyhole contained a mirror, a cot, a small table, and one chair. Dunkel was shocked. Lee sat down in the chair and surveyed his domain. "These conditions are discouraging for an actor," he observed, his voice bleak.

Canada clearly wasn't getting star treatment. Stagehands and the rest of the crew were indifferent, incompetent, even belligerent. "Those fools forgot my gun and my knife last night," Lee complained to Dunkel. "I hope I will be better prepared this matinee. After all, I have to keep kill-ing the woman all week long." To be honest, he said, he'd rather be boxing, "but you know, there's an age factor to consider. And when you have a son of 22, your years are pretty obvious." Canada visibly cheered up as he proudly told the reporter that Carl was following in his old man's footsteps, and would open the following week in Jean-Paul Sartre's play, *The Respectful Prostitute*. Around this time Carl filed for a Social Security number. The original application notes his birth name, Carl Vincent Canegata, and the name he was now working under, Canada

Vincent Lee, Jr. Given that his father's name had just been tainted red, Carl's decision to perform as Canada Lee, Jr., may have been a gesture of love and loyalty. (For most of his professional life, however, the actor used the stage name Carl Lee.)

Canada took some comfort in the glowing reviews captured by *Lost Boundaries*. The film broke box-office records in several northern cities and won best screenplay at the third annual Cannes Film Festival. *Time* called it "not only a first-class social document, but also a profoundly moving film." *Life* named it Movie of the Week, and *Newsweek* claimed it was "one of the best movies made since the war." *The New York Times* chimed in: "Viewed as emotional entertainment, as social enlightenment, or both, it is one of the most effective pictures that we are likely to have this year." However, *Times* reviewer Bosley Crowther pointed out that the story of a black family passing for white "touches the immediate anxieties of only a limited number of Negroes" and "may even be regarded by some Negroes with a certain distaste." Black critics did find themselves on uncertain critical ground, observes film historian Thomas Cripps. While the Associated Negro Press called *Lost Boundaries* a "classic" and an *Afro-American* writer said it "brought tears to my eyes," the *Chicago Defender* chided de Rochemont for failing to "grapple too strenuously with the issues raised," and in the *New York Amsterdam News*, Fredi Washington criticized the filmmakers for slighting blacks.

When Southerners began to attack the film, the black press had little choice but to close ranks and defend it against political censorship. In Atlanta, *Lost Boundaries* was banned after the city's censor decided the film was "contrary to the public good." The censor in Memphis concurred, saying the film was "inimical to the public welfare" because it "deals with social equality between whites and Negroes in a way that is not practiced in the South." De Rochemont prepared to file a lawsuit in federal court against the censors. In the meantime, the picture sold out theaters in Norfolk, Miami, Richmond, Houston, Louisville, Raleigh, San Antonio, and twenty-five smaller Southern towns, earning a string of enthusiastic reviews.

Too bad good reviews didn't pay the rent. Canada could have used the cash.

🐾   🐾   🐾

One evening, Frances and Canada were alone in their apartment when the doorbell rang. Two men claiming to represent the FBI wanted to talk to the actor—alone. Frances waited in another room and Lee later told her what happened.

The agents said they understood Canada was having trouble getting work. They made the actor an offer they were certain he couldn't refuse: "Come out against Robeson, and your name will be in the clear."

Lee immediately assumed this was a shrewd and despicable strategy designed to split the black community into factions and weaken the civil rights movement. "I'm not going to divide my people," Canada replied, hotly. "We are the two biggest Negro names in New York. I may not agree with everything that Robeson says, but I'll be damned if you're going to get me to fight another great American Negro."

You're making a mistake, the mysterious visitors told him: "If you think you were blacklisted before, it will be nothing in comparison to what will happen in the future."

He could save his career, but the price was betrayal.

Canada had been betrayed by his government during the Coplon trial. He was betrayed by the entertainment industry that took away his work and destroyed his dreams. He was betrayed by the media that ruined his name and reputation. He was betrayed by friends and colleagues who believed the worst when they should have known better.

Lee refused to betray his people, and he refused to betray Robeson, a fellow artist, freedom fighter, and friend.

"Get the hell out of here," Canada said, and cursed them so loudly that Frances could understand him in the next room. It was one of the very few times she ever heard him swear. The men left in a hurry. "He was absolutely livid that they should have the nerve to come to him with something like that," she said. Lee was so upset that Frances worried he might become ill; Canada had recently been diagnosed with hypertension.

Accounts differ as to whether or not Canada denounced Robeson. In *Journal of the Plague Years*, Stefan Kanfer claims that Lee did denounce his fellow activist, and Victor Navasky, publisher of the *Nation*, agreed in his 1981 book *Naming Names*; yet neither book lists a source for this information and Frances vigorously denies it. She does admit, though, that her version of the "mysterious visitors" incident can't be corroborated. However, the FBI did pressure other prominent African Americans to

condemn Robeson, including singer Josh White and baseball hero Jackie
Robinson, which lends credibility to Frances's position. Lee also described
the incident to his son. "Canada said to me: I can't do it. Robeson is a
great man," Carl later recalled. Paul Robeson, Jr., has said that he never
found evidence to support the allegation that Lee denounced his father.
But the most convincing proof that Canada didn't smear Robeson to get
off the blacklist is the most obvious: Lee remained out of work.

If the tainted actor had chosen to clear himself, there were a host of
options ranging from excruciatingly expensive to profoundly humiliating
to ethically despicable. He could have paid off American Business Con-
sultants, a clearance racket staffed with former FBI agents. He could
have recanted before HUAC or the FBI, naming names in a public
purge. He could have gone to the Screen Actors Guild; the union helped
clear a few blacklistees, but "only those who could or would swear that
their political past was meaningless, a 'horrible mistake,'" according to
author Larry Ceplair. Or Lee could have gone to the media to make a
splashy confession that he had been "duped" by Commies.

Other people were doing it, and those who didn't were paying a high
price.

"Show business people who couldn't or wouldn't clear themselves
soon became unemployable and ostracized. Some left the country—if
they could get passports," writes historian Ellen Schrecker. "Ultimately,
many of the blacklisted actors had to abandon their careers and take
whatever jobs they could find . . . The blacklist took a personal toll as well.
Broken health and broken marriages, even suicides, were not unknown."

Not long after the mysterious visitors episode, Frances did the books
and found they were eighteen thousand dollars in debt. She wanted to
give up the costly Fifty-seventh Street apartment. Canada said he would
think about it. Frances offered to get a job, even something part-time, but
he refused even to consider it. Frances worried about his health. Lee
continued to suffer from high blood pressure, and she begged him to see
a doctor. "He had these wracking headaches," she remembers. "I'd stand
there and rub his neck. He was just so frustrated, fighting this invisible
enemy. He couldn't even hit or strike out anywhere. There was nothing
concrete for him to attack, to fight against."

Instead, Lee scoured the town, looking for work. He tried to generate
interest in a couple of plays, including *The Reluctant Lady*, still hoping
to bring it to Broadway. He sent Frances to Baltimore to talk to some

backers about financing the project. Upon her arrival, she was handed a note asking her to call home immediately.

"Turn around and come back as fast as you can and get Canada into bed," said her brother, who was a physician. Frances apologized to her hosts, jumped in the car, and drove back to New York City. By the time she got to the apartment, Lee's blood pressure measured 280 over 160. "He could have had a cerebral hemorrhage. That's how high his blood pressure was," she said. "I got him off his feet, into bed."

Canada was a terrible patient. He wasn't used to being sick, and he worried far more about money and work than about his blood pressure. Rent was past due, bills and debts were stacking up. When Lovey pawned Canada's gold cufflinks to raise some quick cash for the couple, Frances realized they were at rock bottom, and she feared for their future. They endured several stressful weeks as Lee's condition gradually improved.

Then, in August, the telephone rang.

Director Zoltan Korda was about to make a film for London Films. *Cry, the Beloved Country* was based on a best-selling book by South African novelist Alan Paton. Korda and Paton were looking for a black actor to play the Reverend Stephen Kumalo, an aging priest whose life is shattered when his son kills a young white man.

Paton, in fact, had spent days peering at dozens of screen tests by black actors through small spectacles that often perched on the very tip of his nose. The writer gave them all a resounding thumbs-down until he saw a clip of Canada in *Lost Boundaries*. Breathing a small sigh of relief, he said: "That's the man I want."

Canada had read Paton's book and was simply ecstatic, Frances said: "He wanted Kumalo. He had dreamed about Kumalo when he read the book. He saw himself as Kumalo. He believed there was not another actor around who could play it like he could."

Better still, Korda wasn't bothered by the blacklist; it held no sway over the British studio financing the film. However, the director *was* a bit nervous about Canada's false eye. He planned to use frequent close-ups and wondered if the glass eye would stand up to such scrutiny. He asked the actor to take a screen test, and Lee eagerly agreed.

The day before the screen test, Canada was anxious and jittery. He had decided that the only thing in the world that could save his career was this film. He paced the floor all afternoon. He didn't sleep all night.

He was completely shattered when he left the apartment to make the test. "And boy, he muffed it," Frances recalled.

Canada came home furious at himself and deeply depressed. He sat and stared morosely into space. Frances sat down with him.

"Go to Korda and ask for a second test," she said.

Lee shook his head. "I can't do that."

"You want me to call him?" asked Frances, reaching for the phone.

Canada called. He got a second test and passed it with flying colors.

Korda explained that he couldn't make a formal offer until all financial arrangements had been sorted out with the studio, but he promised to be in touch. Frances and Canada tried not to worry, they knew film deals could drag on for months. Still, the wait was sheer hell. Lee tried to stay calm and optimistic as the days passed. Paton wanted him. Korda wanted him. He was going to get the part; he was going to beat the blacklist. He just had to be patient and avoid trouble.

But Lee wasn't a patient man, nor could he seem to stay out of trouble.

On August 27, 1949, Paul Robeson was scheduled to perform a concert in Peekskill, New York, to benefit the Harlem chapter of the Civil Rights Congress. Local conservatives protested that they didn't want Robeson. Though he had performed three concerts in Peekskill in past years, things had changed. Always controversial, the singer was now loathed and feared by racists and anti-Communists. Robeson would never make it to the concert. Hours before it was to start, an angry mob wielding clubs, rocks, and knives stormed the site. They smashed chairs, set them afire, burned a cross on a hillside, and threatened to kill Robeson, as well as blacks and Jews in the audience. Injuries were reported by concert staff, including teenager ushers. Days later, Robeson said he would perform the concert on September 4. Canada and other activists championed the cause. At a rally on Lenox Avenue, ten thousand people demonstrated their support. On the day of the concert, Robeson ignored death threats and traveled to Peekskill along with singer Pete Seeger and other artists. They performed before a crowd of twenty thousand people, surrounded by a human wall of unarmed volunteer guards. But when the concertgoers left, they were stoned and beaten as police and state troopers stood by and watched. More than a hundred people were injured. The ugly Peekskill riot made headlines around the country. Robeson, Lee, and civil rights groups angrily demanded a full investigation.

Public sympathy, however, tilted farther to the right as Americans grew more agitated over the expanding power and influence of Communism. On September 23, President Truman gravely announced that the Soviet Union had detonated its first atomic bomb.

That same evening, Canada was booked on *The Barry Gray Show*. Credited as the father of talk radio, Gray was the first to invite listeners to call in and comment during his show. The savvy host attracted thousands of listeners by interviewing showbiz stars on air. He grew so popular, in fact, that Ed Sullivan and Walter Winchell began to view him as competition for their own radio programs. They asked their celebrity friends not to go on Gray's show. As a consequence, Gray began to invite more political figures, engaging them in fierce debates that generated more controversy and attracted even more listeners.

Given the day's news about Russia and the bomb, and knowing the format of Gray's program, Lee surely realized he might find himself in dangerous waters if talk turned to politics. And yet he seemed utterly surprised, even shocked, when Gray opened the program with a direct shot: "I think probably we can get right to it by asking Canada Lee, who has been accused of being many, many things, the reason why."

Lee laughed nervously, tried to make a joke, failed, and finally stuttered out that he really just wanted to act, but nobody seemed interested in his work.

The talk show host said he knew that Lee's name had been attached to controversial groups and causes. Your name has been tainted, he told the actor. "I'm a guy that likes to call things *things*," Gray said, clumsily avoiding *spade a spade*. "I want to find out if we still agree on things politically, or we disagree, and why have you done this?"

Canada insisted he hadn't changed politically. He was a liberal, not a Communist. He reminded Gray that during the war, he and other celebrities believed they were doing their patriotic bit by performing or speaking or lending their names as sponsors to various organizations. Later, he said, when Russia became an enemy instead of an ally, the Attorney General decided some of these groups were actually Communist fronts.

"Have you become a member of any of these organizations?" Gray asked.

"I haven't even joined the Elks!" Canada laughed. "I really am not a joiner. I joined church once when I was a little kid. And I've never joined anything since."

Gray then professed weariness with name-calling and Red-baiting in the press, asserting his firm belief in the Constitution and the right to free speech. But he still wanted to know if the accusation that Canada was a fellow traveler was true. "If you haven't joined any organizations, why then have you been called the names?" he asked.

Canada hedged at first. He said he wasn't sure, "but I've been fighting for the minority peoples because, in fighting for the minority peoples, I again fight for myself."

Gray then brought up Peekskill, asking if Canada thought violence would solve the country's race problem. Lee said he believed education was the answer. "I deplore very much the Peekskill incident," he said. "I deplore it even more because . . ." He obviously saw he was getting into trouble. "Well, I better not go on," he said, nervously backing away from discussing Robeson. But Gray refused to be diverted; he said that despite the constitutional guarantee of free speech, Robeson did not have the right to advocate the overthrow of the American government. (Robeson, in fact, never did so.)

Canada said he believed "the Robeson thing" resulted from irrational fear. White people are taught from birth "the fear of the Negro," he said—the razor-toting, violent, bogeyman. But before Lee could fully connect the Peekskill riot to racism and anxiety, Gray interrupted, arguing that education was taking care of those stereotypes. Canada shot back that minorities and the poor were still "kept down." What Lee tried to say next—despite interruptions and nervousness—is that whenever a black man expresses ideas powerful enough to unite minorities and the poor, it makes the white majority afraid.

Unfortunately, he didn't articulate his point well, and Gray cut him off. "I don't follow you, Canada. Honestly I don't." He insisted on getting back to his initial question: "Why have people given you the taint of being a follower, a leftist, a fellow traveler?"

"I've been right in the forefront of the fight for equal rights," Canada said. "That's all I've been doing." Without specifically mentioning the Coplon trial, the actor referred to the newspaper articles that named him, along with Frederic March and Helen Hayes.

Now more than halfway through the program, Gray's other guest, Mac Clark, joined the conversation by paraphrasing Shakespeare: "I have not come here to bury Canada Lee, nor have I come to praise him."

In Lee's "militancy" for civil rights, Clark said, the actor had aligned himself with groups that took their orders from the Cominform.

When Canada asked how the average actor could possibly know which groups those were, Clark and Gray both rejected ignorance as an excuse. "Canada is not by any means a stupid man," Clark said.

"Nor is he four years old," Gray added.

"Nor is he a child," Clark agreed. "For him to come up and say, 'Well, how was I to know?' is no defense to me."

Canada, who had suddenly become invisible in the cramped studio, interrupted with extreme courtesy: "I don't mean to disagree with you but—"

"Well, I am disagreeing with *you!*" Clark snapped.

"All right then, I'll disagree with you, Mac," Lee said, ever gracious. He briefly described his work with the Southern Conference for Human Welfare to support equal rights and civil liberties for blacks in the South—and then pointed out that this group had been cited as a Communist front.

Gray, who had lived in the South and fancied himself an expert on the region's racial problems, cut Lee off with a diatribe against Northern liberal militants "creating scenes" by flagrantly breaking Jim Crow laws. Clark excitedly chimed in, and the final exchange between the three men was heated and ultimately devastating for Canada.

"Certain groups become so doggone vehement, so doggone militant," Clark said, "they lose all sense of direction and pretty soon mayhem and murder, it all becomes part of the picture, which is the Communist picture. And unfortunately fellows like Canada Lee ... have joined these groups . . . they get in with this violence—"

Violence? Canada interrupted, desperate to put a stop to this. "But Mac—Mac—*Mac,*" he said, raising his voice over Clark's. "I *never* joined a group in my life—"

"But you have!" pounced Barry Gray.

"You've been attached to them!" Clark added. "You've become part and parcel!"

"You have lent your name to advertisements," Gray said, over Canada's protestations. "That is much the same thing."

"That's true," Canada said, hoping for an opening. "That's true, but—"

But the opening vanished as Gray and Clark moved in for the kill, and with a few simple sentences defined the bitter cruelty and bewildering ethics of the blacklist. Don't you see, Canada? they said. It doesn't matter whether you are in fact a member of the Communist Party. If the man on the street, in the subway, and on the bus believes you are a Red, a Pink, a fellow traveler, or a subversive, then you *are*.

"That's a fact!" Clark spat. "So if you don't hold a card, it doesn't matter—"

"You have *joined!*" Gray finished smugly.

When the show was over, Lee realized that no one had actually called him a Communist. They said he joined groups, implied he was a sympathizer. And for most people, that was enough to keep him on the blacklist. "He was the victim of a more nebulous whispering campaign," Walter White later observed, "but no one was more effectively boycotted."

Shortly after the Barry Gray show aired, *Variety* reported that Lee's radio sponsor, the American Tobacco Company, had dropped him because he was a suspected Communist. Furious, Lee wrote to the magazine, denying the charge and accusing *Variety* of "furthering a false and completely vicious rumor." Reporting such items, he said, "only helps to keep alive the attempt to smear my reputation."

"I am not, never have been, nor ever intend to be a Communist," he wrote. "That I have been fighting the un-American practices used against my people, such as lynchings, Jim Crow, utter disregard for the Negro's dignity as a human being, or first-class American citizen, I neither can nor wish to deny."

He admitted to voting and using his right to campaign. He had done his patriotic duty by promoting victory for America during the war. He had raised money to aid those who suffered polio, cancer, heart ailments, multiple sclerosis, and combat blindness. He battled poverty, illiteracy, segregation, and discrimination against all minorities. He conceded support for liberal causes, but denied membership in any subversive group.

Lee told *Variety* that he had lost television, radio, and film roles because of lies and innuendo. "How long can a man take this kind of unfair and unfounded treatment?" he asked. "I am sick and tired of being indicted by unverified implications," he wrote. "If anyone has any proof, not insinuations, let them come forward." In conclusion, he said his "reputation as an American and as an actor" had been greatly damaged by slanderous statements: "If they continue, my only recourse will be to take legal action."

The *Daily Worker* was a bit offended by Canada's stand. A columnist "regretted that in his reply Mr. Lee accepted the assumption that to be a Communist is 'subversive,' or that it cannot be reconciled with 'integrity as a loyal American.' Mr. Lee must know that in fighting for those social advances in which he so deeply believes, loyal American Communists have certainly been on the front lines." But the *Worker* praised the letter as "an impressive indictment" of the blacklist, which sought to silence any dissent that might stand in the way of profits for networks and advertisers. "This, and not any assumed membership in the Communist Party, is the reason for the blacklist against any militant fighter for the people," the columnist concluded.

If Canada had hoped the rumor mill would come to a full stop after his threat of legal action, he had to be thoroughly disappointed when Walter Winchell ran this item in his October 13 column: "Canada Lee, the Negro star, will address a Vets' rally near Peekskill, Nov. 6th. He will wallop Paul Robeson's 'line.'"

Presumably, Winchell meant that Lee's remarks to the veterans would either criticize Robeson's purported statement that black soldiers would never go to war on behalf of their oppressors, or would attack Robeson's well-publicized contention that the American Legion and other veterans groups participated in the Peekskill riots. Certainly, the columnist had insinuated that Canada would denounce Robeson in some fashion.

Would this never end? Lee found out that Winchell's sources were a couple of advertising men who sent the columnist bits of gossip in exchange for a few dollars. Canada wrote the two men and requested a retraction, but they refused. Lee wrote Winchell, demanding a correction. Nothing happened. Meanwhile, columnists at other papers repeated the rumor. Lee wrote letters to their editors, hoping to set the record straight. "I am for complete democracy," he wrote to the *Daily Compass*. The Negro, he said, has a right "to act, sing, speak, or play ball without fear of mob violence any place in these United States. This is a great nation, and at no time in its history has there been any doubt of the Negroes' love, loyalty, and contribution to this nation's safety and culture." But all Americans must share the benefits of democracy equally, Canada argued, and he would continue to oppose "Jim Crow, Klanism, prejudice, lynching, and all other indignities and lack of opportunities that keep the Negro from being a first-class Citizen in this America for which so many had fought and died."

Lee was boxing with shadows, rumors, innuendo, and insult. Those who once praised him now turned against him, including former political allies, journalists, colleagues, and fans. "How can they do this to me?" he asked in letters and press releases and speeches. The answer was as complex as the players in the Red Scare drama.

"Among the supporters of the blacklist in America and Hollywood were those who genuinely believed that Soviet Communism was actually threatening the United States," Larry Ceplair has observed. "They thought American Communists were the pawns of a Moscow-directed conspiracy aimed at conquering the U.S."

Americans believed they had a right to be afraid. The Soviets had the atomic bomb. Communists under Mao Zedong were taking control of China. East Germany was now a Soviet satellite. Communist uprisings erupted from Colombia to Korea. Here at home, eleven American Communists were tried and convicted of conspiring to overthrow the U.S. government. Priests and preachers told their congregations that Communism threatened Christianity. Scientists quoted in *Life* explained ways American cities could prepare for atomic war. Schoolchildren practiced safety maneuvers in their classrooms in case of nuclear attack. Confidence in national and personal security was at a low point.

Many who sought to end Canada Lee's career were convinced that the actor was a Communist who sought to overthrow the American government. Even if he was only a Communist sympathizer, he was still on the wrong side of a clash that was growing more intense and frightening by the day. Others suspected that Canada wasn't, in fact, a Communist, but nevertheless believed him a traitor because he continued to criticize his country at a time when the nation appeared to be in grave peril.

Lee couldn't, or wouldn't, understand the fears that drove the blacklist. In his mind and in his heart, he was doing right and helping others. He refused to end his crusades for civil rights and humanitarian causes. He raised money for Negro schools in Mississippi and for blind soldiers. He encouraged blacks and Jews to work together for social justice. He spoke out in favor of the Jewish state of Israel. He campaigned for black candidates and hosted a dance to benefit his father's beloved charity, the Mayfield Nursery. He fought for integrated seating at the Maryland Theater in Baltimore. He condemned the Ober Law, which outlawed the Communist Party and required public employees to swear loyalty oaths and, in effect, their opposition to radical ideas. He urged citizens to take a stand against "these frightened little men" in Congress who looked for Reds under every bed.

Those frightened little men were listening, and Lee's remarks about them were promptly typed on index cards and dropped into his HUAC file.

In November, Canada managed to get one radio job. He hadn't done any broadcast work since June, and his last acting job had been that hole-in-the-wall *Native Son* in July. The radio script, "Knights of the Golden Circle," concerned a Civil War–era secret society that sympathized with the Confederacy and plotted to create a network of slavery extending from the United States to Mexico and the West Indies. Part of an innovative series called *Destination Freedom*, the show was broadcast on WMAQ-Chicago and other stations.

Soon after the program aired, Lee found his name mentioned in Ed Sullivan's column, provocatively headlined "Red Sails on Broadway." Clearly, Ed had not changed his low opinion of Canada's politics. In this case, the columnist's subject was a dinner in support of peaceful relations between the United States and the Soviet Union; the event at the Waldorf-Astoria Hotel was sponsored by the National Council of American-Soviet Friendship. "For the guidance of theatergoers who have the Commie line sprayed at them from Broadway stages," he wrote, "I've prepared a list of sponsors of the Russian shenanigans at the Waldorf. Some of these sponsors of the Waldorf-Kremlin conference are deluded; most of them aren't on our side and they aren't clowning!" The list included Lee and Robeson. By this point, it's likely that Canada had given up on trying to win a retraction from Sullivan about this column item or any other.

The holidays came and went, the New Year and a new decade arrived, and still there was no word from Korda on *Cry, the Beloved Country*. Then Lovey abruptly announced that he was also up for a part in Korda's film. "His screen test was fantastic," recalls his son, Bill Canegata. Lovey had never acted before. Frances was annoyed. Lee was amused, but it wouldn't be so funny if Lovey got a part and he didn't.

As time wore on, Lee became tormented by the idea that his false eye looked bad in the second screen test. He found out that a clinic in London was producing high quality prosthetics that would photograph better and look more realistic on film. The trouble was money, of course — money to get to London, money to buy the lens.

But the more he thought about a trip to Europe, the better the idea seemed. Other blacklisted actors and writers were leaving the country to seek work in London, Paris, Rome, even Mexico. If he could get to London, he could talk to friends in the entertainment business there and find a way to work abroad.

Frances met with Canada's physician and close friend, John Moseley. They agreed that a trip to Europe might reduce Lee's tension and lower his blood pressure. "Even though it meant borrowing money, the trip was necessary," Frances recalled.

Friends and family loaned the couple all the cash they could spare, and Canada got his plane ticket to London. He would leave on Saturday, March 4, 1950, one day after his forty-third birthday. The couple decided to host a huge birthday-farewell bash and invited nearly a hundred people — old friends like the Moseleys, Billy Butler and his wife, Mary, as well as stars and society folk like Richard Adler, dancer Ray Bolger, and their neighbor, actor Burgess Meredith.

"We couldn't afford a catered affair, so it was necessary to be ingenious," Frances said. "I didn't even have a kitchen, just this blasted two-burner hotplate in a closet."

After stuffing four turkeys and glazing two hams, Frances sweet-talked a chef at a nearby restaurant into baking and slicing them. She cooked side dishes on their small hot plate. Plates, cups, saucers, and silverware were rented; cases of wine and liquor were delivered.

The party was a smash. People danced, sang, ate, and drank all night long. Bolger, slightly inebriated, decided to dance on the windowsills. The ledges were extremely narrow and the apartment was several stories up. Bolger merrily skipped from the sofa to the sills, executing taps, turns, and slides. "My heart was in my mouth the entire time," Frances said. "It took a long time to stop pounding after he climbed down."

The party lasted into the wee hours of the morning. Near dawn, Canada tried to rest as Frances and a few friends collected garbage and stacked dirty dishes. Soon it was time to go. Lee put his suitcase in the car and checked his wallet and passport. As Frances drove him to Idlewild, he talked excitedly about his first trip to Europe, but when they said their good-byes, he felt melancholy about leaving her. "I'll be right here waiting for you to come home," Frances assured him. She swore to be faithful. He promised to write often. They kissed. And then he was gone.

"I went back to the apartment. What a mess!" Frances said. Lacking a kitchen sink, she washed dishes in the bathtub, and after hours on her knees, promised herself that their next apartment might be tiny, but it would definitely have a kitchen.

The next day, Frances got a telegram from Lee. He had arrived safely and checked into the Strand Palace Hotel. He immediately made an appointment with the eye specialist, and arranged meetings with people in the film and theater community. He had also called his friend Leonard Kovin, an artist in Paris he hoped to visit in a week or two.

Frances wrote back, updating him on news and business. She was lonely, especially at night, but she wanted him to be happy and healthy. She urged him to get some rest.

Frances was still trying to sort out Canada's income-tax woes and their debts. Untangling his finances was tedious work, and she was feeling ill; soon she was in bed with a bad case of influenza. Miserable and anxious, Frances got angry and upset when a week passed with no word from Canada. She often found herself in tears. "All of his friends were constantly phoning for news, including his agent," she said. "It was most infuriating not to be able to give them one bit of information."

Finally on March 13 she received a telegram. Lee missed her, he loved her, Paris was wonderful, Lennie was great. Relieved, but not altogether pleased, she wrote back that she was glad to know he had made it to France. Her week had been sheer hell, but she had good news. His agent, Peter Witt, had called to say it was nearly certain that Canada had the part of Kumalo in *Cry, the Beloved Country*. All that remained were final contract negotiations. Shooting was set to begin in June. "I was so thankful," Lee later told a reporter. "I almost cried. I was $18,000 in debt at the time with no real prospects in sight."

In her next few letters, Frances urged Lee to negotiate aggressively on his film contract. She thought his agent bargained too low during initial discussions. She also peppered Canada with questions: how long did he intend to stay in Paris? Had he met with Korda? What about other work? Lee was pursuing several projects, including a show with Josephine

Baker in Paris, a fall production of *Othello* in London, and a screenplay about the nineteenth-century black Shakespearean actor Ira Aldridge. As for news on the home front, Frances told Canada she had filed for an extension on his 1949 income-tax return and fended off the telephone company. She asked Canada to write her more often and told him she loved and missed him.

On March 17, Frances got the news they had been waiting for all these months. The contract for *Cry, the Beloved Country* was agreed upon. Canada would earn a thousand dollars per week for a guaranteed fifteen weeks, all expenses paid. Filming would start in London on June 15, move to South Africa, then return to London for a final two weeks.

Fifteen thousand dollars *plus* expenses! After months of little or no work, it was like winning the lottery. Even though Canada's salary wouldn't cover their debt, it would make a serious and very welcome dent. Frances was giddy with relief. No more fighting shadows and vicious blacklists, she told Lee. You'll be on top again, and those creeps will come crawling back with their tails between their legs.

Canada was happy. He walked the streets of Paris with his friend Lennie, sat in cafés, visited nightclubs. Everywhere he was welcomed; never was he refused a seat, a table, or service. On March 18, he wrote his love a postcard: "Baby, Prepare yourself to live here. This is where we will spend our days. I love it, only I love you more. Canada."

Lee returned to London. He was now determined to move with Frances to Europe, where he could build a new career far from the blacklist. The separation was wearing on him. He had intended to spend a few more days in Paris, but on the spur of the moment, he flew back to New York unannounced. Arriving late on a Friday night, he caught a cab to midtown Manhattan. Quietly, he let himself into the apartment at West Fifty-seventh Street, his heart pounding. His worst fear was that Frances might not be alone. He put his key in the lock, opened the door, and stepped into darkness. He stood there for a moment, just inside the door, listening—all was silent. Rushing to the bedroom, he found Frances asleep by herself and woke her with a kiss.

Later, he confessed to Frances that when he held her, "I thanked divine providence that you were alone. It was a great moment in my life, because I knew that I loved you—and I felt more than I should. That night taught me to trust you."

It was a wonderful, happy, romantic spring. Their troubles weren't over, and they still had creditors to stall. But after weeks of no work and considerable worry, Lee had a starring role and hopes of more work to come in Europe.

His blood pressure was still high, however, and Dr. Moseley remained concerned. Shooting any film is stressful, but Lee was banking all of his hopes for the future on this movie. And he would be filming in apartheid South Africa. The studio had informed black actors in the cast that they would have to be "indentured" to Korda to live and work there. Canada was likely to feel terrible strain under these conditions.

The actor desperately needed rest, but when he was in New York, the phone never stopped ringing, and Lee could never say no to anyone who requested his help for a worthy cause. Frances consulted Dr. Moseley and other friends. Everyone agreed that Canada needed to leave town again. They borrowed more money and arranged for Lee to spend an entire month in Europe before starting work on the film.

In the middle of May, Frances and Canada said their farewells at the airport again. This time proved even more difficult than the last; it would be many months before they saw each other. "I cried," Frances said. "It was very, very hard to see him go."

To console herself, Frances kept furiously busy packing up the apartment. She had finally convinced Canada they needed a more economical place: "The Fifty-seventh Street apartment was expensive, and it was silly for my bones to rattle around while I was waiting for him . . . and just wasting money." She rented a sixth-floor walk-up at 222 East Fortieth Street and put most of their things in storage except for a little bit of furniture and lots of file boxes. Her job, while Lee was away, was to deal with the IRS and oversee payments on his debts once those checks from the studio began rolling in. Before he left, Canada had asked Lovey to help with the move. Lee was worried about Frances; she had been diagnosed with uterine tumors that were benign but still caused her discomfort.

"Don't fall down on this," Canada had warned his brother.

Moving day came. Lovey never showed. After several trips up and down six flights of stairs, Frances was exhausted. When Carl stopped by to help, she sat down suddenly on the steps and cried. "Thank God you're here," she told him. He hugged her and headed up the stairs with a huge load of boxes.

When Canada found out about Lovey, he was furious. "It seems always thus, the people whom you think you can depend on are always never there," he wrote her. "I'm going to write Lovey a scorcher. He promised to be there with you and again he disappoints. This is the first time I have actually been unhappy since I arrived."

Lee was in Paris, staying with Lennie at 6 rue Catulle Mendes in the seventeenth arrondissement. He had fallen in love with the City of Light, especially the nightlife. Decked out in tuxedos, he and Kovin got a ring-side table at the Lido and watched the topless dancers do the cancan. Lee was quick to tell Frances that although the girls were lovely, none was as wonderfully endowed as she was.

Shortly after he arrived in Paris, Canada learned that London Films had pushed the shooting schedule back to mid-July. This was a blow to Frances's carefully laid financial plans, as she had counted on studio checks to begin arriving in June. How would they manage to cover their bills? Canada demanded that the studio pay him a thousand dollars on July 1, plus his expenses during his stay in Europe. The studio declined at first, and Frances had to stall creditors once again. Lee worried about her constantly, and his blood pressure edged upwards.

London Films eventually agreed to give Canada the thousand dollars. Lee wrote Frances that while they had many creditors at their heels, he wanted her to first reimburse family and friends who had loaned them money. He said he had fallen ill with a high temperature and chills after getting yellow fever vaccinations, but was fully recovered. He had moved into a furnished apartment at 26 rue des Plantes. He knew Frances was busy painting the new apartment and wished he could be there to help, even "if I did no more than stand around and say where it isn't painted."

At home, Lovey and Carl were both pursuing acting careers. Lovey auditioned unsuccessfully for the role of Kingfish on the *Amos 'n' Andy* television show, and was disappointed to learn that he wasn't getting a part in *Cry, the Beloved Country*. Carl had more success, winning a summer job at a resort called Chrystal Lodge, where he would perform scenes from *Romeo and Juliet*, *Stranglers*, *Miss Julie*, and *Lysistrata*. "These are things that I've been dying to do," Carl wrote his father.

Though Carl was in his late twenties, his letters show a childlike vulnerability and a need for his father's approval and praise. "I've started taking singing lessons, and I've discovered that I'm really able to sing," he writes. "Gee, Canada, it's so wonderful. I think that within 6 months that

I will be able to do club dates. Isn't it wonderful?" He clearly missed seeing his father, and ends one letter, "I really hope with all my heart that someday you and I could be together in Paris. I'll keep that as a wish for the future."

On Thursday, June 15, the day that shooting was originally scheduled to begin in London, Canada sat contentedly in his little Parisian apartment. He spent the early part of the morning writing Frances a sweet letter. He was sorry for not writing sooner. He had lost his pen and both pairs of glasses. The only thing he hadn't lost was his good eye, he joked, and "there was a time when I thought I had misplaced that." He told her he was growing a beard for his role as Kumalo and that she would positively laugh at him. He loved her, he missed her, he wished she could come to Paris. Nobody could love her as much as her "Canadian."

That night, he hopped a plane to Sweden to visit his friend Ivar Ohman, managing editor of a Swedish magazine, who had known Lee since he was a boxer. The Swedish press gave Canada a warm reception at the airport, snapping dozens of photographs for the next day's newspapers. Ohman's publisher invited the actor to his home for a glass of wine to celebrate his arrival on Swedish ground. The men then went to a party hosted by the American cultural affairs attaché, who perhaps hadn't heard about Lee's FBI or HUAC files, nor his alleged subversive activities. Canada told everyone how much he would like to play Othello, perhaps hoping there might be producers in the crowd.

The next day, Ivar drove Canada to his family's summer farm, or *langsjort*. The men fished, played soccer with the children, and then took a steam bath called a *bastu*. Lee rarely touched liquor, but Ivar induced him to tie one on and he went to bed wonderfully plastered. He woke up after midnight to find the sun still high in the sky. At six, he was out on the lake, fishing in the stillness of Sunday morning. One evening, as Canada and Ivar sat before an open fire just before dinner, Lee fervently wished Frances could be at his side so they could enjoy these moments together. He couldn't wait to bring her to Europe. He didn't think he could ever live in America again.

A week later, Lee traveled to London. Korda had asked him to do some screen tests with an actor who was up for a role in the film. While Lee was in the Big Smoke, banner headlines announced that the North Korean army had crossed the thirty-eighth parallel on June 25. Though the civil war between North and South Korea had been festering for some time, the United States believed Stalin was behind the move, testing American resolve. The escalating tension between East and West made it easier for Hoover, Senator McCarthy, and the rest of the anti-Communist network to convince their fellow Americans of the threat posed by subversives at home. "In a crude but not incorrect way," observes historian Ellen Schrecker, "McCarthyism can be seen as the home front of the Cold War."

Canada was taking a holiday from politics. He went boating on the Thames one Sunday afternoon with friends. Something went wrong with the steering mechanism, so Lee and his pals calmly pulled up a floorboard to get to the guide wires. Picnickers along the riverbank were amazed to see the launch floating magically downriver and navigating three locks with its passengers chatting gaily and no one at the wheel to steer.

By the time Lee returned to Paris in late June, he had gone through two thousand dollars out of their very limited funds. Frances begged him to send her the receipts for his tax records. Canada wrote somewhat sheepishly that he would try to remember what he did with the money.

Two weeks remained before filming started, and Lee was eager to travel. After a one-day trip to London for makeup and other tests, Lennie picked him up at the Paris airport and drove south all night. The next morning, the two men were on the beach at St. Tropez. "It is the most beautiful place in the world," Canada wrote Frances from his room at the Hotel Caste, overlooking the Mediterranean. The two men spent a week in St. Tropez and a few days in Cannes ("glorious, only too many Americans," Canada wrote). On the morning of July 10, they crossed the Italian border. After stopping in Pisa so Canada could see the famous tower, they drove on to Florence. Travel in Europe seemed luxuriously easy to Lee compared to his time on the road with Jim Crow at home. Not a single hotel or restaurant turned him away. He wished he had started traveling earlier, he wrote Frances: "The people are wonderful, and best of all, I don't have to worry about my color."

By mid-July Canada was back in London and preparing to leave for South Africa. When he saw a doctor for his final physical, his blood pressure was 200 over 130. He wrote Frances that he felt quite all right, and that his new glass eye was a great improvement.

South African newspapers announced the cast's arrival. "Canada

Lee, Charles McRae and Sidney Poitier, prominent Negro actors, are to be allowed into the Union to take leading parts in the film *Cry, the Beloved Country*. Their entry is on condition: that they are brought out for the sole purpose of appearing in the film; that accommodation is arranged for them; and that they take no part in politics," *The Dispatch* reported July 19.

That last condition must have been difficult for Lee to agree to, but keeping this job was crucial if he wanted to pay off his debts and build a career in Europe. The actor would frequently and surreptitiously break the rule by collecting papers, photographs, and other evidence of the cruelties of apartheid with the goal of smuggling them back to New York.

On Sunday morning, July 23, Canada took a 9:00 a.m. flight from London to Johannesburg, where he entered the country as a bonded servant of Zoltan Korda. Despite this rather chilling official welcome, Lee soon found himself in fairly luxurious quarters on a five hundred-acre farm with his own car, chef, and a houseboy who called him "Massa." "I told him my name was Lee, but he kept right on with that 'Massa' business," Canada later told a reporter. "So finally I decided it was wasted effort . . . 'Massa' I remained."

Lee stayed in Johannesburg for a week before moving with cast and crew to Ixopo, Natal, in the Midlands region west of Durban. Blacks in the cast had to first get travel permits from the Department of Native Affairs. Traveling through rolling hills, Lee saw farms, paddocks, cultivated fields, and rich grassland with large grazing herds. Along the way, the caravan of cars stopped for gas. Canada had to use the toilet, and so he stepped off the bus and found the Afrikaner who ran the station.

"Where is the gent's room, please?" he asked.

"What's that you want?" the Afrikaner said. Canada spotted a sign on a door saying, "Gent's—Europeans Only." He started for the door.

"You can't go in there!" the Afrikaner called. "That's for Europeans."

Canada was spoiling for a fight, but actor Charles McRae stepped in and convinced Lee to return to the car. They drove on to Ixopo, where the cast registered at the Plough Hotel. Canada was disturbed by the gas station incident, but he was favorably impressed by young Afrikaners he met. One night, he was invited to come over to an Afrikaner's house at 3:00 a.m. to hear a Joe Louis fight on the radio. "I lost six cents on the fight," he told the press, good-humoredly. "I was invited to the homes of

Europeans who are in deep sympathy with the Native problems here, and really looking for answers."

Young people will make changes, he said, but they will need the help of black South Africans and at the moment, that was impossible, for blacks had little education, and no money or political power. Lee's optimism would dim as he got a swift education in local politics from the black South Africans in the cast and crew, including actor and activist Lionel Ngakane, and from his own experiences living under apartheid.

Shooting began August 3, 1950. Frances and Carl sent a telegram telling the actor to break a leg. Lee wrote glowingly about his first day on the set. Zolly is a great director, he said, and is aiming for an Academy Award. Somewhat ruefully, he admitted that he felt ignorant around Korda. He couldn't seem to do what the director wanted, but vowed he would find a way.

His letters home throughout the month of August consistently express the same themes: his insecurity on the set, his inability to meet Korda's demands, and his growing awareness of the nightmare of apartheid. Lee, McRae, and three other black cast members were now lodged at the fifteen-hundred-acre farm of Gary E. Francis, brother-in-law to the novelist Alan Paton. Once again, their quarters were quite comfortable, and Lee was given a horse to ride. But although Francis was a liberal man, his wife was conservative, according to Canada. The black houseguests did not mix much with their white hosts and Lee spent most of his free time in his room. There was nothing for him to do—even the local cinemas were for Europeans only. He figured he could take his passport and try to force his way into the movies, but decided that if black South Africans couldn't go, he wouldn't.

Instead, Lee took to hanging out with young Lionel Ngakane, destined to be a key figure in South African film. Born in Pretoria in 1928, Ngakane became politically active at an early age, joining the African National Congress youth league along with Nelson Mandela. Ngakane was working as Korda's assistant and also played Absalom Kumalo, Lee's on-screen son.

One night, Canada and Ngakane were invited to dinner at a white friend's house. On the way over, "we saw a native woman being brutally beaten," Canada later recalled in an interview. "We both got sick and couldn't go." He told the reporter some of the frightening stories he had heard, including an account of a young boy "prevailed upon to confess larceny by imbibing so much water that eventually his bladder burst and he died." The black South African was treated as "a slave, to be kicked around, and he lives in such mortal fear that even a band of his own people never comes to his defense when he is in trouble."

News from home always cheered Canada up. Frances sent love letters, cartons of Chesterfield cigarettes, and his beloved *Herald Tribune* crossword puzzles. His father sent word that he was about to make a long-awaited trip to his home island of St. Croix. Carl wrote that he had just lost a role in a Theatre Guild production of *Head of the Family* to Harry Belafonte. "When the opportunity does present itself, I will come through with shining colors," he wrote, "the tradition of the Lees in the theater."

Though he was eight thousand miles from home, Canada never lost touch with his old neighborhood. He found out through the grapevine that Beulah Bullock was having a little trouble getting her son to do as he was told. One day the telephone rang at Beulah's home in Harlem. It was Canada, calling from Johannesburg, wanting to know what was up with Oscar. She poured out her heart to him, and Lee listened attentively. "He's a boy!" Canada told her, urging her not to worry. "Look, put him on."

The actor talked to Oscar, and the young man listened.

"I asked Oscar, 'What did he tell you?'" Beulah said. "He would never say. But I would never have a problem with Oscar after that. For weeks, I wouldn't have problems."

Aunt Sylvia Hoist urged Lee to take lots of photos on his travels. She reported that Juanita was feeling well and had taken up painting; Sylvia then praised her nephew for finding the doctor who successfully treated his ex-wife during her bouts with mental illness. Lovey wrote that Pheta, his estranged wife, had come back to him, inspiring him to "do my share and stand on my own two feet (loan me a buck?)." Never a big supporter of Canada's relationship with Frances, Lovey also took care to send news of Lee's ex-girlfriends, to inquire if Lee was enjoying any native girls, and to encourage him to send home a few of those damsels as souvenirs for his little brother.

Canada had no use for that kind of souvenir. After his experience with the blacklist, issues of faith and trust, betrayal and infidelity were nothing to joke about. After receiving a particularly sweet love letter from Frances, he nearly cried. He hadn't been able to put his faith in a lover before, he said. He wasn't a handsome man, and he always thought women only wanted him for his fame or his money. But he loved her with all his heart. "You I trust," he told her. "You I believe in."

He regretted the years they lost when she went away. If they had stayed together, he said, they would have a child by now. They should marry, he announced, and move to Europe where he could work and be able to take care of her. The past year had been so hard, and he didn't want to put her through anything like that again.

Cold winter rains set in, turning the earth into a sea of red mud. Bad weather delayed the shooting schedule and the chilly temperatures lowered everyone's spirits. Canada told the *Cape Times* that he never knew it could be so cold in Africa; he wished he had brought his "winter underwear." Korda injured his back and snapped at the cast. He picked on Lee constantly. Canada grew annoyed, but told himself he had to take it. Too much was riding on this picture.

Apartheid depressed and frightened him. "With my own eyes I saw a native on a motorcycle bump into a white man's car," he later said. "There was no damage done, yet the native was viciously beaten and kicked into a patrol wagon." He wrote his young nephew, Billy, a postcard: "Never come to South Africa."

Canada frequently suffered wracking headaches that he called "attacks," sometimes five or six times a night. He believed these were symptoms of his high blood pressure. Dr. Moseley prescribed medication and Frances airmailed it to Ixopo. Lee later admitted to a reporter that he knew he was ill all the while he was in South Africa, but said "there was nothing I could do but accept it, and hope for the best."

Near the end of August, Carl wrote that he had run into the young actor Sidney Poitier, who had just caused a sensation in his film *No Way Out*. Poitier would soon be on his way to South Africa to join Canada on the set. "He is really a good Joe," Carl told his father. "For the first time, I met a young Negro actor who was thinking . . . not only of himself, but of the tremendous struggle . . . the job we must do to take our rightful place as free men. I feel a little silly writing to you about such things. I guess very few people are more aware of these things than you . . . Take good care of yourself, old Dad. And I know you will bring home the Academy Award."

On September 5, Canada awaited Poitier's arrival. He was looking forward to it, but he admitted he was looking to his laurels, too. Poitier had a very good role and could steal the show, but only over my dead body, Lee wrote Frances a bit wickedly. Korda had initially cast Poitier as Canada's son, Absalom; he then changed his mind and moved Poitier to a more prominent role as the young priest, Msimangu. In the film, Msimangu helps Kumalo search for his wayward boy. "Poitier . . . brought good humor and a relaxed gregariousness to his priest," observes film historian Donald Bogle.

Canada, Poitier, and the rest of the cast moved to Johannesburg. While he was there, Lee had a sudden change of heart about Europe and told Frances to look for a new and larger apartment in Manhattan for them to live in upon his return. He believed that thanks to Korda and this film, he would be able to beat the blacklist and find profitable work on stage and in television. After they saved enough money to pay off their debts and get a little ahead, they could move to Europe and marry. He was eager to take Carl with them; he feared his son might be drafted and sent to the war in Korea.

Canada wrote his father that he intended to marry Frances. James wrote his son back, urging caution, asking Lee to wait and see if his financial situation was better after this picture. But James also seemed to be worried about the viability of the relationship. Please don't mention marriage to her yet, he said—if you change your mind, "she will have nothing on you." Lovey, who had never cared for Frances, was even more adamant: "Don't wash up your career by mixed marriage. You get the milk, why buy the cow?"

Lee dismissed these arguments; his mind was already made up. In early October, he wrote Frances to say happy thirty-first birthday, with the wish that they would never again spend a birthday apart. In the middle of the month, Frances traveled to Rio de Janeiro to transact some business, relax on the beach, and visit friends. Canada tried not to think jealous thoughts.

In November the shoot was finally over, and so was the honeymoon with Korda. Director, cast, and crew could hardly wait for the divorce. According to Lee, nearly everyone on the set hated the director and one script girl suffered a nervous breakdown.

Canada made his farewells to friends in Johannesburg and gave a final press conference. He also sent a warm letter to the *Rand Daily Mail* hoping to mend some fences. British and American papers had reported that Lee was ill-treated during the film shoot, and South African journalists were somewhat miffed. In his letter to the editor, Lee said he had a "wonderful time" and he thanked everyone for their "cordial hospitality." But he also wrote that as a black man, he would be lying if he said everything was fine in their country. What hurts South Africa, he said, is that "everyone is so occupied in this new land with making his fortune," instead of righting wrongs and addressing injustices.

The message was oblique, but clear enough. Joseph Trauneck, director of the Johannesburg Symphony Orchestra, praised Canada for the gracious way he had handled himself in his letter to the editor: "You have put it in a way which again demonstrates the better taste and deeper human concept of life the black people seem to have, but the white people only seldom. We white people should be deeply grateful for it, and grateful to you for expressing it so clearly. But I doubt that they understand."

While Lee was courteous to the South African press, he intended to give the American media an earful. In his luggage, he secreted a few papers and photographs, smuggling home evidence of the little-known atrocities of the apartheid system.

Lee wired Frances that he would arrive in London on November 8 to film some retakes in the studio. The couple was trying to arrange a rendezvous in Europe. The actor had changed his mind and once again was keen to move there. On November 28, he cabled Frances in New York, telling her to come to London. You can't get here fast enough, he said, sending his love and devotion and requesting some American money.

The next day, he cabled her again, instructing her to collect his divorce papers from a trunk at his 555 Edgecombe Avenue apartment, where Billy and Mary Butler were now living, and to bring the papers to London. Clearly, the man had marriage on his mind. Frances arrived in London on December 7, and what a sweet reunion it was after eight months apart. Canada had felt sick and exhausted for several weeks, but now that Frances was at his side, he swore he felt grand. He wanted them to move to Paris just as soon as he finished the retakes at London Films, and he sent her across the Channel to find an apartment.

Or perhaps he sent her to Paris because he actually didn't feel well at all.

"I got an attack in London two days before we finished the film," he later told his brother, Lovey, describing it as intense pressure, as though an invisible horse sat on the middle of his chest. He began to panic.

Heart attacks had killed his mother and sister. Was he going to die? He felt, he said, as though he had started to slowly drown inside: "Try as I might, I couldn't get my breath."

He managed to find his way to a clinic, where he was given a shot of morphine to ease the pain. "I could feel my heart pumping so hard that the area around it was all sore," Lee later recalled. "I was afraid that my heart would stop." Electric jolts of pain shot down his arms, back, and neck as the vise in his chest tightened. Gasping for breath, Canada said he couldn't carry on much longer. The doctor ordered a shot of digitalis, which forces a weakened heart to contract harder and can slow rapid heart rhythms. Immediately, the pressure lessened and Lee began to breathe easier. He would survive.

The day after this episode, the actor was expected at the film studio. Instead, he checked himself into St. Mary's Hospital. Word reached Frances in Paris and Carl in New York that Lee was seriously ill and needed surgery. They both rushed to London. Doctors had advised Canada to undergo a sympathectomy, a relatively new procedure at the time (and rarely performed today). It was used in cases of malignant hypertension, when a patient was in danger of a stroke or other life-threatening complications. Doctors explained that they would cut the sympathetic nerves in Lee's abdominal and thoracic regions in an effort to lower his blood pressure.

The sympathectomy required two separate procedures, which Canada insisted on having in quick succession. "He wanted to be free of the blood pressure that he was certain would kill him," said actor Kevin O'Morrison, a friend for a decade, adding that the procedures were performed dangerously close to each other, "so close that were it not for Canada's outsized stamina, [they] could not have been survived."

Frances and Carl anxiously sat through the first surgery on January 17 and the final one ten days later. When it was all over, Canada was very weak, but he also felt tremendous relief. "It was wonderful—wonderful," he said, "to be rid of the tension."

The surgeons in London and Dr. John Moseley in New York all warned the actor that if he wanted to get well and stay well, he must quit work and give up his activism for the time being, possibly for good.

Canada refused.

"I realized then that I had one role," Frances said. "To keep him in one piece."

THIRTEEN

NO GREATER LOVE

THEN COMES MARRIAGE

C anada and Frances married in his hospital room. The groom simply couldn't wait.

"His mind was made up this time," Frances said. "Nothing was going to stop him, nobody was going to tell him otherwise. In one way, this was a frightening time, because he had been so ill. In another way, it was a beautiful time. We were very much in love." As a wedding gift, Canada presented Frances with an expensive pale-blue moiré dressing gown. "It was one of the most beautiful things I ever owned," she recalled.

Newspapers and gossip columnists back in the States reported that Canada Lee had taken a white wife. Lee's brother and father sent along congratulations, but, as expected, Lovey wasn't altogether pleased about the marriage. Carl, on the other hand, was delighted. Most of the actor's friends were happy for Lee, but there was consternation in certain quarters, especially in Harlem. "There may have been some reservations when we got married," Frances said. "But they didn't hold up very long."

Canada stayed in the hospital to recuperate. When he was discharged, the couple rented a flat in London for three weeks with an extra bedroom for Carl. The weather was rainy and cold, which Lee found uncomfortable, but he still needed to be within easy reach of the doctors and the hospital. Canada and Frances began to plan a trip to a warmer climate, someplace where he could be comfortable and convalesce.

In the meantime, they showed Carl around the city and visited their many friends. Mark Marvin, who had produced *On Whitman Avenue* with Canada, now lived in London with his wife, Blanche, an actress. One night at a party, Frances noticed that Canada had disappeared. She found him in a side room, where their hosts happened to keep a violin. "He never lost his love for the violin," Frances said. "He sat there for about a half hour, fiddling."

Canada's friend and physician John Moseley traveled to London with his wife and daughter at the end of February. Lee was at last deemed well enough to travel, so the two couples headed to Paris with their children. When Frances and Canada decided to travel farther south with the Moseleys, Carl elected to stay in Paris to study French, using the last of his education money from the GI Bill. His father approved of the idea — he thought it might help Carl with his acting career — but he was also sad to leave his son behind. "He's a great guy," Canada wrote Lovey. "We've really gotten to know each other . . . I think this trip will do him an awful lot of good."

The women took a train to Florence with the entourage's luggage. The men drove south by car, stopping at St. Tropez and Cannes before crossing the Italian Alps to Florence. As much as they enjoyed traveling with the Moseleys, Canada and Frances were eager to find a place to put down roots for a while. A friend knew of an inexpensive villa for rent just outside of Torremolinos. At first Lee "didn't want to go because he was anti-Franco," Frances said, "but it was warm and we could afford it." In mid-March, the couple bid farewell to the Moseleys and traveled to Spain.

"Boy, you have never seen such a place," Canada wrote Lovey, describing their four-bedroom house and pool. "The Mediterranean is about a block away. Behind us are the Sierra Madres . . . and all this for $60 a month." Bride and groom took a three-month lease and enjoyed a dreamy honeymoon. "This is Andalusia where you have the Gypsy dancers and the Flamenco dancers," Lee said. "When you wake up in the morning you can hear the song of the laborers singing their Flamenco songs, and this goes on all day."

A young woman cooked dinner for them most nights, which they ate before a huge fireplace. When they wanted entertainment in the evening, they went into town. A far cry from the resort mecca it is today, Torremolinos in 1951 was a relatively small enclave with few hotels, restaurants, and bars. The couple often went to a private club where their landlord was a member. On their first visit, Canada had spotted a piano.

"He saw it and he went right over and started to play," Frances said. "Whenever we went there after that, he would always play the piano for me. I loved to hear him play, and also to sing! He sang well. He was really a talented musician."

Frances was determined that Canada rest and relax, but she couldn't stop him from reading the papers, where the Korean War and the Red Scare generated the biggest headlines. "I understand that the hysteria is getting worse and worse there," he wrote Lovey. "Is it true that W.E.B. Du Bois has been put into jail? If that is so, then everybody is really going crazy there." (The Department of Justice indicted the aging activist as an "unregistered foreign agent," largely because of his appeal for a ban on the atomic bomb. Du Bois was later acquitted.)

Though Lee stayed in touch with the world, at least part of him was glad to be out of the fray for a little while. "Here there is no talk of the war," he wrote his brother. "As a matter of fact you don't even know it exists. I tell you, Lovey, it's going to be difficult being a Negro again. In this part of the world, no one could care less."

Weeks passed; Canada ate well, slept well, and exercised. Frances was thrilled with his progress and good spirits. "Here he was, alive after two surgeries, with all of his old charm, back to his old charismatic self," she said. "I had to pinch myself."

No wonder she felt a pang of dread when a telegram arrived from London. Korda wanted Lee to come back for more retakes. This meant taking a plane, and doctors had instructed the actor not to fly until July at the earliest. Frances urged her husband to reply that the trip wasn't possible. Lee insisted he felt fine and that the picture must be completed. On May 15, he flew to London, sending her a telegram immediately after landing to say he had arrived safely with no ill effects. After a few days, he sent Frances another wire that he would return to her arms very soon.

Canada was still in London a week later when he received devastating news from New York. A telegram stated that his father had died quite suddenly on May 26 of a heart attack. In shock, Lee called Frances and the studio and made arrangements to fly home.

"James C. Canegata, sixty-seven, father of Canada Lee, the actor, died yesterday of a heart attack at Harlem Hospital," read one obituary. "He lived in Riverton Houses, 2255 Fifth Avenue. A native of the Virgin Islands, Mr. Canegata came to the United States fifty years ago. He had been employed by the National Fuel and Gas Corporation as a clerk for the last thirty-one years . . . Mr. Lee, who is in London doing retakes for the film *Cry the Beloved Country*, is expected to arrive home today for his father's funeral and then return to London."

As the family gathered to mourn Pops Canegata, Lee struggled to cope with another difficult blow in a year that had already delivered so many—languishing on the blacklist, going into serious debt, experiencing apartheid, and undergoing major surgery. His blood pressure soared. Newspapers later reported that after his father's funeral "he suffered a heart attack, but it had not been necessary for him to be hospitalized."

When Lee returned to Spain in early June, the lease on the villa was nearly up and he decided they needed a change of scene.

"What shall we do?" Frances asked her husband.

"Go to Italy," Canada said, with a mischievous grin.

After some more sightseeing in France, they headed to Rome. Fickle Canada forgot all about Paris and fell in love with The Eternal City instead; this, he declared, would be home for several months, maybe for good. The couple checked into a hotel on the fashionable Via Veneto and launched a search for the perfect apartment.

Via Veneto was lined with chic shops and restaurants, and its beautiful cafés were watering holes for many American expatriates, including a small community of blacklisted actors. By 1951, the FBI believed that Communists had "given up hope of dominating the industry in Hollywood," and were "attempting to transfer the affection of the stars and top production personnel to foreign, and particularly Italian, production of motion pictures." A COMPIC report stated, "It is now fashionable to go to Europe to make a picture, particularly in Italy, and as a result, they're flocking there, where the film unions are completely dominated by Communists."

One day, as Canada and Frances sat together at a café on the via, Marc Lawrence approached them. Lawrence had been a "friendly witness" before HUAC. He wanted to explain why he had named names. His eyes filled with tears. Canada was uncharacteristically cool. "Your crying about it now is not going to help anything," he told Lawrence.

Lee was elated to discover that two old friends were also in Rome—blues singer Victoria Spivey and her friend Ada Smith. Spivey, a singer from Texas, had owned a blues club in New York that Canada and Frances often visited. Smith was a West Virginia native nearly a decade older than Spivey; her flaming red hair earned her the nickname "Bricktop." Bricktop had owned fashionable jazz clubs in Paris during the 1920s and '30s. She taught the Charleston to Cole Porter and helped make Mabel Mercer and Alberta Hunter famous. Spivey and Bricktop were "temporarily on top of the world," Frances recalled, and throwing "unbelievable parties."

The couple quickly fell in with an international crowd of musicians, actors, and artists. When Lee started talking to people about work in Europe, he got some interesting bites. It was all so thrilling—they were in Rome, they were in love, they were blissfully happy—until Lee got another telegram from Korda. More retakes were needed in London. Once again, Frances pleaded with Canada not to go. Once again, he insisted he was fine, and that he was honor-bound to make the movie the best it could be. While Lee was in London, Frances stayed in Rome to look for an apartment. Korda had promised that the process would be brief, but on July 28, Canada sent Frances a telegram warning her that he wouldn't be home for at least a week.

At long last, retakes were truly finished, and Lee returned to Rome eager to work on his own projects. He had recently met an entrepreneur named Dino who was said to have amassed a great deal of money running cinemas. "Dino said the rest of his family all were bishops," Frances recalled. The movie palace mogul was a colorful figure and so rotund, she said, that he "walked sideways" through doors. Dino was eager to make a movie, and he offered to produce a color version of *Othello* with Canada in the lead.

Lee, of course, loved this idea. "*Othello* is a natural for me," he told *The Ring*, adding that Italy was an ideal place to film it because "there are less limitations on the part." While he didn't elaborate on those limitations, he may have assumed there would be fewer problems shooting intimate scenes between Othello and Desdemona.

Dino hired Max Nosseck to direct. This was an interesting choice for a Shakespearean film in the Bard's native tongue, since the diminutive German director spoke broken English at best. Producer and director discussed casting. Lee was the cinch for Othello, and Dino wanted Italian film actress Anna Vita to play Desdemona.

Now Canada had everything he had ever wanted: an opportunity to play one of the great classical roles, to work as he wished without regard to color or politics, to live with his beloved wife with no fear of prejudice. "I never want to go back to the States," he told Frances. "I can make money here. I can be my own man. We can have the kind of life here we could never have at home."

Unfortunately, by the end of August, little progress had been made on *Othello*. The stumbling block may have been that Dino was not quite what he seemed, according to actor Mickey Knox, a blacklisted actor who happened to know the director. Max Nosseck talked to Knox in Los Angeles and offered him the role of Iago.

"Great!" Knox said. Out of work for months, he was thrilled to get a paying gig, and in Italy, to boot. Toasting his good fortune, he flew to Rome.

"Of course, I didn't know Italians yet," Knox said. "It was all bullshit. Max had found some poverty-stricken producer who, being Italian, put on a great show—nice car, well dressed—and fooled him. The Italian thought Max was going to bring the money. Max thought he was going to put up the money. So nothing happened."

Canada knew Dino was having trouble coming up with enough cash to make the picture, but he remained optimistic. Costumes were designed and publicity stills taken. (Ironically, Lee's old friend Orson Welles was also working on a film version of *Othello* but in black and white, with himself in the lead. Though Welles and Lee had once agreed to collaborate on the play, there is no evidence that Orson considered anyone but himself for the role of Othello in his film. Welles's project was also backed by Italian money that dwindled, although the film was eventually completed and released in 1952.)

On August 31, Canada's half-brother Robert Gadsen and his wife, Mabel, sent a letter to Rome. They had enjoyed their visit with Canada at his father's funeral; it was still hard to believe "Pop" was gone. They seemed pleased about the actor's marriage. "Do hope Lee has luck in Italy with his films," Mabel wrote Frances. "He will, with you, always be keeping his chin up. Without you he would be lost. We are so happy about you. We all know he is well cared for by you. That was all his talk—how wonderful you were before and after and all during his illness. You are just wonderful. May God bless and keep you both with luck and happiness."

Back in the United States, the Red Scare and the blacklist were still going strong. A booklet called *Red Channels: The Report of Communist Influence in Radio and Television* was in wide circulation; it listed 151 performers deemed Communists or fellow travelers and had become the bible of blacklisters. Senator Joseph McCarthy hunted Communists in the State Department, while HUAC launched yet another probe into the entertainment industry, this time under Chairman John S. Wood. Several actors who had worked with Lee, as artists or fellow activists, were called to testify in the spring and summer of 1951, including the major talents involved with *Body and Soul*: writer Abraham Polonsky; actors Anne Revere, Lloyd Gough, and John Garfield; and director Robert Rossen.

There were now well over one hundred index cards, clippings and reports in Lee's HUAC file, including a statement by Louis Budenz, a former managing editor of the *Daily Worker* who defected from the Communist Party in the 1940s and was now one of the government's star witnesses against alleged subversives. The document said:

> Although I had been advised of CANADA LEE's close association with the Communist Party throughout the 1940s and had witnessed one goodwill presentation by him of entertainment for the delegates of the National Convention of the Communist Party, secretly given, it was specifically around 1943 that I was advised officially that he was an adherent of the Communist Party. This information was given to me by Dr. SAM SILLEN and JACK STACHEL. Up to the time I left the Party, I continued to receive official advices [sic] from these men that LEE was an adherent of the Communist Party.

Budenz's credibility would come into question even by the FBI, because the Red-hunter seemed to come up with sensational new allegations primarily to keep his name in the newspapers and to maintain a demand for his paid services as an expert witness on alleged subversives. Nevertheless, the presence of this document in Lee's file indicates that the actor was still under a heavy cloud of suspicion at HUAC.

Rome was definitely a safer place for Lee at the moment.

As Dino struggled to find money for *Othello*, finding a paying job was uppermost on Canada's mind. He was anxious about his own finances. Canada and Frances had moved into an apartment on Via Belluno. In October 1951, Carl wrote them with bad news. Saks Fifth Avenue had filed suit against Frances for nonpayment of a fifty-dollar bill. The City Marshal had tried to confiscate possessions Frances had stored at an apartment leased in her name on 20 Christopher Street. Luckily, Carl had a friend staying there who managed to pay her bill plus a twenty-dollar penalty. "We had some tough moments there for awhile, but everything is now under control," Carl wrote.

The aspiring actor reported he couldn't find any theater jobs. He had worked as a busboy and applied for a position at Bloomingdale's running an elevator "but they concluded that I wasn't the type. Probably figured me for a union organizer, or something almost as deplorable." He was considering taking the Civil Service Test to work in a post office, like his Uncle Lovey. Carl closed his letter on a more cheerful note. He had been invited to see a rough cut of *Cry, the Beloved Country*. "Word is around town that you're sensational," he told his father. "I know you will be in to collect your Academy Award."

The film was set to premiere in January. Korda asked Lee if he would make a publicity tour in the United States before it opened to capitalize on the good buzz the actor was already getting. "I had a bad feeling about it," Frances said. "But Canada wanted to go. He wanted to support the film, and he also wanted to talk to people about the atrocities he saw in South Africa. He felt that people needed to know what was going on over there."

Canada was still determined to make *Othello*, but he was becoming discouraged by the slow progress. Dino and other movie people talked a good game—picture deals, acting, even directing—but Lee hadn't earned a single lira in Rome. He needed to make money. He began to talk about moving back to New York for a little while. He would be in the States for weeks, perhaps months, promoting *Cry, the Beloved Country*. Maybe he could line up some work in theater, where the blacklist held less sway.

Frances and Canada devised a plan. Korda didn't need him in New York until December, and Lee still had loose ends to tie up regarding *Othello*. Frances would go to Paris, convert her plane ticket to a berth on the *Isle de France*, and sail to New York with the household goods they had collected after living some eleven months abroad. Canada would travel to Paris later, stay a few weeks, and in early December he would fly home to join Frances in New York. By then, she would have an apartment ready, and Canada would prepare for his publicity tour.

Carl knew they were worried about the blacklist. "The two of you together have overcome greater problems than this," he assured them. "Once you get back to New York, you will find things on this side resolving themselves." The young actor's fortunes had improved since his last letter. He was rehearsing an Off-Broadway play called *Decision* and was hoping to get some TV work soon; if he did, he promised to help them pay off some of their debts.

Frances took the train to Paris, arriving just past ten o'clock at night without a place to stay or a penny to pay her cabbie. She gave the driver an address on the Champs Elysees, told him to wait, climbed four or five flights of steps, and knocked on a door with a little peephole. A little shuffling behind the door, the sound of keys turning and deadbolts ratcheting open, and there was Pop Landau. A Polish émigré and a true Parisian character, Landau had survived the war by hiding in the city's famed sewer system. He made his living trading dollars for francs on the black market, which was a technically illegal but thriving business in postwar Paris since you could get a third more francs for your dollars. "Everybody went to Pop," Frances said. If you changed a lot of money, the old gent might even give you a pastrami to take home as a bonus. And if you were an artist down on your luck—especially an actor or singer—Pop would always loan you a bit of money to tide you over until your next check came in. Pop had helped Canada before, and he was happy to help Frances now. He paid her cab fare, escorted her to the Hotel Metropole on the rue d'Etoile, paid for her room, and tucked a little extra cash in her pocket. "He was both a friend and a life-saver," Frances recalled. After checking into the hotel, she delightedly discovered she knew two of the guests—that party-loving twosome, Spivey and Bricktop, had also left Rome behind and installed themselves at the Metropole. "They were angels, keeping me sane and helping me to avoid depression at leaving Canada," Frances recalled.

By Thanksgiving, Frances was in Manhattan and Canada was in Paris, staying at the Metropole, borrowing another thousand francs from Pop Landau. He ate his holiday dinner alone at the hotel on a rainy evening and wrote her a beautiful letter giving thanks to his wife for her love, her tender care, her faithfulness.

Canada and Zoltan Korda spent some time together in Paris. *Cry, the Beloved Country* had opened the previous week in South Africa, and reviews were raves across the board. The director was eager for Canada to travel to New York for the PR campaign, and promised to make arrangements for the studio to pay for his trip back to the States.

In the meantime, Lee spent his days pining for Frances and his nights in the clubs. He often went out with Spivey, who was still at the Metropole. Canada got a letter from Frances with enough money to pay his debt to Pop Landau. He wrote her that the funds arrived in the nick of time, but asked that she still send along a blank check from his corporate account. Take a loan with our car as guarantee, he advised, or sell the car outright. We can always get another one if all goes well with the movie, he said.

Frances continued to search for an affordable apartment in New York while Canada worked out a deal with London Films for his passage home and publicity tour expenses. On December 2, 1951, a bleak and rainy Sunday morning, Canada wrote his wife of his loneliness and anxiety. He felt as though every day might be his last. Now that I have you in my life, he said, now that I know love, I am terribly afraid of death. "It is not death itself," Lee told her, "It is really the feeling of leaving you."

He wrote of his desire to have a child with her. Canada had been told that the medication he took for his hypertension might inhibit his fertility. But that afternoon he had met with a medical resident who assured him that the odds of this side effect were slight. "I've been singing ever since," he wrote. "Wouldn't it be wonderful if we could have a child, darling? I think that if we did, I would be happy the rest of my life."

The actor was having trouble sleeping, and often woke in the middle of the night with a headache and pressure on his chest. After taking his pills he would read until daylight. In one letter home, he quoted the Twenty-third Psalm to Frances, and said her love for him had given the verses new meaning: "*Yea, though I walk through the valley of the shadow of death, I shall fear no evil, for* thou *art with me.*"

Lee soon received two letters from his beloved wife—one full of love and longing and the other with good news. She had attended a private VIP screening of *Cry, the Beloved Country* for celebrities, city officials, cast members, and their guests. Canada's performance was the talk of the evening, and many were in tears as the film ended.

At last, Lee reached an agreement with London Films regarding the publicity tour. The studio agreed to cover a one-way ticket to New York plus four hundred dollars in expenses. It wasn't the deal he had hoped for, but he was tired of haggling. He stood firm on one point: when a studio executive told him to keep his mouth shut about South Africa on the publicity tour, he flatly refused.

Frances mailed him a precious check and enclosed reviews of *Cry, the Beloved Country* from South African newspapers. The film had premiered simultaneously in Durban, Cape Town, and Johannesburg. One critic called the film "a screen poem of poignant beauty, unadorned with sensationalism or contrivance, and intensely affecting in the almost Biblical simplicity of its dialogue." The cast was called "first-rate, with Canada Lee setting mood and tempo with a beautiful performance as the Reverend Kumalo. His anguish and the heavy spiritual burden he has to bear are finely indicated, and his gradual return to peace at the end came almost as a Divine benediction."

The *Cape Times* reported that censors had cut just eleven feet from the film, and the trims were made with novelist Alan Paton's "full approval." According to the article, a censor asked for changes in a scene at the end of the film involving Kumalo, Canada's character. The scene as originally shot showed two white characters discussing the return of Kumalo to his village. "The censor thought the comments of the farmer somewhat violent, and so Mr. Paton asked if he could insert a different scene," the article reports. "The scene put in is a very lovely musical one, in which Kumalo is returning to his village and being received by his people."

Because a London newspaper had reported that black Americans in the cast were ill-treated during the film shoot, the *Cape Times* asked Paton to comment. "The actors were told beforehand of the difficulties that would be encountered," he said. "Every effort was made, not only by London Films, but also by the authorities in the Union, to smooth as many of those difficulties away as possible without abrogating the law."

When Lee was asked for a statement on the subject, he supported Paton's party-line position, but seized the opportunity to attack apartheid. "The movie people made provisions for my comfort and well-being," he said. "Still, the racial problems in South Africa made my trip a nightmare. They talk about the race problem in the United States. Compared to South Africa, it doesn't even exist. The terrible caste system over there—it makes things terrible for the natives. All of us who saw it say prayers that some way will be found to bring happiness and understanding to the people of all races in Africa."

Frances finally found a cheap apartment at 235 West Fourth Street in Greenwich Village. It was small, dark, and none too clean, but it was affordable. She and Leslie Nash worked together for days, washing cupboards, floors, and walls to get the rooms ready for Canada's arrival. Then she removed some furniture from storage and began to unpack.

On Saturday, December 15, Canada arrived at Idlewild, his luggage full of presents and his heart full of happiness and anticipation. When the couple arrived at the Greenwich Village apartment, "we shut the door on the world for a little while," Frances recalled. "It was heaven."

But the world eventually came knocking. Friends and family descended on the couple. Carl came, of course, as did Lovey, his wife, Pheta, and son, Billy. Langston Hughes took one look at the cramped, cheerless space and "offered to paint us a window on the wall," Frances said. Canada contentedly reigned over dinners and parties, his beloved wife at his side. He spoke of offers he had received to work overseas, telling Kevin O'Morrison that the governments of Italy, Israel, and Ethiopia had each offered the actor his own theater company. Lee was flattered and grateful, but insisted: "I just want to work *here* as a free man. An artist." While he mulled over offers to perform in Europe and elsewhere, he quietly told a friend he was afraid it was just too good to be true.

He was right. Soon after his return to the United States, Lee's passport expired, and when he applied for a new one, the State Department took his application "under review." This would send chills down the spine of any blacklisted performer. It was common practice for the government to revoke or refuse to issue passports to blacklisted artists. Canada's friends Paul Robeson and Charlie Chaplin were just two of many examples. (Robeson had filed suit in district court to have his passport restored. His legal battle would last eight years.)

"We tried not to worry at first," Frances said. "Canada was optimistic that with *Cry, the Beloved Country* opening, and with good reviews, that he could get it back."

The film premiered January 23, 1952, at the Bijou on Forty-fifth Street. *Newsweek* said Lee's interpretation of the old priest, or *umfundisi*, was "especially evocative." Otis L. Guernsey said Canada gave "a nearly monumental performance of a good old man shaken with grief but preserving his simple-hearted compassion through all his trials." Bosley Crowther wrote: "Mr. Lee, the American actor, does a profoundly moving job in capturing the dignity, the fervor, and the humility of the old Zulu priest, especially when he is shaken by disillusion and despair. He even conveys the impression of being indigenous to the environment in which he plays."

Riding the good notices, Canada carried on with his publicity tour. True to his word, and to the chagrin of some executives at London Films, he told the press about the atrocities of apartheid. One of his first interviews was on NBC radio's *Tex and Jinx Show*, hosted by the husband-and-wife team of Jinx Falkenberg and John "Tex" McCrary. Canada called *Cry, the Beloved Country* a "humane story" and described his character, the Reverend Kumalo, as "a man of a very godlike quality, very Christ-like in his whole attitude toward the world." But he moved on quickly to describe the oppression of black South Africans and said he "would rather be one of the poorest of sharecroppers in the unenlightened South than a rich Negro in South Africa." After this broadcast, NBC received at least four letters from the South African Press Attaché complaining about Lee's "highly derogatory" remarks and "glaring misstatements of fact."

Canada also met with Irene Thirer of the *New York Post* over coffee one day. While the journalist had intended to talk to the actor about his adventures making *Cry, the Beloved Country*, she noticed that Lee mostly "wanted to let off steam about the indignities suffered by the Negro in South Africa."

"My entire experience in South Africa was a nightmare," he told her. "Nothing could ever tempt me to return there." He described the rigid caste system in detail, including the frequent practice of jailing blacks without cause, since as convicts they could be used for slave labor. He compared South African farmers to white racists in the rural American South, but was quick to say that "in Africa, there is even less feeling that the Negro is human. He still is almost completely a slave, to be kicked around, and he lives in such mortal fear that even a band of his own people never comes to his defense when he is in trouble."

At the same time, Canada said he was proud of the work he had done in this film, and grateful to Zoltan Korda. Astonishingly, he didn't shy away from saying exactly why he owed Korda a debt of gratitude. Nor did the *Post* shy away from printing it: "I'd been heavily in debt and out of work for a long time. Why? Because of vicious tongues. They said I was a Communist and I wasn't and never had been. Only I was always in there fighting, God knows, for my race and for other minorities. They linked me as a subversive (he chuckled) with Helen Hayes and Fredric March. Ridiculous? Ridiculous! . . . I had to challenge the stigma and it gave me so severe a case of hypertension that I underwent an operation for high blood pressure."

The article concluded by noting that Canada planned to travel to the Virgin Islands to visit his father's family, hoping the trip would also calm "this thumping heart of mine." After a "sojourn with friends" in New York, Thirer reported, Canada would likely accept two movie bids, "the first one to be made in Italy in April, the other to be filmed in Dutch Guiana."

For all of Lee's wishful thinking, he wasn't going to travel anytime soon. Every time he contacted the Passport Division, his application was still under review. "Canada didn't expect to have the blacklist still in effect when he came back," Frances recalled. "We were both convinced the blacklisting would be finished and he could get back to work."

It's difficult to understand why the couple believed that Canada could beat the blacklist, although it seems they were banking on the success of *Cry, the Beloved Country* and the possibility that Lee would be nominated for an Oscar. But in early 1952, the blacklist network was stronger than ever. If film studios hired blacklisted actors, they risked boycotts by civic and religious groups. If radio or television contracted these pariahs, they could lose thousands of dollars if sponsors took their ads elsewhere. CBS instituted an in-house loyalty oath. Congressional committees continued to investigate Communism in Hollywood, and after the CFA debacle, few in the movie industry were brave enough to protest the hearings. More of Canada's friends and colleagues were being called before HUAC, including playwright Lillian Hellman, who refused to name names, famously arguing, "I cannot and will not cut my conscience to fit this year's fashions." Most who stood fast in their opposition to the committee faced disastrous consequences: income vanished, careers crumbled.

Though Canada and Frances had truly believed the actor could pull free of the blacklist, "obviously, we were terribly, terribly wrong," Frances said, "and Canada paid a terrible price for this mistake." Lee realized that

Cry, the Beloved Country would not save him after all, and now he was trapped in the United States without work and sinking deeper into debt. His blood pressure tested higher. He complained to a reporter that his health problems were a result of "hardships" and "obstacles" put in his way because of "my political activities on behalf of my race and other minorities." Frances was also convinced his illness was exacerbated by the blacklist.

"He was fine in Europe after the operations," she said. "That's why we remained as long as we did. I didn't want to come back. Believe me, if they hadn't insisted on our returning because of the [film's] opening . . . we would not have come back when we did . . . We came back, and we were right back into it."

When Lee told actor Kevin O'Morrison about his surgeries, his recuperation, and the wonderful health he had enjoyed in Italy, he had a pained look on his face. O'Morrison asked how he was feeling now. The actor shook his head.

"Forty-eight hours after I was back in the States, Kev, it was like I never had the operations. I had it back," he said.

"You had *what* back?" O'Morrison asked. "The *nerves* are cut."

"Doesn't matter," Canada said. "I've got it."

Frustrated and desperate, Lee went to see his friend Walter White at the NAACP. "I can't take it any more," he told White. "I'm going to get a shoeshine box and sit outside the Astor Theater. My picture is playing to capacity audiences and, my God, I can't get one day's work!"

"I dissuaded him from carrying out his melodramatic plan," White later reported, "but I am not sure today that I was right." White traveled to Washington in February 1952 to try to help Lee with his passport problem, but the State Department stalled him by claiming that Canada's application was still under review.

Given his health and his troubles, a more cautious man might have laid low, "but Canada went to rallies, in spite of his high blood pressure," his son, Carl, later recalled. Unable to find work as an actor, Lee devoted himself to the only work he had left, donating his time to political and humanitarian causes. He was particularly determined to speak out against apartheid. In February, he appeared before the National Conference of Christians and Jews to deliver an address titled "What Brotherhood Means to Me." In vivid detail, he spoke of police torture and whippings in South Africa; he explained the head tax, the poll tax, and the twenty-odd passes that natives were required to carry to travel even from one village to the next if they wanted to avoid jail. He reminded his audience of America's own history of slave labor, chain gangs, and curfews, not to mention Jim Crow and lynching and poll taxes.

Concluding this speech, Canada returned to the theme of brotherhood. It is particularly moving to find that even in this painful and discouraging time, Lee still had hope; he still believed in his country, and in democracy. "If brotherhood can flourish anywhere, it can in our America," he told his listeners. "Nowhere in the world has the black man advanced like the American Negro. We haven't gotten full equality of opportunity yet, but time and American fair play will make it come true."

Lee participated in a bond drive for the State of Israel along with actress Audrey Meadows and singer Juanita Hall; in the month of February alone, he spoke at three bond rallies. For his efforts, he received a personal thank-you letter from Henry Morgenthau, Jr., former Secretary of the Treasury under FDR and now chairman of an organization handling a $500 million bond issue for the new nation.

On February 22, Lee was scheduled to make a speech in honor of President's Day during a community meeting at George Washington High School on 190th Street in Manhattan, but had to cancel at the last minute. The text of the speech he intended to deliver still survives, full of optimism for the future of democracy and this country. But it carries within it words of caution, too. "Let us not be fooled by words with twisted meanings, no matter how great the heat or the fury with which they are uttered," he said. "[Democracy] must be guarded and protected if it is to live. It must be immunized against the poisonous toxins of all 'isms' including McCarthyism."

On March 3, 1952, Canada celebrated his forty-fifth birthday with Frances. A telegram arrived. It was from Carl. In the past, the young man sent his father birthday telegrams because the actor was always on the road, or in Hollywood, working. Now, Lee was just blocks away, idle, fighting depression. Perhaps Carl hoped to cheer his father by keeping up the tradition.

The lovely gesture may have lifted Canada's spirits momentarily, but he knew the only cure for his blues was a paying job. Luckily, Langston Hughes was concocting just such a remedy.

SO LITTLE TIME

FIGHT TO THE DEATH

Langston Hughes knew Canada was desperate for a job. One day, when he was at the West Fourth Street apartment, Lang had an inspiration. Canada, he said, you don't have to sit around and wait for work. We can put together a one-man show. They began to toss ideas around. Lee wanted to do monologues from Shakespeare, especially *Othello*; Lang suggested a collection of poems he had published in the early 1940s called *Shakespeare in Harlem*. It would make a great title for the show—Lee could perform poems by Lang in the first half and Shakespearean monologues in the second.

"They decided they would do it at the Village Vanguard," Frances recalled. "It wouldn't be much money . . . but it was something."

Lang and Canada met regularly at the apartment to work on the show. "Lang spent about two weeks there," Frances recalled. "And what a fabulous two weeks that was, listening to those two harangue each other over which poem was better. They were good friends, but I was beginning to think they might get into a fist fight!"

At the same time, the two men were also asked to participate in a star-studded NAACP "Great Night" extravaganza at Madison Square Garden. Chaired by Oscar Hammerstein II and Lena Horne, the March 6 event would feature Ella Fitzgerald, Henry Fonda, Yul Brynner, and Tallulah Bankhead, along with a host of other celebrities.

"It was a big fund-raising drive and they asked Canada to appear," Frances recalls. "And Canada said, 'Fine, Fine. So long as I can get up to say a few words about South Africa.' And of course they said yes."

More than fifteen thousand people packed the Garden that evening. Lee's role was to narrate "Toll the Liberty Bell." Many of his good friends were in this pageant, including Rosetta Lenoire and Fred O'Neal from *Anna Lucasta*, and Sidney Poitier. The cast also included a former friend: Ed Sullivan. There is no evidence, however, that the two men crossed paths that night. The production was simply gigantic.

Prominent civil rights leaders and community activists made speeches, including Adam Clayton Powell, Jr., and Walter White. Theater impresario Dick Campbell was in charge of the lineup of orators, which was rather lengthy. Canada had been promised his five minutes to talk about South Africa, and he was bound and determined to take the podium. "How soon can I go on?" Canada pestered Campbell several times, growing more and more anxious as Dick put him off. He paced the floor constantly.

"Boy, this is going to take all night," Lee muttered. "I've got to get up there and tell them something about the horrors of apartheid."

"Canada, relax, your turn will come," Campbell said.

Frances was standing just offstage, and she tried to calm Canada down. "I knew these rallies could go on for hours, and it was 11:30 p.m. already," she said. "Canada is walking back and forth every five minutes or so, saying, 'Well, Dick says it will be just a few more minutes.'"

Finally, at the very end of the evening, Campbell gave Lee the thumbs-up. When he was introduced, the applause was tremendous — after all, he had a very successful picture still playing in cinemas around town.

A draft of Lee's speech exists, more poetic than militant as it describes the life of blacks under apartheid. "They are an ancient people, with ancient traditions, and a heritage of bravery and nobility," Lee said. "For them, there is only the land. They have precious little of it left." He praised the efforts of rebels fighting for change in South Africa, and urged Americans to support their efforts. He also made a plea for education and tolerance. Our country isn't perfect, but we should be thankful, he said: "We have made more progress in all phases of the race question than any other part of the world."

Frances recalled that her husband spoke for only five minutes, but other people said he talked much longer and practically had to be dragged offstage. Exhausted after the marathon event, many in the audience started making their way out of the building during his speech, ready for home and bed. "It was a beautiful, moving speech," Frances said. "But the people who were listening were no more interested than the man in the moon!"

Disappointed by the lackluster response, a dejected Canada found Frances offstage and wondered sadly, "Well, it didn't do much good, did it?"

The next day, Langston and Canada went back to work on the one-person show. It bothered Lee to be performing in such a small space, so far from Broadway. "But it was money to take care of us," Frances recalled. Canada and Lang discussed taking the show on the road. According to Frances, "the idea of the tour came up because Canada's passport still hadn't come through."

The actor may have had his reservations about this one-person show, but he loved working with Langston Hughes. In all the years they had been friends, this was the first time they had worked so closely on a project, and they had a ball. "They always found so many things to laugh about," Frances said. "It was a joy to be around them." Nevertheless, she could see that her husband tired easily and suffered terrible headaches. "I was very worried about him," she said.

Canada confided to a close friend that he was feeling a bit ill. He hadn't seen a doctor yet. "Frances doesn't know about this," Lee said anxiously, "and I don't want you to tell her. You've got to promise me you won't tell her."

"But you've got to tell her sometime," his friend insisted.

"I'll tell her in my own way," Canada said. "Maybe I have the flu or something."

He was certain he would feel better if he could just get work and money. He made the rounds at television networks and local stations, still hoping to get past the blacklist. He told Walter White of the NAACP that he "received four lucrative television offers as a result of the acclaim given *Cry, the Beloved Country*, but each sponsor said he would employ him only after he had appeared on some other program. But none had the courage to employ him first." White promised he would do what he could to help.

Lee had to do *something*. Quietly, he sought the advice of Daniel James, editor of *The New Leader*, a social-democratic publication that was virulently anti-Communist. And James in turn contacted Alvin W. Stokes, an investigator for HUAC, on March 31, 1952. James told the investigator that actor Canada Lee wished to talk about his "former left-wing activities." In a memo to his supervisor, Stokes wrote:

> Mr. James reports that Canada Lee has reorientated [sic] his thinking with respect to his former well-known C.P. front activities and may now be in a position to cooperate with the Committee on Un-American Activities . . . A tentative appointment has been scheduled for a meeting with him at a public place on Tuesday, April 8th, 1952 . . . The receipt from the Committee office of a rundown on Canada Lee's C.P. activities, strictly for my own use, will be helpful to me in eliciting and evaluating such information as Canada Lee is willing to give.

Desperate, ill, perhaps even afraid, Canada may have decided to clear himself and save his acting career by using an established method: recantation to HUAC. He appears to have kept his efforts secret from most of his family and friends, including his wife.

And yet, even as he discreetly worked to get his name off the blacklist, he made the fascinating and contradictory decision to continue speaking out against the controversial issue of apartheid. Perhaps he thought that if he prostrated himself before the anti-Communists, he might be permitted to continue his struggle for civil rights, although this would seem a forlorn hope.

Whatever his reasoning, he boldly and repeatedly attacked apartheid as a white supremacist slavery system. He was invited to join the Americans for South African Resistance (AFAR). The ad hoc group organized a "defiance rally" in Harlem on April 6, 1952, the three hundredth anniversary of the white man's arrival in South Africa, and Lee delivered the keynote address, describing the brutality he had witnessed to the eight hundred people gathered at the Abyssinian Baptist Church. Lee never believed in sugarcoating his material. Twice during radio interviews on *Cry, the Beloved Country*, Lee maneuvered his hosts into allowing him to deliver a detailed litany of human rights abuses in South Africa that included dismemberment and castration. On one of these programs, a midnight talk show on WJZ, he said that London Films had recently called him on the carpet "with the demand that I criticize South Africa no more." Studio executives were furious at this remark; Lee received a letter urging him to consider the impact his inflammatory statements might have on his reputation and on their film.

During the second week of April, Canada and Langston were in final rehearsals for the one-man show at the Vanguard. Lang presented his friend with a copy of the book of poems they were using in the show, *Shakespeare in Harlem*. On the inside cover Hughes wrote, "Inscribed especially for Canada, Sincerely, Lang, New York, April 8, 1952."

That very day, according to HUAC records, Canada met with investigator Alvin Stokes at the Hotel Woodstock. Daniel James, the editor, was at Canada's side, along with Howard Rushmore, who, like Louis Budenz, was a former journalist at the *Daily Worker* and had defected from the Communist Party. After changing sides, Rushmore started writing rabid Red-baiting columns for Hearst's *New York Journal-American*.

Because he had not received the "run-down" he had requested from HUAC on Canada's alleged subversive activities, Stokes apparently went into the meeting cold. When the interview was over, he typed a memo to his superior:

> Canada Lee said that:
> He never joined the Communist Party.
> He was invited many, many times to do so. (join C.P.)
> He did sign petitions for C.P. front organizations.
> He did entertain or speak at C.P. front meetings.
> He did associate closely, but not exclusively, with persons who were said to be Communists, or progressives.
> He discovered that he was being used as a "sucker" by persons known as Communists or progressives, sometime in 1948 or 1949.
> He publicly had his name withdrawn as a sponsor of the Waldorf Peace Conference in N.Y.C. in 1949.

He is now anti-Communist and will cooperate with the Committee fully regarding his activities and associations in the past.

Stokes concluded by saying that he planned to interview Canada again during the following week, and he reiterated his request for a "rundown" on Lee's file at HUAC.

Two days later, on April 11, *The New York Times* published a brief listing in the arts section: "Canada Lee will offer a program of readings from Shakespeare, Langston Hughes and the 'Rubaiyat of Omar Khayyam' this evening at the Village Vanguard. Mr. Lee was last seen on Broadway in the Theater Guild production, *Set My People Free*."

How painful it must have been too see that in print—*Set My People Free* had closed in 1948. Then, Canada Lee had been touted as one of the greatest Negro actors of his time; four years later, the only job he could get was reading poetry in a hole-in-the-wall on Eleventh Street in Greenwich Village.

The show sold well enough; there weren't that many seats to fill. Canada found himself making coffee and doughnut money again playing a door gig, just like the bad old days with his struggling band. Frances, however, always tried to make the best of things. One night, to cheer Lee up, she splurged on two small steaks. While she was in the kitchen cooking, the doorbell rang.

"Damn," she thought to herself. "There goes the steak."

She was certain that a hungry mouth was at the door, and equally certain that Canada would happily feed any friend or stranger in need. She quietly slipped into the living room to find Lee talking to an ex-boxer, now down-and-out. According to Frances, "Canada pulled out his last twenty-dollar bill and gave it to him." The actor always felt fortunate that he had managed to make a new life for himself after boxing, when so many fighters ended up crippled and impoverished. "He felt he owed them his help," she said. "That was Canada, always."

After dinner with Frances, Lee headed over to the Vanguard to do his show. It may have been small potatoes, but it was a chance to do what he purely loved: to be on a stage, in the lights, riding out the jazzy rhythms of Lang's poetry, luxuriating in those glorious Shakespearean monologues he had so often read on the stage, riding the subway, or in bed before going to sleep. Yet now, in this difficult time, the words resonated differently. From *Othello* he read the Moor's tragic final speech:

Soft you; a word or two, before you go.
I have done the state some service, and they know
No more of that.—I pray you, in your letters,
When you shall these unlucky deeds relate,
Speak of me as I am; nothing extenuate,
Nor set down aught in malice: then must you speak
Of one that lov'd not wisely, but too well.

Canada had done the state some service; his scrapbooks bulged with certificates of appreciation and thank-you letters. Now that service was discounted, ignored. If only the writers of his time would take up Lee's story, his unlucky deeds, and speak the truth of him, of what he tried to do, without lies, rumors, insinuations, malice. He was a man, he had faults, but he must have wondered if the very thing he was most proud of—his love for his country, for his people—was the very thing that destroyed him.

Each night at the Vanguard, he closed with the words of a medieval Persian poet, a poem he had read and reread over the years, finding in it a reflection of his love of life, beauty, romance, companionship. Now, he found in the poem something he had missed before, the melancholy of a man struggling with his own limitations, his own mortality:

I heard a Voice within the Tavern cry,
"Awake, my Little Ones, and fill the Cup
Before Life's Liquor in its Cup be dry."
And, as the Cock crew, those who stood before
The Tavern shouted—"Open then the Door!
You know how little while we have to stay,
And, once departed, may return no more."

Canada's reading of the "Rubaiyat of Omar Khayyam" was so successful with audiences that he decided to record it with a semi-improvised piano score by the composing team of Wesley and Mischa Portnoff. He may have hoped to market the recording to a radio station for broadcast, or to sell it as a novelty album. To prepare for the taping, he organized a timing rehearsal with Mischa, the pianist; a recording of this session still exists. One hears the same rich baritone familiar to the actor's fans during the peak of his career. But Canada's voice also sounds weary, sorrowful, even lethargic, over the delicate, bright score, and in hindsight it seems apparent that all was not well.

Lee refused to admit he was sick, but Frances was no fool. She urged him to see his doctor and friend, John Moseley. Canada waved away her concerns and then, without telling Frances or Moseley, he reportedly consulted a different physician at New York Hospital in Queens. No one knows exactly what he was told.

The actor was under a great deal of strain trying to decide what to do. He was supposed to meet with investigator Alvin Stokes again in April, but there is no record of the meeting in the actor's HUAC file. Perhaps Lee got nervous and put off the meeting, or perhaps Stokes postponed it, still waiting for his "run-down." Restless, Canada sought out a reporter friend who had helped him organize a press conference after the Coplon trial. "What can I do to clear my name?" Lee asked him.

The reporter suggested another press conference; he believed that many journalists were sick of the Red Scare humbug and might give the actor a fair hearing. But Canada vetoed the idea. According to the reporter, he said "he couldn't afford to buy a few drinks for the boys, and he wouldn't let them waste their time trying to do him a favor."

He probably judged the public mood correctly. Lee had recently been invited to appear at a high school in New Jersey, but when he arrived, school officials apologized and informed Canada that they could not allow him to speak. The actor was too dangerous to lecture students and their families. Gracious as always, Canada took his leave, but it had to hurt. "If he hadn't believed in human dignity and democracy so passionately, he couldn't have fought the battles he did, endured what he did," Frances said.

About this time, Walter White traveled to Washington, D.C., to see a ranking FBI official about Lee's case. According to White, the official said "he had no authority to 'clear' any citizen falsely accused of association with subversive organizations." The official reportedly told White that in any case, there was nothing in the FBI records that would brand Canada as a subversive.

According to Lovey, Lee also went to the FBI to ask whether they had anything against him in their files. "I'll never forget how happy he was when he came out," Lovey later told a reporter. "He said they told him: 'Canada, don't worry about it. We have nothing in our files against you. You are OK.'" It is not known if the FBI disclosed to White or to Lee that the bureau had in fact maintained a file on the actor since 1943, and at one point found Canada's activities worrisome enough to consider custodial detention as well as prosecution on charges that he had violated sedition laws.

Despite any assurances he may have received, Lee knew a cloud still hung over him. At this point, he seems to have confided in his brother about his dealings with HUAC. Lovey later told a reporter that Canada requested a hearing before the committee. "It was all set," Lovey said, "and he was scheduled to testify." To date, nothing has surfaced in HUAC files to corroborate this statement, but if Lee actually contemplated making a public recantation in front of the committee, it indicates how desperate the actor was to clear his name.

Bills stacked up, and his show at the Vanguard would be closing soon. Lee reached out to every person he knew in show business, trying to hustle work. Somehow, he managed to sneak around television's blacklist to win a small part as a boxer in *The Final Bell*, as well as the starring role in *American Inventor*, a biography of George Washington Carver. Publicity stills for the latter show Lee wearing torn pants and a haggard smile.

Canada contacted the State Department yet again. "He was convinced that his passport would come through and we would go back to Italy and he would make *Othello*," Frances said. "But they said his application was still under review."

One morning Lee opened his newspaper to read a horrifying story. Two Negroes had been shot down in cold blood by an ex-policeman in White Plains who resented their presence in a public tavern. Activists were organizing a rally on April 14 to protest these murders and to demand justice, and Lee accepted an invitation to speak, along with Walter White. If Canada worried that making such a speech might undermine his attempts to clear his name, he clearly decided that the speech was more important.

White offered Canada a ride to White Plains, and the two men arranged to meet at 7:00 p.m. That evening, White was sitting in his office, waiting for Lee. Minutes passed until the actor was seriously and uncharacteristically late. It began to rain, and when Lee at last arrived, the usually dapper man was bedraggled and soaked to the skin.

"It was only later that I found out why," White recalled. "He had walked all the way uptown to my office in a torrential rainstorm because he wanted to save the 40 cents in his pocket for food. But even then he was undisturbed by his own plight. He was worried because an old actor had asked him for $10 and he had to turn him down. 'But I'll dig up that $10 somewhere tomorrow.'"

When the two men arrived at the rally in White Plains, they went their separate ways. Walter Kirschenbaum of the Jewish Labor Committee ran into Canada. "He was very hungry and said he'd had to rush up there without dinner," Kirschenbaum recalled. "He was very grateful when someone went out and got him a sandwich." Later, Kirschenbaum said, he learned Lee hadn't eaten because he was broke.

Anger and sorrow and pain filled the room that night when Canada was called to the podium. Many in the audience were grieving family and friends of the two slain men. The actor, too, was full of anger and sorrow and pain. "I try not to be emotional," he told them. He stood for a moment, collecting his thoughts, and quoted *Othello*: "Haply for I am black, and have not those soft parts of conversations that chamberers have." He came before them, he said, no slick politician, no lofty orator: "I am a black man, and black men have been killed, and I must be emotional."

He began to talk of South Africa.

"I have just left a country where black people are virtually in chains, where a black man has to have some seventeen passes to move about in his own country," he said. He spoke of torture and death, of white men cutting off ears or castrating some of their African victims. "My God!" he suddenly cried out. "What am I to do?"

He clenched his fists.

"I don't know whether a white American knows what it means to be a Negro and a good American at the same time," he said. "When I think that America, this great and tremendous country, has been built on the backs and sweat of my people; when I think that in every war my people have died for this country; and when I know that my people cannot walk the streets here in safety, I feel bad."

It was his greatest speech, and his very last.

On April 16, 1952, Canada wrote a letter to Paul R. Reynolds & Son, publisher of *Native Son*. He requested permission to perform a three- to five-minute monologue from the play during a forthcoming tour, something Lee would no doubt have had to organize himself. Shortly afterward he collapsed. At last admitting that he was unwell, he cancelled the rest of his performances at the Vanguard. (According to ads in *The New York Times*, comedian Wally Cox probably took over Lee's spot at the club starting April 24.) Frances took her husband to see John Moseley on or around April 29. Lee described his symptoms—he had headaches, he may have had trouble urinating. Dr. Moseley examined him and performed several tests. Canada, now suffering waves of excruciating pain, was given a sedative to make him more comfortable. When the test results were in, Dr. Moseley found a room where he could speak privately with Frances.

Both kidneys had failed. Uremia had already set in. Nothing could be done.

Canada was going to die.

How long do we have? Frances asked. Ten days to three months, Moseley told her. It was impossible to know for sure. At a critical stage, Canada would slip into a coma. At some point, his heart would simply stop.

Did you tell him he's dying? Frances asked. No, the doctor answered. Canada hadn't asked how sick he was and Moseley hadn't told him.

Is there anything you can do for him at the hospital? she asked. No, he answered. All we can do is give him something for the pain.

"I don't want to send him to the hospital," Frances said. "He'll know he's dying."

They decided to tell Canada that he had kidney trouble and leave it at that. "I felt it was more important that he not know," Frances recalled. "I thought he would be more comfortable. So that was the way we handled it."

She was given medications to ease his pain. Then she took him home to West Fourth Street. Wife, companion, and lover was now also nurse— and actress.

"Canada, the doctor wants you to go to bed so you can knock this thing out," she told him when they were back in their apartment. Lee tried to pull her into bed with him. "Now, you're going to be a good boy," she said. He laughed.

"I didn't believe it, I think, those first few days," Frances later recalled. "I had a shred of hope. I guess I couldn't have made it through otherwise."

If Canada had any inkling of the severity of his condition, he didn't let on. "He always had a difficult time believing that his body could betray him," Frances said. He spoke of going back to Italy to finish *Othello*. He imagined the kind of life they could have in Europe. He laughed and talked with her; he wanted to make love to her. "He was incorrigible," Frances said. "I loved that man so much."

When he felt well enough, friends stopped in. Everyone kept up the pretense that Canada's "kidney problem" would get better. Friends, colleagues, acquaintances, and hangers-on of all kinds stopped by to spend time with Lee. When the crowds got too big, and when Lee needed rest, Frances or Dr. Moseley would shoo people out the door.

Lang stopped in often to keep Lee's spirits up, as did actor Kevin O'Morrison. "I came by to make him laugh, to sing old songs with him and other friends who fell by . . . making the small room even smaller, as we watched Canada's once-magnificent body waste under the sheet that covered his nakedness to just above his loins," O'Morrison said. "Sometimes I succeeded in making him laugh—and when I did, the robustness of his laughter made it even more difficult to believe that we were at a deathwatch."

Under sedation for pain, Canada began to talk less and sleep more. "He couldn't focus," Frances said. "I just wanted him to stay calm, and take the sedatives so he wouldn't be in agony." Carl, now twenty-five, seemed to be in denial about his father's illness. "When Carl came down, Canada was under such sedation he couldn't speak," Frances said. "Carl thought his dad didn't want to speak to him. He got very upset. I tried to explain. It was difficult for everyone."

Lee grew steadily weaker. Frances stopped the parade of visitors and allowed only family and their closest friends in the room. She even turned Bishop Herbert F. Wilke away. "He was an Eastern Orthodox priest and he was in full regalia." Frances told him, "You walk in there in that regalia and Canada's going to *know*."

Frances spent more time alone with her husband, talking to him quietly, tending to him, making him feel comfortable and loved. "He never asked me if he was dying," she said. "I would have told him the truth, if he asked me."

After a week, he slipped into a coma. Frances knew then that the end would come far too soon: "I didn't leave his bed side. I held his hand for hours."

A day or two passed. A letter arrived from Paul R. Reynolds & Son granting Canada's request to perform the Bigger Thomas monologue on his upcoming tour. "This permission is granted up to October 1, 1952," Paul Reynolds wrote. "If you want to do it after October 1, 1952, would you write us again?" Frances carefully filed the letter, clinging perhaps to some scrap of hope that her husband might miraculously recover.

On May 7, the HUAC offices in Washington, D.C., finally acted on Alvin Stokes's request for a "run-down" on Canada Lee. A staff member pulled the actor's HUAC files, including a set of 107 three-by-five-inch file cards, each containing a specific piece of information about Lee—a speech he gave, a piece of letterhead that contained his name, an article about him published in the *Daily Worker*. Someone took these files and the stack of cards and began to type a meticulous, three-columned summary of the actor's allegedly subversive activities documented by HUAC since 1941. When the summary was finished on May 8, it was eight single-spaced pages and indicated that Lee had been involved in some way with twenty-one organizations cited as Communist fronts by either the Attorney General or congressional committees on un-American activities.

That very day, Thursday, May 8, Frances left Canada's side for just a moment to go to the kitchen. She returned to the bedroom to find the bed empty.

"He got out of bed, buck naked," she said. "Here was this invincible man, standing there before me. But of course, he wasn't invincible."

She put her arms around him, walked with him across the room, and tucked him in. He slipped back into unconsciousness and Frances stayed with him all through the night.

The next day, on Friday, May 9, 1952, at 6:30 p.m., just ten days after she had taken him to the doctor to find out what was wrong, Frances sat at Canada's side and held him, and kissed him, and felt his last breath touch her.

"At the end, all pain was disappearing from his face . . . that smooth, young face, so beautiful in death," Frances said. "I got a small mirror and checked his breath. I took the sheet and covered him up to his chin, and then I called John."

Dr. Moseley made the necessary phone calls from his office. Frances sat with Canada in the small, dark room. Almost immediately, it seemed to her, the doorbell began to ring and ring. The doctor came, the coroner came, reporters came, and so did a pair of men on a mission. "We're here to make a death mask," they told her.

"I don't know who asked for it or who paid for it," she said. "It was so strange, but I was in no shape to say yes or no to anything or anyone." A few weeks later, the death mask was delivered to her.

Word of Canada's death spread quickly in Harlem and elsewhere. Loften Mitchell was walking up Seventh Avenue with actor Richard Ward, talking about Canada's illness. They decided to stop off at Sidney Poitier's restaurant, Ribs in the Ruff, for some barbecue. As they crossed 127th Street, Mitchell felt a strange foreboding in the pit of his stomach. He stopped for a moment to talk to someone. Ward walked on over to Poitier, who was leaning against the awning of his shop. "My God! My God! Sidney just told me—Canada's dead!" Ward shouted back at Mitchell.

"The night exploded with tears, endless tears," Mitchell later wrote. "They beat upon the streets in an unrelenting flood that drowned out the car noises and the laughter so familiar to Seventh Avenue. And silence came to Harlem—a silence that was welcomed by none. That night Sidney Poitier faced hundreds of friends who made their way to his shop to offer condolences, to weep with him. The pain-wracked young actor was almost numb. He knew what we all knew—that something had been taken from us which nothing could replace."

Ironically, Billy Butler, one of Canada's closest friends, was at that moment working for one of Canada's principal detractors. He was conducting the orchestra at Ed Sullivan's live television show when he got the news. Butler had to master his grief and get to work; in the world of live television, the show definitely must go on. "That was the most difficult thing I had to do in my whole life," Butler said.

All of the New York daily newspapers as well as major publications throughout the country published obituaries for Canada Lee. His death was variously attributed to a heart attack or to hypertension terminating in uremia. All of the obits paid tribute to his amazing transformations from musician to jockey to boxer to actor. All described his triumphs on the stage and screen and several made careful references to the blacklist.

"In recent years, Mr. Lee complained that he had lost stage and screen jobs because the Communist label had been pinned on him falsely by the guilt-by-association method," wrote *The New York Herald Tribune*.

"Lee had been tagged several times as a pro-Communist—a charge he stoutly denied," wrote the *Daily News*. "He acknowledged that he had lent his name in the past to some organizations which appeared subsequently on the Attorney General's subversive list, but he declared he had done so only because they were anti-Nazi or anti-fascist groups and were 'working for the civil rights of my people.'"

A handful of papers linked Canada's illness and death to the blacklist. "Friends said the actor's health might have been affected by the Communist label which had been falsely pinned on him. Lee admitted that he had lost several stage and screen contracts because of the red tag," one obituary read.

It was Abner Berry at the *Daily Worker* who boldly put into print what many of Canada's friends were thinking, though a number of them were chagrined that it had to come from a Communist. As far as Berry was concerned, racism and the complex social, political, and economic machine known as the blacklist killed Canada Lee.

"From 1934 to 1949, Lee had conducted a fight for his integrity as an actor and a prideful Negro, intent upon attaining first class citizenship for himself and his people," Berry wrote. "In 1949, the long, cold war hand of the Pentagon and the State Department censors clamped down upon Lee, as it had upon every Negro artist dependent upon European appearances and the mass media for a livelihood. 'COMMUNIST!' yelled the war-and-hate-mongers at the Negro actor. And his career, his ability to earn a living, was threatened . . .

"He fought for his dignity, even when he did not understand the nature of that fight. He suffered and he died. And when his friends say that his death was hastened by the hounding of the witchhunters, the facts of his life document the accusation . . .

"Last Friday night, the medical men, in coldly precise and scientific terms, announced that Canada Lee had died of 'a malignant phase of high blood pressure.' But his colleagues and his people who mourn him know just as precisely that malignant Jim Crowism had a lot—much too much—to do with the fact that Lee's great heart stopped just when he should have been at the top of his powers."

In Washington, D.C., the eight-page single-spaced "run-down" on Canada Lee that had been requested by Alvin Stokes was filed away in the actor's dossier with a cover note written on a half sheet of HUAC stationery in red pencil: "Now deceased."

Did the blacklist kill Canada Lee, as Abner Berry suggests?

Doctors aren't certain what causes hypertension. In Canada's lifetime, many believed that stress could elevate blood pressure, but there is no medical proof. Many physicians now suspect that the answer will be found in genetic research. Whatever the case, Lee's chronic high blood pressure damaged his kidneys, and when the actor's kidney failure and uremic poisoning were finally diagnosed, the damage could not be repaired with existing medicines or technology.

Canada's mother, father, and sister all died of heart-related illnesses. African Americans are more likely than whites to have high blood pressure; studies indicate they also are more likely to develop kidney problems from it even when blood pressure is only mildly elevated. In fact, African Americans ages twenty-five to forty-four are twenty times more likely to develop hypertension-related kidney failure than Caucasians in the same age range. Lee may well have inherited what killed him. But the stress imposed on his life by the blacklist would surely have aggravated his condition, and many who admired the man and his work, and those who loved him, were convinced that the blacklist contributed to his illness and his death.

"I believe it was a major factor," Frances said. "He was an idealist. His ideals were being torn down . . . no passport, no money, his bitterness about South Africa . . . all of these things contributed."

"Canada Lee," Ossie Davis has written, "couldn't find a job anywhere and died of a broken heart." Adam Clayton Powell, Jr., concurred: "The real subversives of America broke his heart." Radio historian Howard Blue has stated that his cause of death was "political persecution." Physicians might doubt that diagnosis, but books and scholarly papers about the Red Scare and McCarthyism routinely cite the actor's death as one of a handful directly attributed to the blacklist.

❦ ❦ ❦

Four thousand people, black and white, rich and poor, famous and anonymous, came to Canada's funeral service on Tuesday, May 13, 1952, at Salem Methodist Church, where the actor had gone to Sunday school and learned to box. The organist played as people streamed into the sanctuary, greeted each other, clasped hands, embraced.

The crowd spilled out of the church doors, and soon thousands of mourners jammed the sidewalks up and down Seventh Avenue. Many theater luminaries came to pay tribute to Lee, including Sidney Poitier, Brooks Atkinson, Dick Campbell, Perry Watkins, Frank Silvera, and Frederick O'Neal. Place of honor was of course given to Lee's family, including Frances, Carl, Lovey, and Juanita Canegata. The cover photo of the funeral program showed the actor as a young and handsome man, under the heading: *Funeral Services for James Lionel Canegata "Canada Lee."*

The Reverend C. Y. Trigg motioned for the congregation to stand and sing the first hymn, number seventy-three in the hymnbook, *Be Still My Soul*. The minister said a prayer and read two lessons from the scriptures. Soloists sang. Then friends and colleagues took turns at the pulpit to share their memories of Canada and make their tributes. Lee's childhood friend Billy Butler spoke, along with one of Harlem's great composers, Noble Sissle. "Many wept unashamedly during the services as they heard the eulogies . . . for this splendid human being," a reporter noted.

Arnold Moss, who had played Prospero to Lee's Caliban, read lines from *The Tempest* that Canada had spoken:

> *Be not afraid: the isle is full of noises*
> *Sounds and sweet airs that give delight and hurt not.*
> *Sometimes a thousand twangling instruments*
> *Will hum about mine ears; and sometimes voices*
> *That, if then had waked after long sleep,*
> *Will make me sleep again; and then, in dreaming,*
> *The clouds me thought would open and show riches*
> *Ready to drop upon me, that, when I waked,*
> *I tried to dream again. (Act II, scene ii.)*

"When Canada spoke those lines, each performance, I couldn't help thinking that the 'noisy isle' he was thinking about was the Manhattan where he spent most of his life," Moss said, "and where he would 'wake' and 'cry to dream again' of the possibility of its riches."

Judge Francis E. Rivers, a longtime friend and fellow political activist, said Lee was "a consistent fighter for the rights of every man, and the impact and memory of his personality will be felt for years." Visibly moved, the judge said it was shameful and sad that such a "vivid, great, and generous American" could be deprived of employment on the grounds that he was "un-American."

Adam Clayton Powell, Jr., clergyman and flamboyant politician, stepped to the dais and turned off the reading light. "Canada Lee made his race a badge of military courage," he said. The enemies of America kept the actor from working and broke his heart, he said, concluding: "America has been cheapened by the death of Canada Lee."

The great theater impresario Oscar Hammerstein II opened his remarks by saying, "When we lose a man like Canada Lee, we can choose to emphasize our loss, or to express our gratitude for the time he spent with us and for what he did in that time. The latter choice is the better one." He continued:

> We who knew him well shall remember an energetic, warm-hearted man; the people of the American theater and audiences the world over will remember an artist of vitality and integrity. There are all kinds of artists in the theater and out of it. Some keep their art in one compartment and their lives in another. In the case of Canada Lee, there was a close and deep relationship between the actor and the man. He approached the part on the stage as he approached every problem in life—with a basic, uncompromising honesty. He had no use for cheap theatricalism, nor did he build his career with cool, calculating steps. He chose parts and plays for what they had to say to the public, not merely for what they might do for him. So he became a versatile actor, always interesting to watch and listen to, not merely because of the mastery of any superficial technique, but because he threw his heart and soul into every role he portrayed, and you could feel his heart beating beneath every character he depicted. The last time I had a chance to talk to him, he had just returned from Africa after finishing *Cry, the Beloved Country*. He was most unhappy at

what he had seen there—misery, injustice, poverty, cruelty. He was consumed with pity and bursting with anger. His capacity for feeling the heartbreak of others is what made him a good actor, and an important man. He was no mildly interested spectator in the world's affairs. He lived them. He threw himself into every scene where he was leading. He spent himself on the rest of us. Wore himself out, perhaps. He gave all of himself to us. Let us never forget to be grateful for the gift.

After Lee's friends and colleagues had spoken, Reverend Trigg read Canada's obituary and then delivered his own eulogy, praising Lee for standing up for what he believed in, even when it brought him nothing but abuse. He paraphrased Henry David Thoreau: "If a man does not march in step with his contemporaries, perhaps it is because he hears a different drummer. Let him step to the music which he hears."

"I would like to hang those words in every office of every congressman in Washington," Trigg said. "I would like to pass these words on to everyone who calls himself American, who every time he sees or hears one who follows a different drummer, brands him a Communist." Canada, he said, followed a different drummer and marched ahead, but he never forgot his people, and he fought to make the world a better place.

The choir sang a final hymn as the pallbearers took their places by the casket. They included actor Frederick O'Neal, producer Rod Geiger, painter Leonard Kovin, and Daniel James, the journalist who had accompanied Canada to his meetings with the HUAC investigator. A list of honorary pallbearers in the funeral program is a who's who of actors, directors, entertainers, writers, athletes, politicians, and activists. It includes Bosley Crowther, John Henry Faulk, Lester Granger, Harry Wagstaff Gribble, Joe Louis, David Loew, Gordon Parks, Sugar Ray Robinson, Josh White, and Walter White. Lee was buried at Woodlawn Cemetery in the Bronx, alongside many other cultural luminaries of New York.

In the days and weeks following his death, stories began to circulate about the actor and his many acts of kindness. A man recalled that one day while driving to a funeral he had a flat tire. In a dress suit, he set about changing his tire in the middle of heavy traffic. Suddenly he looked up and there, rolling up the sleeves of his brilliant white shirt to help, was Canada Lee. "I'll never forget it," the man told Beulah Bullock. "I offered to pay him, but he said, it's all right. And I never saw him again."

A woman in Harlem recalled that during the war, she had gone grocery shopping with her children one day. Burdened with a heavy load of packages, surrounded by small and tired children, she realized as she reached the checkout counter that she had left her ration stamps at home. There was nothing to do but leave all her packages in the store and walk home. When she came back to the store, the owner told her that her bill had already been paid by Canada, who happened to witness her plight. "Small acts of kindness travel faster than light," Beulah said. "I don't know how he could do so much for so many."

In a strange twist of fate, Lee's death was rapidly overshadowed in the public eye by another death. John Garfield, Canada's friend and fellow blacklisted actor, died of coronary thrombosis on May 21, 1952. He was thirty-nine. Star of *The Postman Always Rings Twice* and *Force of Evil*, as well as *Body and Soul*, Garfield was one of Hollywood's most popular tough guys before his name was named.

In the final days of his life, the actor had had enough of the blacklist. In an attempt to win pardon and rehabilitation, he was working frantically to finish a sixteen-page apologia called "I Was a Sucker for a Left Hook." It was never printed, although the manuscript was leaked to a few columnists. Garfield's sudden death in the apartment of his mistress was front-page news. Mobbed by thousands of fans, his funeral broke the previously spectacular attendance record set at Rudolph Valentino's funeral in 1926.

Canada's death was suddenly yesterday's news, forgotten in a matter of days by journalists as they wrote about the next big story. Forgotten by all except one, that is—Lee's old friend and betrayer Ed Sullivan couldn't resist kicking a couple of "Commie" corpses:

> The grim and curious coincidence of the deaths of John Garfield and Canada Lee within a few days spotlights the fact that both appeared in *Body and Soul*, made by United Artists in 1947. *Body and Soul*, as a case history, is of tremendous importance to Americans fighting Communism because it illustrates the manner in which Commies and pinks, in the field of communications and

ideas, gave employment to each other. The picture was directed by Robert Rossen, written by Abe Polonsky, included in its cast Garfield, Canada Lee and Anne Revere. All of them later were probed by the House Committee on Un-American Activities. *Body and Soul* is the pattern that the Commies and their sympathizers in TV networks, agencies and theatrical unions would like to fasten on the newest medium. From the director on down, the Commies insert their members, freeze out those who are on the American side of the fence.

The FBI tucked the column into the actor's file. Though Canada was dead and buried, the forces behind the blacklist wouldn't leave him alone.

FIFTEEN

BLUES REQUIEM

SPEAK OF ME AS I AM

C anada Lee died under a cloud of suspicion. While thousands of people from his hometown came to his funeral to pay him tribute, in the public eye, the actor was variously perceived as a traitor to his country, a subversive black activist, a man who betrayed his friend and fellow activist Paul Robeson to save his own skin, a Communist dupe or Red sympathizer.

For several years after Canada's death, a group of friends and admirers, including writers, activists, and labor leaders, tried to do what Lee had failed to do—clear his name and restore his reputation.

Many believed that the first step was to prove to the American public once and for all that Canada was not a Communist; some sought to go farther, to show that Lee was in fact an anti-Communist. Inflammatory articles in the *Daily Worker* blaming the actor's death on the witchhunters were particularly troublesome. While most agreed at least in part with this assessment, they did not want the *Daily Worker* to trumpet it in an effort to transform Canada into a Communist martyr.

"The *Worker* is trying to claim Canada Lee," critic and columnist Leonard Lyons noted indignantly in the *New York Post*. The writer went on to cast Lee as an African American patriot, and wrote that the actor had once told him, "America is the best place for the Negro, for no place else is there any hope for decent living." Lyons went so far as to argue that

Lee spent the last three years of his life fighting subversives tooth and nail, although little evidence exists to support this contention. Syndicated columnist Whitney Bolton echoed Lyons: "I know for truth that his last years were passed in combating Communist influences in this country."

Not long after these articles appeared, radio station WLIB in New York City broadcast a memorial tribute to Canada by Charles R. Iucci, secretary of the musicians' union Local 802. Iucci fondly recalled Lee's early career as a musician and his lifelong love affair with jazz and blues. The labor leader then told his listeners that Communists were "trying to claim Canada Lee as theirs." He declared vehemently, "Canada Lee loathed the Communists" and "knew them for his enemies" because "they would destroy every chance for the artist." Again, there is scant proof of this; on the contrary, the actor had befriended many Communists. He worked with Party members as an artist on films like *Body and Soul*, and as an activist while fighting Jim Crow and other discriminatory practices.

Iucci concluded by hailing Lee as a patriotic freedom fighter: "Canada Lee was the epitome of the free way of life. His every thought, his every act, his every desire was the expression of a man in whom freedom throbbed always. It was because of this that Canada Lee was a great musician, a great actor, and a great American."

The tug-of-war continued a few months later, when the Communist Party published a lavishly illustrated pamphlet seeking funds for the legal defense of black Communists accused of violating the Smith Act by advocating the overthrow of the U.S. government. The pamphlet, which was mailed to hundreds of black community leaders, featured a photo of Canada Lee with a reminder that the actor had been "hounded to death by the Un-American Committee." This time it was Frances who sharply distanced Canada from the Communist Party. She wired the publishers of the pamphlet, demanding they remove her husband's name and picture from their "misleading" appeal. The *New York Post* printed an excerpt from her telegram. Though Frances privately blamed the blacklist for Lee's death, she decided to downplay the humiliating end to Canada's career and emphasize instead her husband's civil rights record: "His premature death resulted from his self-sacrificing devotion to the task of securing basic human rights and decent living conditions for all peoples everywhere." Lovey also proclaimed his brother's patriotism, insisting:

"Canada was no Communist. And when he woke up to how he had been used, when he found out they were listing his name and using it without his permission, he fought them and fought hard."

Few stories hold the attention of the press for very long. Despite energetic efforts to set the record straight on Canada, the man was dead, and reporters soon turned their attention to new issues. Lee's admirers realized they must pursue other strategies. Days after the funeral, Frances was sitting alone in that dark little apartment on West Fourth Street, wondering how she was going to carry on without Canada, when the telephone rang. It was Walter White of the NAACP. "We have an important meeting and you must be there," he told her.

Frances wanted to refuse. Grieving, still in shock, she told herself she was in no condition to think or speak, let alone take part in a meeting. But she found herself promising White that she would come. "Canada Lee, get behind me," she told the shadows in the empty room. "I don't know if I can do this without you."

At the meeting, Walter White and Reverend Adam Clayton Powell, Jr., announced their intention to organize a foundation in Canada's name to preserve the actor's memory and ideals. The Canada Lee Foundation would grant scholarships to young people of color who planned to make their careers in the theater. Additional awards could be presented to community leaders, politicians, and businessmen who promoted integration in the arts. White and Powell believed that Lee's name would live on through these awards.

All of this would require money, of course. Frances could raise money. She had a head for business and had done some fund-raising for various causes before marrying Canada. What better cause could there be than carrying on Lee's good works? She accepted a position as the Foundation's administrative secretary and fund-raiser.

Strangely enough, within a matter of hours, Frances received another offer. An old friend who was a prominent banker in Brazil urged her to move back to Rio, where he and his wife would help her find a job and start a new life. "I would have gone, except for the Canada Lee Foundation," Frances said. John Moseley urged her to reconsider; he believed she would be better off in Brazil. "I can't run away from this," Frances told him. "I have to do it, for Canada's sake." White and Powell put together a distinguished board of directors for the Foundation that included Oscar Hammerstein II and Cab Calloway. But the board members were famous and busy men, and the Foundation became more or less a one-woman enterprise.

Digging in Canada's files, Frances pulled out the actor's old address books. For the better part of a year, she spent most of her waking hours writing, calling, and ringing doorbells from New York to California. Many gave generously and everyone shared fond memories of the actor. "I knew Canada was an extremely wonderful person when I was married to him," she said, "but it was really only after he died that I truly realized his importance, how much he gave to this country." A few times, to her surprise and dismay, she got a slightly chilly reception because of her color, but these incidents were rare. "I went through that whole tour, on radio and on TV, and not one nasty thing was said or written," she recalled. "Small things I didn't let bother me. It was just ignorance. After all, Canada was the epitome of dignity. How could I carry myself any other way?"

Money started coming in, not in barrels, but enough to get started. On November 11, 1952, the Canada Lee Foundation went public. *The New York Times* announced that the new organization would provide "aid to young dramatic artists of all races, via scholarships and grants to institutions, and will work toward establishing an intercultural theater in New York, open to all artists." The Foundation also planned to present annual awards "to those in the theater who have created new opportunities for young actors and actresses without regard to race or creed."

The inaugural fund-raising event, a private screening of *Cry, the Beloved Country*, took place on December 12, 1952. The Foundation also produced a private-edition record album, entitled *The Canada Lee Memorial Record*, a twelve-inch LP that featured dramatic works and poems Lee had recorded, mostly for radio broadcasts. "Although Canada is gone, much of his work survives as a living memorial," stated a letter marketing the record. "The roles he played on stage, screen, radio, and television, and the thoughts he conveyed in his pursuit of universal brotherhood, truly bear repeating. Some will live on beyond all of us." The record was distributed privately at six dollars a copy. Proceeds would support the Foundation and "perpetuate other of Canada Lee's works."

Meanwhile, the blacklist machine began to slowly break down. In 1953, Senator Joseph McCarthy investigated Communist infiltration into the military and attempted to discredit the Secretary of the Army. President Dwight Eisenhower was furious. The army passed unsavory information about McCarthy to sympathetic journalists already fed up with the senator's Red Scare tactics. Eisenhower told his vice president, Richard M. Nixon—a former Red-hunter and HUAC member—to put McCarthy in his place.

On March 4, 1954, Nixon made a speech. He didn't name names, but everyone recognized his intended target: "Men who have in the past done effective work exposing Communists in this country have, by reckless talk and questionable methods, made themselves the issue rather than the cause they believe in so deeply." Radio journalist Edward R. Murrow didn't hesitate to point the finger directly at the senator. On March 9, during his popular and influential television program *See It Now*, Murrow attacked the man and his methods. The Senate censured McCarthy in December, effectively ending his career.

Despite McCarthy's political demise, the Red Scare wasn't over yet, and Lee's name was far from being cleared. On March 18, 1954, the *New York Post* broke the story that a Mrs. Canegata, clerk-typist for the Immigration and Naturalization Service, had been fired because of "continuing sympathetic association" with her late brother-in-law, Canada Lee. (The accused had briefly handled correspondence for Canada; the INS didn't explain how her association had continued with the actor after his death.) The *Post* reported that her husband, William Canegata, feared that the U.S. Government would also take away the post office job he'd held for sixteen years.

So it was that Canada's brother, Lovey, and his wife, Pheta, suddenly found themselves in hot water because they were related to a deceased alleged subversive.

After working at the INS for three years, Pheta had been notified that "termination of your employment in the Department of Justice is necessary or advisable in the interest of national security." But she refused to go away without a fight. While Pheta admitted that her late brother-in-law "was reputed to have been in sympathetic association with Communist causes at a certain point in his career," she argued that this charge was never proved and Lee had categorically denied it. Pheta presented the INS with statements from community leaders defending Canada's reputation. "If these answers, together with the accompanying statements, are deemed insufficient to grant my clearance and reinstatement," she wrote, "I hereby request a hearing before a security hearing board at the earliest possible time."

Lovey told the press that his brother "had been unwittingly used by some of the Communist fronts in the early days," but he insisted that Lee loved his country. The actor tried to do right by his people, Lovey said, and to help anyone who suffered from discrimination and injustice: "If you knew Canada at all, you knew how he felt about the dignity of man. That was his main theme and he would speak on it any chance he got." Pheta eventually prevailed in her fight and was reinstated with back pay, according to her son, Bill Canegata. Lovey kept his job at the post office.

By this time, Frances and the Canada Lee Foundation were struggling to raise funds, and had dispersed only a few grants and awards. In the mid-1950s, activities gradually decreased and the organization eventually disbanded. "We just didn't have the kind of resources we needed to keep it going," Frances said. Foundations need large endowments to sustain themselves, and the big money was not forthcoming. Many wealthy, influential people still believed the actor had been a Communist sympathizer, if not a card-carrying Party member, and declined to donate. Try as they might, the Canada Lee Foundation's supporters could not overcome the damage done by the blacklist.

It would be years, in fact, before the blacklist truly died, releasing its grip on the entertainment industry, as well as labor, education, government, and other economic sectors. Some scholars argue that its chilling effects linger today, discouraging blue- and white-collar workers, artists, and public servants from speaking out on issues for fear of reprisals or dismissal by their employers. Certainly, the power of the blacklist lasted well into the 1960s. Scholars have spent years studying its impact, assessing damage that ranges from the personal (destruction of careers, friendships, marriages, and health), to the aesthetic (reducing art to the bland but safe), to the social and political (weakened civil liberties, reinforced Cold War anxieties).

In the last fifty years, Cold War scholarship and popular response to the blacklist have ridden waves of revisionism and counter-revisionism. Hundreds of books, films, news articles, and scholarly papers have explored how and why the blacklist happened; the truth about Soviet espionage and Communist infiltration; the consequences of the Red Scare and McCarthyism; and the lessons to be learned about national security, political repression, and personal freedoms.

The subject hasn't yet been exhausted, nor has a general consensus been reached. Perhaps that is as it should be. Following the events of September 11, 2001, Americans once again find themselves facing a diffuse and shadowy enemy that seems to threaten us from without and from within. How will we balance the importance of protecting our personal freedoms with governmental responsibility to provide for national security? Can we face our fears about terrorism without practicing intolerance and political repression? Will we examine critically what our leaders tell us? Will we speak out when we have concerns? Will we listen thoughtfully to voices of dissent?

We often mistake criticism for disloyalty. It happens on playgrounds, in families, at work, in governments, in wartime, in public discourse. If you're not with us, you must be against us. America, love it or leave it. But if allegiance and activism are held to be contradictory, if criticism is deemed treacherous, then patriotism becomes blind complacency, a mindless ovine acceptance of the social status quo.

In a 1976 speech, Michael Wilson described what it was like to be a victim of the blacklist, and issued a warning to the next generation of screenwriters:

> Unless you remember this dark epoch and understand it, you may be doomed to replay it. Not with the same cast of characters, of course, or on the same issues. But I see a day perhaps coming in your lifetime, if not in mine, when a new crisis of belief will grip this republic; when diversity of opinion will be labeled disloyalty; and when extraordinary pressures will be put on writers in the mass media to conform to administration policy on the key issues of the time, whatever they may be. If this gloomy scenario should come to pass, I trust that you younger men and women will shelter the mavericks and dissenters in your ranks, and protect their right to work . . . This nation will have need of them if it is to survive as an open society.

When Wilson made that speech, the blacklist was finally over and a new era of reparations and apologies had begun. The Screenwriters

Guild slowly reinstated dozens of credits to blacklisted artists, in many cases posthumously. John Howard Lawson did not receive his writing credit for *Cry, the Beloved Country*, Canada's final film, until October 1997. That same year, which marked the fiftieth anniversary of the infamous Waldorf Statement that launched the blacklist, the Screen Actors Guild formally accepted responsibility for its role in collaborating with the studios, the media, and the government to support and perpetuate the blacklisting of its own members.

Too little and too late for many blacklist victims, including Canada Lee.

Five decades after his death, his story has largely disappeared, his achievements as artist and activist all but forgotten. This man who broke color barriers in the worlds of art and entertainment and the media, who fought for civil rights and aided humanitarian causes at home and abroad—this man was dropped from public discourse so swiftly, so easily, so completely that Canada Lee, once a household name in America, has been virtually erased from memory and history.

His story, his artistic accomplishments, and his contributions to the struggle for civil rights, deserve more than that.

As a boy growing up in Harlem, Canada Lee dreamed of becoming something. The son of a black working-class family, he faced tremendous obstacles. But he simply would not be denied the chance to achieve, and using his talent, charm, and courage, his boundless energy and irrepressible spirit, Lee overcame those obstacles. He worked his way from stable boy to jockey at a time when white riders were determined to keep black jockeys off the racetracks. As a nationally ranked prizefighter, he battled racism in the ring, and though he never won the championship title he so desired, he was universally respected for his honesty, generosity, determination, and sportsmanship—traits that by themselves make heroes of athletes today. When a disastrous injury cost him the sight of his right eye and ended his boxing career, Lee retired from the ring with grace and dignity. He found himself in the middle of the Great Depression, a penniless, partially blind, unemployed black man with a grade-school education.

Refusing to give up his dream of becoming something, Canada determinedly reinvented himself one more time. On the stage of a tiny theater in Harlem, he took a risk, read some lines, and found his calling as an actor. He would leave an enduring though largely unheralded legacy to the artists who followed him by using his fame and his good name to speak out against injustice, to fight for civil rights, to help those less fortunate, to make the world a little better.

For nearly two decades, Lee battled stereotyped roles offered to black artists in theater, radio, film, and television. As a novice actor in the Federal Theatre Project, he helped break down color barriers in American theater by performing Shakespeare and modern masterpieces. His work in the Negro Unit challenged audience expectations—most white theatergoers, and many black theatergoers, were used to seeing actors of color playing butlers, maids, and slaves, singing and dancing merrily as they polished silver or picked cotton. Throughout his career, Lee played complex and dignified characters, including a labor organizer (*Stevedore*); the defiant leader of a Caribbean revolution (*Haiti*); a sailor protesting segregation in the military (*South Pacific*); a black veteran opposing racist housing covenants (*On Whitman Avenue*); and a priest combating apartheid in South Africa (*Cry, the Beloved Country*). When economic necessity compelled him to take menial roles, as in *Mamba's Daughters* and *Set My People Free*, he tried to rise above the stereotype. Canada took his battle to broadcasting, urging black radio and TV workers to take up a militant struggle against dehumanized portrayals of black characters. When he went to Hollywood to film Alfred Hitchcock's *Lifeboat*, Lee bravely spoke out against "nigger" dialogue, putting his newly launched movie career at risk by insisting that black characters and black audiences be treated with respect. He joined advocacy groups to lobby movie studios for fair employment practices, socially progressive scripts, and better roles for actors of color. The battle against stereotypes begun by Canada Lee and other pioneering black performers has not been won yet, observes historian Glenda E. Gill, but "through their incessant struggles, their strong sense of identity, their resistance against racism, and their unrelenting demands that African Americans be represented authentically, they paved a smoother way for the African American performing artists of the twenty-first century."

An early proponent of nontraditional casting, Lee played classical roles never before assigned to artists of color. He became the second black actor (after Paul Robeson) to play Shakespeare on Broadway, starring as Caliban in *The Tempest*. But Caliban was an inhuman creature, and Lee was determined to play a man, not a monster. He got that chance in *The Duchess of Malfi*, and made headlines across the country as the first black actor to play a white character in a classic drama. To be considered believable, Lee was compelled to take the stage in whiteface. Nevertheless, he set an important precedent. Less than a decade after Lee's death, theaters and festivals began to cast actors of color in classical roles without regard to color and without white makeup. Earle Hyman, a greenhorn when he starred with Lee in *Anna Lucasta*, became an eminent Shakespearean actor; James Earl Jones, Morgan Freeman, Gloria Foster, Alfre Woodard, and Angela Bassett have starred in classic plays at the New York Shakespeare Festival and other stages. As for the movies, Hollywood rarely takes on the classics these days, which makes it all the more significant that Denzel Washington (*Much Ado About Nothing*) and Laurence Fishburne (*Othello*) have starred in recent Shakespearean film adaptations. Color-blind casting has its critics, including artists of color, but Canada Lee's fight for nontraditional casting nevertheless stands as an important contribution to increasing artistic opportunities and respect for minority actors.

While battling for the right to play "white" roles in classic plays, Lee also sought to bring black history, culture, and issues to mainstream audiences. He once said that the domination of white culture in the arts and media made black Americans virtually invisible—as though they were a people without a past, without problems, without achievements. Determined to balance this inequity, Canada produced, promoted, and performed in plays and programs that unearthed black history and told the stories of Toussaint L'Ouverture, Marcus Garvey, Frederick Douglass, George Washington Carver, Booker T. Washington, Pearl Harbor hero Dorie Miller, pianist Pinetop Smith, and many others. As the narrator on *Flow Gently, Sweet Rhythm*, he became the first black announcer on a national radio series—a pioneering program that featured artists of color. He also hosted two radio shows that exclusively showcased black musicians. As he raised awareness about black culture, Canada never shied from current events and strived to put social and political issues on the stage, screen, and airwaves. As the star of *Native Son*, he faced down death threats and pickets to portray a victim of social injustice, a performance hailed at the time by prominent critics as the finest ever by a black actor. He made revolutionary radio programs like *New*

World A-Comin' to highlight controversial subjects crucial to the black community, including segregation and poll taxes. He produced and starred in *On Whitman Avenue*, a provocative drama about discriminatory housing practices. His film *Lost Boundaries* took on the topic of blacks "passing" as white, causing censors in some Southern cities to ban the film. His last screen appearance in Zoltan Korda's *Cry, the Beloved Country* was perhaps his greatest triumph—an understated yet deeply moving condemnation of the indignities suffered by people of color living under apartheid.

Lee's interest in creating more accurate portrayals of black people became inextricably tied to his desire for more equitable treatment of black artists and audiences. The actor was inspired by his early experience in the Federal Theater Project, which awarded equal pay to black and white workers and insisted on integrated audiences. At a time when black theatergoers were usually confined to the worst balcony seats in the house, a section known as nigger heaven, Lee fought for integrated seating in venues across the country. On the road with *Native Son*, he faced down theater managers, politicians, and citizens who were enraged at the play's interracial casting and insisted on identical treatment for black and white cast members in hotels and restaurants. In 1946, he broke a color barrier by becoming the first black man to produce a straight play on Broadway, and he urged other artists of color to back meaningful projects. Throughout his career, Lee lobbied for equal pay, better working conditions, and more job opportunities for black actors, directors, producers, designers, and technicians in theater, film, radio, and television.

As his fame and influence increased, Lee extended his activism beyond the arts and into his community. Raised by parents who were committed to aiding those in need, Canada believed he had a moral obligation to ease human suffering. While still a teenager, Lee donated portions of his prizefighting purses to destitute boxers, hospitals, and other charities. As a Broadway star, he generously gave time, money, and energy to humanitarian causes. Though he couldn't serve his country during World War II because of his partial blindness, he supported the war effort by performing at local hospitals and USO stations, rallying folks to buy bonds, and making morale-boosting radio programs and victory films. He worked tirelessly in Harlem and other neighborhoods to support orphanages and homes for the aged. He raised money for health clinics and hospitals, as well as day care centers, summer camps, and youth centers for poor children. Deeds such as these rarely make headlines, but Lee's efforts to improve the lives of the poor and the sick, the injured and the disabled, the young and the elderly deserve recognition, for these countless acts of community service show the actor's wholehearted commitment to helping others. When his political knowledge broadened, and his social consciousness deepened, Canada began to address issues of national and international importance.

Possessed of a beautiful voice, a magnetic presence, and a flair for oratory, Lee rapidly found himself in great demand as a speaker for Democrats and progressives, labor and civil rights organizations, social and humanitarian causes. In city halls and state capitals, Canada made ardent pleas for better schools, housing, jobs, and health care for poor and working-class citizens. He battled Jim Crow and lynching; lashed out at conservatives who opposed civil rights initiatives; and presented a petition in Congress that demanded the expulsion of Senator Theodore Bilbo, an avowed white supremacist. He fought for a Fair Employment Practices Commission to ensure equal job opportunities for minorities. Speaking fearlessly to elected officials, Lee insisted that people of color be given positions of power in local, state, and national government. When Hollywood writers, directors, and actors were summoned to Washington for questioning about alleged subversive activities, Canada joined other prominent film and stage stars in a campaign to support their right to freedom of speech. He urged African Americans to take pride in their heritage; decried the horrors of apartheid in South Africa; and raised money for anticolonialist movements throughout the continent. Lee's powerful and insistent voice of dissent was never completely stifled by the blacklist. Even when his career, his future, and his health were at risk, he continued to speak out against injustice—such was the strength of his commitment to champion the rights of all people who did not enjoy the privileges of this democracy.

As his last public act, Canada traveled to Westchester County, New York, to mourn with local residents after two innocent black men were shot to death by a white ex-policeman. Though he was weak and gravely ill, Lee delivered his finest speech, and in its conclusion there was pain in his voice when he said, "I don't know whether a white American knows what it means to be a Negro and a good American at the same time."

Canada Lee asked white America to understand that a black patriot can love his country even as he angrily demands that his country honor its fundamental promises by treating its people of color with dignity and respect. Forgotten too long by history, he deserves to be remembered as a hero, a man who had the courage to do what he believed was right, though it cost him the only thing he ever wanted, the chance to be somebody. It may also have cost him his life.

Like the heroes in classic tragedies, Canada was a complex man with flaws and contradictions, and faced with many difficult decisions, he made his share of mistakes. He loved and cherished his son, but he was not always around when Carl needed him. He respected women's rights, yet did not want his wife to seek employment outside their home. He worked hard and became a consummate contract negotiator, yet was often in financial straits because he spent money compulsively and often gave it away to family, friends, and the needy. Though he cared deeply about the people in his life, the actor pursued his social and political activism even after he realized it could jeopardize his career, his health, and the security of those he loved and looked after. He knew the risks and fought on; but when his name was named, and the blacklist robbed him of his work, he suffered greatly, in part because he could no longer support his loved ones. This may well be the reason that after determinedly fighting for three years to defend his actions and clear his name, Canada quietly contemplated whether or not he should compromise his principles to salvage his career; perhaps he was desperate to once again be able to take care of the people he loved. He took a few secret steps toward recanting his beliefs before his inquisitors, but we will never know what his ultimate decision would have been.

"I only hope to God that you kids never in your whole life, as long as you live, give up the fight," Lee once told a group of schoolchildren. "It is most important, for the future of the world."

Canada never gave up, and neither did Frances. Decades ago, she began recording and transcribing interviews with people who had known her husband, in a valiant effort to preserve his story. Many of these friends and colleagues were growing old; some had already died. When Lee's papers began to deteriorate, Frances resolved to preserve them. Now in her eighties, she is growing more fragile each year, and still she fights to clear Canada's name, to tell his story, and to restore his honor as artist and activist.

"When Canada died, they tried to make him invisible. They tried to obliterate him, his name," Frances said. "I owe him this fight."

Among the actor's scrapbooks there is an unsigned poem typed on a single sheet of paper titled "Bigger in the Deserted House." These words by an anonymous poet make a fitting epitaph for Canada Lee, a good man who braved and risked and achieved so much, a patriotic American wrongfully accused of disloyalty and tragically punished with the only thing he ever truly feared: anonymity.

Where are your black hands? . . .
Fists are turning 'round and 'round
On your whip-like wrists.
What are they seeking?
What makes them drop with futility at your sides?
Why do you shout?
And, like the threat of a heat storm, rumble?
You take your voice down to yourself and moan.
Why do you run so hard and breathlessly?
When only one more spasm of expression is possible,
Why do you use that final breath in a long intensely rhythmic whisper
That shakes mankind to the roots?

NOTES

PREFACE

xi   *"Overlooked by almost every theatrical or film historian . . .":* Stefan Kanfer, *A Journal of the Plague Years: A Devastating Chronicle of the Era of the Blacklist* (New York: Atheneum, 1973), p. 179.

xvi *"but tell them about the Negro jockey . . .":* Kelly Miller, "Perfect Picture of Harlem," *New York Amsterdam News,* July 30, 1930.

1. ALWAYS CHASING RAINBOWS: The Music

4   *"just a man who worked hard . . .":* Canada Lee, "The Importance of Education in Combating Prejudice," May 4, 1944, speech delivered at Public School 37, 113 East Eighty-seventh Street, Manhattan.

4   *Note on the surname Canegata:* Canegata actually seems closer to a Dutch name, "Cannegieter," than any Danish surname on record. "I have never seen our family name spelled that way, but there are many different spellings to it," amateur genealogist Sharon Mornan-Cangieter e-mailed the author. "I have found some family members in St. Croix, but not with that spelling. One thing that is for certain—the name Cannegieter is of Dutch origin and not Danish."

4   *"The heat along the equator . . .":* Leif Svalsen, *The Slave Ship Fredensborg* (Bloomington, Ind.: Indiana University Press, 2000), p. 9.

6   *"could sit a saddle . . .":* J. Mercer Meredith, "Canada Lee's Racial Heritage," *New York Age,* May 3, 1941.

7   *"and I didn't finish grammar school . . .":* Martha Jackson, "Canada Lee . . . One of the 'Roving Ambassadors,'" *St. Louis Star-Time,* November 1, 1941.

7   *Canegata family history:* Bill Canegata, interview with the author, July 6, 2002.

7   *Canada's name on census roll:* 1920 United States Federal Census, entry for James Canegata, roll T625-1224, ED 1439, Page 26B.

8   *"knew dignity . . .":* "He's Really Lionel Canegatas [*sic*] Of St. Croix, Virgin Islands,"

Brooklyn Daily Eagle, clipping fragment, Canada Lee file, New York Public Library for the Performing Arts.

9   *"seemed to flash into being . . .":* David Levering Lewis, *When Harlem Was in Vogue* (New York: Penguin, 1997), p. 25.

9   *"My grandmother was a healer . . .":* Bill Canegata interview.

9   *"ducked behind something . . .":* William Butler, Jr., interview with Frances Lee Pearson, Harlem, N.Y., 1978.

10   *"a fight almost to the death . . .":* Dr. John Moseley, interview with David Kamara.

10   *"I fought my way . . .":* Sidney Fields, "Only Human: The Spirit of Canada Lee," unsourced clipping fragment, Canada Lee file, New York Public Library for the Performing Arts.

10   *Punching monitor in the jaw:* Canada Lee, "The Importance of Education in Combating Prejudice."

10   *"It was a little game . . .":* John P. Carmichael, "Look Who's Acting! It's Mr. C. with Canada Lee," *Chicago Daily News,* November 29, 1941.

10   *"I was always reading . . .":* Helen Ormsbee, "Canada Lee Finds His Career Just a Series of Exciting Jobs," *New York Herald Tribune,* June 9, 1946.

11   *Professor Butler, music school:* Leslie Nash, Jr., interview with the author, December 9, 2002; William Butler, Jr., interview.

12   *"while other kids . . . competent critics . . .":* Carmichael, "Look Who's Acting!"

12   *"a virtuoso's lot . . .":* "Actor Has Variety of Talents," *New York Sun,* April 5, 1939.

12   *"his inherited spirit of adventure . . .":* "Canada Lee, Actor on Stage, Screen," *The New York Times,* May 10, 1952.

12   *Lee's parents had objected:* "Canada Lee, 45, Is Dead; Stage and Film Star," *New York Herald Tribune,* May 11, 1952.

12   *"to become his own man . . .":* "Canada Lee and Bigger," *The New York Times,* March 30, 1941.

13   *Passing for white:* Leslie Nash, Jr., author interview.

2. RUNNIN' WILD: The Races

14   *"Romance and excitement . . .":* Seymour Freidin, "Boxer, Jockey, Band Leader, Canada Lee Becomes Star Actor," *New York Herald Tribune,* March 30, 1941.

14   *Lure of the track:* "Canada Lee and Bigger."

14   *Men in St. Croix excellent horsemen:* J. Mercer Meredith, "Canada Lee's Racial Heritage," *New York Age,* May 3, 1941.

14   *"I didn't know which end . . .":* Allan Keller, "Bigger Finds a Judge Who Understands," *New York World-Telegram,* April 3, 1941.

15   *"In a month I was wearing . . .":* Keller, ibid.

16   *"about to chuck . . . I finished second . . .":* Carmichael, "Look Who's Acting! It's Mr. C. with Canada Lee," *Chicago Daily News,* November 29, 1941.

16   *"I spurred . . . five lengths ahead.":* Keller, "Bigger Finds a Judge Who Understands."

16   *Note:* Historian Tom Gilcoyne at the National Museum of Racing and Hall of Fame is the source of the only information I could find on Lee's jockey career. Mr. Gilcoyne provided a photocopy of a racing form concerning a race at Dorval on September 16, 1922, in which Lee rode the horse Ardito and finished *dead last.* This would seem to contradict Lee's story in which he won on Ardito; however, it is possible that Lee was recalling a different race in which he won on the same horse. I have chosen to give Canada the benefit of the doubt.

16 *"I really thought . . ."*: Carmichael, "Look Who's Acting!"

17 *"I never had a good hand . . ."*: "Canada Lee and Bigger."

17 *"Pop would just look . . ."*: Bill Canegata, interview with the author, July 6, 2002.

17 *"havens for ex-convicts . . ."*: Ted Carroll, "Canada Lee Scores Stage Triumph," *The Ring*, July 1941, Vol. XX #6, p. 12.

18 *"They paid off in peanuts."*: Sidney Fields, "Only Human: The Spirit of Canada Lee," unsourced clipping fragment, Canada Lee file, New York Public Library for the Performing Arts.

18 *"no experience, no name . . ."*: Carmichael, "Look Who's Acting!"

18 *"My agent would go to a man . . ."*: Canada Lee, "The Importance of Education in Combating Prejudice."

18 *"Those jockeys on those half mile . . ."*: Carroll, "Canada Lee Scores Stage Triumph," pp. 11–12.

18 *"They were ridden . . ."*: Neil Schmidt, "Black jockey's journey spanned different worlds: Prejudice rode ex-Cincinnati rider out of country," *The Cincinnati Enquirer*, April 29, 2002.

20 *"Take a trip . . ."*: Buster Miller, "The Sports Parade, *New York Age*, Saturday, May 4, 1910, archives of the Kentucky Derby Museum.

20 *"About the only racetrack . . ."*: Pohla Smith, "Blacks in Racing," *The Backstretch*, February 1994, p. 24, archives of the Kentucky Derby Museum.

20 *"Soon after that . . ."*: Tom Wilson, "Way Back When: Black Boys Ruled the Turf," unsourced clipping fragment, May 1940, archives of the Kentucky Derby Museum.

20 *"They got to thinking . . ."*: Joyce Trammell, "African American Jockeys," unpublished manuscript, archives of the Kentucky Derby Museum.

21 *"They scared me right out . . ."*: Carroll, "Canada Lee Scores Stage Triumph," p. 12.

21 *"but found no glory . . ."*: "Canada Lee Takes On a New Job," *New York Herald Tribune*, March 16, 1941.

3. LIFE CAN BE SO SWEET: The Ring

22 *"I was wondering . . ."*: Earl Wilson, "Canada Lee: Crazy Guy and Swell Actor," *New York Post*, March 3, 1941.

22 *"I was considered a big shot . . ."*: Canada Lee, "The Importance of Education in Combating Prejudice."

23 *"I had always licked him in school . . ."*: "Actor Has Variety of Talents," *New York Sun*, April 5, 1939.

23 *"Everyone was Dempsey-conscious."*: Seymour Freidin, "Boxer, Jockey, Band Leader, Canada Lee Becomes Star Actor," *New York Herald-Tribune*, March 30, 1941.

24 *Harry Wills controversy*: Hype Igoe, "Mixed Bouts Decision Due from Boxing Board Today," *New York World*, December 21, 1923.

24 *"Why inflict the punishment . . ."*: Hype Igoe, "New York May Sanction 'Mixed' Bouts," *New York World*, December 20, 1923.

24 *Willie Powell meeting*: Carmichael, "Look Who's Acting!"

24 *"There's big money in fighting."*: Nat Loubet, "Two of a Kind," *The Ring*, November 1949, p. 22.

25 *"I loved fighting . . ."*: Freidin, "Boxer, Jockey, Band Leader, Canada Lee Becomes Star Actor."

25 *"one of the luminaries . . ."*: "Canada Lee Touring [sic] Pro," *New York Amsterdam News*, October 6, 1926.

25 *How Lee got his fighting handle:* "Canada Lee," *Current Biography 1944* (New York: H. W. Wilson, 1944).

25 *"Canada Lee, crack colored featherweight . . .":* "Canada Lee Defeats Rival In Coney I'd. Amateur Tournament," *New York Age,* July 31, 1926.

25 *"Some people would say . . .":* Keller, "Bigger Finds a Judge Who Understands."

26 *Background on Lee's matches:* "Canagata [sic] Lee Now Ready To Enter Ranks of Professionalism: Puts Out His Man in Short Order: Colored and White Boys in Fine Showing at Madison Square Garden," *New York Amsterdam News,* October 13, 1926.

26 *Powell fight:* Irving Rudd, "Program for Pugilism," *The Negro Digest,* April 1946, pp. 47–50.

26 *"Here He Is . . ."* through *"Good Luck!":* "Canada Lee Touring [sic] Pro," *New York Amsterdam News.*

26–27 *"I was scared"* through *"and I win.":* "Canada Lee and Bigger."

27 *Note:* Editions of *Nat Fleischer's All-Time Ring Record Book* list "Willie Power" or "Powers" as Lee's first professional boxing opponent, but in *The New York Times* interview Canada states it was "Willie Powell," and as the man was Lee's friend, the author has opted to use the name Lee himself used.

27 *"Everything points . . .":* "Canada Lee Out to Make Another 'Rep.'" *New York Amsterdam News,* October 27, 1926.

28 *"Did Canada happen to be . . .":* "Canada Still Making Good," *New York Amsterdam News,* November 10, 1926.

28 *"Canada Lee got a taste . . .":* "Flowers Whips Murray Elkins," *New York Amsterdam News,* December 22, 1926.

28 *"so that ole Sam . . .":* *New York World,* January 20, 1927, unsourced clipping fragment, Gumby File, Rare Book and Manuscript Library, Butler Library, Columbia University.

29 *"Canada Lee whipped Izzy . . .":* *New York Sun,* January 20, 1927, unsourced clipping fragment, Gumby File, Rare Book and Manuscript Library, Bulter Library, Columbia University.

29 *"I learned new methods . . .":* Freidin, "Boxer, Jockey, Band Leader, Canada Lee Becomes Star Actor."

29 *"Fighting is beautiful . . .":* "Canada Lee and Bigger."

30 *"Blanchard was little else . . .":* "Bruce Flowers Wins Again: Colored Fighters Won All Their Bouts at Opening of New Club," *New York Amsterdam News,* November 2, 1927.

30 *"Willie Harmon, veteran east-side . . .":* James P. Dawson, "Harmon is Victor Over Canada Lee," *The New York Times,* February 14, 1928.

30 *"providing plenty of action . . .":* "Canada Lee in Sensational Draw," *New York Amsterdam The News,* March 28, 1928.

30 *"I had a good punch . . .":* Stanley Frank, "Canada Lee's Love For Ring Is No Act," *New York Post,* May 16, 1941.

30 *"prime favorite . . .":* Nat Fleischer, *Black Dynamite* (New York: C.J. O'Brien Inc., 1947), p. 172.

30 *Note on boxing statistics:* Boxing historian Donald. R. Koss at Richard J. Daley College, who is also a member of the International Boxing Research Organization, plumbed existing records on Lee's fighting career. Mr. Koss notes that records of fights in the 1920s and 1930s were not as scrupulously kept as they are today. He has documented sixty bouts for Canada Lee between 1927 and 1931; of those, the majority (forty-six bouts) took place between 1927 and 1928. Another source, the *Everlast Record Book,* cites

forty-eight bouts for Canada Lee in 1927 to 1928. Newspaper reports describe several bouts not cited in either record. Mr. Koss noted in an April 2001 letter to the author that *Everlast* "did not attempt complete coverage of the sport as *Fight Fax* does today, so inclusion is something of a barometer on a boxer," rather than an exact win-loss statement.

31 *"I was a kid . . .":* Leonard de Paur, interview with Frances Lee Pearson, May 1983.

31 *"loomed large on the pugilistic horizon . . .":* Fleischer, *Black Dynamite*, p. 172.

31 *"practically impossible to drag . . .":* "Canada Lee Has Everything, Says Jim Buckley," *New York Amsterdam News*, July 11, 1928.

31 *"In the final round . . .":* "Lee Right Along With Dundee," *New York Amsterdam News*, December 19, 1928.

32 *"the chocolate youngster . . . real merit.":* Carmichael, "Look Who's Acting!"

32 *"collected wins . . .":* "Newcomers on Boxing Card at Garden Tonight," *Boston Herald*, December 20, 1928.

32 *"perhaps the best welterweight":* "Hard Punching Welterweights," *Holyoke Daily Transcript and Telegram*, November 12, 1928.

32 *"No fighter to appear . . .":* "Lee-Brignolia Clash in Feature Bout In Audi Ring," *Erie* [Pa.] *Daily Times*, November 23, 1928.

32 *"a big hit":* "Lee and Horner Meet in Troy Ring Tonight," *The Troy Record*, August 22, 1929.

32 *"astounding chap":* Ed Sullivan, "Little Old New York," *New York Daily News*, March 29, 1941.

32 *"It wasn't an era . . .":* Fleischer, *Black Dynamite*, p. 172.

32 *"The first stage production . . .":* Helen Ormsbee, "Canada Lee Finds His Career Just a Series of Exciting Jobs," *New York Herald-Tribune*, June 9, 1946.

32 *"Money is meant to be spent.":* Bill Canegata, interview with the author, July 6, 2002.

32 *"I never kept any of that money . . .":* Keller, "Bigger Finds a Judge Who Understands."

33 *"wasn't around much . . .":* Elaine Plenda, telephone interview with the author, May 22, 2002.

33 *"She had breakdowns . . .":* Bill Canegata interview.

33 *"Juanita really dressed him up . . .":* Elaine Plenda interview.

33 *"He saw his father . . .":* Frances Lee Pearson, interview with the author, November 1997.

34 *"It was Canada"* through . . . *"to this day.":* Leslie Nash, Jr., interview with Frances Lee Pearson.

34 *"My dad . . .":* Canada Lee, "Why Theater People Support FDR," *Daily Worker*, October 6, 1944.

35 *"Lee was the [Sugar] Ray Robinson of his day.":* Irving Rudd, "Canada Lee, Former Boxer, Eyes Return," *The Ring*, 1946.

35 *Lee was overrated as a fighter:* Damon Runyon, "The Brighter Side: Box-Fighter Makes Good as an Actor," *New York Journal-American*, November 8, 1946.

35 *"It wasn't the fighters themselves . . .":* Lee, "The Importance of Education in Combating Prejudice."

35 *"cost numerous other boxers . . .":* John P. Lopez, "Those are my heroes," in "Breaking the Barriers: A *Houston Chronicle* Special Section," April 13, 1997.

35 *"A great many . . .";* "Tad," *Evening Journal*, March 22, 1927, unsourced clipping fragment, Gumby File, Rare Book and Manuscript Library, Butler Library, Columbia University.

35 *verge of locking in a championship bout:* Lee, "The Importance of Education in Combating Prejudice."

35 Note: Although Lee says the championship fight would have been with McLarnin, Jackie Fields held the title in the winter of 1929. McLarnin would not secure the title until May 1933.

36 *"Proper treatment would . . .":* Carroll, "Canada Lee Scores Stage Triumph."

36 *"Lee simply held . . .":* "Broadway Paradox," unsourced clipping fragment, spring 1941, Gumby File, Rare Book and Manuscript Library, Butler Library, Columbia University.

36 *"I was pretty sore . . .":* "Canada Lee Aims for Shakespeare and What's More, He'll Get Him, Too," *Brooklyn Daily Eagle*, September 17, 1944.

36 *Algers fight:* "Canada Lee Stops Algers in 5th Round," *The New York Times*, January 12, 1930.

36 *"[Lee] is coming into . . .":* "Lee and Black Bill Winners at Olympia," *New York Amsterdam News*, January 15, 1930.

37 *"Suddenly, all . . ."* through *"authentic champion":* "Canada Lee Hizo Gran Demonstración en el Entrenamiento," Associated Press (Havana, Cuba), February 11, 1930.

37 *"waste his time . . .":* "Regresa Hoy a New York Canada Lee," Associated Press (Havana, Cuba), February 12, 1930.

38 *"Freeman was dazed . . .":* Ray Peebles, "Freeman Earns Decision Over to Lee in Great Scrap: Negro Punches Hard But Tommy's Steady Attack Wins Verdict," *Erie Dispatch-Herald*, August 9, 1930.

38 *"The New York Negro . . .":* Joe Martin, "Freeman Pounds Way to Victory Over Canada Lee," *Erie Daily Times*, August 9, 1930.

38 *Final period of Lee's boxing career:* "Broadway Paradox," unsourced clipping fragment, Gumby File, Rare Book and Manuscript Library, Columbia University.

39 *Lee claims he was never knocked out:* Rudd, "Program for Pugilism."

39 *End of Lee's boxing career:* Frank, "Canada Lee's Love for Ring Is No Act."

39 *"Losing to a greenie . . .":* Johnny Fitzgerald, "Leading Boxer Becomes Leading Actor: Canada Lee Returns To City in Which He Ended Ring Career," *The Evening Telegram*, Toronto, Canada, February 4, 1942.

40 *"He still thinks . . .":* Carmichael, "Look Who's Acting!"

40 *"and told him to quit":* unsourced clipping fragment, *New York Daily Mirror*, July 17, 1934, Gumby File, Rare Book and Manuscript Library, Butler Library, Columbia University.

40 *"Just threw it away . . .":* Carmichael, "Look Who's Acting!"

40 *"Most kids . . ."* and *"I thrilled to every minute . . .":* Rudd, "Canada Lee, Former Boxer, Eyes Return."

40 *"I loved fighting better . . .":* Keller, "Bigger Finds a Judge Who Understands."

40 *"No one ever enjoyed . . .":* Carroll, "Canada Lee Scores Stage Triumph."

4. NICE WORK IF YOU CAN GET IT: The Stage

42 *"instinctive antagonism . . .":* Michael David Harris, *Always on Sunday: Ed Sullivan: An Inside View* (New York: Signet, 1968) p. 36.

43 *"I felt as though a friend . . .":* Canada Lee, draft of a letter to Ed Sullivan, 1949.

43 *"I figured that my popularity . . .":* Canada Lee, speech, "The Importance of Education in Combating Prejudice."

44 *Lee substituted for Duke Ellington:* "Bigger Than Ever," *Pic* magazine, August 5, 1941, p. 28.

44 *"I had to give it up . . .":* Wilson, "Canada Lee: 'Crazy Guy' and Swell Actor."

44 *"I never could take . . .":* Francis, "Canada Lee Aims for Shakespeare and What's More, He'll Get Him, Too."

44 *"Because I had been . . .":* Sidney Fields, "Only Human: The Spirit of Canada Lee," unsourced clipping fragment, Canada Lee file, New York Public Library for the Performing Arts.

45 *"I thought people . . .":* Francis, "Canada Lee Aims for Shakespeare and What's More, He'll Get Him, Too."

45 *"Did you ever come home . . .":* Carmichael, "Look Who's Acting!"

45 *"Enter here":* Fields, "Only Human: The Spirit of Canada Lee."

45 *"I always admired actors . . .":* Wilson, "Canada Lee: 'Crazy Guy' and Swell Actor."

45 *Lee's accidental audition:* Carmichael, "Look Who's Acting!" Also recounted in Freidin, "Boxer, Jockey, Band Leader, Canada Lee Becomes Star Actor," and in Carroll, "Canada Lee Scores State Triumph."

46 *Augustus Smith:* "'Whitman Avenue' Gramps Really Is Gus Smith," *New York Amsterdam News,* July 13, 1946.

46 *"He always felt . . .":* William Butler, Jr., interview with Frances Lee Pearson, Harlem, N.Y., 1978.

47 *Rex Ingram's role in* Stevedore: Frances Lee Pearson, interview with the author, November 1997.

47 *"They have only to give . . .":* John Mason Brown, "The Theatre Union Takes to the Soap Box Once More—Stevedore and the Race Problem in America," *New York Post,* clipping fragment, Canada Lee file, John Golden Archives, Museum of the City of New York.

48 *Bill Robinson at Stevedore anecdote:* Glenda E. Gill, *No Surrender! No Retreat!: African American Pioneer Performers of Twentieth-Century American Theater* (New York: St. Martin's Press, 2000) p. 110; Glenda E. Gill, "Careerist and Casualty: The Rise and Fall of Canada Lee," *Freedomways,* First Quarter, 1981.

48 *"He got nasty . . .":* Wilson, "Canada Lee: 'Crazy Guy' and Swell Actor."

48 *"gleaming gusto":* Brooks Atkinson, "From Broadway to Harlem," *The New York Times,* May 7, 1935.

48 *"Harlem in the 1930s . . ."* Loften Mitchell, *Black Drama* (New York: Hawthorn Books, 1967), p. 100.

49 *"Nobody appreciated . . ."* through *"survey the crowd.":* Leonard de Paur, interview with Frances Lee Pearson, May 1983.

50 *"I was scared . . ."* through *"Louis stunk.":* Frank, "Canada Lee's Love for Ring Is No Act."

51 *"indigenous plays . . ."* through *"come up and direct.":* John Houseman, *Run-Through: A Memoir* (New York: Simon and Schuster, 1972).

52 *"It was really ridiculous . . .":* Leonard de Paur interview, "The Battle Over *Citizen Kane,"* produced by The American Experience, WGBH/Boston, 1997, transcript accessed at www.pbs.org.

53 *"Hernandez would say . . .":* Thomas Anderson, interview with Frances Lee Pearson, Englewood, N.J., May 1978.

54 *Rehearsals of* Macbeth: Bosley Crowther, " 'Macbeth' the Moor," *The New York Times,* April 5, 1936.

54 *"He tried so many . . .":* Thomas Anderson, interview.

54 *"He knew what he wanted . . ."*: Leonard de Paur, interview, "The Battle Over *Citizen Kane*."

54 *"He kept them going . . ."*: Houseman, *Run-Through: A Memoir.*

54 *"I wanted to stay . . ."*: Ormsbee, "Canada Lee Finds His Career Just a Series of Exciting Jobs."

55 *"Then I knew . . ."*: Francis, "Canada Lee Aims for Shakespeare and What's More, He'll Get Him, Too."

55 *"Though Welles's . . ."*: Wendy Smith, "Macbeth: The Play That Electrified Harlem." *Civilization,* January–February 1996.

55 *"The kilt . . ."*; *Macbeth set in Haiti:* Crowther, "Macbeth the Moor."

56 *"Within five . . ."* through *". . . his triumph."*: John Houseman, ibid.

57 *"the audience . . ."*; *"This production proved . . ."*: "Negroes Hail Real Theater as Macbeth Usurps Harlem: All-Colored Cast Plays Shakespeare—Audience Rivals Hollywood's," *New York Age,* April 15, 1936.

57 *"That was magical . . ."*: Orson Welles interview, quoted in "The Battle Over *Citizen Kane*," produced by The American Experience, WGBH/Boston, 1997, transcript accessed at www.pbs.org.

57 *"Shakespeare himself . . ."* through *"its own."*: Ralph Matthews, *Macbeth* review, *Afro-American,* April 15, 1936.

57–58 *"the inability of . . ."* *"an exhibition of deluxe . . ."*: Percy Hammond, "A W.P.A. 'Macbeth,'" *New York Herald Tribune,* April 15, 1936.

57–58 *"awkwardly but . . ."*; *"terrifyingly active"*; *"It was a spectacular . . ."*: Burns Mantle, WPA 'Macbeth' in Fancy Dress," *New York Daily News,* April 15, 1936.

57 *"inept . . ."*: John Mason Brown, "A Not So Voodoo 'Macbeth' Performed in Harlem," *New York Post,* April 15, 1936.

58 *"Banquo played . . ."*: Sylvia Taylor, "Canada Lee Has Many Trades—Master of Them All," *Daily Worker,* August 21, 1941.

58 *"a show out of* Macbeth *. . ."*: Robert Garland, "Jazzed-Up 'Macbeth' at the Lafayette," April 15, 1936.

58 *"logical and stunning . . ."*: Brooks Atkinson, "'Macbeth,' or Harlem Boy Goes Wrong, Under Auspices of Federal Theatre Project," *The New York Times,* April 15, 1936.

58 *"In* Macbeth *the Negro . . ."*: Roi Ottley, *New York Amsterdam News,* clipping fragment, Canada Lee file, New York Library for the Performing Arts.

59 *Macbeth tour background:* Glenda E. Gill, "The Black Actor in the Depression Years." *White Grease Paint on Black Performers: A Study of the Federal Theatre of 1935–1939.* American University Studies, Series IX, History, Vol. 40, p. 17.

59 *"When Macbeth suddenly . . ."*: George Freedley, *Playbill,* July 1, 1946.

60 *"soul in crisis"*: Gill, "The Black Actor in the Depression Years."

60 *"a gift from God . . ."*: Langston Hughes, "Federal Theatre Led the Way to Plenty of Integration on Broadway," *New York Age,* May 2, 1953.

60 *"It was the Federal Theatre . . ."*: Langston Hughes and Milton Meltzer, *Black Magic: A Pictorial History of the Negro in American Entertainment.* (Englewood Cliffs, N.J.: Prentice-Hall Inc., 1967).

61 *"Roosevelt's New Deal . . ."*: Thomas Cripps, *Slow Fade to Black: The Negro in American Film 1900–1942* (New York: Oxford University Press, 1977), pp. 263–264.

61 *"Although the Harlem mummers . . ."*: Brooks Atkinson, "Eugene O'Neill's 'S.S. Glencairn' Series of One-Act Plays Put On by a Negro Troupe in Harlem," *The New York Times Theatre Review,* October 30, 1937.

62 *"insult"; "The Federal Theatre's . . ."*: John Mason Brown, "O'Neill's Sea Plays Acted Up in Harlem," *New York Post,* October 30, 1937.

62 *"even for players . . ."*: St. Clair Bourne, *New York Amsterdam News,* November 6, 1937.

62 *"Lee, as the dying . . ."*: Richard Watts, Jr., "S.S. Glencairn," *New York Herald Tribune,* October 30, 1937.

62 *"an over-genteel . . ."*: "Brown Sugar," *The New York Times Theatre Review,* December 3, 1937.

62 *Brown Sugar background:* Gill, "Careerist and Casualty: The Rise and Fall of Canada Lee."

63 *"Uncle Tom is Dead . . ."*: "Filibuster and the National Negro Congress," *New Masses,* May 24, 1938, p. 31.

63 *"If it is a tale . . ."*: Brooks Atkinson, "William Du Bois's 'Haiti' Opens in Harlem," *The New York Times,* March 4, 1938.

64 *"The smashing climax . . ."*: Howard Barnes, "Haiti," *New York Herald Tribune,* March 4, 1938.

64 *"was the first time . . ."*: Loften Mitchell, *Black Drama,* pp. 102–3.

64 *"I was supposed to . . ."*: Elinor Hughes, "Canada Lee Calls 'Native Son' Role Fun," *Boston Herald,* September 20, 1941.

65 *"on Canada's behalf . . ."*: Gill, "No Surrender! No Retreat!", pp. 113–114.

65 *Federal Theatre hearing, background:* Robert Vaughn, *Only Victims* (New York: Limelight Editions, 1996).

65 *Communists in the Federal Theatre:* Richard M. Fried, *Nightmare in Red: The McCarthy Era in Perspective* (Oxford University Press: New York, 1990), p. 48.

65 *"The killing of the FTP . . ."*: Gill, "No Surrender! No Retreat!," p. 114.

66 *"wreck hundreds . . ."*: Vaughn, *Only Victims,* p. 72.

66 *"I will never forget . . ."*: Canada Lee's speech to the Industrial Union of Maritime & Shipbuilding Workers, October 23, 1944, sections reprinted in the *Independent,* c. October 1944, and in "Why Theater People Support FDR," *Daily Worker,* October 6, 1944.

66 *"people who were running . . ."*: Leonard de Paur, interview with Frances Lee Pearson.

66–67 *"In the theater he has found . . ."*: Carmichael, "Look Who's Acting!"

5. BROADWAY MELODY: Bona Fide Star

68 *"I've always been like a leaf . . ."*: Sidney Fields, "Only Human: The Spirit of Canada Lee," unsourced clipping fragment, Canada Lee file, New York Public Library for the Performing Arts.

68 *"late addition"*: "Negro Actors for *Mamba's Daughters,*" *New York Post,* December 24, 1938.

69 *"lumbering . . . limp . . . plodding"*: Brooks Atkinson, "Ethel Waters Plays Her First Dramatic Role in the Heywards' *Mamba's Daughters,*" *The New York Times,* January 4, 1939.

69 *Mamba's Daughters background:* John Mason Brown, "Ethel Waters Appears in *Mamba's Daughters,*" *New York Post,* January 4, 1939, and Martha Jackson, "Canada Lee . . . One Of The 'Roving Ambassadors,'" *St. Louis Star-Time,* November 1, 1941.

69 *"The ovations . . ."*: "Actor Has Variety of Talents," *New York Sun,* April 5, 1939.

69 *"It was stop-the-show . . ."*: George Freedley, *Playbill,* July 1, 1946.

70 *"If you ever . . ."*: Buddy Moore, note to Frances Lee Pearson.

71 *"ear music"; "Negro talk"*: Max Wylie, *Best Broadcasts of 1940–41* (New York: Whittlesey House, 1942).

71 *Cabaret TAC:* "TAC Opening," *New York Herald Tribune,* October 4, 1940.

72   *"honest portrayals . . ."*: "Negro Group to Reopen Lincoln Theater Oct. 22," *New York Age*, September 28, 1940.

72   *"Canada Lee gives . . ."*: Brooks Atkinson, "Negro Playwrights Company Opens a New Theatre Movement in Harlem with *Big White Fog*," *The New York Times*, October 23, 1940.

72   *Negro Playwrights Company background*: Rena Fraden, *Blueprints for a Black Federal Theater 1935–1939* (New York: Cambridge Theatre Press, 1994), p. 125, and Doris Abramson, *Negro Playwrights in the American Theatre, 1925–1959* (New York: Columbia University Press, 1967), pp. 116–117.

73   *"This was clearly . . ."* through *"the better."*: Simon Callow, *Orson Welles: The Road to Xanadu* (New York: Penguin USA, 1996), pp. 538, 539.

74   *Native Son background*: Margaret Walker, *Richard Wright, Daemonic Genius* (New York: Amistad Press, 1988), and Hazel Rowley, *Richard Wright: The Life and Times* (New York: Henry Holt and Co., 2001).

75   *"A blow at . . ."*: Howe quoted in Callow, *Orson Welles: The Road to Xanadu*, p. 540.

76   *"in a light . . ."*: Richard Wright to John Houseman and Orson Welles, May 19, 1940, Welles manuscripts, Lilly Library, Indiana University, Bloomington.

76   *"a free medium . . ."*: Rowley, *Richard Wright: The Life and Times*, p. 204.

77   *"hurled himself at it . . ."*: Callow, *Orson Welles: The Road to Xanadu*, p. 543.

77   *Dudley's resignation*: "Doris Dudley Withdraws As Opening Nears: Strubling-Spell Episode Given as Real Cause," unsourced clipping fragment, Schomburg Center for Research in Black Culture.

77   *"strictly because . . ."*: Anne Burr, interview with Frances Lee Pearson, Hollywood, Calif., December 1981.

78   *"comparable to . . ."* through *"testimony to that"*: St. Clair Bourne, "Who Should Portray the Role of Bigger Thomas?," *New York Amsterdam News*, August 10, 1940.

78   *"Canada, who was . . ."*: Bill Chase, "All Ears," *New York Amsterdam News*, November 23, 1940.

79   *"A blaze of . . ."*: Dan Burley, "Backdoor Stuff," *New York Amsterdam News*, November 30, 1940.

79   *"Big Joe Turner . . ."*: Harold Lehman, telephone interview with the author, June 4, 2002.

80   *"he spent more sleepless nights . . ."*: Carroll, "Canada Lee Scores Stage Triumph."

80   *"I made it!"*: Buddy Moore note.

80   *"Welles and I . . ."*: Wilson, "Canada Lee: 'Crazy Guy' and Swell Actor."

80   *"to be surrounded by . . ."*: Jean Rosenthal, "Native Son Backstage," *Theater Arts Monthly*, June 1941.

80   *"afraid that it would look . . ."*: Anne Burr interview.

81   *"but never in a comparable situation"*: Edgar T. Rouzeau, "Broadway to Witness Rare Scene in 'Native Son': Play Climax Has White Actress and Colored Star Alone on Stage," *Pittsburgh Courier*, March 1941.

81   *"When Orson Welles . . ."*: *"Native Son*: Orson Welles Stages the Shocker of the Year," *Spot, the Entertaining Picture Magazine*, June 1941.

81   *"go easy on scenes . . ."*: "Broadway Report," *PM's Weekly*, March 16, 1941, p. 45.

81   *"Never in my life . . ."*: Richard Wright interview, copy in Welles manuscripts, Lilly Library, Indiana University, also cited in Callow, *Orson Welles: The Road to Xanadu*.

82   *"It is more than a whisper . . ."*: "Harlem Readies Itself for 'Native Son' Opening," *New York Amsterdam News*, March 15, 1941, p. 20.

82   *"Dearest My Sweet . . .":* Canada Lee, letter to Caresse Crosby, February 1941, Caresse Crosby Papers, Special Collections, Morris Library, Southern Illinois University, Carbondale.

83   *"shot the big fat devil . . ."* through *"we've got two rats.":* Wilson, "Canada Lee: 'Crazy Guy' and Swell Actor."

84   *Picture of Lee in chef's hat:* "Cast of 'Native Son' Grooms for Big Opening on Broadway," *Pittsburgh Courier,* March 8, 1941, photo and caption.

84   *"Every day I come home . . .":* Canada Lee, letter to Caresse Crosby, March 1941, Caresse Crosby Papers, Special Collections, Morris Library, Southern Illinois University, Carbondale.

85   *"Mr. Welles wants everything . . .":* "'Native Son,' Directed by Orson Welles, Opens Monday," *PM's Weekly,* March 16, 1941, p. 44.

85   *"four hours of . . ."* through *"best cast I've ever seen.":* Marvel Cooke, "Orson Welles Conducts 'Native Son' Rehearsal," *New York Amsterdam News,* March 22, 1941.

85   *"I don't have time . . .":* Canada Lee, letter to Caresse Crosby, March 19, 1941, Caresse Crosby Papers, Special Collections, Morris Library, Southern Illinois University, Carbondale.

86   *"I thought I . . .":* Anne Burr interview.

86   *"Here was Canada . . .":* Paul Stewart, interview with Frances Lee Pearson, Hollywood, Calif., December 1981.

86   *"Thanks for my big chance . . .":* Canada Lee, telegram to Orson Welles, Welles manuscripts, Lilly Library, Indiana University; cited in Callow, *Orson Welles: The Road to Xanadu.*

86   *"You are doing . . .":* Orson Welles, telegram to Canada, quoted in Floyd G. Snelson, "Native Son," *New York Age,* June 7, 1941.

86   *"You will wow them . . .":* Paul Robeson, telegram to Canada, quoted in Snelson, "Native Son."

87   *"The audience is as rude . . .":* Ed Sullivan, "Little Old New York," *New York Daily News,* March 27, 1941.

87   *"Come out, you . . .":* Dialogue from *Native Son,* souvenir program, John Golden Archives, Museum of the City of New York.

88   *"I want the play . . .":* Orson Welles, letter to Paul Green, cited in Walker, *Richard Wright, Daemonic Genius.*

88   *Nin at Native Son cast party:* Noël Riley Fitch, *Anaïs: The Erotic Life of Anaïs Nin* (New York: Little, Brown and Co., 1993), p. 242.

88   *"They were unbelievable . . .":* Anne Burr interview.

88   *"the greatest theatrical director . . .":* Sidney B. Whipple, "Native Son Stark Drama Stamped With Genius," *New York World-Telegram,* March 25, 1941.

88   *Four stars; "a perfect selection . . .":* Burns Mantle, "'Native Son' Stirs Audience to Emotional Pitch at St. James," *New York Daily News,* March 25, 1941.

88   *"Here is a sepian . . .":* Ed Sullivan, "Little Old New York," *New York Daily News,* March 27, 1941.

89   *"Mr. Lee's performance . . .":* Stark Young, "Book Basis," *The New Republic,* April 7, 1941.

89   *"superb . . .":* Brooks Atkinson, "The Play," *The New York Times,* March 25, 1941.

89   *"magnificent job . . .":* Wolcott Gibbs, "Black Boy," *The New Yorker,* April 4, 1941.

89   *"a master of . . .":* Richard P. Cooke, "Dark Drama," *The Wall Street Journal,* March 26, 1941.

89 *"The strongest . . ."*: "New Plays in Manhattan," *Time*, April 7, 1941, pp. 76–77.

89 *"one of the season's best . . ."*: Richard Watts, Jr., "Native Son," *New York Herald Tribune*, March 25, 1941.

89 *"fortunate in its Bigger . . ."*: John Mason Brown, "Orson Welles Presents Mr. Wright's 'Native Son,' *New York Post*, March 25, 1941.

89 *"highly emotional . . ."*: William E. Clark, "Broadway Production of 'Native Son' Is Faithful To Novel," *New York Age*, March 22, 1941.

89 *"dominates the stage . . ."*: Ralph Warner, "Stage Version of *Native Son* a Compelling Social Document," *Daily Worker*, March 27, 1941.

89 *"Thank you . . ."*: Paul Muni, quoted in "Theatrical Notes," *New York Age*, April 12, 1941.

89 *"Canada Lee has added . . ."*: Rosamond Gilder, "Glamour and Purpose," *Theater Arts Monthly*, October 1942.

89 *"To most people . . ."*: Atkinson, "The Play."

89 *"selfish humanity's sins . . ."*: Burns Mantle, "'Native Son' Stark Drama Stamped with Genius."

90 *"As it is bad . . ."*: Billy Rowe, "First-Night Audience Cheers Native Son," *Pittsburgh Courier*, April 5, 1941.

90 *"I can only hope . . ."*: Edgar T. Rouzeau, "White Press Loud in Praise for Native Son," *Journal and Guide*, April 4, 1941.

90 *"average, decent . . ."*: Sullivan, "Little Old New York," March 27, 1941.

91 *"What Mr. Sullivan . . ."*: "Native Son Notes," *New York Amsterdam News*, April 12, 1941.

91 Hearst papers gang up on Native Son: John Anderson, "'Native Son' Links Red, Racial Themes," *New York Journal-American*, March 25, 1941.

91 *"the only explanation . . ."*: "The Hearsters Gang Up on Welles' 'Native Son,'" *New York Daily News*, March 26, 1941.

91 Hearst scribes defended themselves: John Anderson, "Critics of Critics Distort Reviews," *New York Journal-American*, March 30, 1941.

91 *"the economic and social . . ."*: Warner, "Stage Version of *Native Son* A Compelling Social Document."

92 *"made a lot of people squirm . . ."*: Howard Cushman, "PM's in New York," *PM*, June 10, 1946.

92 *"I can't believe it . . ."* through *"so hard and so long."*: Carroll, "Canada Lee Scores Stage Triumph," pp. 10–11.

92 *"the producers bought that car . . ."*: "Drama Dept.," *Philadelphia Record*, April 20, 1941.

93 *"Canada is fond . . ."*: "Bigger Than Ever," *Pic* magazine, August 5, 1941, p. 29.

93 *"rejection and isolation"* through *"there wasn't anbody."*: Carl Lee, quoted in a press release for *Gordon's War*, issued by Gordon Armstrong, National Publicity Director, Twentieth Century Fox Film Corp, Carl Lee clipping file, New York Public Library of the Performing Arts.

94 *"My father was a talented man . . ."*: Bill Canegata, interview with the author, July 6, 2002.

94 *"I never could understand . . ."*: Thomas Anderson, interview with Frances Lee Pearson, Englewood, N.J., May 1978.

94 *"I remember him coming . . ."*: Bill Canegata, interview.

95 *"We started out . . ."* through *"second home for him"*: This American Life, "Kindness of Strangers," copyright 1997 Chicago Public Radio. Distributed by Public Radio International, quoted with permission from *This American Life*.

96–97 *"I never felt comfortable . . .":* "Stage Notes," *New York Amsterdam News*, April 12, 1941.

96 *"Canada had the pick . . .":* Dr. John Moseley interview with David Kamara.

96 *"He never told me . . .":* Leslie Nash, Jr., interview with Frances Lee Pearson.

96 *"We talked . . .":* Anaïs Nin, *Diary of Anaïs Nin, 1939–1944, Vol.* 3 (New York: Harcourt Brace Jovanovich, 1969), p. 106. Also, Fitch, *Anaïs: The Erotic Life of Anaïs Nin*, p. 242.

98–99 *"the cream . . ."* through *"She never quite got over it.":* This American Life, "Kindness of Strangers."

99 *"He wasn't the kind . . ."* through *"the whole world.":* Leslie Nash, Jr., interview.

99 *"and then take . . .":* William Butler, Jr., interview with Frances Lee Pearson, Harlem, N.Y., 1978.

99 *"On the nights . . .":* Nell Dodson, "Can Canada Lee Take Success and Keep Head?" American Negro Press syndicated column, April 1941.

100 *"Canada was having . . .":* Anne Burr, interview.

100 *"All you had to do . . .":* Thomas Anderson, interview.

100 *"Judge, everything is going along . . .":* Keller, "Bigger Finds a Judge Who Understands."

100 *"Fighting gave me . . .":* Freidin, "Boxer, Jockey, Band Leader, Canada Lee Becomes Star Actor."

101 *"I would give . . .":* "Canada Lee Would Rather Be Champ Than B'way Star," *New York Morning Telegraph*, March 28, 1941.

101 *"If I had my life . . .":* Multiple sources include Freidin, "Boxer, Jockey, Band Leader, Canada Lee Becomes Star Actor."

101 *"Canada Lee is a Negro . . .":* "Canada Lee and Bigger."

101 *"All my life, see . . .":* "Canada Lee and Bigger."

102 *"I never studied acting . . .":* Wilson, "Canada Lee: 'Crazy Guy' and Swell Actor."

102 *"You can see, in . . .":* Carmichael, "Look Who's Acting!"

102 *"We're making history . . .":* Freidin, "Boxer, Jockey, Band Leader, Canada Lee Becomes Star Actor."

102 *Need for plays on race relations:* "Broadway Paradox," unsourced clipping fragment, Gumby File, Rare Book and Manuscript Library, Butler Library, Columbia University.

102 *"I don't kid myself . . .":* Leighla Lewis, "Canada Lee Remains Sober Above Success," *The Afro-American*, July 12, 1941.

102 *"If I've done nothing else . . .":* Carroll, "Canada Lee Scores Stage Triumph," p. 12.

103 *"has a voice now . . .":* Sidney Fields, "Only Human: The Spirit of Canada Lee," unsourced clipping fragment, Canada Lee file, New York Public Library for the Performing Arts.

6. WHY DON'T YOU DO RIGHT: On the Road with Jim Crow

104 *"What impressed me . . .":* Leonard de Paur, interview with Frances Lee Pearson, New York, N.Y., May 1983.

105 *"I've known guys like Bigger . . .":* Freidin, "Boxer, Jockey, Band Leader, Canada Lee Becomes Star Actor."

105 *"I knew guys who said . . ."*: Keller, "Bigger Finds a Judge Who Understands."

105 *"The* Native Son *sensation . . ."*: Dan Burley, "Back Door Stuff," *New York Amsterdam News*, April 5, 1941, p. 13.

105 *"Lee is being sought . . ."*: Nell Dodson, "Spring Has Come to Harlem," *Philadelphia Tribune*, May 8, 1941.

106 *"Congrats to . . ."*: Floyd G. Nelson, "Harlem," *New York Age*, April 1941.

106 *"Canada was conned . . ."*: Anne Burr, interview with Frances Lee Pearson, Hollywood, Calif., December 1981.

107 *"The goal was to . . ."*: Blue, *Words At War*, pp. 89–90.

107 *Canada Lee's activism:* Canada Lee Master Name Index Cards, House Un-American Activities Committee, Box 392, 9E3/5/92, National Archives, Washington, D.C.

107 *"obviously inclined . . ."*: "Those Who Have Made Good," *Variety* review, May 14, 1941, p. 32.

108 *"The film executives . . ."*: "Screen Rights Sought: MGM In Market For 'Native Son'—Would Make It All-White," *Pittsburgh Courier*, April 5, 1941.

108 *Wright's alleged approval of all-white film:* Michel Fabre, *The Unfinished Quest of Richard Wright*, 2nd ed. (Chicago: University of Illinois, 1993), p. 336.

108 *"just a case history . . ."*: column fragment re: MGM bid, *New York Post*, May 9, 1941, Canada Lee file, New York Library for the Performing Arts.

108 *"If this plan . . ."*: Samuel Sillen, "Bigger Thomas on the Boards," *New Masses*, April 8, 1941.

108 *"horrified"*: Hazel Rowley, *Richard Wright: The Life and Times* (New York: Henry Holt and Company, 2001), p. 247.

109 *"What is going . . ."*: "'Native Son' Notes," *New York Amsterdam News*, April 18, 1941.

109 *"Lee, Negro star . . ."*: Ed Sullivan, "Little Old New York," *New York Daily News*, May 29, 1941.

109 *Lee's desire to start a band:* "Canada Lee's Band Yen," *Variety*, April 30, 1941.

109 *"Nothing definite . . ."*: "'Native Son' Star Planning New Ork," *Downbeat*, May 15, 1941, p. 16.

109 *"wait out the run . . ."*: "Canada Lee May Lead a Swing Band," *Pittsburgh Courier*, May 8, 1941.

109 *"The star of* Native Son *. . ."*: clipping fragment re: missing son, *New York Post*, May 9, 1941, Canada Lee file, New York Public Library for the Performing Arts.

109 *"He was a teenager . . ."*: Bill Canegata, interview with the author, July 7, 2002.

110 *"Not more than . . ."*: "Native Son, In Red for 36G, Closes," *Variety*, July 2, 1941.

110 *Closing of* Native Son: "Native Son Takes $36,000 B.O. Rap," *Afro-American*, July 12, 1941.

110 *"showed the race . . ."*: "Native Son Was $46,000 'In Red' When It Closed," *Pittsburgh Courier*, July 12, 1941.

111 *"Lee has no definite . . ."*: Wilella Waldorf, "Canada Lee's Future Plans; Soft Pedal on Othello," *New York Post*, June 23, 1941.

111 *"Canada Lee is proving . . ."*: "Canada Lee in New Field," *New York Amsterdam News*, August 2, 1941.

111 *"Scores of fan . . ."*: "Radio Work Keeps Canada Lee Busy During The Summer Months," *New York Age*, August 2, 1941.

111 *War Department program:* "Reschedule Broadcast," *New York Amsterdam News*, August 9, 1941.

111 "Realizing that colored . . .": "Canada Lee Launches Ambitious Radio Drive for Negro Talent," New York Age, July 3, 1941.

111 "I will waste no . . .": Edward T. Rouzeau, "Authors Given Splendid Chance By Lee," Journal and Guide, July 12, 1941.

112 "shrewdly": "Canada Lee with Wardell Saunders, Rena Mitchell, Dramatic Skit," Variety, July 9, 1941.

112 "He is now rapidly . . .": "Native Son Breaks Attendance Records At Windsor Theatre," New York Age, August 16, 1941, p. 10.

112 "two things . . .": "Truth About Star's Salary," New York Amsterdam News, August 23, 1941, p. 20.

113 "He needed the Negro . . .": "Canada Lee's Car Causes His Arrest," New York Age, August 23, 1941, p. 10.

113 "She was a super lady . . .": Gill, No Surrender! No Retreat!, p. 108.

114 "It was like being . . .": John Randolph, interview with Frances Lee Pearson, Los Angeles, Calif., November 1981.

114 "little short of perfect . . .": Rudolph Elie, Jr., "Native Son," Boston Herald, September 16, 1941.

114 Uncle Tom's Cabin, broadcast: "Canada Lee in 'Tom' on 'Invisible Theater,'" Variety, September 10, 1941.

114 "the first time . . .": "Radio," New York Mirror, column item on "Uncle Tom's Cabin," September 1, 1941.

114 fifteen hundred striking Gimbel's workers . . . : "Stars Perform At Gimbel Strike Rally," Daily Worker, September 3, 1941.

114 "Now that I have . . .": Elinor Hughes, "Canada Lee Calls 'Native Son' Role Fun," Boston Herald, September 20, 1941.

115 cut the play's profanity . . . : "Bordages Play Goes Into Rehearsal Oct. 1," New York World-Telegram, August 29, 1941.

115 "If they know . . .": Florence Fisher Parry, "I Dare Say: The More (Murders) the Merrier—Folks Like Grisly Humors," Pittsburgh Sun-Telegraph, September 1941.

115 "melodramatic frenzy . . .": Karl Krug, "'Native Son' Uneven Tragedy: Canada Lee Brilliant in Leading Role," Pittsburgh Sun-Telegraph, September 20, 1941.

115 "Although there were . . .": clipping fragment, New York Amsterdam Star-News, October 4, 1941, courtesy Konrad Nowakowski.

115–16 "Canada always" through "the S.O.B.": Thomas Anderson, interview with Frances Lee Pearson, Englewood, N.J., May 1978.

117 "I were not so . . .": James Canegata, letter to Canada Lee, November 14, 1941.

117–118 "That town . . ."; ". . . I was crying.": John Randolph interview.

117 "You're no longer"; "come from.": "Broadway Paradox," unsourced clipping fragment, spring 1941, Gumby File, Rare Book and Manuscript Library, Butler Library, Columbia University.

118 "The only thing I want . . .": Martha Jackson, "Canada Lee . . . One of the 'Roving Ambassadors,'" St. Louis Star-Time, November 1, 1941.

119 "I came away . . .": Gympsey Ison, "Call-Post Columnist Gives Impressions of 'Native Son' Current Hanna Hit," Cleveland Call and Post, November 8, 1941.

119 "a good half . . .": Lloyd Lewis, "'Native Son,' Blend of Horror Pathos and Stump Speeches," Chicago Daily News, November 11, 1941.

119 "At the moment . . .": Lloyd Lewis, "Critics Give Canada Lee Supreme Tribute of the Season: Actor Shoots, Critics Pray, Duck and Run," Chicago Daily News, November 15, 1941.

119 *Standing ovations:* Ashton Stevens, "Thrills, Lulls, and Canada Lee," *Chicago Herald-American,* November 11, 1941.

119 *"The Negro race . . .":* Robert Pollak, "Native Son Comes Home," *Chicago Daily Times,* November 11, 1941.

119 *Stop Hitler meeting:* Harris B. Gaines, National Negro Stop Hitler and Hitlerism Committee, letter to Canada Lee, November 20, 1941.

120 *"Canada, why . . .":* Thomas Anderson interview.

120 *"For the good . . .":* James Canegata, letter to Canada Lee, November 14, 1941.

120–21 *"I am enclosing . . .":* Juanita Waller Canegata, letter to Canada Lee, March 7, 1942.

121 *"He took care . . .":* Beulah Bullock, interview with the author, October 27, 2002.

121 *"Oh my God . . .":* Thomas Anderson interview.

121 *Rewrite of script; "there are no . . ."; "In this war . . .":* John Randolph, "Negro People Will Join Fight Against Axis, Says Richard Wright, Revising 'Native Son,'" *Daily Worker,* December 13, 1941.

122 *"John decided . . . very much.":* Sarah Cunningham, interview with Frances Lee Pearson, Los Angeles, Calif., November 10, 1981.

123–24 *"Every place . . ."; "hands in his pockets"; Two-Gun Pete:* Thomas Anderson interview.

123 *"We didn't have telephones . . .":* Charles Walton, "Bronzeville Conversation: Eddie Flagg, Manager of the DuSable Hotel, Jazz Institute of Chicago," c. 2002, article accessed November 4, 2002, at http://jazzinstituteofchicago.org/.

123 *"Canada Lee" poem:* Canada Lee scrapbook for *Native Son,* Manuscript Division, Schomburg Center for Research in Black Culture.

124 *"lovely letter . . .":* Juanita Waller Canegata, letter to Canada Lee, March 7, 1942.

125 *"Unspoiled by his . . .":* "From Violinist to Actor Via Prize Fighting," *The Chicago Sun,* December 11, 1941.

126 *"good performance . . ."; "Swell reading . . .":* Canada Lee scrapbook for *Native Son.*

126 *"Perhaps the outstanding . . .":* "Hey Buddy! Look at Me! I'm Makin' a Road," *Elm Bark,* Elmhurst College, Chicago, Ill., December 19, 1941.

126 *"I'm single . . .":* Helen M. Scott, "Inquisitive Sal," *St. Paul Recorder,* January 16, 1942.

126 *"reminds you . . .":* Frank Diamond, "Top Negro Actor, But Canada Lee, Native Son Lead, Prefers Fighting," *Minneapolis Morning Tribune,* January 1942.

126 *"I was surprised . . .":* William T. Evjue, "Negroes at Loraine," *Capitol Times,* Madison, Wisc., January 18, 1942.

127 *Canada loaned Jack the money:* Jack Geiger, *This American Life,* "Kindness of Strangers," copyright 1997 Chicago Public Radio, distributed by Public Radio International, quoted with permission from *This American Life.*

127 *"I'm going through . . .":* H. Jack Geiger, letter to Canada Lee, January 23, 1941.

127 *"pleading softly . . .":* "Give Negro Soldiers Equal Rights, Canada Lee Pleads," *Milwaukee Journal,* January 15, 1942.

127 *"I enjoyed your statement . . .":* James Canegata, letter to Canada Lee, January 29, 1942.

128 *"We were sharing . . .":* John Randolph interview.

128 *"of all the hunted . . .":* "'Native Son' Is Basis for Sermon," *The Evening Telegram,* Toronto, February 7, 1942.

128 *"I feel so . . .":* "'Accept Us As We Are,' Canada Lee Asks Students," *Toronto Globe and Mail,* February 6, 1942.

128 *"by a neck":* Script, Crown Brand Sports Club No. 93, Radio CFRB, February 3, 1942.

129 *George "Twistmouth" Ganaway:* Howard C. Hosmer, "It's This Way," *Rochester Democrat and Chronicle,* February 9, 1942.

129 *soft punches; "Someone mentioned . . .":* Jack Andrews, "Canada Lee, Who Fought Here, Returns as Theatrical Star," *The Post-Standard,* Syracuse, N.Y., February 11, 1942.

129 *sergeant stepped in:* Jack Kenny, "'Copper' Friend of Actor Takes Sides Against Law, Nearly Queers Play," *Syracuse Herald-Journal,* February 11, 1942.

129 *"entertain colored . . .";* "*not New York."*: Max Johnson, "Theatre Bias Hits 'Native Son,'" *The Afro-American,* February 17, 1942; John Randolph interview.

130 *"He never, ever . . .":* John Randolph interview.

130 *"Every reference . . .":* John Randolph, "Native Son Down Below," *New Masses,* clipping fragment, February 1942.

131 *"Claudia spent . . ."* : Beulah Bullock, interview with the author, October 27, 2002.

131 *"couldn't make up . . .":* "More of the Week's Washing," *New York Amsterdam Star-News,* April 7, 1942.

132 *"I feel a real . . .":* Anaïs Nin, *The Diary of Anaïs Nin, 1939–1944,* Vol. 3. (New York: Harcourt Brace Jovanovich, 1969), p. 283.

132 *"chilled and thrilled . . .":* John E. Ackerman, "Canada Lee Stars as Central Goes Over to the Legitimate," *Herald News,* Passaic, N.J., July 1942.

132 *Saroyan rehearsals; "Reading the Daily News . . .":* Robert Sylvester, "Saroyan Novelties Include Free Verse and Real Bus Boys," *New York Daily News,* August 1942, clipping fragment, Canada Lee file, New York Public Library for the Performing Arts.

133 *"revolutionary . . .":* Joe Bostic, "Dial Time," *The People's Voice,* August 15, 1941.

133 *"With no 'Oohs!' . . .":* Roxanne Chandler, "Radio Begins Honest Portrayals of Negro," *Daily Worker,* August 11, 1942.

133 *"the author of some . . .":* Wolcott Gibbs, "Back Again, Briefly," *The New Yorker,* August 1942, p. 28.

133 *"artistic hari-kiri . . .":* and *"He is an admirable . . .":* John Mason Brown, "William Saroyan Opens the Saroyan Theater," *New York World-Telegram,* August 18, 1942.

134 *"Canada Lee's poise . . .":* Burns Mantle, "Bill Saroyan's Theater Opens With Two Curious Dramas," *New York Daily News,* August 19, 1942.

134 *"Canada Lee is honest . . .":* Brooks Atkinson, "Saroyan Theater Makes Debut," *The New York Times,* August 19, 1942.

134 *The Saroyan plays:* Howard Barnes, "Undisciplined Exuberance," unsourced clipping fragment, John Golden Archives, Museum of the City of New York, and Richard Manson, "Saroyan Struts His Stuff At the Belasco Theatre," *New York Post,* August 18, 1942.

134 *"All speakers . . .":* Robert Hill, *The FBI's RACON: Racial Conditions in the United States During World War II* (Ithaca, N. Y.: Northeastern University Press, Spring 1995).

134 *"a screen yarn . . .":* "Screen News Here and in Hollywood," *The New York Times,* September 1, 1942.

135 *"triumphant . . .":* Brooks Atkinson, "Canada Lee Giving a Superb Performance in a Revival of 'Native Son,' Put on at the Majestic at Popular Prices," *The New York Times,* October 24, 1942.

135 *From four stars to three:* Burns Mantle, "'Native Son' Offered At Majestic Theater," *New York Daily News,* March 24, 1942.

135 *"At the time . . .":* George Freedley, "Canada Lee's Stirring Performance Makes *Native Son* Revival a Must," unsourced clipping fragment, Canada Lee file, New York Public Library for the Performing Arts.

136 *"When Canada Lee . . .":* Van Vechten letter quoted in Arnold Rampersad, *The Life of Langston Hughes, Volume II: 1941–1967: I Dream A World* (New York: Oxford University Press, 2002), p. 55.

136 *"wanted to avoid..."*: "Canada Lee Fights Closing," unsourced clipping fragment, Canada Lee file, New York Public Library for the Performing Arts.

137 *"I get blamed..."*: "Protests Restore 'Native Son' Drama," December 1942, unsourced clipping fragment, Canada Lee file, New York Public Library for the Performing Arts.

137 *"an important human..."*; *"As long as business..."*: Robert Sylvester, "'Native Son Stays," *New York Daily News*, December 8, 1942.

137 *"The attempt to stab..."*: "Halting of 'Native Son' Thwarted By Protests Of People," *New York Age*, December 12, 1942.

138 "Photo. *Daily Worker...*": Canada Lee Master Name Index Cards, House Un-American Activities Committee, Box 392, 9E3/5/92, National Archives, Washington, D.C.

138 *Contained in FBI/HUAC files:* "Canada Lee to Act at Lenin Rally Revue," *Daily Worker*, December 31, 1942, p. 3, and "Canada Lee Signed to Appear in Big Garden Lenin Meet," *New York Age*, January 9, 1943.

138 *"I would not fight..."*: Canada Lee FBI file, report from FBI Agent E. Conroy to FBI Director J. Edgar Hoover, April 29, 1943.

7. CALIFORNIA, HERE I COME: Hollywood, War, Romance

140 *Note:* Frances Lee Pearson quotes in this chapter are from interviews with the author, November 1997–December 2002.

140 *Victory films, black actors, wartime in Hollywood:* Thomas Doherty, *Projections of War: Hollywood, American Culture, and World War II* (New York: Columbia University Press, 1993), pp. 82–83 and pp. 207–208.

143 *"The agreement..."* and *Office of War Information:* Thomas Cripps, *Slow Fade to Black: The Negro in American Film, 1900–1942* (New York: Oxford University Press, 1977), pp. 376, 379.

144 Lifeboat: Dan Auiler, *Hitchcock's Notebooks* (New York: Spike/Avon, 1999), pp. 128–32.

144 Note: Statistics on U.S. Merchant Marine casualty rate in World War II as compared to other services are available at the Merchant Marine's web site, www.usmm.org.

145 *"casts adrift..."*: Doherty, *Projections of War*, p. 210.

145 *"Man, how I'd love..."*: "Canada Lee Wants 'Blood and Thunder,'" *Yank* magazine, clipping fragment, John Golden Archives, Museum of the City of New York.

146 *"head of an unofficial..."*: Canada Lee FBI files, report on Canada Lee (source censored), April 29, 1943.

146 *violating sedition statutes:* Canada Lee FBI files, Assistant Attorney General Tom Clark, memo to FBI Director J. Edgar Hoover, October 21, 1943.

146 *Double-V concept:* "Benefit Show In Person, Duke Ellington and Canada Lee," *New York Amsterdam News*, May 15, 1943; "Bill Sparkling With Stars, That's Latest On Our Show," *New York Amsterdam News*, December 19, 1942.

146 *"Your stake..."*: "First Graduation of Negro Soldiers at Camp Kilmer Features Canada Lee," *New York Age*, January 2, 1943.

146 *New School for Social Research lecture:* Events Listings, *New York Daily News*, January 29, 1943.

146 *"I speak for all the dead..."*: Ben Hecht, "A Tribute to Gallantry," 1943.

147 *"My head and eyes..."*: Donald Gillies, e-mail to the author, June 26, 2003.

147 *"They are guilty..."*: "Canada Lee At Forum Condemns Treatment Of Negro Artists," *New York Age*, April 10, 1943.

147 *Lee's participation in Newspaper Guild Forum:* "Harrison Honored by Foreign Born," *The New York Times*, April 18, 1943.

147 *"constantly battling . . .":* Alfred A. Duckatt, "Assignment in New York," *New York Age*, May 23, 1943.

148 *"For This We Fight":* Duckatt, "Assignment in New York;" " 'For This We Fight' In Production With Campbell Directing," *New York Age*, May 18, 1943; and "Negro Freedom Rally," advertisements, *New York Amsterdam News*, May 22, 1943, and June 5, 1943.

148 *"They told me . . .":* Seymour Peck, "Lee Put Heart And Soul Into *Body and Soul*," *PM*, September 4, 1947.

148 *"an uneven . . .":* Robert E. Morseberger, "Adrift in Steinbeck's *Lifeboat*," *Film Quarterly*, Vol. IV, #4, Fall 1976.

148–49 *"When they first . . .":* Otis L. Guernsey, Jr., "The Playbill: Canada Lee, Negroes and the War," *New York Herald Tribune*, December 26, 1943.

149 *Darryl Zanuck concerned:* Auiler, *Hitchcock's Notebooks*, pp. 129, 132.

149 *Tallulah never wore underwear . . .:* Michael Mills, "Films: 1940s," copyright 1997, accessed September 30, 2001, at http://www.moderntimes.com.

149 *"that he didn't live . . . I never touched him.":* Peck, "Lee Put Heart And Soul Into *Body and Soul*." (Note: In Peck's article, Canada does not identify the actor. Frances Lee Pearson identified the actor in question as Walter Slezak in an interview with the author.)

150 *"The script . . .":* Peck, ibid.

156 *"like we were Ethel Merman . . .":* Betsy Blair Reisz, interviewed by Patrick McGilligan and Paul Buhle, *Tender Comrades: A Backstory of the Hollywood Blacklist* (New York: St. Martin's Griffin, 1997) p. 547.

156 *Canada and The Sleepy Lagoon Defense Committee:* Petition to Governor Earl Warren of California, "Free the Victims of the Sleepy Lagoon Case" (Canada Lee cited as sponsor), and "The Sleepy Lagoon Case," pamphlet with a foreword by Orson Wells, published by the Sleepy Lagoon Defense Committee, June 1943. Sleepy Lagoon materials courtesy of the Yale Divinity School Library.

157 *FBI believed otherwise:* Canada Lee FBI files, including a report by Agent Robert W. Hollman, July 5, 1944, "Security Matter—C."

159 *"I would talk to him . . .":* Leslie Nash, Jr., interview with Frances Lee Pearson.

159 *Sister Claudia inquired:* Claudia Reilly, letter to Canada Lee, August 16, 1943.

159 *Lovey told him:* William "Lovey" Canegata, letter to Canada Lee, October 5, 1943.

159 *"From reports in the papers . . .":* Carl Vincent Canegata (Carl Lee), letter to Canada Lee, September 20, 1943.

159–60 *"I was supposed . . . pray.":* Guernsey, "The Playbill: Canada Lee, Negroes and the War."

160 *"The history of blacks . . .":* Donald Bogle, *Toms, Coons, Mulattoes, Mammies, and Bucks: An Interpretive History of Blacks in American Films* (New York: Continuum, 1991), p. xv.

160 *The film's climactic scene:* Robin Wood, *Hitchcock's Films Revisited* (New York: Columbia University Press, 1989), pp. 75–77.

161 *"Canada Lee was enamored . . .":* Anaïs Nin, *Diary of Anaïs Nin, 1939–1944, Vol. 3*, pp. 269, 271–272.

163 *"It's not one of those . . .":* Guernsey, "The Playbill: Canada Lee, Negroes and the War."

164 *"garden-variety plot . . ."*: Lewis Nichols, "The Play," *The New York Times*, December 30, 1943.

164 *"Howard Rigsby and Dorothy . . ."*: Lewis Kronenberger, "An Honest Try on a Good Theme," *PM*, December 30, 1943.

164 *"trite and tedious . . ."*: Frank Gill, "South Pacific," unsourced clipping fragment, Canada Lee file, New York Public Library for the Performing Arts.

164 *"Lee has a vivid . . ."*: Burton Rascoe, "South Pacific is Amateurish," *New York World-Telegram*, December 30, 1943.

165 *"Dear Sirs . . ."*: Robert Wallsten (Ed.), Elaine Wallsten Steinbeck, John Steinbeck, *Steinbeck: A Life In Letters* (New York: Viking, 1975).

165 *gala invitation-only preview:* Irene Thirer, " 'Lifeboat' — Event of The Week," *New York Post*, January 11, 1944.

166 *"Drastic eliminations . . ."*: Auiler, *Hitchcock's Notebooks*, p. 129.

166 *"one of the most pertinent . . ."*: Howard Barnes, "On The Screen: Lifeboat — Astor," *New York Herald Tribune*, January 13, 1944.

166 *"there's no place to hide"*: Archer Winston, "Alfred Hitchcock's *Lifeboat* Opens at the Astor Theater," *New York Post*, January 13, 1944.

166 *"Joe stands aside . . ."* and *"vital and realistic . . ."*: cited in Thomas Cripps, *Making Movies Black* (New York: Oxford University Press, 1993), p. 79.

167 *"ten days to get out of town"*: Dorothy Thompson, review cited in Clayton R. Koppes and Gregory D. Black, *Hollywood Goes to War: How Politics, Profits, and Propaganda Shaped World War II Movies* (New York: The Free Press, 1987), p. 309.

167 *"It's final, insidious . . ."*: Bosley Crowther, "Adrift in *Lifeboat*: The New Hitchcock-Steinbeck Drama Represents Democracy at Sea," *The New York Times*, January 23, 1944.

167 *"If we have failed . . ."*: Kenneth Macgowan, "The Producer Explains," *The New York Times*, January 23, 1944.

167 *"Please convey . . ."*: Wallsten (Ed.), et. al., *Steinbeck: A Life In Letters*.

168 *"I don't honestly . . ."*: Guernsey, "The Playbill: Canada Lee, Negroes and the War."

168 *"If the Negro . . ."*: "Canada Lee Talks About 'Lifeboat,'" *PM*, March 8, 1944.

8. STORMY WEATHER: Boy Gets Girl, Girl Disappears

169 Note: Frances Lee Pearson quotes in this chapter are from interviews with the author, November 1997–December 2002

169–70   *"Man, how I'd love . . ."*; *"Here is a message . . ."*: "Canada Lee Wants 'Blood and Thunder,'" *Yank* magazine, clipping fragment.

170 *"for dramatizing . . ."*: Quoted in Howard Blue, *Words at War*, p. 154.

170 Ballad of a Man Who Went To War: Arnold Rampersad, *The Life of Langston Hughes, Volume II, 1941–1967: I Dream A World*, p. 82.

170 *"I should like . . ."*: John Salt, letter to Canada Lee, February 22, 1944.

171 *"the contributions . . ."*: Blue, *Words at War*, p. 286.

171 *"I visualized . . ."*: Duke Ellington, *Music is My Mistress*. (New York: Da Capo Press, 1988).

171 *"a public invitation . . ."*: *New York Times* article quoted in "Canada Lee," *Current Biography 1944* (New York: H. W. Wilson, 1945), p. 396.

172 *"Canada Lee is more . . ."*: "Canada Lee, Songs-Comedy," *Variety*, April 12, 1944.

172 Note: The Dramatic Workshop, which nurtured talents including Tennessee Williams and Marlon Brando, remained an important creative force in New York until 1951, when the director's Communism became a liability; after Erwin Picator's application for U.S. citizenship was denied, he moved to West Germany.

172 *Lee as Othello at the New School:* "Canada Lee," *Current Biography 1944*, p. 396.

173 *"Of such a stature . . .":* Rudolph Elie, Jr., review, *Variety*, October 1943, cited in Paul Robeson, Jr., "Paul Robeson: Voice of a Century," *The Black Collegian Magazine*, copyright © 1997, accessed at www.black-collegian.com.

173 *"His Othello was the greatest . . .":* Harry Haun, "Miss Daisy's Driving Force: Earle Hyman," *Playbill*, Vol. 89, #3, March 1989.

173 *"a tendency to spit . . .":* Wilella Waldorf, "A Streamlined *Macbeth*, a New *Othello*, and a Broadway Audition," *The New York Times*, April 3, 1944.

174 *"It was Canada Lee's evening . . .":* Bob Francis, "Dram Workshop Proves 2 Things With *Macbeth*," *Billboard*, April 3, 1944.

174 *Dorie Miller:* Blue, *Words at War*, p. 285.

175 *Dorie Got a Medal:* Brad Miller, Library Systems Manager, Norman Corwin collection, Thousand Oaks Library System, e-mail to the author, October 24, 2001.

175 *"the absence . . .":* Horace Clayton, *The Courier*, May 13, 1944, cited in Blue, ibid., p. 292.

175 *"so that those . . .":* William Marshall, interview with Frances Lee Pearson, Pasadena, Calif., November 1981.

175 *"There is no such thing . . .":* Canada Lee speech, "Racial Prejudice," undated, c. 1943–1944.

175–76 *"I don't know . . . I only hope to God . . .":* Canada Lee, "The Importance of Education in Combating Prejudice."

176 Carry on, America: Arnold Rampersad, *The Life of Langston Hughes, Volume II: 1941–1967: I Dream A World*, p. 105.

177 *"strongly resents . . .":* Report by Special Agent Robert W. Hollman, July 5, 1944, Department of Justice case file 146-1-12-774, National Archives and Records Administration, Washington, D.C.

177 *a number of radio jobs:* "Canada Lee," *Current Biography 1944*, p. 396.

178 *"What a night that was!":* Hilda Haynes, interview with Frances Lee Pearson, Los Angeles, Calif., November 1981.

178 *"the most important . . .":* Burton Rascoe, "Anna Lucasta," *New York World-Telegram*, August 31, 1944.

178 *"a tedious charade . . .":* Howard Barnes, "Tedious But Well Acted," *New York Herald Tribune*, August 31, 1944.

178 *"Broadway needed a lift . . .":* Ruby Dee, *With Ossie and Ruby: In This Life Together* (New York: Quill, 2000), p. 158.

179 *"a hit that's turning away . . .":* Francis, "Canada Lee Aims for Shakespeare And What's More, He'll Get Him, Too."

179 *"They were a happy crew":* Loften Mitchell, *Black Drama* (New York: Hawthorn Books, 1967), p. 122.

179 *"He was the greatest . . .":* Haun, "Miss Daisy's Driving Force: Earle Hyman."

179 *lucrative contract:* Anna Lucasta files, including files of financial records filed by the firm of Klein and Ziegler, John Golden Archives, Museum of the City of New York.

179 *"Broadway producers saw . . .":* Ossie Davis, *With Ossie and Ruby: In This Life Together*, p. 162.

180 *sweeping floors:* Canada Lee speech, "Let's Build a City," c. 1944.

180 *"on well developed . . .":* Canada Lee speech, Philadelphia, c. fall 1944.

181 *"Even today . . .":* Canada Lee speech to the Industrial Union of Maritime & Shipbuilding Workers, Baltimore, Maryland, October 29, 1944.

181 *"The best way . . ."*: "Harlem Tribute Paid Wilkie as Great Liberal," *New York Herald Tribune*, October 30, 1944.

181 *"I am an American of African descent . . ."*: Canada Lee speech at the Wendell L. Wilkie tribute, "Africa and A New World A-Coming," African Academy of Arts and Sciences, October 29, 1944.

181 *"I trust you . . ."*: K. Ozuomba Mbadiwe, letter to Canada Lee, November 3, 1944.

182 *"He knew who he was . . ."*: Leslie Nash, Jr., interview with Frances Lee Pearson.

183 *"not to let the Robeson-Othello precedent . . ."*: Margaret Webster, *Don't Put Your Daughter on the Stage (Dear William)* (New York: Alfred A. Knopf, 1972), p. 120.

183 *"He seemed an inevitable . . ."*: Cheryl Crawford, "Such Stuff As Dreams Are Made Of," souvenir program from *The Tempest, or What You Will*, January 1945.

183–84 *"Shakespeare! That's what I've wanted since . . ."*: Francis, "Canada Lee Aims for Shakespeare And What's More, He'll Get Him, Too."

184 *"I do not intend to make Caliban . . ."*: Hermine Rich Isaacs, "This Insubstantial Pageant," *Theater Arts Monthly*, February 1945, pp. 89–93.

184 *[Canada] was torn*: Webster, *Don't Put Your Daughter on the Stage (Dear William)*, p. 121.

185 *"Caliban yearns . . ."*: Margaret Webster, "The Tempest, Or What You Will," souvenir program from *The Tempest*, January 1945.

185 *"I covered the floor . . ."*: interview with Margaret Webster, unsourced clipping fragment, John Golden Archives, Museum of the City of New York.

185 *Webster commanded tremendous respect in rehearsal*: Ormsbee, "Canada Lee Finds His Career Just a Series of Exciting Jobs."

185 *"He was terribly hard to work with . . ."*: Gill, *No Surrender! No Retreat!*, p. 121.

185 *"They Were Tops . . ."*: Ed Sullivan, "Little Old New York," *Daily News*, December 31, 1944.

186 *"The Boston matrons . . ."*: Webster, *Don't Put Your Daughter on the Stage (Dear William)*, p. 124.

186 *"He was lying peacefully behind the rock . . ."*: Webster, ibid., pp. 124–125.

187 *"certainly one of the stars . . ."*: John Kieran, unsourced clipping fragment, John Golden Archives, Museum of the City of New York.

187 *"Lee's portrayal of the monster . . ."*: John Chapman, *New York Daily News*, January 27, 1945.

187 *"Mr. Lee, in costume . . ."*: Lewis Nichols, " 'The Tempest' With Vera Zorina and Canada Lee Opens at the Alvin for a Limited Stay," *The New York Times*, January 27, 1945.

187 *"with uncouth power"*: Otis L. Guernsey, Jr., *New York Herald Tribune*, clipping fragment, John Golden Archives, Museum of the City of New York.

187 *"both articulate and monstrous . . ."*: "Tempest on a Turntable," *Newsweek*, February 5, 1945, pp. 82–83.

187 *"I suspect Mr. Lee . . ."*: Burton Rascoe, "Margaret Webster Puts On a New Kind of Tempest," clipping fragment, *New York World-Telegram*, New York Public Library for the Performing Arts.

187 *"the only Shakespearean actor . . ."*: *Variety*, March 6, 1945.

188 *"One eye was slightly defective . . ."*: Jack Harris, "Regular Fella," *The Hobo News*, clipping fragment, Gumby File, Butler Library, Rare Book and Manuscript Library, Columbia University.

189 *"a towering figure..."*: Canada Lee, "Why Theater People Support FDR," *Daily Worker*, October 6, 1944.

189 *"the leading Communist front..."*: Transcript, Investigation of Un-American Propaganda Activities in the United States, House of Representatives, Subcommittee of the Special Committee to Investigate Un-American Activities (HUAC), Thursday, October 5, 1944, pp. 10331–10349.

189 *"interlocking fronts"*: George E. Sokolsky, "These Days: Political Action Committee," October 24, 1944, King Features Syndicate.

190 *"political persecution..."*: "An Open Letter to Governor Thomas E. Dewey," *New York Sun*, September 27, 1944.

190 *Lee's files at the FBI and HUAC*: Canada Lee Master Name Index Cards, (Box 392), 9E3/5/9/2, House Un-American Activities Committee, National Archives, Washington, D.C.; Canada Lee Investigative Name File, First Series (Box 30), 9E3/4/11, House Un-American Activities Committee, National Archives, Washington, D.C.; Canada Lee FBI files; and *Communist Activity in the Entertainment Industry: FBI Surveillance Files on Hollywood, 1942–1958*, University Publications of America (microfilm).

191 *"Canada could not reach me..."*: Frances Lee Pearson, e-mail to the author, February 12, 2003.

9. NO BUSINESS LIKE SHOW BUSINESS: White Way and Whiteface

193 *"We will win..."*: Canada Lee speech, "Wallace for Secretary of Commerce," c. February 1945.

194 *"Sunday night..."*: Linda Dahl, *Morning Glory: Biography of Mary Lou Williams* (New York: Pantheon Books/Random House, 1999), accessed online in *Jazz Education Journal*, www.iaje.org.

194 *"They went crazy..."*: "Barney Josephson," *Artist and Influence*, Vol. XX, 2001, edited by James V. Hatch, Leo Hamalian, and Judy Blum, courtesy Hatch-Billops Collection.

195 *"may be summed up..."*: Canada Lee speech, "The Negro and the Peace," May 7, 1945.

196 *"disunity of the most..."*: Canada Lee, "Canada Lee Tells What An FEPC Means to Him," *Daily Worker*, July 5, 1945 (reprint of Canada Lee speech "Save the FEPC" of June 19, 1945).

196 *"want to belong..."*: "Harlem Girl Scouts Open Play Center," *The New York Times*, July 3, 1945.

197 *early draft of speech; "You can't tell..."*: Drafts of Canada Lee speech, "Independence Day," July 4, 1945.

198 *Benjamin J. Davis bid for reelection*: "Thousand Artists, Writers Back Davis," *Daily Worker*, September 25, 1945.

198 *"Who will permit..."*: Canada Lee speech to the Baltimore Industrial Union Council, September 3, 1945.

199 *"a first-class job"*: *Chicago Times*, clipping fragment, October 1945, Canada Lee file, New York Library for the Performing Arts.

199 *"but who was I..."*: William Branch, telephone interview with the author, June 27, 2002.

199 *"By the way..."*: Carl Canegata, letter to Canada Lee, October 15, 1945.

200 *"I felt guilty..."*: Ormsbee, "Canada Lee Finds His Career Just a Series of Exciting Jobs."

201 "On Whitman Avenue *was years . . .*": Richard Adler, *You Gotta Have Heart* (New York: Donald Fine, 1989), pp. 158, 162–3.

201 *"contributions toward . . .":* "Four Noted Americans to Receive Awards for Meritorious Work," *Daily Worker,* January 7, 1946.

201 *"The voice of Lenin . . .":* "Lenin Rally Hears Strike Aid Plea," *Daily Worker,* January 16, 1946.

202 *"dashed into the corridor . . .":* C. P. Trussell, "Mead Takes Hand At Filibustering: New Yorker Gets Petition From New York Negroes for Expulsion of Bilbo," *The New York Times,* February 1, 1946.

203 *"When you see . . .":* Fredi Washington, "Fredi Says," *People's Voice,* June 1, 1946.

203 *Jimmy Cannon . . . invited Lee on his radio show:* Variety, March 6, 1946, clipping fragment, Canada Lee files, New York Public Library for the Performing Arts.

203 *"Me, a producer . . .":* George Freedley, "On Whitman Avenue," *Playbill,* July 1, 1946.

203 *"Maxine dearest . . .":* Canada Lee and Mark Marvin, telegram to Maxine Wood, April 10, 1946, Maxine Finsterwald Papers, Special Collections Department, University of Iowa Libraries, Iowa City, Iowa.

203 *left "many a sophisticate . . .":* "On Whitman Avenue," *The Buffalo Courier-Express,* April 11, 1946.

203 *"Like many other . . .":* Rollin Palmer, "Erlanger Play is Sincere Plea for Racial Understanding," *The Buffalo News,* April 11, 1946.

203 *"decidedly limited":* "On Whitman Avenue," *Variety,* April 17, 1946.

204 "On Whitman Avenue *is not . . .":* Annie Oakley, "The Theater and Its People: *On Whitman Avenue," The Windsor Daily Star,* Windsor, Ontario, Canada, April 16, 1946.

204 *"This play, through its . . .":* Eleanor Roosevelt, "My Day," syndicated column, April 1946.

204 *"With the exception of one backer . . .":* Theater column, *New York Amsterdam News,* April 20, 1946.

205 *Gough anecdote:* Blue, *Words at War,* p. 62.

205 *"You start to put on your shoe . . .":* Ormsbee, "Canada Lee Finds His Career Just a Series of Exciting Jobs."

205 *"the façade . . .":* Charles Humboldt, "Lynching Bee, Northern Style," *New Masses,* May 28, 1946.

205 *"the fact remains . . .":* Lewis Nichols, "The Play," *The New York Times,* May 10, 1946.

205 *"While it rates . . .":* Howard Barnes, "Rocky Street," *New York Herald Tribune,* May 10, 1946.

205–6 *"eyes are raised . . .":* Walter Winchell, "Walter Winchell on Broadway," syndicated column, May 1946.

206 *"The play has three producers . . .":* Irving Hoffman, *Daily Reporter* (Hollywood), May 9, 1946.

206 *"vital and immediate . . .":* Louis Kronenberger, "A Vital Theme is Ill Handled," *PM,* May 10, 1946.

206 *"Broadway lynching":* Fredi Washington, "Fredi says," *People's Voice,* May 18, 1946.

206 *"Loaded with dynamite":* St. Clair T. Bourne, column, *New York Age,* May 18, 1946.

206 *"brought tears . . .":* Ralph Matthews, "Whitman Avenue," *The Afro-American,* May 18, 1946.

206 *"the most effective play I have ever seen . . .":* Langston Hughes, review, *Chicago Defender,* June 22, 1946, cited by Gill, *No Surrender! No Retreat!,* p. 122.

206 *penned a glowing testimonial:* Eslanda Goode Robeson, letter to the *Daily Worker*, May 19, 1946.

206 *"I can understand...":* Eleanor Roosevelt, "Racial Problems," *New York World-Telegram*, May 18, 1946.

206 *"This is our play...":* Charles Humboldt, "This is Our Play," *New Masses*, April 21, 1946.

206 *"Canada Lee, who...":* Ed Sullivan, "Little Old New York," *New York Daily News*, May 19, 1946.

207 *"Critics rejected us...":* Beth McHenry, "Canada Lee Is Determined That *On Whitman Avenue* Must Live," *New York Daily Worker*, May 21, 1946.

207 *PM stood by its review:* Louis Kronenberger, "Going to the Theater," *PM*, May 21, 1946.

207 *The paper sponsored a public forum:* "Forum to Discuss *On Whitman Avenue*," *PM*, May 22, 1946.

207 *"Harlem Whets Sharp Ax...":* "Harlem Whets Sharp Ax Vs. 'Whitman'" Nixers; Calls New York Crix 'Fascists,'" *Variety*, May 22, 1946.

207 *scuffles occasionally broke out:* Michael Carter, "New York Diary," *The Afro-American*, May 25, 1946.

207 *Canada invited Senator Bilbo:* Richard Dier, "In the Big City," *The Afro-American*, May 25, 1946.

208 *Lee helped Paul Robeson rally:* "Big 3 Unity for Colonial Freedom," advertisement, *Daily Worker*, May 19, 1940.

208 *"We have every right...":* "Jersey City Most Democratic in State, Says Canada Lee," Jersey City N.J. *Jersey Journal*, June 4, 1946.

208 *"Intolerance is undemocratic...":* "Jersey City Is Most Tolerant Community in State, Lee Says," Hoboken, N.J. *Jersey Observer*, June 4, 1946.

208 *"Unbeknown to the speakers...":* Nancy Wolcott Ebsen, "Blacklist," *Los Angeles Times*, November 8, 1987.

208 *"the benefit of much...":* "Theater Round-up," *Rocky Mountain News*, June 2, 1946.

209 *"We talked to teachers...":* Canada Lee and Mark Marvin, "More 'Fight' Needed: Co-Producers Say Energy and Faith Can Aid the 'Special Appeal' Play," *The New York Times*, August 11, 1946.

209 *Efforts to save play:* "Canada Lee to Speak," *Brooklyn Citizen*, May 22, 1946.

209 *"People know all about me...":* Harriet Van Horne, column, *New York World-Telegram*, June 13, 1946.

209 *"I was dispatched...":* Adler, *You Gotta Have Heart*, pp. 162–163.

210 *"This interview came...":* Ormsbee, "Canada Lee Finds His Career Just a Series of Exciting Jobs."

210 *"lay off the subject...":* Howard Cushman, "PMs in New York," *PM*, June 10, 1946.

210 *"I am happy...":* Canada Lee, "It's Turned the Corner," advertisement, *New York Age*, June 15, 1946.

211 *"a brilliant account...":* U.S. Congress House Committee Hearings, 80th Congress, Senate Library, Vol. 1138, 1947, card 13.

211 *"a top Hollywood director":* "*On Whitman Avenue* May Be Screened," *Pittsburgh Courier*, June 29, 1946.

211 *"and negotiate...":* "New Play Bought By Lee and Marvin," *New York World-Telegram*, July 25, 1946.

212 *"The wilting summer heat . . ."*: Canada Lee, letter to Caresse Crosby, July 11, 1946, Caresse Crosby Papers, Special Collections, Morris Library, Southern Illinois University, Carbondale.

212 *"No astute showman . . ."*: Vernon Rice, *"Whitman Avenue's* Story Is One of Faith And Miracles," *New York Post,* August 10, 1946.

212 *"The chief reason . . ."*: "Nose Thumbers Three," *Newsweek,* July 15, 1946.

213 *Lee carted everyone off to a USO:* "Canada Lee to Give Show," *Asbury Park Press,* July 26, 1946.

213 *"You would think . . ."*: Howard Fast, "Four Brothers and You," *New Masses,* April 2, 1946.

213 *Lynching in Moore's Ford; "Fire in a canebrake"*: Laura Wexler, *Fire in a Canebrake* (New York: Scribner, 2003).

214 *"Each of us has strings . . ."*: John Hudson Jones, "Harlem Seethes at Ga. Lynchings; Huge Rallies Demand U.S. Action," *Daily Worker,* July 29, 1946.

214 *"The Blinding of Isaac Woodard"*: "Blinding of Isaac Woodward," by Woody Guthrie. © 1965 (renewal) by Woody Guthrie Publications, Inc. All rights reserved. Used by permission.

215 *"Your presence on platform . . ."*: Telegram, Canada Lee to Orson Welles, August 31, 1946, Welles manuscripts, Lilly Library, Indiana University.

215 *"special appeal . . ."*: Lee and Marvin, "More 'Fight' Needed: Co-Producers Say Energy and Faith Can Aid the 'Special Appeal' Play.

215 *"Nothing I or anybody . . ."*: Adler, *You Gotta Have Heart,* pp. 162–163.

216 *They mailed letters . . .* : Canada Lee and Mark Marvin, letter to investors, November 1, 1946, Caresse Crosby Papers, Special Collections, Morris Library, Southern Illinois University, Carbondale.

216 *They sent pitches to a hundred studios . . .* : A. H. Weiler, "By Way Of Report: Producers Seek Funds to Make Racial Picture," *The New York Times,* December 1, 1946.

216 *"on a real old fashioned . . ."*: Press release on *Othello* tour, 1946, Canada Lee file, New York Public Library for the Performing Arts.

216 *"My reigning ambition . . ."*: "Art in Ebony!" *Swank* magazine, September 1941.

217 *Impressive credentials:* Press release on *The Duchess of Malfi* issued by Jean Dalrymple, September 17, 1946, Canada Lee file, New York Public Library for the Performing Arts.

217 *"If we only could get . . ."*: Elliot Norton, "Dearth of Actors Gave Opportunity to Canada Lee," *Boston Sunday Post,* September 29, 1946.

218 *"Police quickly spirited . . ."*: "Police Rescue White Man from Negro Mob," Associated Press, published in *The Boston Traveler,* September 17, 1946.

218 *"first time in theatrical history . . ."*: "Negro Actor Will Portray White Man," United Press, September 24, 1946.

219 *"There's nothing at all . . ."*: Sam Zolotow, "Canada Lee to Act White Role in Play," *The New York Times,* September 16, 1946, p. 9.

219 *"The practice had originated . . ."*: Bogle, *Toms, Coons, Mulattoes, Mammies, and Bucks,* p. 25.

219 *"Bosola . . . is a Spaniard . . ."*: Bradford F. Swan, "Negro Star to Portray White Man in Play Here," *Providence Bulletin,* September 20, 1946.

220 *"Watching the make-up . . ."*: Bill Chase, "All Ears: Ring Out The News," *New York Amsterdam News,* clipping fragment, Gumby File, Rare Book and Manuscript Library, Butler Library, Columbia University.

NOTES ⚜ 397

220 *"For a time it looked . . .":* Grace Davidson, "Put Up Bars to Colored Stage Star," *Boston Post,* September 23, 1946.
220 *"The answer seems to be . . .":* Norton, "Dearth of Actors Gave Opportunity to Canada Lee."
221 *"can open up vast new . . .":* "Negro Actor Will Portray White Man," United Press, September 24, 1946.
221 *"I hope it will be . . .":* clipping fragment, *Berkshire Eagle,* Pittsfield, Mass., September 18, 1946, Canada Lee file, New York Public Library for the Performing Arts.
221 *"Theoretically there is no reason . . .":* Elliot Norton, "Actor Canada Lee Has Great Chance In White Role," *Boston Sunday Post,* September 22, 1946.
222 *"the presentation of an actor . . .":* Bill Chase, "Canada Lee Made White for Broadway: Canada Lee Makes 'White Man' Debut," *New York Amsterdam News,* October 5, 1946, clipping fragment, Gumby File, Rare Book and Manuscript Library, Butler Library, Columbia University.
222 *third act was still a bit shaky:* "Canada Lee Misses Play: Does Not Take Role at Opening in Boston of *Duchess of Malfi,"* *The New York Times,* September 25, 1946.
222 *"I don't want to mess this up . . .":* "Negro Actor Will Portray White Man," United Press.
222 *"He showed that . . .":* *Billboard* quote cited in Chase, "Canada Lee Made White for Broadway: Canada Lee Makes 'White Man' Debut."
222 *"So far as his appearance . . .":* "Canada Lee Takes Role of Bosola In 'Duchess of Malfi,'" *Christian Science Monitor,* September 30, 1946.
223 *"In profile, there was no hint . . .":* Elliot Norton, "Makes History On Stage In Hub: Colored Man Takes White's Role and Result Is Interesting and Good Performance," *Boston Post,* September 26, 1946.
223 *"Canada Lee's turning 'whiteface' . . .":* Lew Sheaffer, "Brooklyn and Broadway Night Life," *Brooklyn Eagle,* October 6, 1946.
223 *"You always felt that . . .":* Ed Sullivan, "Little Old New York," *New York Daily News,* September 30, 1946.
224 *"It is my unpleasant duty . . .":* John Gassner, *Forum,* clipping fragment, Canada Lee file, New York Public Library for the Performing Arts.
224 *"Historians say . . .":* John Chapman, "Duchess of Malfi a Slow, Long And Unimportant Theater Relic," *New York Daily News,* October 16, 1946.
224 *"Even the research student . . .":* Howard Barnes, "Next Week 'East Lynne,'" *New York Herald Tribune,* October 16, 1946.
224 London Daily Telegraph *called Lee: London Daily Telegraph,* cited by Peter Noble in *The Negro in Films* (New York: Arno Press, 1970).
224 *"delight . . . has acquired mastery . . .":* Brooks Atkinson, "The Play," *The New York Times Theatre Review,* October 16, 1946.
224 *"He presents a rather comical . . .":* Ward Morehouse, "'The Duchess of Malfi,' a Gory Melodrama, Is Slow-footed and Ponderous," *New York Sun,* October 16, 1946.
224 *"Tour-de-force":* Richard Watts, Jr., "Villainy Not Very Exciting In 'Duchess of Malfi,'" *New York Post,* October 16, 1946.
224 *"stinker":* Runyon, "The Brighter Side: Box-Fighter Makes Good as an Actor."
224 *"Our blackface white men . . .":* Westbrook Pegler, "As Pegler Sees It," King Features Syndicate (Hearst), May 7, 1947.
225 *an eye-catching and obviously staged . . . :* "Boot-Out Bilbo Affair," *Daily Worker,* November 19, 1946.

225 *The note-takers hadn't slackened . . .* : Canada Lee Master Name Index Cards, (Box 392), 9E3/5/9/2, House Un-American Activities Committee, National Archives, Washington, D.C; Canada Lee Investigative Name File, (Box 30), 9E3/4/11, House Un-American Activities Committee, National Archives, Washington, D.C.; and "Report To FBI Director," New York Committee for the Preservation of the First Amendment to the Constitution, October 25, 1947, "Communist Activity in the Entertainment Industry: FBI Surveillance Files on Hollywood, 1942–1958," University Publications of America.

226 *"This was beyond the realm of a stunt . . ."*: Leonard de Paur, interview with Frances Lee Pearson, New York City, May 11, 1983.

10. BODY AND SOUL: Red Scared

228 *Note*: Frances Lee Pearson quotes in this chapter are from interviews with the author November 1997–December 2002.

228 *"A year went by . . ."*: Seymour Peck, "Lee Put Heart and Soul Into *Body and Soul*," *PM*, September 4, 1947.

229 *"A friend of mine at Enterprise . . ."*: Abraham Polonsky, quoted in press release, "Blacklisted Writer Illuminates Our Time," California State University, Northridge, April 24, 1946, accessed March 2003 at www.csun.edu.

230 *"He had remembered me . . ."*: Peck, "Lee Put Heart and Soul Into *Body and Soul*."

230 *"The element common . . ."*: Alan Casty, *The Films of Robert Rossen* (New York: Museum of Modern Art, 1969).

231 *"For the first time . . ."*: "Canada Lee: Ex-Pug Makes Comeback," *Ebony*, August 1947.

231 *"an almost catalytic effect . . ."*: "Canada Lee: Ex-Pug Makes Comeback," ibid.

232 *"You rarely find . . ."*: Peck, "Lee Put Heart And Soul Into *Body and Soul*."

232 *"I wanted an effect . . ."*: Bill Cady, "Oscar® Gets in the Ring," March 12, 2002, accessed April 30, 2002, at www.turnerclassicmovies.com.

232 *"When I'm acting . . ."*: Erskine Johnson, "In Hollywood: Behind the Scenes," NEA Columnist, January 12, 1947.

232 *"really battled it out . . ."*: "Canada Lee: Ex-Pug Makes Comeback."

233 *"I'm against communism . . ."*: Lloyd Gough, letter to Frances Lee Pearson, Los Angeles, Calif., 1981.

233 *"The funny thing . . ."*: Peck, "Lee Put Heart And Soul Into *Body and Soul*."

234 *"It's remarkable . . . a lot of guts."*: Peck, ibid.

234 *"Don't say a word . . ."*; *Charlie Chaplin incident*: Henry and Sylvia Blankfort, interview with Frances Lee Pearson, Los Angeles, Calif., December 1981.

235 *"He was very upset . . ."*: Beulah Bullock, interview with the author, October 27, 2002.

235 *"This picture I think . . ."*: Peck, "Lee Put Heart And Soul Into *Body and Soul*."

235 *The Red Scare*: Richard M. Fried, *Nightmare in Red: The McCarthy Era in Perspective* (New York: Oxford University Press, 1990), p. 73.

237 *"dazzle"*: Congressman Karl E. Mundt, "Extension of Remarks," May 28, 1947, Congressional Record, Vol. 93, Part II, 80th Congress, First Session, p. A2538.

238 *[Canada Lee and] Lena Horne*: "Lena Horne to Do Movie Short," *Daily Worker*, September 16, 1947, p. 11.

238 *"In Macbeth, Negro actor . . ."*: "Canada Lee's 2-Toned Shakespearean Rep," *Variety*, April 2, 1947.

239 *"They asked if . . ."*: Vincent Curcio, "The Do-It-Yourself Queen," *The Freeman*, a publication of The Foundation for Economic Education, Inc., June, 1991, Vol. 41, No. 6.

241 *"an indictment against . . ."*: Sondra Gorney, "Garfield's *Body and Soul* Prizefight Film Packs Punch," *Daily Worker*, August 28, 1947, p. 11.

241 *"Don't look for . . ."*: *Newsweek*, September 15, 1947, p. 13.

241 *"We have to fight fire . . ."*: Glenn Lovell, "Marsha Hunt," Special Edition of *National Screen Actor*, January 1998.

241 *"The threat of a blacklist . . ."*: Philip Dunne, *Take Two: A Life in Movies and Politics* (Limelight: New York, 1992), p. 196.

242 *"mass hysteria was no way . . ."*: John Huston, *An Open Book* (New York: Da Capo Press, 1994), p. 131.

242 *"outlined with sarcasm . . ."*; *"Mr. [name blacked out] . . ."*: Earl Scheidt, Letter to FBI Director, October 18, 1947, "Communist Activity in the Entertainment Industry: FBI Surveillance Files on Hollywood, 1942–1958," University Publications of America.

243 *"All speakers denounced . . ."*: Earl Scheidt, FBI Teletype to FBI Director J. Edgar Hoover, October 17, 1947, "Communist Activity in the Entertainment Industry: FBI Surveillance Files on Hollywood, 1942–1958," University Publications of America.

243 *Meeting of Committee on First Amendment Defendants*: Quarterly report to FBI Director, March 23, 1948, "Communist Activity in the Entertainment Industry: FBI Surveillance Files on Hollywood, 1942–1958," University Publications of America.

243 Variety *called them the "Red Quiz . . ."*: "Red Quiz Barnum Show," *Variety*, October 20, 1947.

243 *"Scores of correspondents . . ."*: *The New York Times*, October 21, 1947.

244 *"voluminous and unruly . . ."*: Guy Hottel, memo to J. Edgar Hoover, October 23, 1947, "Communist Activity in the Entertainment Industry: FBI Surveillance Files on Hollywood, 1942–1958," University Publications of America.

244 *"Not one? . . ."*; *"Swarmed down here . . ."*: Earl Wilson, "Forget It," *New York Post*, October 1947.

244 *"I told Mr. Wilson . . ."*: J. Edgar Hoover memo of October 23, 1947, "Communist Activity in the Entertainment Industry: FBI Surveillance Files on Hollywood, 1942–1958," University Publications of America.

245 *"How can they talk about . . ."*: Kanfer, *A Journal of The Plague Years*.

245 *"Humphrey Bogart, his sultry . . ."*: Frank Holeman, "Stars Drop in to Fight Red Probe," *New York Daily News*, October 27, 1947.

245 *"We were revved up . . ."*: Marsha Hunt, interviewed by Glenn Lovell, *Tender Comrades: A Backstory of the Hollywood Blacklist* (New York: St. Martin's Press, 1997), p. 316.

246 *testimony given by the witnesses*: U.S. Congress, House Un-American Activities Committee, Hearings Regarding the Communist Infiltration of the Motion Picture Industry, 80th Congress. First Session, 1947.

247 *"so shrill and defiant . . ."*: Marsha Hunt, in *Tender Comrades: A Backstory of the Hollywood Blacklist*, p. 317.

247–48 *"The most un-American . . ."*: Samuel Goldwyn, statement, press release issued October 30, 1947.

248 *"Commie Carnival Closes . . ."*: "Commie Carnival Closes: An Egg is Laid," *Variety*, October 31, 1947.

248 *"We had won . . ."*: Kenneth Lloyd Billingsley, *Hollywood Party: How Communism Seduced the American Film Industry in the 1930s and 1940s* (New York: Forum, 2000), p. 198.

248 *"this blustering and shouting . . ."*: Dunne, *Take Two*, p. 199.

248 *"We woke up . . ."*: Paul Henreid, with Jules Fast, *Ladies' Man* (New York: St. Martin's Press, 1984), p. 185.

248 *"star chamber . . . leery"*: Ed Sullivan, "Little Old New York," *New York Daily News,* October 28, 1947.

248 *"The Commies not only . . ."*: Ed Sullivan, "Little Old New York," *New York Daily News,* October 29, 1947.

249 *"It is Canada Lee . . ."*: Bosley Crowther, *"Body and Soul* Exciting Story of Prizefighting, Starring John Garfield, at Globe," *The New York Times Film Review,* November 10, 1947.

249 *"exceptionally well"*: *"Body and Soul," Variety,* August 13, 1947.

249 *"Pathos and anger . . ."*: Gorney, "Garfield's *Body and Soul* Prizefight Film Packs Punch."

249 *"the manner in which . . ."*: Ed Sullivan, "Little Old New York," cited in Kanfer, *A Journal of the Plague Years,* p. 178.

250 *"It is not as hot . . ."*: Report to the FBI Director, September 12, 1947, "Communist Activity in the Entertainment Industry: FBI Surveillance Files on Hollywood, 1942–1958," University Publications of America.

250 *"confirmed fellow traveler"*: Canada Lee Master Name Index Cards, (Box 392), 9E3/5/9/2, House Un-American Activities Committee, National Archives, Washington, D.C.

250 *"Ten witnesses refused to answer pertinent questions . . ."*: Richard Nixon, speech to Congress, November 27, 1947.

250 *The Waldorf Statement*: Charles McHarry, "Film Biggies to Purge All Reds," *New York Daily News,* November 26, 1947.

251 *"Only Sam Goldwyn . . ."*: Larry Ceplair, "SAG and the Motion Picture Blacklist," Special Edition of the *National Screen Actor,* January 1998.

251 *"blacklisted"*: *Newsweek,* December 8, 1947, p. 12.

251 *"Far from being offered . . ."*: Lovell, "Marsha Hunt."

251 *Westbrook Pegler singled out CFA members; "Developed something called . . ."*: Westbrook Pegler, "As Pegler Sees It," King Features Syndicate, December 19, 1947.

252 *"The public is beginning to think . . ."*: Robert Sklar, *City Boys: Cagney, Bogart, Garfield* (Princeton, N.J.: Princeton University Press, 1992), p. 196.

252 *"foolish" expedition*: Humphrey Bogart, "I'm No Communist," *Photoplay,* March 1948, p. 86.

252 *"Sullivan stated he . . ."*: FBI files cited in Sklar, *City Boys: Cagney, Bogart, Garfield,* p. 196.

253 *"Humphrey Bogart caved . . ."*: Gary Giddins, *Faces in the Crowd* (New York: De Capo, 1992), p. 130.

253 *"To be leftist was . . ."*: Richard M. Fried, *Nightmare in Red: The McCarthy Era in Perspective* (New York: Oxford University Press, 1990), p. 78.

11. TROUBLE, TROUBLE: Russian Spies and Pink Paint

254 Note: Frances Lee Pearson quotes in this chapter are from interviews with the author, November 1997–December 2002.

254 *The Venona Project*: William P. Crowell, "Introduction to the VENONA Project: An Effort to Digitize and Enhance the VENONA Documents," accessed at the National Security Agency Web site, www.nsa.gov/docs/venona.

254 *"This is the stuff . . ."*: John M. Deutch, Director of Central Intelligence, U.S. Central

Intelligence, speech delivered at the VENONA press conference, July 11, 1995, accessed at www.cia.gov.

255 *"We were inside the enemy's . . ."*: Robert J. Lamphere, with Tom Schachtman. *The FBI-KGB War: A Special Agent's Story* (Macon, Ga.: Mercer University Press, June 1995), pp. 96–97.

256 *he was campaigning for Henry Wallace:* "26 Civic Leaders Join Plea to Vote for Isacson," *Daily Worker*, February 9, 1948.

256 *"Wallace is Stalin's . . ."*: FBI report, "Communists and Pro-Communists for Wallace," undated, author and recipient unspecified. 1948 Campaign File, Wallace Folder, Truman Presidential Museum and Library, National Archives and Records Administrations, accessed March 25, 2003, at www.trumanlibrary.org.

256 *"Henry Wallace's Man . . ."*: "Leo Isacson: Fourth of a Series of Reports on the Communists and Pro-Communists for Wallace," 1948 Campaign File, Wallace Folder, Truman Presidential Museum and Library, National Archives and Records Administration, accessed March 25, 2003 at www.trumanlibrary.org.

256 *HUAC added more:* Canada Lee Master Name Index Cards, (Box 392), 9E3/5/9/2, House Un-American Activities Committee, National Archives, Washington, D.C.

256 *"theatrical bigwigs . . ."*: Walter K. Lewis, "Behind the Asbestos Curtain," *Plain Talk*, June 1947, pp. 15–16.

257 *"witch hunts"*: John Hudson Jones, "'All-Arts' Rally Maps Fight on Unamericans," *Daily Worker*, March 26, 1948.

257 *Mad Arts Ball:* "Mad Arts Ball in Harlem April 2," *Daily Worker*, March 29, 1948, p. 13.

257 *Canada presented an award to Arthur Gaeth:* "UE to Get Radio Award Monday," *Daily Worker*, June 22, 1948, p. 6.

258 *"At a time . . ."*: Jack Gould, "Programs In Review: 'Amateur Hour' Comes to Television—Canada Lee and Danny Thomas," *New York Age*, clipping fragment, Gumby file, Rare Book and Manuscript Library, Butler Library, Columbia University.

258 *"In music and text . . ."*: Saul Pett, "Yule Records For Junior," Associated Press column, December 10, 1948.

259 *"Canada Lee, in restraint . . ."*: Pat Keasby quote cited in e-mail to the author from Frances Lee Pearson, May 2, 2002.

259 *Fat Man in Famine:* Fred Russell, "Passing Show," *Bridgeport Post*, August 11, 1948.

259 *"Mr. Mostel appeared . . ."*: Fred Russell, "Passing Show," *Bridgeport Post*, August 17, 1948.

259 *"Yadda yadda yadda"*: "Yadda, yadda, yadda": Harold Wentworth and Stuart Berg Flexner, *Dictionary of American Slang* (New York: Thomas Y. Crowell Co., 1960).

259–60 *the actor had filed as a candidate:* campaign notices, *The New York Times*, July 28, 1948, p. 6, and *Daily Worker*, August 15, 1948, p. 11.

260 *"spy scare . . ."*: "End 'Spy' Scare, Asks Arts, Science Group," *Daily Worker*, August 18, 1948.

260 *Notes in Lee's HUAC file:* Canada Lee Master Name Index Cards, (Box 392), 9E3/5/9/2, House Un-American Activities Committee, National Archives, Washington, D.C.

260 *Withdrawal from Senate Race:* Campaign notice, *The New York Times*, August 22, 1948, p. 45; "ALP Names Lee Substitute," *The New York Times*, August 22, 1948, p. 32.

260 *Lee had been inked for the role . . .*: E. B. Rea, "Encores and Echoes," *The Afro-American*, October 4, 1948, p. 6.

261 *"President Truman . . . Negro people in the South.":* "Arrests of '12' Assailed by 395 Negro Leaders," *Daily Worker*, August 23, 1948, p. 11.

261 *HUAC kept close tabs:* Canada Lee Master Name Index Cards, (Box 392), 9E3/5/9/2, House Un-American Activities Committee, National Archives, Washington, D.C.

262 *"for whom a Negro . . .":* David Levering Lewis, *W.E.B. Du Bois: The Fight for Equality and The American Century, 1919–1963* (New York: Henry Holt and Company, 2000), pp. 532–533.

263 *"That stare would wilt . . .":* William Marshall, interview with Frances Lee Pearson, Pasadena, Calif., November 1981.

264 *"Get back!"* through *". . . I will not be there.":* William Marshall, ibid.

265 *"It is ironical . . .":* "Denounces Ban on Canada Lee," *Daily Worker*, October 28, 1948.

268 *"Mr. Lee suggests with . . .":* John Lardner, "Set My People Free," *New York Star*, November 5, 1948.

268 *"Canada Lee as the . . .":* "When the Slaves Rose," *Newsweek*, November 15, 1948.

268 *"a fresh and powerful . . .":* Richard Watts, Jr., "An Arresting Stage Portrait Of an Early American Rebel," *New York Post*, November 14, 1948.

268 *"The costumer has rigged . . .":* Wolcott Gibbs, *The New Yorker*, November 1948.

268 *"really hamming it . . .":* John Chapman, "'Set My People Free' Promises An Uprising, But It Fizzles Out," *New York Herald Tribune*, November 1948.

268 *"Since Negro actors . . .":* Brooks Atkinson, "Set My People Free," *The New York Times*, Sunday, November 14, 1948.

268 *"A serious person . . .":* Venona decrypted message accessed at http://www.nsa.gov/docs/venona/venona_docs.html.

269 *"There can't be any doubt . . .":* Lamphere, *The FBI-KGB War*, p. 98.

269 *"When I had all these data . . .":* Lamphere, ibid., p. 103.

270 *"We had one hell . . ."; "I decided to bait a hook . . .":* Lamphere, ibid., pp. 104, 105.

271 *"he did not like . . .":* David Chudnow, letter to Canada Lee, February 2, 1949.

271 *more index cards:* Canada Lee Master Name Index Cards, (Box 392), 9E3/5/9/2, House Un-American Activities Committee, National Archives, Washington, D.C.

271 *Othello tour plans:* "*Othello* Bond Posted," *New York Herald Tribune*, February 21, 1949, and *Othello* press release, February 1949, Canada Lee file, New York Public Library for the Performing Arts.

271 *"There is not a single Negro . . .":* Bob Lauter, "Around the Dial: 'Voice of Freedom' Campaigns For Negro News Commentator," *Daily Worker*, February 16, 1949, p. 13.

272 *"BORN: Lucky Lionel . . .":* Bobby Dorsey, "Character-tures," *New York Age*, March 19, 1949, p. 6.

273 *"rebellious, biting . . .":* "Destination Freedom: Richard Durham," accessed December 14, 2002, at www.blackradiodays.com.

273 *"Happy birthday . . .":* Carl Lee telegram to Canada Lee, March 12, 1949.

273 *"no Soviet spy could afford . . .":* Lamphere, *The FBI-KGB War*, pp. 107–8.

274 *"She had taken the bait!":* Lamphere, ibid., p. 109.

274 *"Coplon's case was the first . . .":* Fried, *Nightmare in Red:*, p. 91.

274 *"most controversial meetings . . .":* *The New York Times*, March 27, 1949.

275 *Russian composer Dmitri Shostakovich:* "Shostakovich to Visit U.S. for Peace Parley," *Daily Worker*, February 21, 1949, p. 9.

275 *Opposition to peace conference:* Editorials, *New York Journal-American*, March 23–24, 1949.

275 *"bunch of woozy Americans . . ."*: Editorials, *New York Daily Mirror*, March 23–24, 1949.

276 *"his name had been listed . . ."*: Charles Grutzner, "Police Lift All Restrictions On Culture Meeting Pickets," *The New York Times*, March 25, 1949.

276 *"The letter of acceptance . . ."*: Gill, *No Surrender! No Retreat!*, p. 127.

276 *"in the hands of CP members . . ."*: FBI report on COMPIC, May 2, 1949, "Communist Activity in the Entertainment Industry: FBI Surveillance Files on Hollywood, 1942–1958," University Publications of America.

277 *"There was a transformation . . ."*: Leslie Nash, Jr., interview with Frances Lee Pearson.

277 *"That apartment was like a palace . . ."*: Bill Canegata, interview with the author, July 6, 2002.

278 *The true story of Dr. Albert C. Johnston . . .* : Margaret Lillard, "Film Has a Happy Epilogue," *The Bergen Record*, Bergen, N.J. July 28, 1949.

279 *"the handling of . . ."* : "Lost Boundaries," *Ebony*, June 1949, cited in Cripps, p. 228.

279 *"Economics prevailed . . ."*: J. Dennis Robinson, "NH Film: The Making of *Lost Boundaries*," copyright 1997, accessed at www.SeacoastNH.com.

279 *"You are fighting for . . ."*: Alexander Feinberg, "City College Puts Attendance at 85%," *The New York Times*, April 20, 1949.

279 *Note on the Coplon trial:* The author frequently referred to the invaluable detailed account of the Coplon trial found in Marcia and Thomas Mitchell's *The Spy Who Seduced America: The Judith Coplon Story* (Montpelier, Vt.: Invisible Cities Press, 2002).

280 *"gauged the temper of mild . . ."*: Lamphere, *The FBI-KGB War*, p. 111.

281 *"He knew we didn't want . . .", "The smell of disaster   "*: Lamphere, ibid. pp. 114–16.

281 *"I am not charged with the responsibility . . ."*: "Film 'Communists' Listed in FBI File in Coplon Spy Case," *The New York Times*, June 9, 1949.

282 *"Actors Fredric March . . ."*: Frank Holeman, "Movie Stars Tagged As Reds in FBI Files, *New York Daily News*, June 9, 1949.

283 *Media coverage of Coplon Trial:* "F.B.I. Report on Reds Lists Film Figures," *New York Herald Tribune*, June 9, 1949.

283 *"conspicuously followed or appeased . . ."*; *"Movie figures, writers . . ."*: *New York World-Telegram* (AP wire story), June 9, 1949.

283 *Canada and Fredric March apparently came under fire:* "'Absurd,' Says March of FBI 'Red' Charge," *Daily Worker*, June 9, 1949.

283 *"I have by now publicly stated . . ."*: "Never Were or Would Be Reds, Fredric March and Wife Assert," *The New York Times*, June 10, 1949.

284 *"We cannot tell . . ."*: "Freedom Comes First," June 10, 1949 by The New York Times Co. Reprinted with permission.

284 *"High Justice Department officials . . ."*: *New York Daily News*, June 13, 1949.

285 *"Archibald Palmer said . . ."*: Paul Healy, *New York Daily News*, June 14, 1949.

285 *including the left-wing Daily Compass:* "Canada Lee Wants Democracy; Hit Red-Baiting 'Smoke-Screen,'" *Daily Compass*, June 20, 1949.

286 *"There comes a time . . ."*: "A Red Tint is Rubbed Off and Rights Are Defined by Canada Lee," *New York Herald Tribune*, June 22, 1949.

287 *"A packed audience . . ."*: "'Lost Boundaries' Premiere: Stirring Address By Canada Lee Marks Ceremony," *Portsmouth Herald*, June 23, 1949.

12. BABY, IT'S COLD OUTSIDE: Friendships Betrayed

289 *Note:* Frances Lee Pearson quotes in this chapter are from interviews with the author, November 1997–December 2002.

289 *"When a black artist . . .":* Bogle, *Toms, Coons, Mulattoes, Mammies, and Bucks,* pp. 94–95.

289 *"anti-Negro stereotyping . . .":* "Canada Lee Has Own Idea For Negro Film," *Variety,* June 29, 1949. *Note:* A veteran writer for radio and film, Arnold Perl was blacklisted until the early 1960s. He made a documentary on Malcolm X, but died in 1971 while it was still in production; the writer received a posthumous screenplay credit with Spike Lee on the 1992 bio-pic *Malcolm X.*

290 *"I freely admit . . .":* "Canada Lee Wants Democracy; Hit Red-Baiting 'Smoke-Screen,'" *Daily Compass,* June 20, 1949.

290 *"I remember when I was down . . .";* "*Nothing or no one . . .";* "*Tell me, Ed . . .":* Canada Lee, draft of a letter to Ed Sullivan, 1949.

291 *"Declaring that he . . .":* "Canada Lee Explains: Actor Denies He Is a Member of the Communist Party," *The New York Times,* July 7, 1949.

291 *"If there was one . . .":* Gill, *No Surrender! No Retreat!,* p. 109.

292 *Hotel Theresa Conference:* "Group to Seek Place for Negro in Radio," *Daily Compass,* July 8, 1949, p. 16.

292–93 *"lynch mentality . . .";* "*militant struggle":* "Radio Held Biased On Negro Problem: Canada Lee Charges Owners Distort Issues, Refuse to Hire Members of Race," *The New York Times,* July 10, 1949.

292 *"The ideology of White Supremacy . . .":* Saul Carson, "Lee, Robeson Blast Bias in Radio," *Daily Compass,* July 11, 1949, p. 19.

293 *"made a violent attack . . .":* Investigative Name File, Canada Lee, First Series (Box 30), National Archives, Washington, D.C.

293 *"These conditions . . .":* Nadia Dunkel, unsourced clipping fragment, date likely August 3, 1949, Canada Lee file, New York Public Library for the Performing Arts.

293 *Carl filed for:* Original application for the Social Security number for Carl Vincent Canegata (Carl Lee), obtained from Social Security Administration by the author.

294 *"not only a first-class . . .":* *Lost Boundaries* review, *Time,* July 4, 1949.

294 *"one of the best . . .":* "Superior Documentary," *Newsweek,* July 4, 1949, p. 72.

294 *"Viewed as an emotional . . .":* *Lost Boundaries* review, *The New York Times,* July 4, 1949.

294 *Crowther review and black critics:* Cripps, pp. 203-31.

294 *"inimical to the public . . .":* "De Rochemont Maps Campaign Against *Boundaries'* Bans," *Portsmouth Herald,* August 24, 1949.

295 *FBI agents offer to clear Lee's name:* Blue, *Words At War,* pp. 355, 379, and interviews with Frances Lee Pearson.

296 *"Canada said to me . . .":* Gill, *No Surrender! No Retreat!,* p. 109.

296 *Paul Robeson, Jr., has said:* Blue, *Words At War,* pp. 355, 379.

296 *"only those who could or . . .":* Larry Ceplair, "SAG and the Motion Picture Blacklist," Special Edition of the *National Screen Actor,* January 1998.

296 *"Show business people who . . .":* Ellen Schrecker, *The Age of McCarthyism: A Brief History With Documents* (Boston: St. Martin's Press, 1994).

297 *"That's the man I want":* "Canada Lee—*Beloved Country* Star," unsourced clipping fragment, Canada Lee file, New York Library for the Performing Arts.

298 *Peekskill riot:* Marilyn Elie, "The First (Peekskill) Concert—August 27, 1949," accessed at www.highlands.com/robeson/first.htm.

299 *Canada on* The Barry Gray Show: Recording of *The Barry Gray Show*, September 23, 1949.

302 *"He was the victim of . . .":* Ted Poston, "Plight of His Kin in U.S. Job Recalls How 'Whispers' Broke Canada Lee: Canada Lee Went Hungry on the Doorstep of Fame," *New York Post*, March 19, 1954.

302 *"furthering a false . . .":* "Canada Lee Resents Red Smear Via Unfounded Sources; Cites Jobs Lost," Canada Lee letter to the editor, *Variety*, November 30, 1949.

303 *"regretted that in his reply . . .":* Bob Lauter, "Around the Dial: Canada Lee Fights Radio Blacklist," *Daily Worker*, December 15, 1949.

303 *"Canada Lee, the Negro star . . .":* Walter Winchell, "Walter Winchell in New York," *New York Daily Mirror*, October 13, 1949.

303 *columnists at other papers repeated the rumor:* Paul Denis, "New York Tell-Tales," *Daily Compass*, October 14, 1949, p.12.

303 *"I am for complete democracy . . .":* "Lee Corrects Winchell," Canada Lee letter to the editor, *Daily Compass*, October 20, 1949, p. 9.

304 *"Among the supporters . . .":* Ceplair, "SAG and the Motion Picture Blacklist."

304 *He fought for integrated seating at the Maryland Theater:* Canada Lee speech on behalf of the Citizen's Committee to End Segregation, Maryland Theater, Baltimore, November 7, 1949.

305 *"frightened little men . . .":* "Baltimore AFL to Fight Anti-CL Law," *Daily Worker*, November 18, 1949.

305 *"For the guidance of theatergoers . . .":* Ed Sullivan, "Little Old New York: Red Sails on Broadway," November 1949, quoted by Cholly Knickerbocker (a.k.a. Igor Cassini), *New York Journal-American*, February 3, 1950.

305 *"His screen test was . . .":* Bill Canegata, interview with the author, July 6, 2002.

307 *Letters:* Canada Lee correspondence files. These files support text throughout the chapter.

307 *"I was so thankful . . .":* Irene Thirer, "Canada Lee—*Beloved Country* Star," *New York Post*, January 27, 1952.

312 *"In a crude but not incorrect . . .":* Schrecker, *The Age of McCarthyism*.

312–13 *"Canada Lee, Charles McRae . . .":* *The Dispatch*, Cape Town, South Africa, July 19, 1950.

313 *Lee enters South Africa as a servant:* Glenda E. Gill, "Black Actor in Non-Traditional Roles," *Journal of Popular Culture*, Vol. 25 No. 3, Winter 1991, p. 89.

313 *"I told him my name was Lee . . .":* Thirer, "Canada Lee—*Beloved Country* Star."

313 *"I lost six cents on the fight . . .":* Canada Lee, "Canada Lee Surveys Life in Union," *Rand Daily Mail*, November 8, 1950.

314 *"we saw a native woman . . .":* Thirer, "Canada Lee—*Beloved Country* Star."

315 *"He's a boy! . . .":* Beulah Bullock, interview with the author, October 27, 2002.

316 *"With my own eyes . . .":* Thirer, "Canada Lee—*Beloved Country* Star."

316 *"Never come to South Africa":* Bill Canegata interview.

316 *"there was nothing I . . .":* "Last Curtain for Canada Lee," *The Ring*, July 1952, p. 23.

317 *"Poitier . . . brought good humor . . .":* Bogle, *Toms, Coons, Mulattoes, Mammies, and Bucks*, p. 179.

318 *"wonderful time . . .":* Canada Lee, "Canada Lee Surveys Life in Union."

318 *"You have put it in . . .":* Joseph Trauneck, letter to Canada Lee, November 8, 1950.

318 *"I got an attack . . ."* through *"would stop.":* Canada Lee letter to William "Lovey" Canegata, March 17, 1951.

319 *"He wanted to be free of the blood pressure . . .":* Glenda E. Gill, "Careerist and Casualty: The Rise and Fall of Canada Lee," *Freedomways,* First Quarter, 1981, p. 24.

13. NO GREATER LOVE: Then Comes Marriage

320 *Note:* Frances Lee Pearson quotes in this chapter are from interviews with the author, November 1997–December 2002.

321–22 *"He's a great guy . . . no one could care less":* Canada Lee, letter to William "Lovey" Canegata, March 17, 1951, The Canada Lee Research Material Collection, Schomburg Center for Research in Black Culture

322–23 *"James G.* [sic] *Canegata . . .":* "James C. Canegata," obituary, *New York Herald Tribune,* May 27, 1951.

323 *"he suffered a heart attack . . .":* "Canada Lee Dead, Stage, Film Star," *The New York Times,* May 11, 1952.

323 *"given up hope . . .":* Report to FBI Director 100-15732, COMPIC, "Communist Activity in the Entertainment Industry: FBI Surveillance Files on Hollywood, 1942–1958," University Publications of America.

324 "Othello *is a natural . . .":* "Last Curtain for Canada Lee," *The Ring,* July 1952, p. 23.

325 *"Of course, I didn't know Italians . . .":* Mickey Knox, interviewed by Patrick McGilligan, *Tender Comrades: A Backstory of the Hollywood Blacklist,* p. 370.

326 *Letters:* Canada Lee correspondence files. These files support text throughout the chapter.

326 *"Although I had been advised . . .":* Louis Budenz statement, Investigative Name File on Canada Lee, First Series (Box 30), House Un-American Activities Committee, National Archives, Washington, D.C.

330 *"A screen poem of poignant . . .":* "Cry, the Beloved Country: Poignant Beauty in Paton Film," *Cape Times,* November 16, 1951.

330 *"The censor thought . . .";"abrogating the law":* "Only 11 Ft. Cut in Paton Film," *Cape Times,* November 1951.

330 *"The movie people made provisions . . .":* "Last Curtain for Canada Lee," p. 23.

331 *"I just want to work* here *. . .":* Gill, *No Surrender! No Retreat!,* p. 129.

332 *"especially evocative":* "New Film," *Newsweek,* clipping fragment, Canada Lee file, New York Public Library for the Performing Arts.

332 *"a nearly monumental performance . . .":* Otis L. Guernsey, Jr., "Africa in Half-Light," *New York Herald Tribune,* January 24, 1952.

332 *"Mr. Lee, the American actor . . .":* Bosley Crowther, "Alan Paton's 'Cry, The Beloved Country' With Canada Lee Opens at Bijou Theater," *The New York Times Film Review,* January 24, 1952.

332 *"would rather be one of the poorest . . .";* *"highly derogatory . . .":* Letters to Tex and Jinx McCrary and NBC, January–February 1952, Schlesinger Library, Radcliffe Institute for Advanced Study, Edith Spurlock Sampson Collection.

332 *"wanted to let off steam . . ."* through *"filmed in Dutch Guiana.":* Thirer, "Canada Lee — 'Beloved Country' Star."

334 *"hardships"; "obstacles"; "my political activities . . .":* "Last Curtain for Canada Lee," p. 23.

334 *"Forty-eight hours after I was back . . .":* Gill, "Careerist and Casualty: The Rise and Fall of Canada Lee," p. 24.

334 *"I can't take it . . .":* Kanfer, *A Journal of the Plague Years,* p. 179.

334 *"I dissuaded him . . ."*: Poston, "Plight of His Kin in U.S. Job Recalls How 'Whispers' Broke Canada Lee."

334 *White traveled to Washington:* Walter White column, *Philadelphia Bulletin*, May 16, 1952, cited by Blue, *Words at War*, p. 365.

334 *"but Canada went to rallies . . ."*: Gill, *No Surrender! No Retreat!*, p. 109.

335 *"If brotherhood can flourish . . ."*: Canada Lee speech, International Brotherhood Week, February 19, 1952.

335 *"Let us not be fooled by words . . ."*: Drafts of Canada Lee speech, George Washington High School, scheduled for February 22, 1952.

14. SO LITTLE TIME: Fight to the Death

336 *Note:* Frances Lee Pearson quotes in this chapter are from interviews with the author, November1997–December 2002.

337 *"They are an ancient people . . ."*: Drafts of Canada Lee speech, NAACP "Great Night" at Madison Square Garden, March 6, 1952.

338 *"Frances doesn't know about this . . ."*: Leslie Nash, Jr., interview with Frances Lee Pearson.

338 *"received four lucrative television . . ."*: Poston, "Plight of His Kin in U.S. Job Recalls How 'Whispers' Broke Canada Lee."

339 *"Mr. James reports . . ."*: Memo, Alvin W. Stokes, April 3, 1952, Canada Lee Investigative Name File, First Series (Box 30), House Un-American Activities Committee, National Archives, Washington, D.C.

339 *Invited to join the Americans for South African Resistance; Lee delivered the keynote address:* George M. Houser, statement at a meeting of the UN Special Committee against apartheid on June 25, 1982, transcribed from a tape in the E.S. Reddy collection and published at www.anc.org.za.

340 *dismemberment and castration:* Transcript of WOR radio program (New York), "Canada Lee Gives Views on South Africa," March 6, 1952, p. 5, Schlesinger Library, Radcliffe Institute for Advanced Study, Edith Spurlock Sampson Collection.

340 *"with the demand that I . . ."*: Transcript of WJZ radio program (New York), "Combs Round Table on the Union of South Africa," March 27/28, 1952, p. 4, Schlesinger Library, Radcliffe Institute for Advanced Study, Edith Spurlock Sampson Collection.

340 *Lee received a letter:* Morris Helprin of London Films, letter to Canada Lee, April 4, 1952, Schlesinger Library, Radcliffe Institute for Advanced Study, Edith Spurlock Sampson Collection.

340 *"Canada Lee said that . . ."*: Alvin W. Stokes, memo to Louis J. Russell, Canada Lee Investigative Name File, First Series (Box 30), House Un-American Activities Committee, National Archives, Washington, D.C.

341 *"Canada Lee will offer a program:"* "Lee Offers Readings Tonight," *The New York Times*, April 11, 1952.

343 *"he couldn't afford to buy a few drinks . . ."*: Poston, "Plight of His Kin in U.S. Job Recalls How 'Whispers' Broke Canada Lee."

343 *"he had no authority . . ."*; *"got him a sandwich."*: Poston, ibid.

345 *"I try not to be emotional . . ."*; *"I don't know whether . . ."*: Abner W. Berry, "The Heavy Burden of Canada Lee," *Daily Worker*, May 13, 1952.

345 *"I have just left a country . . ."*: Kanfer, *A Journal of the Plague Years*, p. 179.

347 *"I came by to make him laugh . . ."*: Gill, "Careerist and Casualty: The Rise and Fall of Canada Lee," p. 25.

349 *"My God! . . ."*: Loften Mitchell, *Black Drama* (New York: Hawthorn Books, 1967), p. 149.

349 *"That was the most difficult . . ."*: William Butler, interview with Frances Lee Pearson.

350 *"In recent years . . ."*: "Canada Lee, 45, Is Dead; Stage and Film Star," *New York Herald Tribune*, May 11, 1952.

350 *"Lee had been tagged . . ."*: "Canada Lee Dies at 45; Noted Stage Performer," *New York Daily News*, May 10, 1952.

350 *"Friends said the actor's health . . ."*: "Canada Lee, Noted Actor, Dead at 45," unsourced clipping fragment, Wisconsin center for Film and Theater Research.

350 *"From 1934 to 1949 . . ."*: Berry, "The Heavy Burden of Canada Lee."

351 *"Canada Lee couldn't find a job . . ."*: Ossie Davis, *With Ossie and Ruby: In This Life Together*, p. 234.

351 *"The real subversives of America . . ."*: Powell quoted in Mitchell, *Black Drama*, p. 149.

351 *"political persecution"*: Blue, *Words at War*, p. 365. *Note:* Deaths most often attributed to the blacklist are those of Canada Lee, John Garfield, Philip Loeb, Mady Christians, and J. Edward Bromberg. Examples of publications linking these deaths to the blacklist include: Stefan Kanfer, *A Journal of the Plague Years*; Dan Georgakas, in Buhle, Buhle, and Georgakas, ed., *Encyclopedia of the American Left*; Richard M. Fried, *Nightmare in Red: The McCarthy Era in Perspective*; Glenda E. Gill, *Canada Lee; Black Actor in Non-Traditional Roles, Journal of Popular Culture*, Vol. 25 No. 3 Winter 1991 and "Careerist and Casualty: The Rise and Fall of Canada Lee," *Freedomways*, First Quarter, 1981, p. 16.

352 *"Many wept unashamedly . . ."*: David Platt, "Thousands Pay Last Tribute to A Beloved Actor—Canada Lee," *Daily Worker*, May 16, 1952.

352–53 *"When Canada spoke those lines . . ."*: Gill, *No Surrender! No Retreat!*, pp. 131–132.

353 *"a consistent fighter . . ."*: Platt, "Thousands Pay Last Tribute to A Beloved Actor—Canada Lee."

353 *"Canada Lee made his race . . ."*: "Final Tribute Paid to a Great Actor, Canada Lee," *The Afro-American*, May 24, 1952.

354 *"If a man does not march . . ."*: Platt, "Thousands Pay Last Tribute to A Beloved Actor—Canada Lee."

355 *"I'll never forget it . . ."*: Beulah Bullock, interview with the author, October 2002.

355 *"The grim and curious . . ."*: Ed Sullivan, "Little Old New York," *New York Daily News*, May 1952, clipping fragment, Canada Lee FBI files, also cited in Kanfer.

15. BLUES REQUIEM: Speak of Me As I Am

357 *Note:* Frances Lee Pearson quotes in this chapter are from interviews with the author, November 1997–2002.

357 *"The Worker is trying to claim . . ."*: Lyons quoted in Kanfer's *A Journal of the Plague Years*, pp. 180–81.

358 *"I know for truth . . ."*: Whitney Bolton, "Looking Sideways," McNaught Syndicate Inc., May 29, 1952.

358 *"trying to claim Canada Lee . . ."*: Charles R. Iucci, "In Memoriam: Canada Lee," WLIB broadcast reprinted in *Allegro*, Local 802 newsletter, June 1952.

358 *"misleading"*: Ted Poston, "Reds Try to Lure Negroes to New 'Front,'" *New York Post*, October 6, 1952.

359 *"Canada was no Communist . . ."*: Poston, "Kin of Canada Lee Losing U.S. Job for 'Associating' With Late Actor."

360 *"aid to young dramatic artists . . ."*: "Canada Lee Memorial: Foundation Is Set Up to Help Young Artists of All Races," *The New York Times*, November 11, 1952.

361 *"continuing sympathetic association"*: Poston, "Kin of Canada Lee Losing U.S. Job for 'Associating' With Late Actor."

361 *"termination of your employment"* . . . : Poston, "Plight of His Kin in U.S. Job Recalls How 'Whispers' Broke Canada Lee."

361 *she refused to go away without a fight*: "Canada Lee's Sister-in-Law Hounded Off Job," *Daily Worker*, March 16, 1954, p. 3.

362 *Pheta eventually prevailed*: Bill Canegata, interview with the author, July 6, 2002.

363 *"Unless you remember this dark epoch . . ."*: Michael Wilson, quoted in Larry Ceplair, "SAG and the Motion Picture Blacklist," Special Edition of the *National Screen Actor*, January 1998.

364 *Lawson did not receive his writing credit* . . . : Bernard Weinraub, "For the Blacklisted, Credit Where Credit Is Due," *The New York Times*, October 1, 1997, p. E3.

364 *The Screen Actors Guild formally accepted responsibility*: "50 Years Ago: SAG Remembers the Blacklist," Special Edition of the *National Screen Actor*, January 1998.

365 *"through their incessant struggles . . ."*: Gill, *No Surrender! No Retreat!*, p. 17.

368–69 *"I don't know whether . . ."*; *"I only hope to God . . ."*: Canada Lee speeches, May 1944 and April 1952, quoted in previous chapters.

370 *"Where are your black hands? . . ."*: Canada Lee scrapbook, Schomburg Center for Research in Black Culture.

INDEX